CHRISTIANITY
at the
RELIGIOUS ROUNDTABLE

CHRISTIANITY *at the* RELIGIOUS ROUNDTABLE

Evangelicalism in Conversation with Hinduism, Buddhism, and Islam

TIMOTHY C. TENNENT

Baker Academic
A Division of Baker Book House Co
Grand Rapids, Michigan 49516

Published by Baker Academic
a division of Baker Book House Company
P.O. Box 6287, Grand Rapids, MI 49516–6287

Printed in the United States of America

Library of Congress Cataloging-in-Publication Data

Tennent, Timothy C.
Christianity at the religious roundtable : evangelicalism in conversation with Hinduism, Buddhism, and Islam / Timothy C. Tennent.
p. cm.
Includes bibliographical references (p.) and index.
ISBN 0-8010-2602-4 (pbk.)
1. Christianity and other religions. 2. Christianity and other religions—Hinduism. 3. Hinduism—Relations—Christianity. 4. Christianity and other religions—Buddhism. 5. Buddhism—Relations—Christianity. 6. Christianity and other religions—Islam. 6. Islam—Relations—Christianity. I. Title.
BR127 .T46 2002
261.2—dc21 2002021569

For information about Baker Academic, visit our web site:
www.bakeracademic.com

Contents

Acknowledgments 7

1. Interreligious Dialogue: An Evangelical Perspective 9

Part 1 Christianity and Hinduism

2. Doctrine of God: Brāhman 37
3. Doctrine of Creation: Līlā, Māyā 63

Part 2 Christianity and Buddhism

4. Doctrine of God: Dharma-kāya (Śunyatā/Citta) 89
5. Doctrine of Ethics: Karuṇā, Maitrī, and Dāna 115

Part 3 Christianity and Islam

6. Doctrine of God: Allah 141
7. Doctrine of Christ and the Incarnation: ʿĪsā, Ḥulūl 169

Part 4 Case Studies and Conclusion

8. Was Socrates a Christian before Christ? A Study of Justin Martyr's Use of *Logos Spermatikos* 199
9. Can the Hindu Upanishads Help Us Explain the Trinity? A Study of Brahmabandhav Upadhyay's Use of Saccidānanda 211
10. Can *Sola Fide* Be Understood Apart from the Specific, Historic Revelation of Jesus Christ? A Study of A. G. Hogg's Distinction between Faith and Faiths 231

Epilogue: Closing Thoughts about Evangelicals and Interreligious Dialogue 239
Glossary 245
Bibliography 259
Subject Index 265
Scripture Index 269

Acknowledgments

I am indebted to the trustees and faculty of Gordon-Conwell Theological Seminary for granting me a sabbatical to write this book. The particular encouragement I received from Haddon and Bonnie Robinson during my months away from the seminary will long be remembered. I would also like to express my gratitude for two of my former professors and now colleagues, David Wells and Garth Rosell. David Wells first taught me the importance of theology in understanding, interpreting, and responding to the ongoing challenges that the church faces. Garth Rosell's ability to ignite one's passion for church history is well known. I am particularly indebted to him for the broad, global view of the church's life that he so ably gives to his students. As a missiologist at Gordon-Conwell, I now find myself striding the two wonderful worlds of theology and church history. Under the able leadership of Garth Rosell, the Division of Christian Thought at Gordon-Conwell nurtures a wonderful—and needed—relationship between missions, theology, and church history. As my dear colleague Peter Kuzmič is fond of declaring at our divisional meetings, "Good missions must be theologically grounded, and good theology must be missiologically focused!" To work alongside Christian leaders like David Wells, Garth Rosell, and Peter Kuzmič in this kind of cooperative environment is truly one of the greatest joys of my professional life.

I also appreciate my students at Gordon-Conwell. Without the interaction with students in my classes over the years, many of the ideas in this book would not have been realized. I am particularly indebted to Sean Doyle, Allen Yeh, and Jeremy John who have served as my Byington research assistants over the last three years. They have each spent many hours in the library on my behalf, and, undoubtedly, this book reflects their hard work.

I divided my sabbatical between the Overseas Ministries Study Center in New Haven, Connecticut, and the New Theological College in Dehra Dun in Uttaranchal, India. I am indebted to Jonathan Bonk, the director of OMSC, and his staff for their encouragement and support during my studies at Yale.

Likewise, the time spent each year in Dehra Dun is always a time of intellectual and spiritual refreshment. I am deeply grateful to the founder of NTC, George Chavanikamannil, whose missionary vision and heart for church planting in India is, in my mind, without parallel.

I am dedicating this book to my wife Julie, whose steadfast commitment to Jesus Christ and joyful spirit remain a constant source of inspiration and encouragement. Besides being a gifted musician, she has brought music and joy into my life and the lives of our two children, Jonathan and Bethany, in more ways than can be recounted here.

Timothy C. Tennent

1

Interreligious Dialogue

An Evangelical Perspective

I confess that although I have read dozens of books on interreligious dialogue, I have enjoyed precious few of them. Yet I am now in the curious position of writing such a book. Upon reflection, the basic reason for my dissatisfaction is that the average Christian would hardly recognize the Christianity that is often presented in such works. Certainly, the apostles—the eye- and ear-witnesses of Christ's life and the first to testify about him—would go away scratching their heads in bewilderment. The Christian gospel is often presented as one among many different paths to God. Christianity is ranked side by side with religions such as Islam, Hinduism, and Buddhism in much the same way as films are displayed at a multiplex cinema. The Islamic Qurʾān or the Hindu Upanishads are as likely to yield spiritual light as the Sermon on the Mount.

I do not believe that the authors of such books distort the gospel message intentionally or maliciously. Rather, most of them simply do not affirm the historic Christian confessions; yet curiously they continue to identify themselves as Christians. Even scholars among the non-Christian religions have begun to recognize this phenomenon. For example, Grace Burford, a practicing Buddhist scholar, comments on this in a recent Buddhist-Christian dialogue titled *Buddhists Talk about Jesus—Christians Talk about the Buddha.*[1] Her chapter is insightfully titled "If the Buddha Is So Great, Why Are These People Christians?" She bluntly asks about these scholars, "If they

1. Rita Gross and Terry Muck, eds., *Buddhists Talk about Jesus—Christians Talk about the Buddha* (New York: Continuum, 2000).

were so taken by Buddhism, why did they hang on to Christianity?"[2] Her remarks are limited to the Buddhist-Christian dialogue but could easily be observed throughout the whole field of interreligious studies. Why would people be prepared to surrender every central claim of historic Christianity and yet be so doggedly determined to remain spokespersons for Christianity? The same point is made by evangelical scholar Ron Nash in his excellent book *Is Jesus the Only Savior?*[3] He points out how John Hick, who is widely regarded as one of the leading voices in the Christian dialogue with other religions, continues to call himself a Christian despite having abandoned the historic faith. Nash goes on to say, "I mean no ill-will when I say that Hick is not a Christian in any historical, traditional, or biblical sense of the word. This is not being unkind; it is only being accurate."[4] These observations from a Buddhist scholar and a leading evangelical scholar testify to the current state of interreligious dialogue. People who stand outside the boundaries of historic Christianity are representing Christianity. The tragic result is that many readers assume that the positions taken by these scholars reflect a broad consensus among Christians around the world.

This is not to say that there have not been several excellent books written to defend historic Christianity in light of the particular challenges of world religions. Lesslie Newbigin's *The Gospel in a Pluralist Society,* J. N. D. Anderson's *Christianity and Comparative Religion,* and Ravi Zacharias's *Jesus Among Other Gods,* are a few examples of excellent contributions to this field.[5] However, these books are not examples of interreligious dialogue per se. They are defenses of historic Christianity in light of growing religious pluralism. These books are extremely important and we need more like them, but we also need more evangelical Christians involved in genuine dialogue with members of other religions. This book seeks to meet that need and to prepare Christians as they begin to take more seriously our obligation to listen and respond to the objections of non-Christian religions.

Genuine dialogue can occur in a way that is faithful to historic Christianity while being willing to listen and genuinely respond to the honest objections of those who remain unconvinced. This underlying premise for the

2. Ibid., 131.

3. Ronald Nash, *Is Jesus the Only Savior?* (Grand Rapids: Zondervan, 1994).

4. Ibid., 99. John Hick, for example, flatly denies the incarnation as historically affirmed in Christian confessions, stating that it is an impossible and logical inconsistency. Christianity, as with any other religion, has the right to police its own borders. This debate has become particularly important in the Islamic community in the wake of the terrorist attacks in the United States. Because a group claims to be Islamic does not automatically guarantee it a place in the household of Islam.

5. Lesslie Newbigin, *The Gospel in a Pluralist Society* (Grand Rapids: Eerdmans, 1989); J. N. D. Anderson, *Christianity and Comparative Religion* (Downers Grove, Ill.: InterVarsity, 1971); Ravi Zacharias, *Jesus Among Other Gods* (Nashville: Word, 2000). See also Lesslie Newbigin, *The Finality of Christ* (Richmond: John Knox; London: SCM, 1969).

current work serves to challenge the perspective of both conservative and liberal Christians for several reasons.

Conservative Christians and Interreligious Dialogue

Many Christians who have embraced the historic Christian confessions and who hold fast to the faith remain reluctant to listen and respond to the objections of Hindus, Buddhists, and Muslims. Dialogue is discouraged because non-Christian religions are dismissed out-of-hand as examples of human blindness and the fruit of unbelief. Sometimes non-Christian religions are regarded as the direct work of Satan. The result has been to avoid any serious dialogue lest Christians unwittingly place the gospel on equal footing with other religions. It is one thing to personally hold fast to the faith; it is entirely different to share it with another person. This is even more daunting if the person belongs to another religion and has many questions about Christianity. The temptation is to go on the defensive and to avoid such encounters. This "safety box" approach has the initial appearance of preserving the gospel. Because the gospel is so valuable, we should lock it up for safekeeping. But the gospel is not nearly so fragile. Christianity is a faith for the world. It flourishes when challenged by unbelief, ridicule, and skepticism. Early Christians defended their faith in the face of martyrdom, and in this context Tertullian first observed that "the blood of the martyrs is the seed of the church."[6] Nevertheless, many of these staunch defenders of orthodoxy were also creatively seeking to effectively communicate the gospel amid the particular cultural, philosophical, and religious challenges of their Hellenistic environment.

It is comforting to know that Christianity can handle the tough questions even if we sometimes feel inadequate. Some readers may already be convinced of the need for evangelicals to become more seriously engaged in dialogue but are genuinely apprehensive because of the paucity of their knowledge about other religions. Perhaps you are afraid that your own faith is not strong enough to stand up against the difficult questions that members of other religions often pose. If that is your situation, these dialogues will introduce some of the key theological and ethical issues that separate Christianity from the non-Christian religions and will expose many of our own false stereotypes.

Because this book is based on many conversations I have had with Muslims, Hindus, and Buddhists from all over the world, it will help to prepare you for some of the more difficult questions that may arise. Unfortunately, much of the literature concerning world religions produced by evangelical Christians has been embarrassingly superficial. There are, of course, several notable exceptions, such as Sabapathy Kulandran's extensive study of the

6. Tertullian, *Apology*, chap. 50, Alexander Roberts and James Donaldson, eds. (*ANF* 3:55).

doctrine of grace in Christianity and Hinduism.[7] More often, however, grappling with the views of other religions is reduced to simplistic charts or sweeping generalizations that operate at a superficial level. Mercifully, in recent years more substantial material is beginning to emerge from evangelical pens. For example, Norman Geisler and Abdul Saleeb's *Answering Islam* provides an excellent resource for those seeking to understand how to respond to Muslim objections to Christianity.[8] However, once Geisler and Saleeb give their answers, there is no opportunity to hear what a Muslim would say in response. As anyone knows who has spent time in dialogue, it is in the actual give-and-take of a full conversation that our ability to understand the basis for an objection finally begins to emerge.[9] In my experience, a Christian response to a question posed by a Hindu, Muslim, or Buddhist often raises surprising follow-up questions which expose new issues that cry out for our attention and reflection. This happens several times in the dialogues contained in this book.

Thus, despite all the risks and the vulnerability involved, our confidence in the gospel demands that we can no longer give space to any kind of cultural, ideological, or religious apartheid whereby we conveniently isolate ourselves from the beliefs and practices of the world we live in. Our Lord has sent us out into the world. It is not some generic world to which Christ calls us, like a distant planet where no one lives. We are called to bear witness to Christ in the Hindu world, the Islamic world, the secular world, and so forth. This book seeks to make the journey easier by charting a fresh path to follow as we go out.

While the command to go out into the world has always rested with the church, until recently it has been all too easy to ignore the implications of this command for the Christian interface with world religions. There are two main reasons for the unique position we are facing in the twenty-first century. First, to make light of the claims and challenges of non-Christian religions is to fail to recognize the changing religious context of the modern world. There was a time when encounters with Muslims, Buddhists, and Hindus were the domain of the foreign missionary who lived in some dis-

7. Sabapathy Kulandran, *Grace: A Comparative Study of the Doctrine in Christianity and Hinduism* (London: Lutterworth, 1964).

8. Norman Geisler and Abdul Saleeb, *Answering Islam: The Crescent in the Light of the Cross* (Grand Rapids: Baker, 1993).

9. One example of a full conversation along the lines of this book is Dom Aelred Graham, *Conversations: Christian and Buddhist* (New York: Harcourt, Brace and World, 1968). Unfortunately, the Christian representatives in Graham's book do not represent or defend historic Christianity. Alas, the need for a conversation in which the Christianity being discussed is the historic Christianity of the Scriptures as proclaimed by the apostles, the content of which has been preserved by the historic creeds of the church. A new release that is beginning to take up this challenge from an evangelical perspective is Ravi Zacharias, *Jesus Talks with the Buddha: There Is One God and Who Is His Prophet?* (Sisters, Ore.: Multnomah, 2001).

tant place. He or she was presumably more prepared for such encounters, so we did not think we needed to study those strange, far-off religions. Certainly, we would never come face to face with living, breathing Hindus, for example, and be forced to respond to any of their questions or objections. However, the twenty-first century does not afford us the luxury of such excuses or isolation. The majority of Christians now live in the southern continents of the non-Western world, not in North America and Western Europe. Today the gospel is growing and thriving in places where other religions have long held sway. As for the Western world, Muslims, Buddhists, and Hindus are now our coworkers, our schoolmates, and our neighbors. It is not unusual to see Hindus celebrating dewali or Muslims keeping Ramaḍān in many cities throughout North America and Western Europe. Islam has recently passed Judaism as the largest non-Christian religion in North America. This new atmosphere of religious pluralism has dramatically influenced how Christians think about their faith, and certainly it has forced us to rethink what is required to witness to the gospel in today's world.

Second, ignoring the challenge of other religions fails to take the biblical witness seriously. Paul's spirited defense of the gospel on Mars Hill (Acts 17) and John's creative application of the *logos* to the incarnation (John 1) demonstrate how deeply the earliest Christians understood the context to which they were called to witness. This book challenges conservative Christians to far more intentional, serious engagements with an increasingly diverse and pluralistic world. In this respect, we are in a position not unlike those in the first century who first heard the Great Commission in the context of a religiously and culturally pluralistic world. Undoubtedly, the earliest Christians understood what it was like to be a minority faith in a pluralistic context.

Liberal Christians and Interreligious Dialogue

Because of the lack of engagement that has characterized much of conservative Christianity, interreligious dialogue has been sustained and participated in primarily by Protestants and Catholics who identify themselves with various liberal positions, several of which will be explored in more detail. From an evangelical perspective, it is safe to say that it is rare for any of these dialogues to defend historic Christianity. Unfortunately, they are often characterized by a lack of vigilance in defending the gospel, and frequently they have conceded ground that lies at the heart of the Christian message. When this occurs, it is often because of several faulty presuppositions that are in force long before the dialogue ever begins.

First, books on interreligious or interfaith dialogue often insist that participants suspend their own faith commitment before coming to the table. It is assumed that a commitment to the truth claims in one's own religion results in disqualification for genuine dialogue with someone from another religion. For example, in *Muslims in Dialogue* Paul Knitter writes, "No matter how much truth and good one recognizes in another religion, if one enters the dialogue convinced that by God's will the final, normative, unsurpassable truth for all religions resides in one's own religion, that is *not* a dialogue between equals."[10] I respectfully disagree with Knitter. I do not see how adopting his view actually assists in genuine dialogue. In fact, I see it quite the opposite. How can one have genuine dialogue *without* a faith commitment? How can interfaith dialogue exist without faith? That is like asking salt to become temporarily saltless so that someone can discover what salt is like in a nonthreatening atmosphere. But if salt is not salty, then it is not salt. I am convinced that genuine dialogue must bring persuaded people together. If convinced Muslims, Hindus, and Buddhists are willing to sit down with a convinced Christian, how is that not a dialogue between equals? When Paul stood up in the meeting of the Areopagus on Mars Hill and engaged with the Stoic and Epicurean philosophers, he did not suspend his faith, he proclaimed it. Yet Paul did so with sensitivity to their concerns and their writings and proved himself to be an able listener. He did not force them to come to God through Judaism; he appealed to general revelation and even quoted their own poets (Acts 17:28). Nevertheless, although the text indicates that one member of the Areopagus named Dionysius became a Christian, most of the Areopagus presumably remained unconvinced by Paul. In contrast to Knitter, I affirm the Zurich Consultation's document on interreligious dialogue which states, "In the context of dialogue with men of other faiths, which demands genuine openness on both sides, the Christian is free to bear witness to the risen Christ, just as his partner of another faith is free to witness to what is most important in his own existence."[11]

The second presupposition frequently found in books on interreligious dialogue is an odd view of truth. Before anyone ever sits down at the table of dialogue, there is often an underlying conviction that there are no absolute truths. Nothing can be asserted as true but only as true for me or true in my experience. Only in the context of relativity can participants avoid inflamed passions and narrow-minded dogmatism that tries to—and here I must invoke the well-worn phrase—cram something down someone's throat. In this way, all transcendent truths get washed up on the shore of human experience, and all truth claims are regarded as having equal value. Religious differences are not real differences, but only *apparent* differences due to

10. Paul Knitter, "Hans Küng's Theological Rubicon," in *Muslims in Dialogue: The Evolution of a Dialogue*, ed. Leonard Swidler (Lewiston, N.Y.: Edwin Mellen, 1992), 279.

11. "Christians in Dialogue with Men of Other Faiths," *International Review of Mission* 59, no. 236 (October 1970): 382–91. This is a reprint of the statement of the Zurich Consultation in reflection on the March 1970 Consultation of the World Council of Churches held at Ajaltoun, Lebanon. The quotation cited is the opening line of section three of the document. My agreement with this portion of the document should not be taken to imply agreement with the document as a whole. Stephen Neill, in his *Christian Faith and Other Faiths* (London: Oxford University Press, 1961), makes the same point in chapter one where he insists that real dialogue is possible only if all participants are committed, resolute, and uncompromising.

cultural perceptions and individual experiences. How many times have we heard the refrain that all religions are basically the same? Yet I have never seen convincing evidence that there is a common root or goal of the world religions. Indeed, most serious students of world religions know this to be false. It is only possible to talk in these terms when the participants invoke this highly subjective understanding of truth. Such a view effectively removes the transcendent from all interreligious dialogue. Transcendent, absolute truths are demoted to the level of human perceptions in a form of dialogue called interior dialogue.[12] The result is that anthropology quietly replaces theology as the focus of the dialogue. In other words, we are no longer speaking about a transcendent God; we are discussing equally valid individual experiences or a particular culture's religious projections that they identify as God or ultimate reality. The whole discussion is man-centered, not God-centered. Anthropology has trumped all theology before the first word of dialogue begins. The universality of subjective experience has replaced all claims to objective truth.

Once truth is reduced to subjective experience, all religious truth claims can be harmonized. The Hindu who experiences ultimate reality as impersonal Brāhman and the Muslim who experiences ultimate reality as righteous Allah calling the world to obedience can be viewed as two subjective perspectives differing only in their vantage points. Subjectively speaking, both are equally valid.[13] This way of thinking is what allowed the Hindu apologist Swami Vivekananda to declare, "If one religion be true, then all the others also must be true."[14] However, from an objective point of view, God either is or is not personal. Either God became incarnate in Jesus Christ or he did not. Either Allah spoke to Muhammad through Gabriel or he did not. This is a very different view of truth. From this perspective, there are genuine points of departure among the world's religions. Undoubtedly, we will also discover places of honest agreement. In either case, it is a dialogue that has the courage of convictions. Jesus, at his trial, told Pilate that he "came into the world, to testify to the truth. Everyone on the side of truth listens to me" (John 18:37). Pilate responded by asking, "What is truth?" Pilate's question continues to be of tremendous consequence when we sit down at the table of dialogue.

The third presupposition dominating much of the current literature on interreligious dialogue is that no one is allowed to use the "c" word—*conversion.* Any reference to the missiological or evangelistic dimensions of one's faith is normally a violation of the terms of dialogue. Any desire to convert a

12. A defense of interior dialogue may be found in such works as Bede Griffiths, *Christian Ashram* (London: Darton, Longman and Todd, 1966) and H. LeSaux, *Hindu-Christian Meeting Point* (Bangalore: National Press, 1969).

13. One of the most well-known books that sets out to demonstrate the ultimate harmony of the most radical differences in world religions is J. A. T. Robinson, *Truth Is Two-Eyed* (London: SCM, 1979).

14. Swami Vivekananda, *Essentials of Hinduism* (Mayavati: Advaita Ashrama, 1947), i.

person is regarded as a narrow-minded, arrogant belief that one's own religion is somehow superior to another. Because of the subjective view of truth, it amounts to saying that one's personal experience is more valid than someone else's. If, as some Hindus claim, there are many different paths to God, how can we as Christians arrogantly assert that our path is better than another? The apologetic, evangelistic side of dialogue becomes impossible because any persuasive speech can be interpreted as crass proselytizing. However, why can't genuine dialogue involve people speaking persuasively to one another from faith to faith? As a committed Christian, I would like to see every Hindu and Buddhist and Muslim in the world fall on their faces before the living Christ and confess him as their Lord and Savior. Does that make me ineligible to sit down at the table of dialogue? I don't think so. I fully expect—and would be shocked if it were not so—that the committed Muslim would equally like to see me fall down before Allah and confess him as Lord and Muhammad as his prophet.

In short, I take a different point of departure when it comes to the evangelistic side of dialogue. Rather than viewing conversion as a taboo, I fully expect Muslims or Hindus or Buddhists to do their best to convince me that they have more coherent worldviews and clearer visions of God or reality than the Christian faith has. Likewise, I am free to make the best case I can for the Christian gospel, realizing that in the end I may remain the only convinced Christian. On the other hand, there is the possibility that I or one of the other participants may become convinced by the compelling truth of Christianity or Islam or Hinduism. It is unprincipled to rule out from the start the possibility of conversion, since the very nature of the dialogue assumes we are discussing weighty matters of life-changing significance.

Spectrum of Views Regarding Christianity and Non-Christian Religions

I have outlined two very different perspectives on interreligious dialogue. I have labeled these positions as simply liberal and conservative and have portrayed them in stark and sometimes provocative terms in order to help readers see how divergent the perspectives within the Christian community are when it comes to the topic of interreligious dialogue. However, the conservative and liberal positions represent only two points along a broad spectrum of responses. A brief survey of the major points along the spectrum of Christian attitudes toward non-Christian religions will further help to clarify why a fresh approach is needed in the area of interreligious dialogue.

Exclusivism

More conservative views are generally grouped together in a category known as exclusivism.[15] A position is categorized as exclusivist if it affirms

15. Sometimes called restrictivism or christocentric exclusivism.

three nonnegotiables. First, exclusivists affirm the unique authority of Jesus Christ as the apex of revelation and the norm by which all other beliefs must be critiqued. This position points out that the early church rejected the option of remaining a *cultus privatus* (private cult), which would have permitted Christianity to survive as a privatized religion accepting equal footing with other religions. The early church insisted on challenging the entire Roman Empire with its many religions by claiming that Christ was not only head of the church, but Lord of the entire cosmos. Drawing on texts such as John 14:6, Acts 4:12, and 1 John 5:11–12, Jesus is not just one of many lights in the religious cosmos; he is *the* light. Those who are without Christ are, to use the words of the apostle Paul, "without hope and without God in the world" (Eph. 2:12). Second, exclusivists affirm that the Christian faith centers around the proclamation of the historical death and resurrection of Jesus Christ as the decisive event in human history (Acts 2:31–32). The Scriptures declare that "God was reconciling the world to himself in Christ" (2 Cor. 5:19) and "making peace through his blood, shed on the cross" (Col. 1:20). Third, exclusivists believe that salvation comes through repentance and faith in Christ's work on the cross and that no one can be saved without an explicit act of repentance and faith based on the knowledge of Christ (John 3:16–18, 36; Mark 16:15–16).

The most well-known and uncompromising defense of the exclusivist position was articulated by Hendrick Kraemer in his landmark book *The Christian Message in a Non-Christian World*.[16] The book was written to provoke discussion for the World Missionary Conference in Madras, India, in 1938. Kraemer's work has become a classic exposition of the exclusivist position. He advocated what he called a "radical discontinuity" between the Christian faith and the beliefs of all other religions. Kraemer refused to divide revelation into the categories of general and special which might allow for the possibility of revelation outside the proclamation of the Christian gospel.[17] For Kraemer, the incarnation of Jesus Christ represents the "decisive moment in world history."[18] Jesus Christ is the decisive revelation of God that confronts the entire human race and stands against all attempts by other religions or philosophies to "apprehend the totality of existence."[19] Kraemer's attack on what he calls "omnipresent relativism" includes dismantling anything that would chip away at the vast gulf between God and the human race. This involves the complete separation of nature and grace or reason and revelation.

16. Hendrick Kraemer, *The Christian Message in a Non-Christian World* (London: Edinburgh House, 1938).

17. Kraemer's disdain for general revelation is clearly influenced by Karl Barth. However, to borrow a metaphor from a letter A. G. Hogg wrote to Lesslie Newbigin in 1937, the Barthian bull pursued the matador of modernism into the china shop and disposed of him there at a destructive cost of many precious things. A proper view of general revelation is certainly one of the more unfortunate losses in Barth's neoorthodoxy.

18. Kraemer, *Christian Message*, 74.

19. Ibid., 113.

A more recent exposition of the exclusivist position may be found in Ron Nash's *Is Jesus the Only Savior?*[20] Unlike Kraemer, Nash accepts the distinction between general and special revelation but argues that general revelation "performs the function of rendering man judicially accountable before God."[21] Nash brilliantly exposes overly optimistic views of the salvific power of general revelation but does not clearly demonstrate how general revelation might assist or prepare one to receive special revelation.

Other views, still clearly within the exclusivist camp, are not convinced that maintaining the three nonnegotiables necessitates a position of such radical discontinuity or a completely negative assessment of other religions. These views tend to be more optimistic about the role and function of general revelation. While acknowledging that there is no salvation in Hinduism, Buddhism, or Islam and that general revelation is incapable of saving anyone, some exclusivists nevertheless believe that God provides truths about himself and humanity through general revelation that are accessible to all. They hold that some of these truths have been incorporated into the beliefs of other religions, providing points of continuity whenever there is a consistency with biblical revelation. This view has been recently advocated by Gerald McDermott in *Can Evangelicals Learn from World Religions?*[22] This perspective does not see Christian truth as completely detached from other truths found through general revelation; nevertheless, it holds that other religions ultimately fall short and cannot provide salvation because they do not accept the centrality of Christ's revelation and his work on the cross. Furthermore, exclusivists insist that the biblical message calls for an explicit act of repentance and faith in Christ, which is obviously not part and parcel of the message or experience of non-Christian religions.[23]

Some who hold to the three nonnegotiables have also advocated a position known as fulfillment theology. The concept goes back as far as the second century with figures like Justin Martyr and his creative use of the *logos* concept.[24] Unlike Kraemer, the governing idea behind fulfillment theology is to demonstrate the continuity between human philosophies or religions and the supernatural religion of Christianity. While affirming the final revelation of Christ, fulfillment theologians saw God working through philosophy and non-Christian religions to prepare people to hear and respond to the gospel.

20. See note 3.

21. Nash, *Is Jesus the Only Savior?* 21. Nash is quoting Bruce Demarest, *General Revelation* (Grand Rapids: Zondervan, 1982), 69–70.

22. Gerald R. McDermott, *Can Evangelicals Learn from World Religions?* (Downers Grove, Ill.: InterVarsity, 2000).

23. For modern treatments of exclusivism, see John P. Newport, *Life's Ultimate Questions* (Dallas: Word, 1989). For a vigorous defense of exclusivism, but one that ultimately leaves the fate of the unevangelized as a mystery known only to God, see Lesslie Newbigin, *The Gospel in a Pluralist Society.*

24. Martyr's use of *logos* will be explored in more detail in chapter 8.

Fulfillment theology arose out of the nineteenth-century fascination with applying Darwinian ideas of evolution to science, sociology, religion, and ethics.[25] In the writings of Max Müller (1823–1900), the concept of fulfillment robbed Christianity of all claims to revelation, and the origins of religion were viewed as an expression of universal human experience.[26] All religions were arranged in stages from the lower religions to the higher, monotheistic religions culminating in Christianity. However, there were scholars and missionaries who adopted the fulfillment concept within an evangelical framework. The most well-known scholar to do this was Monier Monier-Williams (1819–1901) at Oxford. Monier-Williams argued for the supremacy of historical Christianity as divinely revealed. He was convinced that, in time, all other world religions would someday crumble as they came into contact with the truth of the Christian gospel. However, he developed a far more positive attitude toward world religions, arguing that Christianity would not be victorious because it refuted all religions but because it fulfilled them. He argued that all religions reveal universal, God-given instincts, desires, and aspirations which are met in the Christian gospel. The missionary community, particularly in India where they were meeting stiff resistance from Hinduism, latched on to fulfillment ideas and began to explore them with earnest in the early years of the twentieth century. The most notable and articulate expression of fulfillment thought came from missionaries working in India such as T. E. Slater (1840–1912) in his work *The Higher Hinduism in Relation to Christianity* and J. N. Farquhar (1861–1929) whose landmark book *The Crown of Hinduism* was published in 1913. Farquhar and Slater were two of the earliest scholars to produce major works that ambitiously set out to compare the doctrines of Hinduism with doctrines in Christianity, demonstrating a fulfillment theme.[27] Farquhar sought to establish a nonconfrontational bridge for the Hindu to cross over to Christianity because, he argued, all of the notable features and aspirations within Hinduism find their highest expression and ultimate fulfillment in Christianity. He based the fulfillment theme on Christ's claim in Matthew 5:17 that he had not come to abolish or destroy but to fulfill.

The fulfillment motif among evangelicals was largely snuffed out with the 1938 publication of Kraemer's *The Christian Message in a Non-Christian World,* which reasserted a more rigid, uncompromising stand toward world religions. On the liberal side, the ongoing rise of rationalistic presuppositions further encouraged evangelicals to close ranks. However, the idea of a

25. Charles Darwin (1809–1882) published his landmark *On the Origin of Species by Means of Natural Selection* in 1859. Later, Herbert Spencer (1820–1903) demonstrated how evolution should be applied to all areas of human existence.

26. See, for example, Max Müller, *Origin and Growth of Religion* (Varanasi: Indological Book House, 1964).

27. See J. N. Farquhar, *The Crown of Hinduism* (1913; reprint, New Delhi: Oriental Books Reprint Corporation, 1971).

radical positive assessment of world religions without relinquishing the supremacy of Christianity found new expression in the second major attitude toward world religions known as inclusivism.

Inclusivism

Inclusivism affirms the first two of the three nonnegotiable positions held by the exclusivists. Thus, inclusivists affirm without qualification that Jesus Christ is the definitive and authoritative revelation of God. Furthermore, they affirm the centrality of Christ's work on the cross, without which no one can be saved. What makes the inclusivists distinct from the exclusivists are their particular views regarding universal access to the gospel and the necessity of a personal knowledge of Jesus Christ. Inclusivists argue from texts like John 3:16 and 2 Peter 3:9 that God's universal love for the world and his desire to save everyone imply that everyone must have access to salvation. Stuart Hackett, an advocate of inclusivism, makes the case for this in *The Reconstruction of the Christian Revelation Claim,* where he states that if every human being has been objectively provided redemption in Jesus Christ through the cross, then "it must be possible for every human individual to become personally eligible to receive that provision."[28] In other words, universal provision demands universal access. Therefore, since the majority of people in the world do not have viable access to the Christian message, inclusivists believe that access has been made available through general revelation, God's providential workings in history, and other religions. Inclusivists affirm that Christ's work on the cross is ontologically necessary for salvation but that it is not epistemologically necessary. In other words, you do not need to know about Christ personally to be the recipient of his work of grace on your behalf. Probably the most well-known articulation of this view occurs in the Vatican II document titled *Constitution of the Church,* which declares, "Those also can attain to everlasting salvation who, through no fault of their own, do not know the Gospel of Christ or his Church, yet sincerely seek God and moved by grace, strive by their deeds to do his will as it is known to them through the dictates of conscience."[29]

Inclusivists generally point to examples of God's working outside of the covenant with Israel as examples that faith, and even salvation, can be found among Gentiles. Biblical examples that are often cited include Melchizedek (Gen. 14), Rahab (Josh. 2), the Ninevites (Jon. 3), the Queen of Sheba (1 Kings

28. Stuart Hackett, *The Reconstruction of the Christian Revelation Claim* (Grand Rapids: Baker, 1984), 244.

29. *Lumen Gentium,* 16, as quoted in "Dialogue and Mission: Conflict or Convergence?" *International Review of Mission* 75, no. 299 (July 1986): 223. In another Vatican II statement, the *Constitution* declared that "since Christ died for all men, and since the ultimate vocation of man is in fact one, and divine, we ought to believe that the Holy Spirit in a manner known only to God offers to every man the possibility of being associated with his paschal mystery" (*Gaudium et Spes.,* 22).

10), and Cornelius (Acts 10).[30] Inclusivists also draw heavily from Paul's statements that God has not left himself without a witness (Acts 14:17) and that the Gentiles have the requirements of the law written on their hearts (Rom. 2:15). They interpret this witness as more than a *preparatio evangelica,* that is, a preparation to receive and respond to the special revelation which follows. They see it as an independent salvific witness, because Christ works not only explicitly through the Christian church but anonymously in countless hidden ways to draw people to himself through creation, history, and the testimony of world religions. In short, salvific grace is mediated through general revelation, not just through special revelation.

The belief in universal access to the gospel and the expanded efficacy of general revelation has led inclusivists to make a distinction between a Christian and a believer. Both are saved through the completed work of Christ on the cross. However, the Christian has explict knowledge of this, whereas the believer has only experienced Christ implicitly and does not even realize he or she has been saved by Christ. The most well-known proponent of inclusivism was the Roman Catholic theologian Karl Rahner, who called these implicit believers "anonymous Christians." Rahner taught that even though non-Christian religions contain errors, God uses them as channels to mediate his grace and mercy and ultimately to apply the work of Christ.[31] The basis for the explicit-implicit or ontological-epistemological distinction is linked to the Jews themselves. They argue that the believing Jews of the Old Testament were reconciled to God through Christ, even though they could not possibly have known about Christ explicitly. Paul, for example, argues that Christ accompanied the Israelites during their wilderness wanderings (1 Cor. 10:4) even though they could not have been explicitly aware of it. This, by extension, is applied to peoples around the world who, although they are living chronologically after Christ, are epistemologically living as if Christ had not yet come. It is these people, in particular, for whom the inclusivists want to hold out hope. Several leading Protestants have followed the new openness exhibited by Vatican II and with some qualifications have fully endorsed inclusivism. Two of the more prominent Protestants who advocate

30. For a full treatment of the inclusivist position, see Clark Pinnock, *A Wideness in God's Mercy: The Finality of Jesus Christ in a World of Religions* (Grand Rapids: Zondervan, 1992) and John Sanders, *No Other Name: An Investigation into the Destiny of the Unevangelized* (Grand Rapids: Eerdmans, 1992).

31. Karl Rahner, "Christianity and the Non-Christian Religions," in *Christianity and Other Religions,* ed. John Hick and Brian Hebblethwaite (Philadelphia: Fortress, 1980). Rahner's most complete treatment can be found in volumes 5 and 6 of his twenty volume *Theological Investigations* (New York: Seabury, 1966–1983). A more accessible defense of inclusivism may be found in Ed Hillman, *The Wider Ecumenism: Anonymous Christianity and the Church* (New York: Herder and Herder, 1968). A well-known application of inclusivism specifically to the Hindu context may be found in R. G. Panikkar, *The Unknown Christ of Hinduism* (London: Darton, Longman and Todd, 1964).

inclusivism are John Sanders in *No Other Name* and Clark Pinnock in *A Wideness in God's Mercy.*

Pluralism

Pluralism rejects all three of the nonnegotiables held by exclusivists. Pluralists such as Paul Knitter, William Cantwell Smith, W. E. Hocking, and John Hick believe that the world's religions provide independent access to salvation. Conflicting truth claims are reconciled through relocating them from the level of objective, normative truth to subjective experience. John Hick, in *An Interpretation of Religion,* wrote that world religions merely "embody different perceptions and conceptions of, and correspondingly different responses to, the Real from within the major variant ways of being human." He goes on to say that world religions all provide "soteriological spaces" or "ways along which men and women find salvation/liberation/ultimate fulfillment."[32] Christianity is just one among many religions and has no unique claim as the final or authoritative truth. According to the pluralists, Christianity is not necessarily the most advanced religion, and it is not the fulfillment of other religions. In short, all claims to exclusivity have been surrendered. For example, both John Hick and Paul Knitter refer to the claim of Christian exclusivity as a myth that must be radically reconstructed into a statement of personal meaning, not historical fact. They argue that christocentric views should be abandoned for a more global oriented theocentric view that allows all religions to participate as equal players.[33]

Pluralists, unlike exclusivists and inclusivists, do not accept the necessity of demonstrating biblical support for their view, because that would concede to Christianity some kind of adjudicating role over other religions. The New Testament may be authoritative for Christians, but the Qurʾān holds its own independent authority for Muslims, the Vedas for Hindus, and so forth. For the pluralists, the only universal standard of criteria rests in human experience, not in any particular sacred text. This is in marked contrast to Kraemer and many of his followers who tended to downplay general revelation altogether. Pluralists go the opposite direction, either denying special revelation outright or seriously degrading it to a kind of general revelation through universal religious consciousness.

Evaluation

It is beyond the scope of this work to present a detailed critique of these three views.[34] Nevertheless, a general evaluation is necessary to establish the perspective from which the ensuing dialogues emerge.

32. John Hick, *An Interpretation of Religion* (New Haven: Yale University Press, 1989), 240.

33. See John Hick and Paul F. Knitter, eds., *The Myth of Christian Uniqueness* (Maryknoll, N.Y.: Orbis, 1987).

34. For a full critique of the inclusivist and pluralist positions from an exclusivist perspective, see Nash, *Is Jesus the Only Savior?*

From my vantage point, the pluralist position is untenable for two main reasons. First, the God of the pluralists is so vague that it cannot be known. John Hick has forcefully called Christians to abandon a christocentric view of reality. In its place he asks the church to put a theocentric center, a concept so vague he cannot even use the word *God* to describe ultimate reality lest he offend nontheistic religions like Buddhism and Taoism, which his position insists he regard with equality. The result is that Hick's "noumenal" or "the Real" (as he prefers to call the ultimate reality) is broad enough to encompass the strict theism of Judaism and Islam as well as the atheism of Buddhism and Taoism. Hick's noumenal encompasses both the personal conception of God in Jesus Christ and the impersonal conception of God in the *nirguṇa Brāhman* of Hinduism. This resulting fog gives us a God and a no-God who is unknown and unknowable and about whom we can make no definitive statement.

Second, the pluralist position is ultimately based on the subjectivity of human experience, not on any objective truth claims. Human experience is the final arbiter of all truth. Therefore, revelation as revelation is struck down. The deity of Christ, for example, is not an objective truth that calls for our response. It is merely a subjective expression of what Jesus meant to his disciples, which may or may not affect us because every human conceives of truth differently. Early in his writings, Hick sought to define salvation vaguely as the movement from self-centeredness to reality-centeredness.[35] However, this definition came under the withering fire of feminist theologians who argued that defining the lack of salvation as being self-focused and self-assertive is a characteristically male assessment. Females, they argue, are finding salvation by being more assertive and self-projecting. Hick conceded that female salvation may indeed be the opposite of male salvation.[36] This kind of unbridled subjectivity that seeks to replace biblical theology based on the assurance of divine revelation with the ever changing subjectivity of human experience is, in my view, untenable. Indeed, Clark Pinnock has gone so far as to say that the very term *pluralist* is an inaccurate label for this position. He points out that "a true pluralist would accept the differences of the various world religions and not try to fit them into a common essence. It would be better to call them relativists."[37]

The inclusivist position is to be commended for its strong affirmation of the centrality of Jesus Christ and the indispensable nature of his death and resurrection for salvation. Furthermore, inclusivism has keenly discerned how God has worked in the lives of those outside the boundaries of the covenant such as Rahab and Naaman. The more positive view of the relationship between general and special revelation is a welcome relief from the

35. Hick, *An Interpretation of Religion,* 46–47.

36. Ibid., 52.

37. Clark Pinnock, "Toward an Evangelical Theology of Religions," *JETS* 33, no. 3 (September 1990): 363 n. 12.

complete separation of nature and grace as seen in Kraemer. On this particular point, the inclusivists do not necessarily fall outside the parameters of Christian history and tradition. Indeed, Thomas Aquinas advocated a more open attitude toward general revelation with the dictim *Gratia non tollit sed perficit naturam* (Grace does not abrogate but perfects nature). However, inclusivists have embraced additional views that are clearly at odds with historic Christian faith.

First, the inclusivist attempt to drive a wedge between the ontological necessity of Christ's work and the epistemological response of repentance and faith cannot be sustained. Inclusivists can be very selective in their use of the biblical data. For example, they often quote 2 Peter 3:9, which says that God is "not wanting anyone to perish," but they fail to quote the rest of the verse, which says that he wants "everyone to come to repentance." God's universal salvific will is explicitly linked to human response. Inclusivists cite Paul's powerful statement about the universality of revelation in Romans 10:18, which says that the "voice" of revelation has "gone out into all the earth," but they fail to point out that this affirmation is in the context of Paul's assertion that "everyone who calls on the name of the Lord will be saved" (Rom. 10:13). Paul goes on to establish a chain that begins with the sending church and the preaching witness and leads to the one who hears, believes, and calls upon the name of the Lord (Rom. 10:14–15). Inclusivists want to separate the links of this chain and argue that the witnessing church is not necessary for believing. In other words, implicit faith can be present apart from the explicit knowledge of Jesus Christ. However, if the inclusivist position is true, then it would mean that non-Christian religions have brought more people to the feet of Christ (implicitly) than has the witnessing church in the world.

Second, for the inclusivists to argue that the object of all genuine faith is Christ shifts the emphasis from a personal response to Christ to the experience of faith regardless of its object. In this view, salvation comes equally to the Hindu who places faith in Krishna, the Buddhist who places faith in Amitabha Buddha, or the Christian who places faith in Jesus Christ. Moving from the worship of Krishna to the worship of Christ does not involve a turning away from Krishna but merely a clarification that it was Christ being worshipped all along. However, Paul says in Acts 20:21, "I have declared to both Jews and Greeks that they must turn to God in repentance and have faith in our Lord Jesus." What would the inclusivists have recommended to Wynfrith when he confronted the Frisian religion in 754? Would they have counseled Wynfrith to point out that the human sacrifices offered to Njord the god of the earth were actually symbols or types of the Lamb of God? Was Thor just another name for Jesus Christ?[38] This is not to deny that there are examples in the Old Testament of people who have faith outside of the Jewish covenant

38. J. A. van Rooy, "Christ and the Religions: The Issues at Stake," *Missionalia* 13, no. 1 (April 1985): 9.

such as Jethro, Naaman, and Rahab; but the object of their faith is explicitly the God of Israel, not the indigenous gods that they formerly worshipped.

Finally, to call Hindus or Muslims or Buddhists anonymous Christians has long been regarded as an insult to those within these traditions. It is patronizing to tell a devout Hindu who worships Krishna that he or she is really worshipping Christ and is temporarily in an epistemological gap. Couldn't the Buddhist or the Hindu respond that Christians are actually anonymous Buddhists or anonymous Hindus? Indeed, there are Buddhist and Muslim groups who have made that very claim.[39]

The strength of the exclusivist position is that it affirms the authority of Scripture, the unique centrality of Jesus Christ, and the indispensability of his death and resurrection. Furthermore, exclusivism takes seriously the call to repentance and the need to turn to Jesus Christ as the object of explicit faith. Exclusivism affirms the key tenets of the historic Christian proclamation as delivered to us in the ancient creeds. The problem with exclusivism comes when, in a desire to protect the centrality of these truths, it overextends itself into several potential errors.

First, in a desire to affirm the centrality of special revelation and the particular claims of Christ, exclusivism sometimes fails to fully appreciate God's activity in the pre-Christian heart. It is one thing to affirm that Jesus Christ is the apex of God's self-revelation; it is entirely another to say that Jesus Christ is the only revelation from God. Since all general revelation ultimately points to Christ, exclusivists need not be threatened by the signs God has placed in creation and in the human heart. God is not passive or stingy in his self-revelation but has left footprints behind, whether in the awe-inspiring expanse of the universe, in the recesses of a solitary heart groping after God, or in the depths of the reflective human mind as it explores fundamental questions that have gripped philosophers and theologians throughout the ages.

Second, exclusivists have sometimes taken a defensive posture and have been unwilling to honestly engage with the questions and objections of those from non-Christian religions. Yet the Great Commission clearly commands Christians to "go into all the world" (Mark 16:15–16). The early Christians boldly proclaimed the gospel amid a dizzying array of cults, mystery religions, emperor worship, and more. The apostles would have surely found the defensiveness that has often characterized exclusivists as incomprehensible in light of our global mandate. Put simply, the match cannot be played if the players remain in the safety of the locker room. The creeds of historic Christianity are not bunkers in which to hide; they are the basis for a global proclamation. The incarnation is the greatest example of God's ini-

39. This claim is made by several Islamic leaders, including the Indonesian Association of Muslim Intellectuals (= Ikatan Cendekiawan Muslim Indonesia or ICMI) leader Nurcholis Madjid, as well as the more well-known view of the Hindu, Vivekananda, who claimed that all the religions of the world are contained within Hinduism.

tiative to enter into our context. Jesus did not enter some vague history, but a particular history at a particular time. Likewise, Christians must fully engage with the particular challenges and contexts to which God has called us. The way forward is to embrace our convictions regarding the truthfulness and uniqueness of the Christian gospel while fully engaging in honest, open interactions with members of other religious traditions. This book is an attempt to do just that.

Of the three positions outlined above, I identify with the exclusivist position because I affirm without qualification the three nonnegotiables. The inclusivist and pluralist positions cannot, in my view, be considered consistent with historic Christianity. I remain convinced, along with other exclusivists, that the historic affirmations of the major creeds are a faithful and trustworthy summary of the basic teachings of Scripture.[40] However, in order to clarify my view in light of the concerns outlined above, I prefer to use the phrase *engaged exclusivist.* This position affirms "the faith that was once for all entrusted to the saints" but, unlike Kraemer's exclusivism, also includes the following two emphases: First, this position emphasizes a more open stance regarding general revelation as a *preparatio evangelica.* John Calvin pointed out that God himself "has endued all men with some idea of his Godhead, the memory of which he constantly renews and occasionally enlarges."[41] In this context, the Reformer refers to the "sense of the Divine" *(sensus divinitatis)* and the universal "germ of religion" *(semen religionis).* Likewise, in his *Confessions* Augustine speaks of the "loving memory" of God that lies latent even in unbelievers.[42] In short, while we must be careful not to allow general revelation to swallow up special revelation (inclusivism), we must not relinquish the basic truth that there is a continuity between the two.

Second, engaged exclusivism affirms the notion that good theology must be missiologically focused. Christianity is not a mere collection of static formulas or propositions to which we give mental or private assent. Good theology compels us to be fully engaged with the world. This is a departure from Tertullian, the early Christian apologist, who once asked, "What has Athens to do with Jerusalem?" But it is consistent, in my view, with the Scriptures. Indeed, the apostle Peter connects the inner conviction of Christ's centrality with this kind of vigorous engagement with the world when he writes, "In your hearts set apart Christ as Lord. Always be prepared to give an answer to everyone who asks you to give the reason for the hope that you have, but do this with gentleness and respect" (1 Pet. 3:15). Cer-

40. I am referring to the historic Apostles' Creed as well as the more precise formulations of Nicaea (325) and of Chalcedon (451).

41. John Calvin, *Institutes of the Christian Religion,* vol. 20, book 1, chapter 3.1. For an English translation of the Institutes, see John T. McNeill, ed., *Calvin: Institutes of the Christian Religion* (Philadelphia: Westminster, 1960).

42. Augustine, *Confessions* 7.17.23 (*NPNF*[1] 1:111).

tainly, there are a number of notable evangelical Christians within the exclusivist camp who have been very engaged and have taken this verse seriously. Examples may be found in such works as Harold Netland's *Dissonant Voices* and Vinoth Ramachandra's *The Recovery of Mission.*[43]

The Distinctiveness and Format of This Book

Engaged exclusivism provides the foundation and stimulus for the kind of engaged, spirited conversations this book attempts to bring together. What makes this book distinctive is that it is more than a one-way defense of historic Christianity. The upcoming dialogues allow for a vigorous, two-way exchange of ideas. In chapters 2 through 6, a Christian engages in conversations with two Hindus, two Buddhists, and four Muslims, all committed to their respective faiths and all with their own particular challenges to the Christian proclamation. The conversations are designed to be animated and vigorous discussions while maintaining congeniality and friendliness, remembering Martin Luther's observation that "if I fight with dirt I shall always get dirty, whether I win or lose."[44]

Such dialogues are not without precedent in Christian and non-Christian literature. One of the earliest examples was written by the Christian scholar, missionary, and martyr Raymond Llull, considered the father of Islamic apologetics. His work *The Book of the Gentile and the Three Wise Men* was written in 1275 and describes a Gentile's search for true religion. This leads him into a conversation with three sages—a Jew, a Christian, and a Muslim. Each of the fictional participants commends his religion in the most positive and courteous terms. Each is full of conviction without being polemical.[45] Several contemporary dialogues similar to the format of Llull's book may also be found. In *World Religions: A Dialogue,* Ninian Smart creates a fictional conversation between six participants: a Christian, a Jew, a Muslim, a Hindu, and two Buddhists.[46] While Smart does an excellent job of creating a dynamic interchange among the participants, the book's fictional Christian moderator makes no attempt to represent or defend historic Christian-

43. See Harold Netland, *Dissonant Voices* (Grand Rapids: Eerdmans, 1991); Vinoth Ramachandra, *The Recovery of Mission* (Carlisle, England: Paternoster, 1996).

44. Theodore Tappert, trans. and ed., *Luther's Works,* vol. 51, *Table Talk* (Philadelphia: Fortress, 1967), xxii.

45. Anthony Bonner, ed. and trans., *Selected Works of Ramon Llull (1232–1316),* vol. 2 (Princeton: Princeton University Press, 1985), 303.

46. Ninian Smart, *World Religions: A Dialogue* (Baltimore: Penguin Books, 1966). Smart's dialogues cover a much wider range of topics in a book less than half the length of this one. The discussions, therefore, tend to be general and at times superficial in their eagerness to find harmony among the world's religions. The topics covered are as follows: polytheism and monotheism, rebirth and salvation, nirvāṇa and mysticism, the worship of God, Buddhism and the Trinity, incarnation and history, and good and evil. The book ends with the Christian moderator declaring to the participants that "you've half persuaded me to look upon doctrines in a more Hindu way" (p. 140).

ity. A contemporary Catholic attempt at a nonfictional dialogue similar to this work may be found in *Christianity and World Religions.* This book represents a dialogue between Roman Catholic theologian Hans Küng and advocates of Islam (Josef van Ess), Hinduism (Heinrich von Stietencron), and Buddhism (Heinz Bechert).[47] This volume, while notable in several of its features, also does not defend historic Christianity. Finally, the general format of this book is also present in other religious traditions. In Hinduism, for example, philosophical reasoning was frequently done through argument and counterargument until a conclusion or resolution was reached.

The great Protestant reformer Martin Luther had a practice of holding animated discussions around the table in his home. These were recorded and became known as *Table Talk.*[48] Most of these conversations took place in the Black Cloister in Wittenberg where he lived even after his marriage to Katherine von Bora. Luther's home was a busy place, frequented by "exiled clergymen, escaped nuns, government officials, visitors from abroad, and colleagues of Luther in the university like Philip Melanchthon, John Bugenhagen, and Justus Jonas."[49] Supper in Luther's household was generally served around 5 p.m. During the meal, Luther would frequently "throw out a question" that would begin a vigorous discussion on issues ranging from serious theological discussions about the nature of Christian conversion, to ethical issues such as whether someone who commits suicide can be saved, to practical matters such as the benefits of a mother's milk. Luther would often make a point, and someone might take exception or ask for clarification about what was said. Luther patiently listened to the objection and then attempted a refutation of the challenge. These conversations were so interesting that the students who lived in Luther's home began taking notes, which are the primary sources for *Table Talk.* The present work, *Christianity at the Religious Roundtable,* seeks to emulate the give-and-take of Luther's talks in an informal, noncombative way for the mutual edification of all who participate.

Of particular interest is Luther's perspective on the great challenges the Christian church faced in the sixteenth century. The Reformer frequently made passionate remarks concerning humanists such as Erasmus, religious enthusiasts such as Andrew Karlstadt and Thomas Munzer, and political leaders such as Elector Frederick of Saxony and Archduke Ferdinand of Austria. The range of topics in Luther's *Table Talk* is relevant because it gives us a glimpse into the issues that Luther regarded as the most formidable challenges facing the church in his day. He was so concerned, for example, about Zwingli's views that in November 1531, he remarked that Zwingli's

47. Peter Heinegg, trans., *Christianity and World Religions* (Maryknoll, N.Y.: Orbis, 1993).

48. See note 44. This 476-page volume represents only one tenth of what is known as *Table Talk.*

49. Tappert, *Luther's Works,* vol. 51, ix.

death was the judgment of God because "if his error had prevailed, we would have perished and our church with us."[50] Luther was also concerned about the threat posed by the spread of Islam. He made numerous references to the Turks and his concern about the "advance of the Turks" who were, in his day, threatening to overrun Austria. Certainly, from our vantage point nearly five hundred years after the conversation, the spread of Islam has posed a far more serious and ongoing threat to the existence of the Christian church than have the views of Zwingli. It is humbling to realize that every generation, including our own, suffers from a degree of myopia. Some issues which concern us may, in the long run, be of little moment while other issues continue to be significant in the ongoing discussions about the life and future vitality of the church.

Especially notable for this current work is the realization that other religious beliefs have been a constant challenge since the church's inception. This is not to demean or discount other challenges that the contemporary church faces. Only time will tell how significant some of the current challenges will be. But the challenge of world religions has always been relevant. The global mandate of the Great Commission assures us that it will always be relevant, but it has grown even more so in the last century. Indeed, the latter half of the twentieth century witnessed global religious renewal coupled with the advance of the church in the non-Western world, and the trend continues in these early years of the twenty-first century. The contemporary church is no longer confined to Western Europe as it was in the days of Luther. Today the globalization of the church is, to borrow a phrase from William Temple, "one of the great facts of our time." For example, when William Carey, the father of the modern missionary movement, went to India at the turn of the nineteenth century, only 1 percent of the world's Protestants lived in all of Asia, Africa, and Latin America combined. Today the majority of both Catholic and Protestant Christians live in Asia, Africa, and Latin America. The church is now predominately nonwhite and non-European in its cultural and ethnic heritage and is living in areas dominated by the other major world religions.[51] The church must now sit at a religious roundtable that is global in its dimensions if we are to engage seriously in the living context of much of the church of Jesus Christ.

Although based on numerous formal and informal conversations that the author has had with non-Christians around the world, this book pre-

50. Ibid., 11.

51. *Christian History,* vol. 36, 20. See also Dana Robert, "Shifting Southward: Global Christianity since 1945," *International Bulletin of Missionary Research* 24, no. 2 (April 2000): 50–58; Andrew Walls, "Origins of Old Northern and New Southern Christianity," in *The Missionary Movement in Christian History: Studies in the Transmission of Faith* (Maryknoll, N.Y.: Orbis, 1996), 68–75; and Andrew Walls, "Eusebius Tries Again: Reconceiving the Study of Christian History," *International Bulletin of Missionary Research* 24, no. 3 (July 2000): 105–11.

sents fictional conversations between an evangelical Christian and members of the three largest non-Christian religions—Hinduism, Buddhism, and Islam. Because of the diversity that is present in all religions, each non-Christian religion will be represented by at least two proponents from varying perspectives within their particular tradition. To avoid the superficiality so often present in books that summarize entire religious traditions in a dozen or so pages, these conversations will focus on two key doctrines within each tradition. For the sake of consistency and a common reference point, the doctrine of God or ultimate reality (however that may be defined within the tradition) will be explored with all participants in all three non-Christian religions.

A second doctrine will then be discussed with each religion. Special care has been taken to select a doctrine that is of particular importance to that religion and is of special significance in the history of Christianity. With the proponents of Hinduism, for example, after we discuss the doctrine of ultimate reality *(Brāhman)*, we will focus on the doctrine of creation *(māyā)* in Hinduism. The nature of the world remains a key area of discussion between Christians and Hindus and forms the basis from which numerous other doctrines can be properly understood. Despite the importance of this doctrine in both Christianity and Hinduism, the Hindu perspective on the creation is widely misunderstood by Christians in the West. With the proponents of Buddhism, the second doctrinal focus will be Buddhist ethics. The role of ethics has long been regarded as one of the most important contributions of Buddhists around the world. Finally, with the proponents of Islam, the second doctrinal focus will be on Christ and the incarnation. The Qurʾān has its own doctrine of Christ that is not only important within Islam itself but is important in understanding the frontier separating Christianity from Islam.

The format of each section will be as follows. First, a general introduction to the theme will be provided. This will give readers who may not be familiar with either the evangelical Christian perspective or the particular views of the non-Christian religion the background necessary to benefit from and follow the upcoming dialogue. It is not essential that readers have an extensive background in the study of world religions, although the conversations sometimes explore unfamiliar territory with a new worldview and a number of new vocabulary words.

Second, the latter half of each chapter contains a section titled "Religious Roundtable" where dialogue takes place. Typically, the conversation begins with my offering a single point that demonstrates why Christianity, in my view, is distinctive from the non-Christian religion. The proponents who are then present will, of course, be given ample space and time to defend, refute, or clarify points that I have made. In the process, if something needs to be clarified or if a caricature of the opponent's position is being addressed rather than the actual doctrine, then everyone is free to interrupt and ask for or provide the necessary clarification. After the non-Christian rebuttal, I will be required to respond to their points. Further questions or clarifications may be raised by either side in the form of a rejoinder at the conclusion of the central exchanges.

As noted earlier, these conversations are based on actual exchanges that typically followed certain guidelines. It is helpful for readers to know these ground rules up front so they can understand the limits of these conversations and so they can have guidance when entering into dialogue with adherents of non-Christian religions. Four ground rules will be rigorously adhered to in these dialogues.

First, all differences of opinion or perspectives should be shared honestly without being pejorative. Kindness and humility should accompany all interactions along with an earnest attempt to listen attentively to what the other person is saying. True dialogue is never passive but requires active listening. While I have argued that this does not necessitate suspending our own faith or surrendering essential features of the historic Christian proclamation, I nevertheless affirm that we can and should be challenged by all those who come to the religious roundtable. There will certainly be many places where our own understanding of the other religion will be brought into sharper focus, and cherished stereotypes may prove to be false or misleading. I also believe that in the context of listening to the objections and questions of those from other religions, believers will be forced to examine their own faith from angles that, heretofore, have been left largely unexamined. In this way, our own faith may very well be enriched because of the encounter.

Second, no one is permitted to exploit abuses present in a religion that are at odds with widely accepted beliefs and practices. All religions have been embarrassed by poor representations of their faith by particular followers. As much as humanly possible, we should avoid stereotypes and gross caricatures of the other religions. For example, in her book *Muslims and Christians Face to Face,* Kate Zebiri has documented how Muslim and Christian dialogue has been consistently plagued by distortions and misperceptions of the other religion's self-understanding.[52] The whole purpose of these conversations is to engage in honest dialogues with the actual positions of other religions and to hear their real objections. Setting up straw men that can be easily knocked down or not allowing Hindus, Buddhists, and Muslims to register authentic objections would defeat the whole purpose of the dialogues.

Third, the questions, responses, clarifications, and rejoinders must all pertain to the central theme being discussed. It is easy for any discussion to drift off the main focus. While there are innumerable points of doctrine or history that could captivate our interest, the central theme will not be well served if this guideline is not adhered to.

52. Kate Zebiri, *Muslims and Christians Face to Face* (Oxford: One World, 1997).

This raises an important point about the choice of themes that will be pursued in these conversations. One of the first questions some may raise concerning these dialogues is why the doctrine of salvation is not discussed. This is an important and strategic omission that is intentional. Having taught courses on world religions to Christian students for many years, I have observed that students often ask soteriological questions first when they reflect on the beliefs of world religions. They want to know immediately how a Hindu or Buddhist or Muslim understands salvation. This is a natural and appropriate question to raise. However, I strongly believe it is virtually impossible to really explore this question without understanding it within the larger worldview and context of the religion. Thus, these dialogues will not discuss the issue of salvation. In the future, I hope to devote a follow-up volume to dialogues that discuss conceptions of salvation as this volume centers around the doctrine of God, but for now we must be patient and learn to be good listeners who seek to understand the larger context.

Finally, while it would be disingenuous for any truly Christian communication not to earnestly desire that all persons come to know Jesus Christ, I freely accept the famous Muslim dictum in the Qurʾān that says, "There can be no compulsion in religion" (sūrah 2:256). After the dialogue is complete, a Buddhist, for example, is free to remain a committed Buddhist without being told that our differences are only semantic. Dialogue should never be a path to sweep major differences under the rug of pluralism. Furthermore, it would be equally irresponsible to tell people that they are, after all, anonymous Christians, thereby swallowing up their faith in the seemingly limitless expanse of inclusivism.

After the three dialogues are complete (parts 1–3), part 4 will focus on three case studies that highlight key features of the relationship between Christianity and the non-Christian religions. The case studies will stretch from the second century to the twenty-first century and will include four Christians from three different continents, each struggling in his own context with the interface of the Christian faith with non-Christian beliefs. We will engage in a historical dialogue with an apologist from Syria, a teacher from Africa, a journalist and theologian from India, and an Egyptian-born missionary from Scotland. After each case study, questions will be raised to help focus on the key issues.

I hope that through these conversations and case studies readers will see how important our historical and theological traditions are in properly responding to the challenges posed by non-Christian religions. Throughout history the church's mission has been effective only so far as it was properly rooted in good theology. Yet proper theology alone cannot preserve the church if it is not engaged in mission with the world. As my colleague Peter Kuzmič is fond of declaring to his classes, "Good missiology must be theologically grounded, and good theology must be missiologically focused!"[53] I heartily agree. This book seeks to preserve this balance by challenging twenty-first-century evangelicals to engage in interreligious dialogue as committed Christian witnesses.

53. Peter Kuzmič is the Paul E. and Eva B. Toms Professor of World Missions and European Studies at Gordon-Conwell Theological Seminary.

PART 1

Christianity and Hinduism

2

Doctrine of God

Brāhman

"In the beginning God . . ."

Genesis 1:1

"In the beginning there was One, without a second . . ."

Chāndogya Upanishad VI.2.1

The One and the Many

Most Western Christians commonly assume that Hindus believe in a vast pantheon of gods and goddesses. Even a casual visitor to India cannot help but be overwhelmed by the array of gods found in homes, shops, temples, and fields. As you walk the city streets or village pathways of India, you will most certainly see images of the playful Krishna with his famous flute, the four-armed dancing Śiva, or Śiva's son, the elephant-headed god Gaṇeśa. But these are just a few of the gods worshipped in India. If you are bold enough to take one of the famous yellow and black three-wheeled auto rickshaws into the gridlocked streets of one of India's great cities, you would likely see small pictures of deities pasted onto the dashboard or dangling crookedly from the rearview mirror with incense sticks burning beneath them. As you board a crowded bus, you might think the strange words written in Hindi above the windshield are, as is traditional in the West, the destination or route name of the bus. It might surprise you to find out that they are a declaration of praise to Hanuman, the famous monkey god who protects his devotees from harm on the road.

Not only is India noted for its gods, but also for its goddesses. If you ever visit India during a time of national or regional celebration, you will find special emphasis on goddess worship. The great goddess of India, Māhā Devi, is manifested in many different ways depending on where you are in the country. She may appear as the blood-drinking Kali who is garlanded with severed heads and arms and dances on the corpse of her husband Śiva or as Durga the warrior goddess who is famous for slaying a buffalo demon *(mahisa)* by piercing his chest with a trident. Yet these experiences would be only the beginning of your introduction to the many gods and goddesses of India.

Indian lore contains a well-known tale about a Hindu man who spent his entire life as a kind of theistic census taker. He went from village to village, house to house, occupation to occupation, caste to caste, inquiring at every location about which deities were worshipped at that place by those people. After traveling throughout India and recording the names of all the deities who were worshipped, tradition states that he chronicled the list in a great book. The number is traditionally held to have been 330 million. When the weary traveler finally returned to his home village, exhausted and in his ninety-third year, he was asked to count how many gods were in his book. He spent seven years counting the gods, and at the end of the book he wrote the grand total—one. He declared in his dying breath that there is "one God worshipped in India."[1]

This story symbolizes the classic problem concerning Hindu theism, and it is the reason why the Western assumption that Hindus are polytheistic is not as simple as the observations of a casual visitor to India might indicate. On the one hand, popular Hinduism seems to have no end to gods and goddesses who are worshipped and adored.[2] On the other hand, India is known throughout the world for its intricate and sublime philosophy that teaches there is only one ultimate reality. The Upanishads (Classical Upanishads date from 600 B.C. to 300 B.C.) and commentaries on them by renowned theologians like Śaṅkara (A.D. 788–820) and Rāmānuja (A.D. 1017–1137) are widely regarded by scholars as among the greatest theological and philosophical works ever written. To categorize Śaṅkara and Rāmānuja merely as philosophers is to overlook the fact that they were both deeply committed to producing systems of thought and theology that have provided the religious basis for much of what is today called Hinduism.[3] However, as in the

1. L. J. Baillas, *World Religions: A Story Approach* (Mystic, Conn.: Twenty-Third Publications, 1991), 158.

2. B. Kumarappa, *The Hindu Conception of Deity* (London: Luzac, 1934); N. Macnicol, *Indian Theism* (Oxford: Oxford University Press, 1915); and N. Macnicol, "Some Hindrances to Theism in India," *The Indian Interpreter* 7, no. 2 (July 1912): 81–88.

3. I appreciate and concur with Julius Lipner's comment in the preface to his excellent study on Rāmānuja that he seeks "to disabuse those scholars who maintain that all the sustained critical work of the Hindu tradition is 'philosophical' in nature. The time has come, I believe, to rehabilitate 'theology' as an apt description for a substantial part of the intellectual tradition of the Hindus." See Julius Lipner, *The Face of Truth* (Albany, N.Y.:

famous story, these major philosophical and theological traditions, while acknowledging the diverse theistic traditions in India, assert there is but one supreme God.[4]

This paradox of the "one and the many" is a classic tension in Indian theology and undergirds a great deal of the discussion concerning theism in the Indian context.[5] This theme is of particular interest to those who study the Upanishads, because it is in these texts that the theology of the one Ultimate Being, known as Brāhman, is most clearly expressed.[6] Those systems of thought that focus on the Upanishads are known as *Vedānta,* which means "end of the Vedas" because the Upanishads were attached as an appendix to the earliest of Hindu writings, a collection known as the Vedas.[7] The Upanishads were originally an oral tradition only, but eventually they were written down and today can easily be purchased in a good English translation as a separate collection.[8] Followers of Vedānta have wrestled with the paradoxical complexities of Hindu theism for many centuries and have resolved this tension in various ways that have evolved into separate schools of Vedantic thought. The two largest and most challenging to the Christian worldview are known as *advaita* (nondualism) and *viśiṣṭādvaita* (modified nondualism).[9] These positions must be understood if we are to enter into a meaningful discussion with Hindus about the doctrine of God.

SUNY Press, 1986), ix. He prefers to call Śaṅkara and Rāmānuja "philosophical theologians" (p. 1) since neither uses any abstract human model of epistemology as a starting point but only the revelation of Hindu scriptures, particularly the Upanishads and the *Bhagavad-Gītā.*

4. See, for example, Moti Lal Pandit, "Śaṅkara's Concept of Reality," *Indian Theological Studies* 17, no. 4 (December 1980): 8–16. See also Julius Lipner, "The Christian and Vedantic Theories of Originative Causality: A Study in Transcendence and Immanence," *Philosophy East and West* 28 (1978): 1–16.

5. For an excellent overview of some of the issues involved, see G. Feuerstein, "The One and the Many: A Fundamental Philosophical Problem in the Principal Upanishads," *Hinduism* 88 (1980): 1–10. See also Richard King, "Brāhman and the World: Immanence and Transcendence in *Advaita Vedānta,*" *Scottish Journal of Religious Studies* 12 (autumn 1991): 107–26.

6. The word *Brāhman* originally meant "sacred power" but gradually came to be identified as the Supreme Absolute.

7. There are four Vedas: *Rig* (hymns), *Sama* (chants), *Yajur* (sacred formula), and *Atharva* (secret formulas). When properly understood, these are not four separate books but (particularly the *Sama* and the *Yajur*) are various recensions and variations of the earliest work, the *Ṛg-Veda,* which is composed of 1,028 hymns to various gods in an early Vedic pantheon. The Vedic religion is an early precursor to what would eventually develop as Hinduism.

8. Perhaps the most accessible translation is S. Radhakrishnan, ed., *The Principal Upanishads* (Delhi: Harper Collins, 1996). All translations of the Upanishads in this book will be taken from Radhakrishnan's translation.

9. *Advaita* literally means "not two," from the word *dva* meaning "two" with the privative *a* prefix. In the West the term *monism* is frequently used rather than the negative *non-*

Advaita Vedānta

The first school of Vedānta, and by far the most familiar to those in the West, is known as advaita or nondualism. The most important thinker in the history of advaita was the late seventh- and early eighth-century philosophical theologian Śaṅkara.[10] Śaṅkara based his teaching on the Upanishads and is widely believed by the advaitins to be the greatest expositor of the Upanishads. Śaṅkara observed the theological tension in the Upanishads between the one Ultimate Being and the many gods who are worshipped. For example, there is a well-known passage where a high-caste Brahmin named Sakalya asks the sage-king, Yajnavalkya, how many gods there are. A most revealing dialogue ensues beginning with the sage responding,

> "As many as are mentioned in the *nivid* of the hymn of praise to the Visvedevas, namely, three hundred and three, and three thousand and three."
>
> "Yes," he said, "but how many gods are there, Yajnavalkya?"
>
> "Thirty-three."
>
> "Yes," he said, "but how many gods are there, Yajnavalkya?"
>
> "Six."
>
> "Yes," said he, "but how many gods are there, Yajnavalkya?"
>
> "Three."
>
> "Yes," said he, "but how many gods are there, Yajnavalkya?"
>
> "One and a half."
>
> "Yes," said he, "but how many gods are there, Yajnavalkya?"
>
> "One."[11]

---

dualism. For the purpose of this dialogue, no distinction will be made between the two terms. There is a third, smaller branch of Vedānta founded by Madhva known as *dvaita* (dualism). This thirteenth-century development of Vedānta was influenced by the ancient Christian presence in southwest India. Due to the limitations of space, this smaller and less influential movement falls outside this particular study.

10. For an overview of Śaṅkara's thought, see the three-volume series edited by A. J. Alston (London: Shanti Sadan): *Śaṅkara on Creation* (1980), *Śaṅkara on the Absolute* (1980), and *Śaṅkara on the Soul* (1981). See also E. Deutsch and J. A. B. van Buitenen, eds., *A Source Book of Advaita Vedānta* (Honolulu: University of Hawaii Press, 1971).

11. *Bṛhad-Āraṇyaka Upanishad* 3.9.1–2. The conversation concludes with the sage saying that the three hundred and three and the three thousand and three are but manifestations of the thirty-three gods. This is a classic example of the way the Upanishads can demonstrate continuity with the past yet introduce new philosophic and metaphysical ideas that later form the basis for Vedantic thought. The sage identifies the number of gods as thirty-three, which is clearly taught in the *Ṛg-Veda*, but manages in the process to introduce the idea of the plurality of gods being merely manifestations of the one.

This kind of intriguing ambiguity about the relationship of the one and the many is a tension frequently found in the Upanishads.[12]

Nirguṇa-Saguṇa Distinction in Advaita

According to Śaṅkara, this tension is resolved by the recognition that the Upanishads speak of the Supreme Absolute in two ways or, more accurately, at two different levels of reality. The highest level is known as *nirguṇa Brāhman.* The lower level of reality is known as *saguṇa Brāhman. Brāhman* is the designation in Indian thought for the Supreme Absolute. The terms *nirguṇa* and *saguṇa* are added as a prefix to the word Brāhman to distinguish between the two levels. The distinction is drawn from the Upanishads and is found in the *Bṛhad-Āraṇyaka,* which declares that "there are two forms of Brāhman, the formed and the formless" (II.3.1), and in the *Śvetāśvatara,* which declares that Brāhman is "devoid of qualities [nirguṇa]" (6.11) and yet is "the possessor of qualities [saguṇa]" (6.18). Śaṅkara himself sums up the basic problem when he writes that in the Upanishads one meets Brāhman, who on the one hand "is qualified by limiting conditions" and on the other hand is "the opposite of this, i.e., One which is free from all limiting conditions whatsoever."[13] He reconciles this paradox by insisting that in the Upanishads, God (Brāhman) is spoken of on two distinct levels. On the highest level, Brāhman cannot be spoken of as having any qualities or relationships. Brāhman is, to use Śaṅkara's language, "non-connected with the world and is devoid of all qualities."[14] When Hindus speak of Brāhman in this way, they are speaking of Brāhman as nirguṇa Brāhman, that is, Brāhman without *(nir)* attributes or qualities *(guna).*[15]

Whenever the Upanishads speak of a multitude of different gods *with* various qualities or attributes, they are speaking, according to Śaṅkara, on a lower level of reality. When Brāhman is spoken of in this way, it is designated

12. See, for example, *Bṛhad-Āraṇyaka* 1.4.10, which declares that "Brāhman, indeed, was this in the beginning. It knew itself only as 'I am Brāhman.' Therefore it became all. Whoever among the gods became awakened to this, he indeed, became that." See also 2.5.1–15, which declares in part that in Brāhman, "All beings, all gods, all worlds, all breathing creatures, all these selves are held together." Other well-known passages are in *Chāndogya Upanishad* 6.1.4–7 and 6.2.1. The latter text asserts that "in the beginning, my dear, this was Being alone, one only without a second," then develops how this one Brāhman entered the many deities. This doctrine is perhaps best summed up in the *Taittrīya Upanishad,* which records that the one Brāhman declares, "Let me become many" (II.6.1).

13. Deutsch and van Buitenen, *Source Book,* 160.

14. Ibid., 197, 162. The editors are quoting Śaṅkara's *Brahmasutrabhasya.* This is a major work of Śaṅkara's and is a commentary on a classic but more esoteric commentary on the Upanishads known as the *Brahma Sūtras.*

15. See also *Śvetāśvatara* 6.11, which declares Brāhman as "devoid of qualities" and five verses later declares that "He is . . . possessor of qualities" (6.16). The genius of Śaṅkara brings these various strands of Upanishadic teaching into a consistent system of thought. Sometimes these two levels of Brāhman are referred to as *para* Brāhman (higher) and *apara* Brāhman (lower).

as saguṇa Brāhman, that is, Brāhman with *(sa)* attributes or qualities *(guna)*. For Śaṅkara, one encounters a personal God only at the level of saguṇa. Advaitins designate this personal God with the name Īśvara, but are careful to qualify that Īśvara, because he is located in saguṇa Brāhman, has no final or ultimate reality. Īśvara is merely a projection of imperfect and limited human descriptions of God.[16]

In summary, the nirguṇa-saguṇa distinction serves two basic purposes within the theistic framework of advaitism. First, it is a way of reconciling the monotheistic and polytheistic statements of the Upanishads into a consistent, unified system of thought. The paradoxical tension between the one and the many finds a logical meeting point in the nirguṇa-saguṇa distinction. The staggering array of gods and goddesses in India does not violate the oneness of God, because all of those gods and goddesses with their many attributes and qualities belong to the lower level of reality, namely, saguṇa Brāhman. Yet nothing that is characterized as saguṇa has any ultimate or certain reality, since it serves as a mere pointer or indicator of the one Brāhman who remains beyond any description. Second, it serves as a firewall to protect the great mystery of God's nature, the *mysterium tremendum* that, according to advaita, defies all explanation or description.

What are the implications of this distinction for the Christian doctrine of theism? While a full discussion and dialogue with advaitism appears later in the chapter, two points should be noted at the outset. First, any propositional truth statements that appear in Christian theologies, such as "God is Almighty" or "God is the Creator," will be relegated by the advaitin to the level of saguṇa, which is illusory and not ultimately real. Indeed, in the advaitin tradition, any attempt to define, describe, or set parameters concerning God is rejected and is met with the Upanishadic expression "neti, neti" which means "not this, not this."[17] Therefore, revelation as we know it is never exact and precise, only approximate and general. Revelation does not make statements of facts or truths with clear boundaries; it only points to mysteries that transcend human description.

Arundhatī Principle in Advaita

This brings us to a second general observation about how the discourse concerning Hindu theism actually takes place. The "neti, neti" of the Upanishads may give the mistaken impression that Hindu theologians are discouraged from writing or reflecting about Brāhman. But Hindu theologians join the neti, neti principle with a hermenutical principle known as

16. For more on the personhood of God in advaitism, see R. G. Panikkar, "The Brāhman of the Upanishads and the God of the Philosophers," *Religion and Society* 7, no. 2 (September 1960): 12–19, and B. Malkovsky, "The Personhood of Śaṅkara's *Para Brāhman*," *The Journal of Religion* 77, no. 4 (October 1997): 541–62.

17. Literally, "na iti, na iti." See *Bṛhad-Āraṇyaka* 2.3.6. See Radhakrisnan, *The Principal Upanishads*, 194.

Arundhatī. Arundhatī is an interpretive device that allows Hindu theologians to make what seem like direct, positive statements about Brāhman while still clinging to the mystery of Brāhman who is nir-guṇa—without qualities. This principle is more popularly referred to as "pointing to the star." Arundhatī is actually the Indian name for a dim star in the Great Bear constellation. A normal observer finds it difficult, indeed nearly impossible, to see the star because it is so dim. So a wiser, more experienced Indian will help him locate the dim star by first showing him a few brighter stars in the vicinity of Arundhatī. Bright stars in the near vicinity of the obscure star can be used as pointers to the correct star.[18] This has become an interpretive metaphor for Indian theologizing. Statements by Indian theologians such as Śaṅkara are often taken in the West as exact statements reflecting doctrinal precision when, in fact, they are only pointing to various indicators *(lakṣaṇa)* of a mystery that cannot be fully articulated. Ignorance of this hermeneutical device has led to significant misunderstandings in the West regarding the doctrine of God as taught and discussed by Hindu theologians.

Viśiṣṭādvaita Vedānta

The second major way Vedantic theologians have reconciled the tension between the one and the many is through a system of thought known as viśiṣṭādvaita or modified nondualism. This system of thought was articulated by the eleventh-century Indian philosopher-theologian named Rāmānuja. He is famous for his vigorous denunciation of Śaṅkara's philosophy, which he describes as a "fictitious foundation of altogether hollow and vicious arguments . . . from one whose intellect is darkened and who has no insight into the meaning of words and sentences."[19] Śaṅkara's position, as we have seen, resulted in a rigid form of absolute nondualism that will not allow any descriptive and determinitive words to be spoken about Brāhman. Rāmānuja agrees with Śaṅkara that in the final analysis only Brāhman has ultimate reality, which is why both systems are, broadly speaking, expressions of nondualism or monism. However, from this point on, Rāmānuja radically departs from Śaṅkara in how he reconciles the tension between the one and the many. There are three key areas in which Rāmānuja challenges Śaṅkara's advaitism.

The Nirguṇa-Saguṇa Distinction Is Rejected

First, Rāmānuja does not accept the nirguṇa-saguṇa distinction that is so crucial to advaitic thought. He does not think it is necessary to place all of

18. G. A. Jacob, *Handbook of Popular Maxims* (Bombay: Tukaram Javaaji, 1907), 5–6.

19. W. S. Urquhart, *Vedānta and Modern Thought* (London: Oxford University Press, 1928), 58–59. One recent exponent of Rāmānuja's viśiṣṭādvaita said, "I would rather see all India abandoning Hinduism altogether than that it should fall prey to the Vedānta of Śaṅkara" (quoted in Robert W. Frazer, *Indian Thought* [London: T. F. Unwin, 1915], 72).

the deities of India, each with its descriptive language about God's attributes and qualities, into the illusory level of saguṇa. Instead, Rāmānuja insists that Brāhman is a personality who "comprehends within itself all plurality."[20] The result is a "monism of the differenced"; that is, the entire created order, including all of the gods and goddesses, are placed *within* the one body of Brāhman. In short, Brāhman is one, but contains within himself all of the plurality and differentiation of the universe.[21] Rāmānuja's theology is based on his exegesis of the third chapter of the *Bṛhad-Āraṇyaka Upanishad,* which asserts, "He who dwells in all beings, who is within all beings, whom all beings do not know, of whom all beings are the body, who controls all beings from within, he is your Self, the inner Controller, the immortal One."[22]

Brāhman Is a Personal God with Countless Attributes

Second, in his commentary on the *Brahma Sūtras,* the esoteric commentary on the Upanishads that the philosophers traditionally exposited, Rāmānuja describes Brāhman as possessing a "host of auspicious qualities, which are countless and of matchless excellence."[23] Rāmānuja took his cue from the opening words of the *Īśa Upanishad,* which declares, "Whatever moves in this moving world, is enveloped by God *[isavasya].*"[24] Rāmānuja understood this phrase to teach "the essential unity of the Deity and the world."[25] Rāmānuja sees the same doctrine taught in the *Śvetāśvatara* Upanishad, which teaches that the many gods *(devas)* of the Vedas were actually only aspects or manifestations of the one God (Rudra or Śiva). In order to reconcile the one and the many, Śaṅkara had relegated all of these texts to the illusory level of saguṇa. Rāmānuja, in contrast, sees the theistic many as located *within* the one Brāhman. The term *nirguṇa,* according to Rāmānuja, should not be interpreted to mean that Brāhman is without qualities, but only that all the attributes and qualities are united in the one Brāhman and that no quality or attribute can ultimately exist apart from or detached

20. F. K. Lazarus, *Rāmānuja and Bowne,* (Bombay: Chetane, 1962), 19–20.

21. In viśiṣṭādvaita theology, this is known as "identity-in-difference," whereas Śaṅkara's advaita is simple "identity," that is, everything is identified with Brāhman without differentiation. To consult Rāmānuja's own argument against Śaṅkara's view that Brāhman cannot be differentiated, consult his *Brahma Sūtra Bhasya,* ed. S. Vireswarananda and S. Adidevananda (Calcutta: Advaita Ashrama, 1995), 1.1.1. Unless otherwise indicated, I use this edition of Rāmānuja's commentary throughout.

22. *Bṛhad-Āraṇyaka* 3.7.15.

23. *Brahma Sūtra Bhasya* 1.1.1 and 1.2.1; John Carman, *The Theology of Rāmānuja* (New Haven: Yale University Press, 1974), 67. See also George Thibaut, *The Vedānta Sūtras with the Commentary by Rāmānuja,* Sacred Books of the East, vols. 34 and 38 (London: Oxford University Press, 1904), 4.

24. *Īśa* 1.1.1. This opening word, *isavasya,* is where the title of the Upanishad derives its name.

25. J. L. Brockington, *Hinduism and Christianity* (New York: St. Martin's, 1992), 7.

from Brāhman. Rāmānuja declares, "The Supreme Brāhman is by his inherent nature such that his essential nature is opposed to impurity and consists solely of infinite knowledge and bliss. He is an ocean of generous qualities that are immeasurable. . . . Since he is the Inner Controller of his whole creation; he has all things as his body and his modes."[26]

Descriptive language that ascribes qualities to God is no longer an entanglement of ignorance; actually, it is essential to true knowledge. If, Rāmānuja argues, a child sees a cow, he recognizes it as such precisely because the cow has qualities that are manifested (saguṇa) and that distinguish it from a dog or a cat. Rāmānuja believes that this applies to all knowledge, even ultimate knowledge.[27] For Śaṅkara differentiation is the essence of ignorance; for Rāmānuja it is the basis for true knowledge. Indeed, this is a fundamental dividing line between Śaṅkara and Rāmānuja. Once the nirguṇa-saguṇa wall of separation has been torn down, there is no longer any theological basis for separating, as Śaṅkara does, the absolute Brāhman and the personal Īśvara of popular Hinduism. Rāmānuja equates the two. Supreme Brāhman *is* the personal Īśvara.

Brāhman Extends Grace and Receives Devotion and Worship

Third, now that the frontier between supreme Brāhman and personal Īśvara has been opened, there is a way to enter into a relationship with God. The "It" of Śaṅkara has become the "Thou" of Rāmānuja. Rāmānuja even opens the boundaries between Indian castes by providing a way for all to enter into relationship with God. For the high castes, the way of devotional meditation *(bhaktiyoga)* allows one to enter into a profound state of trust and self-surrender to God. For the masses, Rāmānuja recommends a form of complete surrender *(prapatti)* whereby one simply trusts in God alone in an act of faith for salvation, recalling the moving words of the *Bhagavad-Gītā*, "Abandoning all Dharmas, come unto Me alone for shelter; sorrow not, I will liberate you from all sins."[28] The devotee is now a recipient of an unearned act of grace.

Conclusion

This brief outline of the philosophies of Śaṅkara and Rāmānuja demonstrates the vast differences between nondualism and modified nondualism in Indian theism. The intense opposition, often antagonism, between the two groups has not diminished over the centuries. The theologies of these men, both rooted in the Upanishads, continue to set the tone for the vast

26. *Vedarthasamgraha*, para. 42, quoted in Carman, *The Theology of Rāmānuja*, 70.

27. *Brahma Sūtra Bhasya* 1.1.1.

28. *Bhagavad-Gītā* 18:66. Unless otherwise indicated, I am using Annie Besant, trans., *Bhagavad-Gītā* (Wheaton: Theosophical Publishing House, 1998). There is some debate about whether Rāmānuja himself made this distinction or if it was made by his immediate disciples.

majority of Hindus. Śaṅkara is often the starting point for much of the discussion concerning Hindu philosophy, and Rāmānuja provides the philosophical and theological foundations that could potentially legitimize any number of expressions of worship in India. As Max Müller once said,

> It must be admitted that in India, instead of one Vedānta philosophy, we have really two, springing from the same root but extending its branches in two very different directions, that of Śaṅkara being kept for unflinching reasoners who, supported by an unwavering faith in monism, do not shrink from any of its consequences, . . . another, that of Rāmānuja, trying hard to reconcile their monism with the demands of the human heart that required, and always will require, a personal God, as the last cause of all that is, and an eternal soul that yearns for an approach to or a reunion with that Being.[29]

It is with these varying streams of Vedantic thought that we must now enter into a discussion about the relationship of Hindu theism to Christian theism.

Religious Roundtable

Now that I have set out a brief overview of the complexity of Hindu theism, it is time to dialogue. The general format will be the same for each of the dialogues in the book. The Religious Roundtable section will begin with my sharing how as an evangelical Christian I have benefited from the study of the other religion. I will point out, if applicable, areas of significant agreement where evangelicals may share a similar perspective or theological concern. At times I may point out areas where I think we can benefit from points made by our partners in dialogue or where I think we may have misunderstood their positions and need to clarify our own understanding of what the other religion actually teaches. However, the heart of the Religious Roundtable section in each chapter will focus on my issuing one or two major objections to the opposition to stimulate the subsequent conversation. I will state an objection and explain why, from an evangelical perspective, the opposing view is incompatible and lies outside the boundaries of the historic Christian proclamation. Then, the opponents will be given ample opportunity to interrupt me and clarify their positions if necessary, as well as an op-

29. As quoted in Urquhart, *Vedānta and Modern Thought,* 63–64.

portunity to give a full response to each objection. Hopefully, the result of the dialogue will be a clearer understanding of how Christianity is distinctive when compared with other religions and also an honest theological engagement with the actual positions, not caricatures, of other religions.

This first dialogue focuses on Hindu and Christian views of theism. Because of the dramatic differences between the two schools of Vedānta, which in my view demand different kinds of responses from Christians, I will converse with Śaṅkara's advaitism and Rāmānuja's viśiṣṭādvaitism separately, beginning with Śaṅkara.

Śaṅkara's Advaitism

Humility and charity are biblical as well as scholarly virtues. Therefore, I want to begin the conversation by acknowledging several ways in which Śaṅkara's writings about theism in the Hindu context have helped me as an evangelical Christian. First, I want to commend Śaṅkara for his unwavering commitment to the absolute freedom of God (Brāhman). One cannot spend time with Śaṅkara without being deeply moved by his willingness to risk everything to safeguard the absolute freedom of God. For Śaṅkara, Brāhman's independence from us and his self-subsisting completeness and perfect freedom apart from us is the pearl of great price to which everything else must be predicated. In our own time, when it seems we are constantly bombarded by pulpit and press with a steady stream of self-help Christianity that seems never to tire of making God's existence and goodness dependent on our happiness and well-being, Śaṅkara is a much needed breath of fresh air.

One of the most remarkable verses in the Upanishads, and a favorite of Śaṅkara, is the declaration in *Chāndogya* 6.2.1 that in the beginning there was only "One without a second" *(ekam evādvītiyam)*. The phrase serves as the Upanishadic equivalent of the opening words of Genesis, "In the beginning God" (Gen. 1:1) or the opening words of John's Gospel, "In the beginning was the Word" (John 1:1). Śaṅkara would ask us to pause for a moment before reading that God created or that the Word became flesh and simply stand in awe at the mystery of God who was free *not* to create and who was not obligated to become incarnate.

Second, Śaṅkara reminds me of how much evangelicals have neglected the aseity of God in our theologizing. *Aseity* is a category of theology focusing on God as he is in himself, apart from us or anything specific he has done on our behalf. This is certainly related to the freedom of God noted earlier, but it is a broader point about the whole way we structure and teach theology. Aseity is a way of stepping back and acknowledging that God was still God in all his fullness before he created the universe, before we were created, or before we needed to be redeemed. Not only was God free not to create, but God did not *need* to create to fulfill something lacking in himself. Another way of putting it is that aseity is concerned with God's ontology, that is, God's *being* apart from God's *doing*. It emphasizes who God is in himself apart from and prior to his gracious acts of creation and redemption.

As evangelical Christians committed to spreading the gospel around the globe, sometimes we risk viewing the gospel as something that can be marketed. We risk presenting a popular gospel focusing almost exclusively on how we can benefit. We have been guilty, at times, of presenting a form of utilitarian theism, unwittingly communicating that God is good, not simply because he is, but because of the good things he has done and continues to do for us. The Christian gospel is thereby marketed as good news because it works for us.

How, then, do we respond when we meet a Hindu who is perfectly content to remain a Hindu because, from his perspective, the gods have treated him well and Hinduism works well for him? Utilitarianism is a dangerous foundation on which to build a worldwide proclamation of the gospel. Śaṅkara understood this point. He was never interested in popularizing Hinduism but in setting forth the unassailable, indescribable mystery of Brāhman. In the process, Śaṅkara has helped me to appreciate the apostle Paul's words with fresh clarity when he proclaims,

> Oh, the depth of the riches of the wisdom and knowledge of God! How unsearchable his judgments, and his paths beyond tracing out! "Who has known the mind of the Lord? Or who has been his counselor?" "Who has ever given to God, that God should repay him?" For from him and through him and to him are all things. To him be the glory forever! Amen. (Rom. 11:33–36)

I would now like to offer two major objections to the Hindu theism found in Śaṅkara's advaitism. I will then explain why, in my view, Śaṅkara's thought is incompatible with Christian theology.

Objection #1: Advaitism is overly pessimistic about the adequacy of human knowledge to speak about God.

First, Śaṅkara's theology does not permit divine revelation that can be spoken of with assurance and confidence. It is one thing to defend the absolute freedom and independence of God; it is entirely another to do so at the expense of revelation. Śaṅkara's theology isolates the nature of God from human knowledge. His theism, however well intended, leaves us with a God who is unknown and unknowable. To put it even more forcefully, Śaṅkara's God is mute. We can know nothing of Brāhman nor assert anything about Brāhman because of the inadequacy of human language to make any meaningful statements. Brāhman does not speak, because there are no words that can even begin to convey meaningful knowledge about Brāhman. As Julius Lipner has noted, "Language—no less scriptural language—as constituted from words and sentences is intrinsically incapable of making known pure, non-differentiated being, such as Brāhman of the *advaitins*."[30]

30. J. Lipner, *The Face of Truth*, 27.

Advaita clarification:

As a contemporary follower of advaitism, I would like to interrupt the Christian presentation to clarify a possible point of misunderstanding. Our position is that human language is an inadequate vehicle for describing true knowledge about God only at the highest level, namely, nirguṇa Brāhman. Śaṅkara and those of us who follow advaita are not arguing that saguṇa Brāhman as Īśvara is mute. From this lower perspective, human language is useful both for describing God and for ascribing attributes to him. Indeed, this serves an important, practical religious need for us. Only in the final sense must we recognize that our words about God are inadequate, shallow, and untrustworthy.

Evangelical rejoinder:

Thank you for that clarification. However, it remains to be seen if the distinction concerning how language is used about God at the two levels is significant. Please clarify this point further. What is the relationship between the descriptive words spoken about Īśvara, however religiously comforting to their followers, and *true* knowledge about nirguṇa Brāhman? Can we with any certainty make truth statements about Īśvara that can, in turn, be meaningfully applied to nirguṇa Brāhman? Let me apply the question to a common experience in India that, for the sake of those reading this dialogue, I will explain in some detail.

Throughout India one can find followers of what is known as *bhakti* Hinduism. The term *bhakti* comes from the Sanskrit word *bhaj,* meaning "to be devoted to." Bhaktism, or devotional Hinduism, refers to a form of Hinduism whereby the devotee worships a particular deity (usually Viṣṇu or Śiva or one of their incarnations) whose presence is normally mediated through the use of icons. The worshipper will offer an appropriate sacrifice and express words of devotion and praise. Bhakti worship of a personal deity is prevalent in India today. Is Śaṅkara saying that a bhakti worshipper who ascribes attributes to a deity (an expression of Īśvara) is speaking meaningfully about nirguṇa Brāhman? Or should followers of bhakti abandon these expressions as ignorant for the sake of the true insights of advaitism?

Advaita reply:

Śaṅkara would certainly acknowledge that a bhakti Hindu is sincere in his or her devotion and worship, but he would be equally firm that a bhakti Hindu or any other Hindu who speaks about God descriptively cannot be assured that he or she speaks accurately or meaningfully. As an advaitin, let me give my own example to clarify our position. If we insist it is meaningful, for example, to say as a propositional truth statement that God is just, what possible reference point do we have to understand a word like *just* except that of human judges and the justice system we live under? This assumes that a corollary can be made between a human judge (for the sake of argument, we will assume an honest, upright judge) and God as judge, for we have no other way to speak meaningfully than to associate such a statement with what we already know. Advaitins insist that any use of a human judge—however honest and upright—to understand God's justice or God as a judge is inherently flawed and cannot be trusted. This, by extension, is applied to all descriptive utterances about God.

From our perspective, this is essentially what has been taught by the Desert Fathers within your own Christian tradition. For example, John of Damascus wrote, "It is plain, then, that there is a God. But what he is in his essence and nature is absolutely incomprehensible and unknowable."[31] Gregory of Nyssa told his followers that "anyone who tries to describe the ineffable Light in language is truly a liar—not because he hates the truth, but because of the inadequacy of his description."[32] This is why we insist that descriptive language not be directed toward nirguṇa Brāhman and why all such language used even to describe Īśvara is ultimately misleading and illusory.

Evangelical reply:

These objections have raised two serious points. First, how adequate are human words in expressing meaningful statements about God? Despite the limitations of human language, can we speak meaningfully about God? Second, how different is Śaṅkara's theism from the theism of Gregory of Nyssa, John of Damascus, and the Desert Fathers who pioneered apophatic theologizing, avoiding positive affirmations about God and preferring to speak by way of negation?

The Adequacy of Human Language in Theologizing

As to the adequacy of human words to express meaningful statements about God, the advaitin objections have propelled us into a modern argument within the Christian tradition about whether revelation is propositional or personal. Evangelicals have been accused of putting so much emphasis upon defending the written words of Scripture that we have forgotten the Christian faith is not about words written in any book (including the Bible), but about the historical intervention of God in human history, culminating in Christ himself. This debate has resulted in two different views of revelation. The first view argues that revelation is fundamentally the acts of God in history. The fact that these acts were recorded in the Bible for our benefit and instruction should not distract us from the central fact of revelation, which is not found in a book but in the acts of God in the world. A second view insists that revelation is about God speaking words of knowledge to humanity in a free act of self-disclosure. In obedience to this revelation, God's servants have faithfully recorded these words in the Bible. Is rev-

31. John of Damascus, *Exposition of the Orthodox Faith*, 4.3 (*NPNF*[2]).
32. Gregory of Nyssa, *On Virginity*, 10.2.355 (*NPNF*[2]).

elation embodied in words or in events? Clearly, proponents of these two views would answer the question quite differently. Even though this is a modern debate, it is important that we reflect on it further because it is vital for properly responding to the issues raised by advaitins.

In 1917 the German scholar Rudolph Otto (1869–1937), who taught at the University of Marburg, published a book titled *Das Heilige* (translated into English as *The Idea of the Holy*).[33] The book is subtitled *An inquiry into the non-rational factor in the idea of the divine and its relation to the rational.* Otto, who also wrote extensively about Hinduism, argued that orthodox Christianity has failed to recognize that God's holiness contains within it a "moment" that he describes as "inexpressible" and that "completely eludes apprehension in terms of concepts."[34] In *Das Heilige* the Latin word *numinous* entered the religious vocabulary to capture the ineffable mystery of a God who cannot be contained in propositional truth statements but remains in the *mysterium tremendum.* Otto's landmark book helped to stimulate a much broader discussion in theological circles about the nature of revelation, especially through the writings of well-known theologians such as Karl Barth and Emil Brunner. These neoorthodox theologians argued that revelation can never be limited to information about God expressed in propositional truths in a book; rather, revelation is a dynamic, existential, personal encounter with God in one's own life. God is not concerned, they argued, with revealing information about himself, but with revealing his own living person in a personal encounter. This emphasis began to cast doubt on the value and reliability of human language as an appropriate vehicle to speak accurately about God. Although this twentieth-century theological debate took place with only scant reference to the Hindu theistic tradition, it is clear that if the neoorthodox theologians are correct, then our ability to respond to Śaṅkara and the advaitins is significantly weakened.

Propositional Truth Defended

There are three reasons why this attack on propositional truth is unwarranted. First, the whole debate mistakenly assumes it is an either-or question. The modern argument presupposes that revelation is either personal or propositional.[35] Either God reveals himself, or he reveals truths about himself. But the great decisive acts of God in history—whether the self-disclosure of his character to Moses at the burning bush or the giving of the Ten Commandments on Mount Sinai—are all communicated to us through words as well as propositional truths about those events. Either God spoke to Moses from the burning bush, or he did not. The statement that God spoke to Moses

33. Rudolph Otto, *The Idea of the Holy,* 5th ed., trans. John W. Harvey (London: Oxford University Press, 1928).

34. Ibid., 5.

35. It should be noted that the modern argument that revelation is *either* personal or propostional may be in part a development from Barth, but is inconsistent with Barth's own view of how personal and propostional truths relate to one another.

at the burning bush is a proposition that is either true or false, yet it is also a decisive act of God in history. Likewise, Scripture uses words to predict later events in history. The prophets predicted the coming of Christ in history. In short, it is not possible to separate the events themselves from the statements about those events. Revelation is both personal and propositional.

Second, if revelation is personal and not propositional, how does God reveal himself personally? We find that he reveals himself through truths about himself and also directly. The incarnation of Jesus Christ is the single greatest act of revelation in history, and Jesus Christ is certainly not a propositional truth statement. He is a person. Yet, the truths about Jesus Christ and the incarnation are communicated to us through the language of truth statements, that is, propositional statements that are either true or false. To persist in the dichotomy, you would have to assert that the incarnation happened, but you could never say anything positive or reliable about the incarnation. The result would be that, despite the personal intervention of God in Jesus Christ, he remains unknowable because we cannot make any statements about him.

Finally, the position is logically self-refuting. The statement that God does not reveal himself through words but only through personal encounter is itself a propositional truth statement about God. None of the proponents who favor personal truth over propositional truth are asking us to accept their viewpoint only if we encounter it existentially as a personal truth. They are arguing on logical grounds that the position is defensible and is either true or false. Śaṅkara has given us, to borrow a poignant phrase of Ravi Zacharias, "a philosophical solvent that dissolves itself."[36] Clearly, personally appropriated truths are closely linked with propositional truth statements.

None of this is to say that human language is fully adequate to express the fullness of God's nature and being. Human language can never fully describe the nature of anything. However, admitting the limitations of human language is quite different from concluding that all human language falls to the ground and cannot be used to speak about God at all. God has chosen to reveal himself in human language. Śaṅkara's pessimism about the usefulness of human language is unwarranted.

Advaitism and Eastern Orthodox Theologizing

This brings us to the advaitin claim that their unwillingness to speak about God in words is no different from some in the Christian tradition who, like Gregory of Nyssa, stated that "God is incapable of being grasped by any term, or any idea, or any other device of our apprehension."[37]

The Eastern tradition to which the advaitins want to compare themselves makes a vital distinction between the comprehension of God and the

36. Ravi Zacharias, *Jesus Among Other Gods* (Nashville: Word, 2000), 63. Zacharias uses the phrase in reference to David Hume, but it is applicable here as well.

37. Gregory of Nyssa, *Against Eunomius*, 1.42 (*NPNF*² 5:99).

knowledge of God. Eastern theologians do agree that it is impossible to comprehend God's essence, but they believe we can have a true knowledge of him, even if incomplete. Their position is summed up well by the apostle Paul's statement that "even though we see through a glass darkly, we *know in part.*"[38] Indeed, Orthodox theology repudiates those "heretics who introduced the idea that God is entirely incomprehensible, inaccessible to the understanding. They built their affirmations upon the idea that God is a simple Essence, making from this the false conclusion that, being a simple Essence, he has *no inward content or qualities.*"[39] In contrast, Orthodox thought teaches that "the simplicity of God's essence is united to the fullness of his attributes."[40] As St. Cyril of Jerusalem said,

> If someone says that the essence of God is incomprehensible, then why do we speak about him? But is it really true that because I cannot drink the whole river I will not take water from it in moderation for my benefit? Is it really true that because my eyes are not in a condition to take in the whole sun, I am therefore unable to behold as much as is needful for me? If, when going into some great garden, I cannot eat all the fruits, would you wish that I go away from it completely hungry?[41]

Śaṅkara has fallen into this error and has left us "hungry" for a true knowledge of God. Let it be clear, therefore, that the advaitins cannot take refuge in the Eastern Orthodox tradition to demonstrate the compatibility of their thought with Christian theology.

Objection #2: Advaitism marginalizes Jesus Christ before dialogue begins.

The second major objection to advaitism is that Jesus Christ, the central fact of Christianity, cannot be spoken of except as the illusory expression of saguṇa. Three major implications arise from this. First, the whole basis for a genuine dialogue with advaitism is seriously eroded. All serious dialogue between religions has been demoted to a secondary category because any truth claims or theological boundaries, however important or decisive for dialogue, are ultimately lost in the sea of saguṇa. As Vinoth Ramachandra has said so well in *The Recovery of Mission,* "My respect for another is tested only when there is a *genuine* clash of basic beliefs and values. A religion that *a priori* refuses to recognize fundamental disagreements can hardly be called tolerant, for it simply refuses to respect the 'otherness' of the other."[42]

38. M. Pomazansky, *Orthodox Dogmatic Theology* (Plantina, Calif.: St. Herman of Alaska Brotherhood, 1983), 51, Pomazansky's emphasis. See also 1 Corinthians 13:12.

39. Pomazansky, *Orthodox Dogmatic Theology,* 53, emphasis added.

40. Ibid., 54.

41. As quoted in ibid., 54.

42. Vinoth Ramachandra, *The Recovery of Mission* (Carlisle, England: Paternoster, 1996), 17.

The second implication, as mentioned earlier, is that all propositional truth claims about Jesus Christ are automatically rendered out-of-court. It should be noted, however, that by denying propositional truth statements, Śaṅkara has built his entire system around a single, unassailable propositional truth: Brāhman is impersonal and cannot be known.

The third implication of the nirguṇa-saguṇa framework for theism is that all possibility of a relationship with God has been foreclosed because Śaṅkara has severed religious experience from true knowledge. Not only has Śaṅkara cut off meaningful theological self-disclosure of God, but he has silenced any genuine worship, because Christian worship can never rise above symbolic pointers. The advaitins have lost all confidence that God can receive or respond to such worship, because Brāhman is "inaccessible to all human wants and sympathies."[43]

Advaita reply:

As an advaitin, let me point out that the statement "Brāhman is impersonal and cannot be known" is only arrived at indirectly and intuitively, not because any particular truth claims can be proven false and this one alone proven true, but because Brāhman transcends the smallness of our insights and utterances.

Let me tell a well-known story to make my point. Once there were five blind men from Savatthi who were asked to describe (that is, articulate truth claims about) an elephant. The problem is that one man grabbed the elephant's tail, the second man felt its leg, the third man touched its side, the fourth man held its ear, and the fifth man felt its tusk. Because they were all blind, each one described the attributes of an elephant to his companions. The first man insisted the elephant is like a rope. The second man was certain an elephant is like a tree. The third man was convinced an elephant is like a broad, mud-baked wall. The fourth man was shocked when the others could not understand that the elephant is like a banana leaf. The fifth man denounced them all, insisting that an elephant is like a brandished sword. Advaita insists that these statements and attributes are all true at a certain level and, though contradictory, they point mysteriously to a truth transcending description. This truth forms the basis of advaitic theism.

Evangelical reply:

The evangelical perspective on this famous story is quite different from the advaitic view. We argue that revelation brings about a certainty of knowledge, even though incomplete. The whole story assumes it is, in fact, an elephant and not some other animal that is being described with accurate, albeit incomplete, language. Upon what epistemological basis does Śaṅkara know that it is an elephant the blind men are seeking to describe?

43. B. Malkovsky, "Personhood of Śaṅkara's *Para Brāhman*," 546.

The whole parable is built on the assumption that there really is an elephant and that at least fragmentary knowledge about the elephant is attainable. The story assumes that the elephant has genuine attributes that each man can describe. In advaitism, however, we are given no confidence that the descriptive language of the five blind men actually corresponds to the elephant. Finally, the whole analogy is flawed because there are actually six men in the famous parable, not five. The sixth is, obviously, the narrator of the story who objectively observes the five men and who sees the entire elephant and how the men are blindly experiencing only a part of the whole. In Śaṅkara's scheme, the whole story is quite unintelligible, for there cannot be a sixth man to tell us with any certainty that there even is an elephant nor how each of the five blind men relates to the elephant.

Conclusion

In conclusion, it is impossible to escape the great gulf between evangelical and advaitin theism. The former is built on the reliability of human language, however incomplete, to make meaningful statements about God that are consistent with divine self-disclosure as located in the Scriptures. Evangelicals assert that because the Scriptures give us reliable knowledge of God, we can be confident that God can be known, because he has chosen to reveal himself to us. The advaitins, in contrast, have no such confidence in the adequacy of human language, and by rejecting propositional truth, they leave us with a God who is unknown and unknowable. If a person asks whether Brāhman is more like Mother Teresa or Adolph Hitler, the advaitin can only say, "Neti, neti." If the same person asks what the Christian God is like, we can point to the person of Jesus Christ as revealed in Scripture.

Rāmānuja's Viśiṣṭādvaita

As with Śaṅkara, Rāmānuja has several praiseworthy elements in his theistic scheme. First, Rāmānuja extols and worships a God with innumerable attributes and qualities. Whereas Śaṅkara is focused almost entirely on the ontological reality of God, Rāmānuja is concerned with the knowability of God in the lives of average worshippers, and he seeks to promote true religious devotion to a God who is knowable. Śaṅkara refers to Brāhman as "It," whereas Rāmānuja addresses Brāhman as "Thou." It is difficult to overestimate the significance of this, and I can only commend him.

Second, I appreciate Rāmānuja's emphasis on our utter dependence upon God. Western Christianity, with its emphasis on individuality, could benefit from a reminder of our dependence on God for our very existence and of our connectedness to one another. Certainly, the body of Christ is a powerful biblical metaphor that, like Rāmānuja's body of Brāhman analogy, reminds us of the dependent nature of all that is truly Christian.

Third, Rāmānuja affirms a more viable perspective concerning revelation than Śaṅkara does. While we as evangelicals do not accept the inspiration and authority of the Upanishads, nevertheless, we must commend Rāmānuja for his positive views about the reliability of revelation and for taking seriously those Upanishadic verses that teach a personal God. Indeed, according to viśiṣṭādvaita, this personal God, Īśvara, is no mere stepping-stone to the true insight of the nondualistic nirguṇa Brāhman. Īśvara is Brāhman.

Finally, we must commend Rāmānuja's respect for the vast religious traditions in India. The Hindu search for salvation is normally divided into three separate paths: the way of knowledge *(jñāna),* the way of works *(karma),* and the way of devotion *(bhakti).* Rāmānuja was able to unite all of these paths together, for in his view the way of works and the way of knowledge are useful aids to bring the devotee onto the path of devotion.[44] Thus, Rāmānuja provided a philosophical framework that has enabled India's diversity to unite as a coherent whole. Undoubtedly, under Rāmānuja's hand many new theistic concepts are introduced into the Hindu veins: God is personal, salvation is through grace, and God is the object of worship, devotion, and adoration. These are all vital building blocks for any potential Christian proclamation in India. Indeed, in viśiṣṭādvaita we discover a dramatic departure from the theistic framework that we encountered with the advaitins. There are, however, two serious objections that I would like to pose to the followers of Rāmānuja.

Objection #1: Rāmānuja's theism is relativistic.

First, by seeking to embrace the full diversity of India's theistic traditions, Rāmānuja opens himself up to a radical form of relativism. Rāmānuja affirms a staggering range of beliefs, expressions of devotion, and religious symbols, for they are all located within the body of Brāhman. All of the *avātars* (incarnations) of Viṣṇu, the popular bhaktism (devotional worship) with its temples, images, holy places, and pilgrimages, as well as goddess worship are included in the body of Brāhman. The implications for Christian theology are profound. Rāmānuja makes no significant religious distinction between the one who worships Jesus Christ and the one who worships Krishna. He is only concerned with how each of these referents inspires the believer to more dedicated devotion and to a deeper understanding of total dependence upon Brāhman. For Rāmānuja, personal devotion and a sense of utter dependence upon God are the highest religious ideals.[45] How one is moved to this devotion is completely relative, since all worship is found within Brāhman.

44. For the full argument, see *Brahma Sūtra Bhasya* 3.4.5.

45. For Śaṅkara, knowledge is the highest religious ideal. For Rāmānuja, even right knowledge must lead to devotion. For Śaṅkara, devotion is only a stepping-stone to proper knowledge, and then the devotion may be discarded.

Viśiṣṭādvaita reply:

As a follower of Rāmānuja, I want to clarify that we do not see all acts of worship as relative or as having equal value to the worshipper. Unlike Śaṅkara, Rāmānuja taught that Brāhman may be known by five defining attributes: reality *(satya)*, knowledge *(jñāna)*, bliss *(ānanda)*, purity *(ānalatva)*, and infinitude *(anantatva)*.[46] Therefore, there are religious expressions that do not recognize the five defining attributes and are therefore unlikely to produce a meaningful devotion to a personal God. Thus, all religions (or even all religious acts) are not entirely relative for Rāmānuja.

Evangelical reply:

Accepting this point, let me clarify my objection. Rāmānuja holds to a modified relativism concerning religions. I concede that Rāmānuja rejects certain nontheistic (Theravāda Buddhism) or nonpersonal theistic (advaitism) understandings of deity as deficient, but he would not be able to critically distinguish between a zealous bhakti follower of Krishna, a devoted evangelical who worships Jesus Christ, and a member of a Ṣūfi sect of Islam who has been inspired to love Allah and give his life in complete devotion to him. This seriously blurs the boundaries between faiths, and it uproots Christianity from its historical moorings, casting it into a sea of cultural and experiential relativity. The historic death of Jesus Christ on the cross is no longer necessary for salvation but is merely one of many culturally conditioned responses to the Ultimate which inspires devotion among his followers. Rāmānuja has quietly turned a theology of God's self-disclosure in the incarnation into a form of anthropology concerning our witness about Jesus Christ who has inspired in us a deeper devotion to God.[47] Rāmānuja gives us no other window to transcendence beyond the bhakti experience.[48]

Objection #2: There is ontological confusion in Rāmānuja's theism.

Rāmānuja's theism does not make a clear ontological distinction between the Brāhman who receives worship and the devotees who offer the worship. This is not easy to demonstrate without going into more detail about Rāmānuja's theism. As we have seen, Rāmānuja's theism is *monistic* from the ontological perspective, because ultimately he does not affirm that anything exists outside the being of Brāhman. On the other hand, Rāmānuja is *dualistic* in the sense that he allows for an I-thou devotional relationship between the believer and personal Brāhman or Īśvara. This tension, as

46. Lipner, *The Face of Truth*, 80.

47. Obviously, the body of Brāhman framework can be used to argue that everything is theology since all is contained within his body. However, practically speaking, this is anthropocentric and experience based.

48. Eric J. Lott, "The Conceptual Dimensions of *Bhakti* in the Rāmānuja Tradition," *Scottish Journal of Religious Studies* 2, no. 1 (spring 1981): 103.

we have pointed out, is reconciled because the dualistic worship occurs within the monistic body of Brāhman. At this point in the discussion, it is essential to clarify precisely what Rāmānuja means by the term *body,* since it is obviously a metaphor that transcends mere materiality. In Rāmānuja's famous commentary on the *Brahma Sūtra,* he defines *body* as "any substance of a conscious being which can entirely be controlled and supported by that being for the latter's own purposes, and whose proper form is solely to be the accessory of that being, is the 'body' of that being."[49]

We are Brāhman's body. Brāhman is the soul that completely controls and supports us, and we are dependent upon him for our continued existence. However, Rāmānuja is so determined to reestablish the relational and devotional link between God and his worshippers that he ends up linking them together in a way that violates the freedom of God that Śaṅkara so nobly defended. Rāmānuja argues that our existence is "incapable of being realized" apart from that which gives ontological support. In other words, we have no existence apart from the being of God. On this point, we are entirely in agreement with Rāmānuja; the world has no independent existence. On the other hand, he argues that we cannot speak about ontology in the abstract. Just as you cannot speak about a cow without encountering specific characteristics and attributes that belong to a cow, so Brāhman is only known and recognized through individual expressions.

Rāmānuja created a model of dependence, but because of his desire to distance himself from Śaṅkara, he actually undermined the independence of Brāhman. Because in Rāmānuja's system everything that exists is in God, his doctrine of theism is linked inextricably to his doctrine of creation. The one who walks into the temple and the one worshipped at the temple are all part of the body of Brāhman. The I-thou relationship so fundamental to true worship turns out to be only functionally real, because in the final analysis, there is no ontological distinction between the Brāhman who is worshipped and the person who is worshipping. For a Christian, this is an ontological confusion of the highest magnitude.

Viśiṣṭādvaita reply:

It is true that Hinduism does not separate the Creator and the creation in the same way as Christian theology. It is a regular feature in Hinduism for the gods to take on human form and become part of the creation. However, don't Christians accept this same ontological confusion in their doctrine of the incarnation? Jesus, as a full member of the Triune God, is the Creator, yet in the incarnation he walks on the beach along the Sea of Galilee as a part of the creation. Jesus worshipping at the temple is also Lord of the temple. If Christians accept the doctrine of incarnation without flinching, then why would they begrudge the same doctrine as embraced by Hindus? What is wrong with worshiping Śiva in the temple while acknowledg-

49. *Brahma Sūtra Bhasya* 2.1.9.

ing that Śiva transcends the temple? What is wrong with allowing the functional worship of Śiva in the temple even if we know that ultimately Śiva and the temple and the worshipper at the temple are all in the body of Brāhman?

Evangelical reply:

This is an important objection. How is the incarnation distinct from the Hindu view of avātars? The word *avātar* means "to descend" or "to come down." Popular Hinduism is filled with avātars. Śiva is thought to have twenty-eight different avātars, though the ten avātars of Viṣṇu have been more important in the religious life of India.[50]

I will point out three vital differences between the doctrine of avātar and the Christian doctrine of incarnation. First, avātars are repeated endlessly throughout each cycle of history, whereas the incarnation is a unique, singular act in history. Chapter 4 of the *Bhagavad-Gītā* says that,

> Whenever there is a decay of righteousness [dharma], O Bharata, and there is an exaltation of unrighteousness [adharma], then I Myself come forth. For the protection of the good, for the destruction of evil-doers, for the sake of firmly establishing righteousness [dharma], I am born from age to age.[51]

Thus, whenever the practice of dharma or righteousness declines, an avātar emerges to destroy the evil and to reestablish righteousness. This cycle continues without end, and therefore the number of avātars is also unlimited.

In contrast, the incarnation is a unique event in history. Jesus Christ does not just appear for a short time and then pass away until the next one arrives. Aldous Huxley once criticized "the error of Christianity" because we only believe in one avātar.[52] In fact, we do not believe in *any* avātars, because, unlike Hindu avātars that arise out of epic mythology, the incarnation is fully historical. Jesus Christ became a first-century Jew in Palestine. History does not repeat itself, and therefore "history is essentially the sphere of the singular, the unique."[53] Second, an avātar comes forth because of accumulated karma and is therefore not a free act of God, whereas the incarnation is an expression of the freedom of God to act and to save. Though it may be a response to human sinfulness, it is certainly not *caused* by human sinfulness or karma. Third, an avātar is a mixture or "blending of the divine

50. The ten avātars of Viṣṇu are fish, tortoise, boar, dwarf, Parasurama, man-lion, Rāma, Krishna, Buddha, and a future avātar, Kalkin, who appears at the end of time. Rāma and Krishna are the most important of the ten, Rāma being the ideal ruler and Krishna being the great teacher and expounder of the *Bhagavad-Gītā*.

51. *Bhagavad-Gītā* 4:7–8.

52. As quoted in Geoffrey Parrinder, *Avātar and Incarnation* (Oxford: One World Publications, 1997), 120.

53. Ibid., 120.

and human."[54] In contrast, the Christian incarnation is a union of two natures, divine and human, into one person who is fully man and yet fully God. This third point particularly addresses the specific point raised by the advaitins in this dialogue. Jesus Christ is fully identified with the Supreme Absolute in an eternal and ontological sense, and in that capacity he comes to earth. There is no ontological confusion in Jesus Christ. Even though the two natures are united into one person, there is no mixing of the two natures. Unlike the avātars, Jesus Christ is not a partial appearance of the divine or a mixture of the divine and human, but a full manifestation of God in bodily form. As Paul declares in Colossians, "In Christ all the fullness of the Deity lives in bodily form" (Col. 2:9). Thus, even though it is a great and wonderful mystery that the Creator of the universe actually lived and walked in the universe he created, there is no ontological confusion once the Christian position is properly understood.

Now that the doctrines of incarnation and avātar have been distinguished, I will continue my argument about the ontological deficiency of the pantheon in Rāmānuja's theistic universe. Rāmānuja understands the gods who are the immediate objects of devotion in bhaktism to be nothing more than types projected from the mind and word of Brāhman. They are not particular individuals. Listen to Rāmānuja's own words concerning this as found in his commentary on the *Brahma Sūtras:*

> The Creator creates the god Indra by uttering the Vedic word "Indra." The words "Indra" etc. do not mean particular individuals but a type. So each Vedic word has a counterpart, an object which is a type, class or species, that have the same form and as such is eternal and does not depend on the birth and death of individuals belonging to that type . . . So when one Indra dies the Creator remembers the particular form of Indra and creates another Indra of the same form etc. even as a potter creates a new pot when an earlier one is destroyed.[55]

In the final analysis, even though the deities of viśiṣṭādvaita are given an ontological foundation in the body of Brāhman, they are actually only types that have no inherent eternality. Thus, the doctrine of dependence actually compromises Rāmānuja on both ends of the spectrum. On the one hand, it ties Brāhman to his own creation and compromises the freedom and independence of God. On the other hand, the deities are not given any independent ontology. Thus, there is a vast ontological gulf between the deities as understood by Rāmānuja and the doctrine of Christ as embraced by evangelical Christians.

54. For a full discussion of the differences between avātar and incarnation, see ibid., 120–27, and Timothy Tennent, *Building Christianity on Indian Foundations* (Delhi: ISPCK, 2000), 323–27.

55. *Brahma Sūtra Bhasya* 1.3.27.

Conclusion

A careful examination of Śaṅkara's advaitism and Rāmānuja's viśiṣṭādvaitism has revealed, despite key insights, major differences between dominant Hindu teachings concerning the doctrine of God and the evangelical view. This overview has sought to establish where some of the clear boundary lines fall between the various schools of thought. The scope of this chapter has focused almost exclusively on Christian theism without a strong emphasis on the doctrine of the Trinity because the borders between Hinduism and Christianity lie mostly on the general frontiers of the doctrine we share with Judaism and Islam. Nevertheless, the language of the Upanishads has been utilized by several notable Indian Christian theologians to articulate the Christian doctrine of the Trinity. This aspect of the doctrine of theism will be developed in part 4, which explores several case studies in how Christian theology has been reformulated in settings dominated by the faith and worldview of non-Christian religions.

3

Doctrine of Creation

Līlā, Māyā

"And God said, 'Let there be light,' and there was light."

Genesis 1:3

"Let me become Many. . . . Having created it, He entered into it."

Taittrīya Upanishad 2.6.1

One of the best ways to gain genuine insight into another religious community is to understand its doctrine of creation. Many evangelical Christians would heartily agree but think it unwise to focus on the Hindu doctrine of creation because, as is so often said, Hindus do not even believe that the created order is real. So they consider this doctrine a nonstarter as far as dialogue is concerned. I disagree with their pessimism and regard the doctrine of creation as a place where Hindus and Christians can meet for a genuine dialogue. In fact, I am convinced this is one of the more fruitful places to begin since the discussion serves to unmask many common misconceptions regarding Hindu thought and cosmology.

The difficulty in introducing someone to a genuine discussion concerning the Hindu doctrine of creation is similar to what we faced in the last chapter in dialoguing with Hindu theists. Hindus do not speak with one voice regarding the doctrine of creation any more than they do with the doctrine of God. Nevertheless, there are two dominant streams of thought that must be explored and with which we must be familiar before we can engage a Hindu in any serious discussion about the nature of the created world. The first stream consists of cosmological traditions that *identify* the creation with God in some way. The second stream consists of traditions that completely *separate* the creation from God, so that creation is somehow unreal.

Identification of God with Creation

Vedic Cosmology: Cosmic Puruṣa Man

Hinduism traces its origins to a series of migrations from central Asia into the northern plains of India by people groups known as Aryans. They migrated into the subcontinent around 1600–1500 B.C. and spoke an Indo-European language that eventually developed into Sanskrit, the classical language of Hinduism. Prior to the Aryan migrations, a flourishing civilization existed along a thousand-mile stretch of the Indus River and its tributaries, with major cities at Mohenjo-Daro and Harappa (located in modern-day Pakistan) and the port city of Lothal (located in Gujarat, India). The remains of this Indus Valley civilization were discovered by Indian archaeologists but were excavated by Sir John Marshall (1876–1958) in 1926. Due to the careful planning of its cities, experts have concluded that the Indus Valley or Harappa civilization was quite advanced. But many mysteries remain about the religious beliefs of these people, as the religious artifacts are mainly confined to several remarkable statues and a number of carvings on hundreds of small seals. Between 1800 and 1700 B.C., the civilization rapidly declined, probably due to climatic changes, leaving behind small settlements. Only then did the Aryan migrations move slowly into the region. Nevertheless, the Aryans encountered the indigenous people along with their religious beliefs, and anthropologists now believe the development of this pre-Hindu Vedic religion of the Aryans contains several influences from the Harappa sources.

It is beyond the scope of this book to survey early Vedic religion. Nevertheless, a major stream of Hindu thought concerning creation traces its origin to the Vedic period. The Aryans who settled in northwestern India began to compose an important body of religious literature between 1200 and 800 B.C. known as the Vedas. The Vedas were recited with great precision into three recitations *(saṃhitās)* known as the *Ṛg-Veda,* the *Samaveda,* and the *Yajurveda.* Eventually, a fourth was added known as the *Atharvaveda.* The *Ṛg-Veda,* the most important of the saṃhitās, contains 1,028 metrical hymns in ten books *(maṇḍala)* that invoke a wide range of deities (traditionally the number is thirty-three) who dwell in groups belonging to several distinct pantheons. Indra, the warrior god, Varuṇa, the guardian of the cosmic principle of order *(ṛta),* and Agni, the god of sacrificial fire, are three of the most prominent of the Vedic gods.

One of the key themes of Vedic literature is the role of ritual sacrifice. Thus, it is no surprise that the creation of the universe itself is described as emerging from an ancient primeval sacrifice of a cosmic man known as *Puruṣa*. The Puruṣa Man was dismembered like a sacrifice, and the various members of his body became the physical universe, stimulated the reemergence of the sacred texts, and formed the basis for the entire social order. The hymn in *Ṛg-Veda* 10.90 is widely regarded as the most important Vedic creation hymn because it links the creation of the physical world to the emergence (or sanctioning) of the caste system.[1] It also marks the reemergence of the sacred texts, which are eternally sounding in the universe but are heard afresh by the sages during each creation cycle.[2] Here is an excerpt from the hymn:

> The Man [Puruṣa] has a thousand heads, a thousand eyes, a thousand feet. He pervades the earth everywhere . . . the Man himself is all this, whatever has been and whatever is to be. . . . All creatures make up a quarter of him; three quarters are the immortal in heaven. With three quarters the Man has risen above, and one quarter of him still remains here, whence he spread out everywhere . . . From that sacrifice in which everything was offered, the verses *[Rig]* and the chants *[Sama]* were born, the meters were born, and the formulas *[Yajur]* were born. From it horses were born; cows were born from it, and goats and sheep were born from it. When they divided the Man, into how many parts did they disperse him? What became of his mouth, what of his arms, what were his two thighs and his two feet called? His mouth was the Brahmin *[Brahmins]*, his arms were made into the nobles *[Kṣatriyas]*, his two thighs were the populace *[Vaiśyas]*, and from his feet the servants *[Śūdras]* were born. The moon was born from his mind; the sun was born from his eye. From his mouth came Indra and Agni, and from his vital breath the wind *[Vāyu]* was born. From his navel the atmosphere was born; from his head the heaven appeared. From his two feet came the earth, and the regions of the sky from his ear. Thus they fashioned the worlds.[3]

For our purposes, the most important aspect of this cosmological hymn is that the universe is not made by a Supreme Being, but is rather a sophisticated rearrangement of the divine Puruṣa figure so that there is no essential differ-

1. The caste system almost certainly predates *Ṛg-Veda* 10.90, but this text provided the theological support for the system of social division.

2. The Hindus do not link revelation to a decisive beginning point occurring in time. Rather, the content of revelation is eternally reverberating in the universe and is heard afresh by sages at various points in the cycle of creation. The highest category of revelation is called *sruti*, which means "that which is heard." The initial sound is the famous *om* (pronounced *aum*), which is still sounded at the beginning of Hindu prayers, chants, and meditations. A lower level of revelation is known as *smriti*, meaning "that which is remembered." The great epics of India, including the *Bhagavad-Gītā* portion of the *Mahabharata*, technically belong to smriti, though many regard them as sruti.

3. The four castes are the *Brahmins*, the *Kṣatriyas*, the *Vaiśyas*, and the *Śūdras*. Wendy O'Flaherty, ed., *Hindu Myths* (New York: Penguin, 1975), 27–28. For a full translation and copy of all the hymns of the *Ṛg-Veda*, see Ralph Griffith, trans., *The Hymns of the Ṛg-Veda*, 2 vols. (Delhi: Low Price Publications, 1995).

ence between the substance of Puruṣa and the substance of the universe. In short, Puruṣa *is* the universe. As important as the various pantheons of Vedic gods are, they emerge *after* the creation and (in this creation theme) are not in any way the cause of it. In another creation hymn, the *Ṛg-Veda* declares,

> Who knows and who can declare it . . . whence comes this creation? The gods are later than this world's production. Who knows then when it first came into being? He, the first origin of this creation, whether he formed it all or did not form it, whose eye controls this world in the highest heaven, he verily knows it, or perhaps he does not know.[4]

Instead, creation is linked to a dismemberment theme of a cosmic man known as Puruṣa. This serves theologically to underscore the central theme in Hindu cosmology, namely, there is a continuity between the essence of Puruṣa and the essence of the universe. This theme is further developed in the Upanishads, which, as noted in chapter 2, were attached to the end of the Vedas.

Cosmology in the Upanishads

In the Upanishads, the theme of dismemberment prevails over the sacrificial theme as the creation motif is developed. In the *Bṛhad-Āraṇyaka,* Puruṣa Man is identified as the World Soul or *Ātman:* "In the beginning, this universe was Soul [Ātman] in the form of the Man [Puruṣa]."[5] In the Upanishadic version, only the Puruṣa Man exists in the beginning. The size of the Puruṣa Man is described as the same size as a man and a woman together in a close embrace. The Puruṣa Man then "caused himself to fall into two pieces," resulting in the first man and woman. From his union with her, explain the Upanishads, the human race finds its origin. The woman then begins to flee from the Puruṣa Man and changes herself into a cow. He then changes himself into a bull and unites with her. She then changes herself into a long succession of earthly creatures, only to find that each time the Puruṣa Man changes himself into her natural mate. They thereby become the origin of all life: "Thus, he created all the pairs, even down to the ants."[6] The precise details of the story are not nearly as important as the theological point at the conclusion of the story. The text declares, "I indeed *am this creation* for I produced all this. Therefore, he *became* the creation."[7] There is clearly an identification between the Creator and the creation.

Even at this early stage in the discussion of Hindu cosmology, several important questions arise. Do Hindus who embrace this view of creation be-

4. *Ṛg-Veda* 10.129.6–7.
5. *Bṛhad-Āraṇyaka* 1.4.1.
6. *Bṛhad-Āraṇyaka* 1.4.4.
7. *Bṛhad-Āraṇyaka* 1.4.5, emphasis added.

lieve that the world is the same as God and are therefore pantheistic? If it is true that Hindus have a nonlinear, nonhistorical, cyclical view of time, then how does this or any doctrine of creation make sense? Does a doctrine of creation imply a belief in linear history? These are just a few of the questions that will need to be raised in the course of our dialogue with Hindus.

Emphasis on the immanence of God and the continuity between God and creation found its full flowering in the theology of Rāmānuja. As explored in chapter 2, Rāmānuja believed that the entire world is contained in the body of Brāhman. Thus, for Rāmānuja, the doctrine of God and the doctrine of creation are closely related. Brāhman is both the efficient and the material cause of the universe. The word *efficient* refers to the sovereign cause of creation, whereas the *material* refers to the substance of creation itself. Let me illustrate this with an analogy of a carpenter building a wooden table. The carpenter is the efficient cause of the table because he or she has made it. A tree is the material cause of the table because the table is brought into existence from the material of a tree. For Rāmānuja, Brāhman is both the efficient and the material cause of the universe.

However, Rāmānuja's doctrine of creation must respond to two potential problems if it is to be consistent with his doctrine of God. First, how can Rāmānuja reconcile a God who does not change (immutable) with a world that is constantly changing? Second, how does Rāmānuja reconcile his belief in a personal God known through the purity of his five defining attributes with a creation filled with misery, pain, and suffering? If, as noted earlier, *everything* in the universe is part of the essence of Brāhman, then the changing of the world involves modification of God's essence; therefore, Brāhman is no longer immutable. Furthermore, since pain and suffering are inconsistent with the divine bliss reflected in the five defining attributes, by implication God would be the author of evil. If this is true, then God is not worthy of our devotion, which would strike at the very heart of Rāmānuja's religious system.

Rāmānuja answers both of these concerns through the development of the Sanskrit word *līlā,* which is central to his understanding of creation. *Līlā* (pronounced *lee-lah*) means "sport" or "play." This term appears in both philosophical and popular Hindu traditions in reference to creation, but Śaṅkara and Rāmānuja use it to preserve God's independence from the world. The world cannot be the result of any desire or purpose by God, for that would violate his utter independence from the world. Brāhman must create without motive, and therefore his creative acts are likened to līlā or play. Creation is a form of spontaneous self-expression. It is like a divine dance or dalliance, not characterized by grand planning or logical sequences, but spontaneous and unpremeditated. Creation is simply a by-product of this dance. It is as involuntary as breathing. Another metaphor used to illustrate līlā is that of a great king who has his every need met but still goes out into the forests to hunt game. He does so not because of physical need, but merely out of play or sport (līlā).[8] Rāmānuja writes,

> Even as kings engage themselves in activity, like playing with a ball, without any motive but for mere amusement, or even as children play out of fun, so also Brāhman, without any purpose to gain, engages Itself in creating this world of diversity as a mere pastime.[9]

The dilemma is that if creation emerges because of a divine purpose, then a consistent nondualistic (monistic) system would entangle God in both evil and change. However, once planning and premeditation are removed, God is untouched by the changes in the universe and by the evil in creation, because creation is an unintended by-product and is not the result of any direct creative will or act. Thus, the doctrine of līlā is the way Rāmānuja seeks to avoid Brāhman's culpability in the problem of evil. Simply put, the so-called problem is that the obvious presence of evil in the world means that God must be either all-powerful or all-good, but he cannot be both. The problem of evil can only be explained if God is not good and is therefore unconcerned about the presence of evil or if he is all-good but lacks the power to change it.

In summary, the identification of God with creation is a dominant theme dating back to the *Ṛg-Veda*. However, linking the doctrine of God so closely with the doctrine of creation raises several theological problems that Vedantic theologians address by seeing the creation not as an act of divine will, but as līlā or divine play, preserving the independence of God in an otherwise monistic system.

Separation of God from Creation

The second major Hindu approach to creation is to completely distance Brāhman from the world. Any nondualistic (monistic) worldview, which affirms that Brāhman is the only reality, must account for the seeming plurality of the universe. All theistic systems encounter this tension between the transcendence and the immanence of God. Responses range from deism, which opts for extreme transcendence, to pantheism, which opts for extreme immanence. Rāmānuja is certainly on the pantheistic side of the spectrum, though we have yet to fully address the issue of pantheism as it relates to Rāmānuja. However, the advaitic response championed by Śaṅkara represents yet another point along the spectrum, but on the side of transcendence. In advaitic cosmology, we find the other major attitude toward creation.

Śaṅkara maintains his nondualism and the absolute independence of Brāhman from creation through his own development of the word *māyā*,

8. See both Śaṅkara and Rāmānuja's comments on *Brahma Sūtra* 2.1.32–36.
9. *Brahma Sūtras Bhasya* 2.1.33.

which has been called "the key concept around which his entire system revolves."[10] The word comes from the root *ma* meaning "to measure, fashion, make, or exhibit."[11] In early Vedic texts, māyā refers to the "uncanny power" whereby deities like Varuṇa and Indra created the world. Occasionally, the term appears in a context that could be interpreted as illusion, as sometimes the deities used māyā to deceive the other deities with whom they were fighting. Śaṅkara, however, uses the word to argue that the world only has the *appearance* of reality. Our ignorance or misperception causes us to view the universe the way we do. The false illusion of māyā produces all the visible phenomena of the external world, the idea of an individualized self, and (as we have seen in the previous chapter) a personal God (Īśvara) or Brāhman with qualities (saguṇa). Any observation of change (which would violate God's immutability) or evil is only the appearance of change or evil, as the only reality is Brāhman, who is completely aloof from the world. This is why māyā is usually translated as "illusion."

For Śaṅkara, only Brāhman truly exists. Our entire experience of the world is only the illusion of accumulated karma, the impersonal law of cause and effect, which blinds us to true reality. Therefore, just as Śaṅkara was prepared to relegate all embodied expressions of God—whether the Jesus of Christianity or the elephant-headed god Gaṇeśa in popular Hinduism—to the realm of saguṇa, so the entire created order falls into the illusory realm of māyā. A famous story about Krishna is known all over India and has inspired countless poems, movies, shows, and books. As a young child, he mischievously sneaks into his mother's kitchen and steals butter from a butter pot, and then in sheer abandonment, he smears it all over his face. In one particularly scandalizing rendition of the story, Krishna even declares he would rather be known as the butter thief than as Brāhman.[12] The story has been subjected to a host of theological interpretations. For our purposes, we only need to be reminded that Rāmānuja would love the story of Krishna and the butter thief, for he is committed to maintaining a nondualism that contains within itself the full expressions of village bhakti worship. There is plenty of room within Brāhman for Krishna and a host of other gods and goddesses. In contrast, Śaṅkara fearlessly holds the line against this kind of popular Hinduism. It is all an expression of ignorance, for Krishna has no real existence. There is no Krishna, there is no butter pot, there is no created world. There is only Brāhman. It is with these two different streams of Hindu cosmology that we must now dialogue.

10. John Grimes, "Radhakrishnan and Śaṅkara's Māyā," *Scottish Journal of Religious Studies* 10 (spring 1989): 51.

11. A. Macdonell, *A Practical Sanskrit Dictionary* (London: Oxford University Press, 1954, 1969), 223.

12. J. Hawley, "Thief of Butter, Thief of Love," *History of Religions* 18, no. 3 (February 1979): 206.

Religious Roundtable

Now that I have set forth the two major doctrines of creation in Hinduism, it is time to engage as an evangelical in a meaningful conversation with our Hindu friends. As before, I will begin by exploring areas of agreement and then engage in an honest assessment of what I see as deficiencies in the Hindu doctrines, allowing for response and rebuttal where appropriate. For the sake of clarity, I will address each of the two streams of thought separately, though sometimes the objections to one might equally apply to the other.

Rāmānuja's Identification of God (Brāhman) with Creation

Let me begin by stating the strengths of what I will call the identity approach, that is, Hindus who identify God with creation. Setting aside any discussion concerning the historicity of the creation stories in Hinduism, the theological point of the identity theme is intended to avoid the dangerous consequences of a world separated from its creator. The postmodern world we now live in has certainly lost sight of this connectedness and lives as if God does not exist. The border crossings between the world of the senses and the unseen world have been closed, and most people live out their lives unaware of the immanence of God in creation and the daily ways we enjoy his sustaining grace. In a debate with an atheist, Rāmānuja would be our steady ally in his insistence that the world is not self-existent. Christians would happily join with the identity approach in our common assertion that God is the efficient cause of the universe and that without his sustaining power, it would cease to exist. Indeed, the close connection between a personal Creator and his creation opens the door for the possibility of divine grace in a way that is alien to some streams of Hindu thought.

Furthermore, we must be equally generous in acknowledging that the identity view rejects anything less than a real world. Creation is neither an illusion nor the mere appearance of something. Our lives and actions, including our prayers and acts of worship, have real meaning. However, despite these positive points of contact, several formidable difficulties are inherent in the identity view of creation, two of which will now be offered.

Objection #1: The identity view confuses the creation with the creator.

While the identity view does assert that creation is real, its proponents are not prepared to state that creation is the emergence of *new* being, that is, the thrusting forth of something that previously did not exist. Christian theology asserts that creation occurs *ex nihilo*, "out of nothing." God brings into being that which previously had no being. In the identity view, nondualism will not permit anything other than Brāhman, so the entire created world eternally exists in a latent form in the body of Brāhman. Creation is an emanation from him, an overflow of his own being, not the creation of anything new. This confusion of the creation with the creator seems to tilt the scales so far toward the immanence end of the spectrum that one might wonder if this position is pantheistic. Indeed, well-known Indologist R. C. Zaehner in his classic study of Hinduism repeatedly asserts that Rāmānuja's cosmology is, indeed, pantheistic.[13]

Identity objection:

As a representative of the identity view espoused by Rāmānuja, I want to make clear that I object to the term *pantheism* as a description of our position. Let me clarify why pantheism is not an accurate term to apply to viśiṣṭādvaita. Pantheism is generally used to express a cosmology of total immanence. In other words, Brāhman and the universe are regarded as identical: Brāhman equals the universe. However, this kind of complete immanence is not what is affirmed in the identity position, for that would mean Brāhman is another word for the universe and would completely contradict the body-soul analogy that serves as the basis for a true I-thou devotional relationship of the worshipper with Brāhman. It may seem like a subtle distinction, but there is an important difference between affirming that the divine is all and affirming that all is divine. The former makes no distinction between Brāhman and the universe; the latter acknowledges that the universe is contained within Brāhman but that the fullness of Brāhman also transcends the universe. This is not pantheism, but pan*en*theism, that is, all is *in* God, but not all *is* God. The textual support for this is found in the famous passage from *Ṛg-Veda* 10.90 quoted earlier in the chapter. The creation hymn declares that "all creatures make up a quarter of him; three quarters are the immortal in heaven. With three quarters the Man has risen above, and one quarter of him still remains here, whence he spread out everywhere."[14] The universe only represents one-quarter of the cosmic Puruṣa Man in the sacrificial dismemberment. Thus, the world can never fully encompass the transcendent Brāhman. In short, Brāhman has an existence outside the world, but the world has no existence outside of Brāhman.

Indeed, our position merely states what Paul meant when he declared that God "is not far from each one of us, for in him we live and move and have our being" (Acts 17:28). Even a contemporary evangelical theologian has written that "no atomic particle is so small that God is not fully present to it, and no galaxy so vast that God does not circumscribe it."[15] If God is

13. R. C. Zaehner, *Hinduism* (Oxford: Oxford University Press, 1966), 7, 10, 38–40, 52, 67, 127, 139.

14. *Ṛg-Veda* 10.90.3–4.

15. Thomas C. Oden, *The Living God,* vol. 1 of *Systematic Theology* (San Francisco: Harper and Row, 1987), 67.

fully present in creation and the entire created world is circumscribed by God, then how is this different from the identity position?

Evangelical reply:

In reply, let me begin by saying that I accept the helpful clarification that the identity position is more properly described as panentheistic than pantheistic. Nevertheless, this does not change my overall objection that the identity position unduly confuses the creator with the creation. Panentheism still maintains that the creation was not made out of nothing *(ex nihilo)* and that matter emanating (a word that literally means "to flow out") from God in the form of creation is, in fact, coeternal with God, even if we concede that it is not the sum total of God's being. My argument is not that God has been completely conflated with the world, but that there remains an undeniable confusion between the world and its Creator. The clear distinction between the infinite, eternal Creator and the finite, temporal creation is not vivid enough. Hebrews 11:3 teaches that "by faith we understand that the universe was formed at God's command, so that what is seen was not made out of what was visible." The Christian view is that God spoke the world into existence. The emphasis in both the Old and New Testaments on God's word bringing forth creation closes the door on any notion that God merely fashioned the world through preexisting materials or that it emanated from his own being. St. Augustine said it most clearly when he declared that the world was not put together "out of pieces of God."[16]

As to the passage in Acts 17 where Paul (quoting a secular source) declares that "in him we live and move and have our being," it must be read in its proper context. Paul is addressing a meeting of the Areopagus after observing dozens of altars and shrines to various gods, including one to an unknown god. Paul proceeds to demolish the smallness of their view of God by chastising them for thinking that the Creator "who made the world and everything in it" could possibly be "like gold or silver or stone—an image made by man's design and skill." In the passage, Paul unequivocally affirms the transcendence of God who is separate from creation. In the identity view, the gold and silver and stone that Paul denounces are actually identified with Brāhman. Contradicting Paul, the identity view would argue that Brāhman is nondifferent from these objects of worship. Having affirmed God's transcendence, Paul does not want to leave it there, but wants his hearers to put their faith in the living Lord Jesus Christ. He declares that God wants men and women to "seek him and perhaps reach out for him." It is in this context that Paul declares the immanence of God who is, as Augustine said, "closer to us than we are to ourselves." To deny God's presence *in* anything or the fact that he encompasses all things is to deny his omnipresence as well as his immanence and transcendence, all of which Christians embrace. All finite things must exist in a certain place. God, being infinite, is

16. Augustine, *Confessions* 11.5.7; 12.7.7 (*NPNF*[1] 1:165, 177).

present everywhere. However, his presence in creation is not to be interpreted by identifying the essence of God with the created order. We are quite right to flee from the extreme transcendence views of the deist who, in a famous analogy, pictures God as the divine, aloof clockmaker who made the universe, wound it up, and then left. But to grant that God and the universe have the same ontological status is a grave error. The alternative is not to identify the universe with God or any part of God, but to affirm a transcendent God who is immanent as the sustainer of his created order.

Objection #2: Creation as līlā or divine play does not satisfy the problem of evil.

As previously noted, Rāmānuja's identity cosmology faces two major difficulties if it is to be consistent with his doctrine of God. Rāmānuja must reconcile the obvious changing nature of creation (he refused to go the route of Śaṅkara and demote creation to some lesser level of reality) with the fact that Brāhman is immutable. Brāhman cannot change, for change implies improvement or decline, and God is perfect. Second, Rāmānuja has to reconcile how Brāhman could be absolutely pure and free from any imperfections while the world with which he is ontologically identified is full of evil, suffering, and pain.

Rāmānuja meets these serious objections with the development of the doctrine of līlā or divine play. This doctrine deserves careful scrutiny because it is unclear how it answers these objections, and it seems to raise additional problems that are not addressed by Rāmānuja.

In Rāmānuja's view, the universe is nothing more than divine reflex, as involuntary as exhaling, or divine play, as motiveless as a child playing with a stick in the mud. Otherwise Brāhman could be found to have desires, which would indicate something lacking in the Divine Being, or he could be viewed as the cause of evil and suffering. However, the analogy only masks the obvious connection between a perfect Brāhman and an imperfect world. Even though a game has no real purpose outside of our own enjoyment, all play is preceded by purposeful decisions. To follow up on Rāmānuja's analogy, the king could have decided to play with the ball, or he could have decided not to play with the ball. Even purposeless play must be preceded by definite decisions that bring about the act of play. Furthermore, Rāmānuja has only described the creation from Brāhman's point of view and therefore does not avoid the problem of evil. Undeniably, līlā has produced embodied individuals who experience various forms of suffering, misery, and cruelty. Why are some people born poor or blind or lame and others are not? The problem of evil remains. Either God is all-powerful or all-good; he cannot be both, for if he were all-powerful, he would eradicate all evils.

Christianity faces this dilemma as well since we affirm both the absolute goodness of God and the absolute sovereignty of God in a world filled with suffering and evil. Essentially, the Christian response to the presence of evil in the world is to affirm two truths. First, God in his sovereignty has chosen not to shield us from the consequences of our free choices, even when the result may be disastrous for ourselves and for those around us. Second, Jesus Christ is the only truly innocent sufferer in the world. As the incarnation of God, he alone is without sin, yet he bore the full weight of the world's evil and suffering and sin on the cross. Thus, for the Christian, the problem of evil finds its meeting point in the cross of Jesus Christ, where the full weight of a world of sinful choices is overcome through the innocent suffering of Jesus Christ.

Identity reply:

As a lifelong Hindu, let me say that we have a deep and abiding respect for Jesus Christ, and we find the unfolding drama of his incarnation on earth to be powerful. However, I would like to clarify a few misunderstandings about līlā before we proceed any further. First (and here is another example of the Arundhatī principle), it is too harsh to characterize līlā as purely purposeless, as if that completely captures the heart of the concept, for indeed, there is some level of purpose even in play. The doctrine of līlā falls somewhere between purposeful and purposeless. Līlā carefully steers a course, to borrow an analogy from Homer's *Odyssey,* between the Scylla of purposefulness and the Charybdis of purposelessness. Moving too far in either direction violates the doctrine. If creation is purposeful, then Brāhman is connected with evil. But if it is purposeless, then Brāhman is disconnected from the world in a way that violates the body-soul analogy. Thus, līlā is a third alternative, falling between action and nonaction, intention and nonintention.

Second, the doctrine of līlā is intended to describe creation from Brāhman's point of view only. From the perspective of creation, all evil and misery is the result of karma that has been incurred due to our actions. In his famous commentary on the *Brahma Sūtras,* Rāmānuja taught that "the Lord takes into consideration the past karma of various beings before creating them as gods, man, or lower animals and therefore partiality cannot be attributed to him . . . So their karma accounts for the difference in their condition and not the Lord's partiality."[17]

Evangelical clarification:

Before I offer any response, it would be wise to define exactly what karma is, since this represents a strong rebuttal that, if successful, could nullify my second objection to the identity view of creation. The law of karma states that every action in a person's life has effects that must be reaped in either this life or the next. Therefore, all differences can be attributed to previous karma. The doctrine of karma in turn provides the basis for the endless cy-

17. *Brahma Sūtra Bhasya* 2.1.34.

cle of reincarnations until all karmic debt has been satisfied. The implications of this doctrine are profound. Indeed, if any and all evil can be attributed to karma and not to Brāhman, then there is no longer a problem of evil. Indeed, to cite a worst-case scenario, even a young infant with terminal cancer is suffering from karma earned in a previous lifetime. So the problem of an innocent sufferer is removed.

Evangelical reply:

It is true that both Rāmānuja and Śaṅkara rely heavily upon the doctrine of karma to satisfy the problem of evil and to keep Brāhman from being responsible for any evil. Śaṅkara insightfully compares Brāhman to the rain, which causes both rice and barley to grow. The difference in the two has nothing to do with the rain but with "the different potentialities inherent in their seeds." He applies this to the staggering inequalities and injustices in the human race, concluding that the only cause is "their own different actions."[18]

On the surface, the doctrine of karma seems to resolve the potential problem of Brāhman becoming sullied by the evils of the world. However, this solution only raises a new question as to the origin of karma. If evil acts and deeds performed in previous lifetimes are responsible for my present sufferings, then where did the evil acts and deeds originate? An infinite regression argument simply will not suffice. One can argue karma back through hundreds or even thousands of lifetimes, but eventually the Vedantists arrive at the creation (emanation) and are forced to answer the fundamental question, Where did evil come from? In the beginning there was no karma, only Brāhman. Thus, the first creation or emanation should have been free from all injustices, inequalities, and evil.

Identity objection:

This line of reasoning, so common among Christians, is based on a Western reckoning of linear time, and thereby it appears to trap the Vedantists into the logical fallacy of an infinite regression argument. However, Rāmānuja clearly taught that there was no beginning. The emanation or flowing out of creation from Brāhman has continued from all eternity in an endless stream. Therefore, the ātman (soul) and the transmigration of the soul from one life to the next with all its accumulated karma is without beginning. Indeed, this objection is as old as the *Brahma Sūtras,* which answered as follows: "If it is objected, that in the beginning there could have been no differences, and that the Lord must then be responsible for the differences (good and evil) that came, then we counter, there is no beginning."[19]

18. *Viṣṇu Purāṇa* 1.4.51–52, as quoted in A. L. Herman, "Indian Theodicy in Śaṅkara and Rāmānuja on *Brahma Sūtra* 2.1.32–36," *Philosophy East and West* 21 (1971): 272.

19. *Brahma Sūtra* 2.1.35.

Evangelical clarification:

Before I respond to this argument, I need further clarification about the precise meaning of the statement, "There is no beginning." Does this mean that *creation* has no beginning but has existed from all eternity? If so, how are we to interpret the famous dismemberment of the Puruṣa Man and the many ways the Vedas speak about the origins of the created order? If the statement "there is no beginning" does *not* refer to creation, to what does it refer?

Identity clarification:

Technically speaking, the statement "there is no beginning" does not refer to creation but to souls (ātman). Individual souls are not part of the creation, but before the creation emerged, they existed in Brāhman in a state almost indistinguishable from Brāhman. It is true that although we believe this particular creation had a beginning, we also believe it is itself only one of an infinite number of creations and an infinite number of beginnings. Traditionally, Hindus teach that the world passes through four successive stages, known as *yugas,* one thousand times before the world is dissolved by Brāhman and returns to its subtle state within Brāhman whereby the cycle begins all over again.[20] The karma that has been accumulated during the yugas passes with the individual souls into a subtle form within Brāhman until at the next creation cycle it reemerges and again takes on name and form. This position is affirmed by Rāmānuja when he said, "Creation also is beginningless, and when the scriptures talk of the beginning of creation they mean only the beginning of a new cycle. This is born out by texts like, 'The Lord devised the sun and the moon as before' (*Ṛg-Veda* 10.190.3)."[21]

Evangelical reply:

Let me retrace the line of argumentation that has led to this point in the discussion. I began with the challenge that the identity view has no adequate response for the problem of evil. My Hindu friend responded by developing the doctrine of līlā or divine play. When several critical problems in this doctrine were pointed out, the doctrine of karma was introduced as a trump card, since all evil and suffering can be accounted for through karma.

20. The four cycles begin with the perfect or *kṛta* age which lasts for 1,728,000 years, followed by the *tretā* age (1,296,000 years), the *dvāpara* age (864,000 years), and the dark or *kali* age (432,000 years). Thus, one turn of the wheel of saṃsāra takes 4,320,000 years and is collectively called a *manvantara.* However, only after one thousand manvantaras or cycles is the universe destroyed. It then resides in this subtle state for another thousand manvantaras before the process begins again. These two thousand-manvantara periods are known as the day of Brahmā and the night of Brahmā, and they equal 8.649 billion years. The entire day and night of Brahmā is known as a *kalpa.*

21. *Brahma Sūtra Bhasya* 2.1.35. It is interesting to note that Griffith translates the critical phrase "as before," which is central to Rāmānuja's point, as "in due order." See Griffith, trans., *The Hymns of the Ṛg-Veda,* vol. 2, 610.

This, in turn, led to a discussion about the origin of evil, for karma itself must have a beginning. However, it was pointed out that such linear origins are not acceptable. The karma solution remained intact because in Hindu cosmology an argument of infinite regression is plausible, for we are not arguing back along a line but round and round in a circle. A line, by definition, has a beginning; a circle does not.

I contend that the identity argument neither preserves a changeless Brāhman nor satisfies the problem of evil. In my first objection to the identity view, I pointed out how the creation is confused with the Creator. Hindus reject the doctrine of creation *ex nihilo* because they will not accept a time when matter was not. In fact, one must seriously question whether the word *creation* is even appropriate since we are actually discussing an emanation. It is only called creation because that which remains almost indistinguishable from Brāhman takes on name and form at a certain point and therefore appears to be a creation event. However, since all matter is eternal—either unmanifested in Brāhman or manifested in the observed order and diversity of the world—it is only an emanation. Therefore, this position does not seem to preserve a changeless Brāhman, for if individual souls make daily decisions that are constantly altering the state of karma, then Brāhman must also be subject to change, and change is inconsistent with the perfections of God in both Hindu and Christian theologies.[22]

This same observation applies to the problem of evil. Denying a true creation and opting for a beginningless world places the evils of karma within Brāhman, either in subtle form before the emanation or in observed form after the emanation. In both cases, karma is brought into direct contact with Brāhman. Either the worldview is nondualistic or it is not. The doctrine of līlā creates a dualistic smokescreen. It tries to reap the benefits of a dualistic system while remaining nondualistic. The doctrine of karma tries to sit on the human side of this false dualism and leave the divine side untouched. It is therefore important to return to two key Upanishadic texts and clarify their meaning in light of Rāmānuja's position.

First, when the Upanishads declare that "in the beginning there was One only, without a Second" (*Chāndogya* 6.2.1), it appears that this verse is roughly equivalent to the opening four words of the Bible, "In the beginning God." It is now clear that the "One" actually refers to Brāhman who eternally contains innumerable souls within himself, making creation *ex nihilo* an impossibility. Furthermore, the beginning is not really a beginning at all, but merely the start of a new point along the eternal cycle of emanations. Thus, the expression "without a Second" does not mean that Brāhman alone existed apart from the countless souls that make up the observed order. All these souls were present in some kind of latent form within Brāhman. How, therefore, can Brāhman remain separate from the evils of karma

22. "Change" in this context refers to change in God's being—ontological change.

since the karma is retained in both the unmanifested and manifested states? Whatever the answer to this question may be, it cannot involve any compromise to nondualism, which is a fundamental starting point of both Rāmānuja and Śaṅkara.

This brings us to the second Upanishadic text, found in *Taittrīya* II.6.1: "May I become many, may I grow forth." This passage is cited to support the one Brāhman becoming many in the creation. Rāmānuja argues that the "I" in the first part of the phrase must be kept consistent with the "I" of the second half of the clause. Thus, it is a statement of nondualism despite the apparent diversity in the world. In fact, Rāmānuja argues this point against another group of philosophers known as the Vaiśeṣika.[23]

In the course of his argument, Rāmānuja admits to four differences between the "I" of Brāhman and the "I" that has grown forth in creation. There is a difference in *time*. Brāhman is before the emanation; creation is after. There is a difference in *shape*. Brāhman has no form or shape; creation has innumerable shapes and forms. There is a difference in the appearance of the *number*. Brāhman is one; creation appears as many. Finally, there is a difference in *language*. We refer to Brāhman as one, but we speak of items on earth individually, such as a table or a tree. Rāmānuja insists that these differences do not violate the essential identity of Brāhman and the world. He declares that "there is not the least trace or sign in these texts of any difference in substance (essence)."[24] Rāmānuja is a consistent nondualist in this argument. However, one cannot have dualism and nondualism. If one separates souls from Brāhman so that he is untouched, then nondualism is compromised. If there is no real separation, then it is difficult to see how Brāhman is not identified with change and evil. For Rāmānuja to declare (as he does in his commentary on the *Brahma Sūtras* 2.1.35) that the latent souls within Brāhman prior to emanation are "almost non-distinguishable"[25] seems to hedge the point. Either the souls are united to Brāhman in pure nondualism or they are not, and we must have the honesty to concede that this is a form of dualism. In short, how does Rāmānuja consistently maintain *both* nondualism and a Brāhman free from the effects of karma? It cannot be both ways.

Identity reply:

The apparent contradiction lies in not properly distinguishing between the soul and the body. Rāmānuja's position is that precisely because Brāhman is free from all imperfections, the ātman or soul is by nature free from all imperfections as well. Karma is never identified with the soul, only with the body, and it can be manifested once the ātman is united with a body

23. The Vaiśeṣika are one of six orthodox schools of Hindu philosophy. The six orthodox schools (*darsanas*) are: Sāṃkhya, Yoga, Mimamsa, Vedānta, Nyaya, and Vaiśeṣika.

24. *Brahma Sūtra Bhasya* 2.1.15.

25. *Brahma Sūtra Bhasya* 2.1.34.

during the period of the emanation. The imperfections are not part of the true nature of the soul. Since Brāhman never takes on form, he remains untouched by the karma. Rāmānuja goes on to argue that once a soul attains Brāhman, then it manifests its true nature apart from the accretions of karma. This true nature is not a new form but, to use his words, "the manifestation of a thing already existent." Thus, Brāhman remains unchanged because karma and ignorance are merely obscuring the soul's true nature. A liberated soul does not *become* free from evil; it merely recognizes its true nature which *is* free from evil. In the same way, a precious gem covered with dirt does not change its essence when it is cleaned but is seen for what was always there.[26] Thus, Brāhman remains both unchanged and unaffected by evil.

Evangelical reply:

After a rather lengthy discussion, we have finally arrived at the root of the identity position. It would be unproductive, in my view, to press the current argument further by asking how the karma is retained by Brāhman during the unmanifested state so it can be reattached to the embodied forms at the point of emanation. This would only further delay getting to the real issue, which is that the harsh reality of evil is effectively denied. In the identity view, suffering, cruelty, and evil are not real but are only external experiences that do not touch our true natures. For the evangelical, this is an unacceptable diminishing of the reality of evil and suffering in the world. The Christian gospel declares that God became embodied in the person of Jesus Christ and died on the cross precisely because the problem of evil was so real and pervasive. For the Christian, the problem of evil finds its solution in Jesus Christ who bore all the sins of the world on the cross and who is the only truly innocent sufferer. I began this dialogue by complimenting the identity position for embracing a real world and not an illusory one. By decisively rejecting the nirguṇa-saguṇa distinction, Rāmānuja seemed prepared to face the harsh realities of the world and to offer a comprehensive solution that put God in meaningful contact with the world. Instead, we have seen a system that utilizes a subtle distinction between manifested karma attached to bodies and forms and unmanifested reality unattached to bodies and forms. This pushes Rāmānuja dangerously close to the position of Śaṅkara he so vehemently denounced. It creates a twofold distinction concerning creation that functions similarly to the nirguṇa-saguṇa doctrine. The result is a subtle denial of the reality of evil. After refuting Śaṅkara and a host of other challengers, Rāmānuja concludes his famous commentary on the *Brahma Sūtras* with the final statement that now "ev-

26. *Brahma Sūtra Bhasya* 4.1.1 and 4.4.4. It should be noted, though it is beyond the scope of this book to elaborate, that the inability of Brāhman to take on form in the real world has serious implications for the Christian view of the incarnation. It is yet another major boundary that separates Hinduism and Christianity.

erything stands relevant, consistent and explained." I must confess that I, for one, remain unconvinced.

Śaṅkara's Separation of the Creation from God (Brāhman)

The second major creation theme in Hindu thought does not identify Brāhman with the world, but completely distances Brāhman from the world. For the purpose of this dialogue, the position as taken by Śaṅkara and the advaitic form of Vedānta will be referred to as the separation view.

Śaṅkara's separation view of creation moves to the opposite end of the spectrum from Rāmānuja's identity view. Rāmānuja moved his followers dangerously close to pantheism, whereas Śaṅkara moves toward absolute transcendence. We saw in the last chapter how important protecting the absolute freedom and independence of God was to Śaṅkara, so it is not surprising that he brings the same kind of rigorous application to his cosmology. Śaṅkara is fully prepared to sacrifice the reality of the world if that is what it takes to preserve the absolute independence of God. One cannot help admiring Śaṅkara for his single-mindedness. In fact, in our own time when it seems that the world is the only reality most people will recognize and the only altar upon which many knees ever bow, it is refreshing to have such a formidable thinker as Śaṅkara remind us that our vision of God has grown dim and our vision of the world is out of proportion.

Even though Śaṅkara and adherents of the separation view come to a different conclusion than Rāmānuja and adherents of the identity view, in the process of developing their ideas they sometimes use similar arguments. Śaṅkara, for example, develops the doctrine of līlā and karma in ways very similar to Rāmānuja. Those arguments were used by Rāmānuja to protect the nondualistic flank of his position and so would naturally help Śaṅkara in the same way. Therefore, most of the arguments made in response to Rāmānuja's writings concerning līlā and karma would equally apply to Śaṅkara and need not be repeated in this discussion.

Nevertheless, there are some key differences in how Śaṅkara understands the two doctrines. First, when Śaṅkara refers to the divine play of Brāhman, his argument sounds almost identical to that of Rāmānuja. But we must remember that Śaṅkara is referring to the personal god Īśvara (a manifestation of saguṇa Brāhman) and not to the supreme Brāhman of the Upanishads. Thus, when Śaṅkara affirms that Brāhman is both the efficient and material cause of the universe, it is important to remember that he is only speaking from the perspective of saguṇa Brāhman. Śaṅkara's unwillingness to speak of the supreme Brāhman as the material cause of the universe is a clear rejection of the identity view, despite the similarity in argumentation. Second, while Śaṅkara also uses the doctrine of karma to protect Brāhman from being the author of evil and to explain the problem of evil, he does not believe in the presence of eternal, individual souls (ātman) within Brāhman. Thus, creation does not emanate from nirguṇa Brāhman. Indeed, Śaṅkara rejects the whole idea of individual souls dwelling within Brāhman as ignorance.

It is now my opportunity to offer two major objections to the separation view.

Objection #1: God created the world as a positive good; it is not an illusion of our ignorance.

For someone who is a committed nondualist like Śaṅkara, the creation itself represents a theological problem that must be overcome. Simply put, if Brāhman is the only reality there is, then how do we account for the world? Rāmānuja did it by placing the world within Brāhman. Śaṅkara does it through the doctrine of māyā, which teaches that the world is a false illusion and only has the appearance of reality. The separationists arrive at their doctrine through a simple syllogism: Brāhman alone is real and undifferentiated. The world is differentiated. Therefore, the world must be unreal. Indeed, if the world were real, then it would have to be the effect of some cause. But this would link the world to Brāhman, making God subject to change and responsible for the evil in the world. Thus, the doctrine of māyā provides a theological space for Śaṅkara to put everything that is not Brāhman.[27]

What a vivid contrast to the biblical account of creation. The Bible begins with, "In the beginning God created the heavens and the earth" (Gen. 1:1). The constant refrain through the subsequent account of creation is the powerful phrase, "and God saw that it was good" (Gen. 1:4, 9, 12, 18, 21, 25, 31). This establishes a positive relationship between the Creator and his creation, for the creation not only came from God, but he continues to sustain it. The New Testament affirms the Jewish view of a creation that resulted from the spoken word of God who called forth new existence out of nothing *(ex nihilo)*. The apostle Paul even declares that God's invisible nature is made known through the visible created order (Rom. 1:20). It is, therefore, unacceptable from an evangelical point of view to embrace a world that is not positively good or that is illusory.

Separation reply:

On behalf of advaitism, let me say how glad I am for this opportunity to expose one of the more glaring deficiencies in how Hinduism is often portrayed in Western textbooks. It is too simplistic to state without any qualification that advaitism teaches that the world is illusory, at least in the sense that most Westerners understand that term as some kind of subjective delusion. Śaṅkara, in his careful explanation of māyā, adopts a classic Arundhatī

27. The doctrine of māyā is so important in Śaṅkara's theology that his opponents (most notably Vallabha, who identifies Krishna with Brāhman) say that Śaṅkara has created a form of dualism by positing two realities: Brāhman and māyā.

teaching style[28] and uses three distinct classes of metaphors that, only when taken together, can point to the meaning of the mystery of māyā.

The first class is best represented by the famous rope-snake metaphor and does fit the stereotype about māyā by presenting the world as a subjective delusion. Śaṅkara tells the story of a man who walks into a hut at dusk. He looks down and to his horror he sees a snake. The man jumps back in fear; however, upon closer examination with a lantern, he realizes it was not really a snake but only a rope. If isolated (as many Western textbooks on Hinduism do), this metaphor would imply that the advaitic position believes the world is merely a subjective delusion. In other words, on the subjective level, we think we see something for which there is no objective basis. We think we are experiencing the world, but upon closer examination under the light of advaitism, we see that we were deluded and that the world has no reality.

There is another class of metaphors, however, that present māyā as an objective illusion. Śaṅkara compares Brāhman to a cosmic magician who produces the world as mere play (līlā). A magician creates an illusion which everyone collectively sees as something other than it really is. The metaphors are objective in the sense that the magician is using real, observable items, and the illusion is collectively experienced by the audience. In this case, objective Brāhman, not the subjective experiencer of the world, is the source of the illusion. In the first class of metaphors, there is no guarantee that every person who walked into the hut would mistake the rope for a snake. In the second class of metaphors, the props used by the magician are essential to the show and are observed by all. Both classes of metaphors emphasize the unreality of the world, though from differing perspectives.

Yet Śaṅkara is careful to distance himself from Buddhist ideas that do not provide any basis for the world's existence. Therefore, Śaṅkara set forth a third class of metaphors that can be labeled as "non-different from Brāhman."[29] The leading example in this class of metaphors is waves on the ocean. When waves, foam, or bubbles appear on the water, they seem to be modifications of the sea even though they are, to use Śaṅkara's words, "non-different from the sea-water."[30] The waves only appear to be distinct from the ocean. This last class of metaphors, if taken by itself, would be close to

28. The Arundhatī hermeneutic was discussed in chapter 2. It refers to indirect argumentation where major ideas only point to a truth that elludes direct argumentation. It is commonly referred to as "pointing to the star" because people use brighter stars in the vicinity of a dim one to help find the dim star. In the same way, the deeper, more complex truths are viewed as dim stars and must be spoken of indirectly.

29. I am indebted to Richard King for pointing out the different classes of metaphors used by Śaṅkara. See "Brāhman and the World: Immanence and Transcendence in *Advaita Vedānta*," *Scottish Journal of Religious Studies* 12 (autumn 1991): 107–26.

30. Śaṅkara, *Brahma Sūtras Bhasya* 2.1.13. For a fuller discussion of māyā in the context of advaitism, see Timothy Tennent, *Building Christianity on Indian Foundations* (Delhi: ISPCK, 2000).

Rāmānuja's view that seeks to demonstrate the continuity of Brāhman with the world. The first class of metaphors, if taken in isolation, would represent the world as a complete delusion and would be close to Buddhist cosmology.[31] But because of our use of the Arundhatī hermeneutic, Western Christians must remember that these classes of metaphors are merely pointers to a mystery that transcends them all. Taken together, the metaphors show māyā to be a temporary misapprehension of unity as multiplicity, and they expose the false tendency to superimpose ultimate reality on that which has a lesser level of reality. Śaṅkara is not arguing that the world has no reality, that it is pure illusion. Rather, he argues that it has no *ultimate* reality and that it is illusory to impose on creation a greater reality than it actually has. In short, māyā is a false way of looking at the world.

Evangelical reply:

This has been an illuminating and helpful clarification. As a Christian, I can affirm that it is wrong to impose on the world a reality it does not have. In our own tradition, Thomas Aquinas has argued that only God has ultimate or necessary existence and that the world's existence is dependent or contingent upon God's existence. We also distinguish between the reality of God and the reality of the world. God has an independent reality that existed before the world was created and that is in no way dependent on anything outside himself. On the other hand, the world is totally dependent upon God's sustaining power, and it cannot continue to exist apart from him, for Scripture declares that he sustains "all things by his powerful word" (Heb. 1:3). In that sense, we agree it is wrong to impose on the world the same kind of reality that belongs only to God.

However, while we both agree that the world is contingent, there remains a great gulf between Śaṅkara and historic Christianity concerning the nature of the world's contingency. First, Christianity holds that we are dependent upon God precisely because he is the maker of the universe. In the separation view, the world exists because of the illusion of accumulated karma, not because of a creative act of Brāhman. According to separationists, the creation exists because of our karma-laden actions, not God's prior free action. Creation is not the realm in which we first come to know God but is a ghastly trap from which we must escape if we are ever to achieve union with God/Brāhman. In contrast, Christians affirm that God has freely chosen to create and sustain the world as a basis for working out his divine plan, which includes entering into a relationship with us.

Second, the separationists are wrong to assume that because the world is changing it must therefore be evil. This is to confuse transitory with evil. We are ready to agree that the world is transitory and belongs to a lesser order of ontology than God's existence. Nevertheless, this should not obscure the fact that, despite this world's transience, it is part of God's good order, and it

31. See chapter 4.

has exactly the reality God intended it to have. Transitory does not mean worthless or illusory. The value of something is related only to God's design. We can delight in an insect that lasts a day, a person's earthly sojourn that lasts a lifetime, or a cathedral that lasts a millennium because they are all part of God's good order.

Objection #2: This view of creation robs the world of design and purpose.

We have seen that in order to maintain nondifferentiated supreme Brāhman, Śaṅkara will not ascribe any meaningful reality to the world, and the creation is relegated to the unreal category of māyā. However, let it be clear that the creator (Īśvara) also is part of māyā. In short, ultimate Brāhman is not the creator of the world, for if he created it he would need a purpose, and if he had a purpose he must have desired something, and to desire something is to admit that God is lacking. Thus, Śaṅkara teaches in his commentary on the *Brahma Sūtras* that "it is incongruous to hold that creation stems out from an intelligent being."[32] If there is no true intelligent being behind the creation, then this is more troubling than Rāmānuja's real but playful creator who at least finds enjoyment in the creation, though it lacks any grand purpose or design. In the separation view, there can be no design or purpose since there is no intelligence behind creation at all. This view robs the entire world of purpose and effectively makes all ethical choices relative.

Separation reply:

As I see it, there are two main problems with this second objection. First, Christians make the mistake of assuming that purpose and ethics are only derived from a personal God who creates and reveals his will through specific commands or promises. The doctrine of karma is an unalterable and universal law that maintains Brāhman's purity from creation and also provides an ethical basis for life. Karma is the ultimate law of sowing and reaping. Every act has specific consequences, either to liberate from the cycle of life (saṃsāra) or to further ensnare in the world's illusive unreality. Far from not having any basis for ethics, it may be the best ethical system the world has ever known, since none other is more exacting or impartial.

Second, if Christians truly ascribe the world's design to God, then God must be playing favorites because of the wide diversity of human endowments. Two children sitting side by side in the same mathematics class under the same teacher are often very different. One excels and becomes a great mathematician; the other drops out of school and becomes a common laborer. The separation view places the cause of the differences wholly on the human side. The differences in these two children are due to the ex-

32. S. Gamghirananda, trans., *Brahma Sūtras Bhasya of Shankaracharya* (Calcutta: Advaita Ashrama, 1993), 361. Śaṅkara is commenting on 2.1.33.

acting law of karma. According to your explanation, since God is the designer of the universe, he must be charged with divine favoritism because he gave greater intellectual endowments to one than to the other.

Evangelical reply:

On the surface, the doctrines of karma and transmigration (rebirth of souls) provide an answer to the problem of evil, since they assert that there is no such thing as innocent suffering. All observed inequalities are the result of karma accumulated in earlier lifetimes and currently being manifested in a person's life. All suffering is attributed to previously committed evil. However, there are four major problems with this seeming solution to the problem of evil.

First, how is it just to punish someone in this life for the sins of a past life of which he or she has no memory? It would be like arresting someone for a crime, but prior to the trial, the prisoner, the judge, the guards—indeed, everyone involved—are given a special potion so that no one has any knowledge of the original crime. In order to be just, punishment must be linked to specific, known offenses. In advaitism no one is aware of the specific actions or deeds that caused a particular transmigration.

Second, the advaitic view of karma confuses the simpler expressions of creation with evil. In the *Manusmṛti,* the standard Hindu work that sets forth the doctrines of karma and transmigration, worm life is ranked lower than bird life because the worm seems to be suffering from a greater evil. Likewise, all creation is viewed as a scale that measures material existence as a greater evil than vegetable life, vegetable life as a greater evil than irrational life, irrational life as a greater evil than rational life, and so forth. The scale of being becomes, in effect, a scale of evil. Therefore, the creation cannot be the act of a just God, but is the result of various expressions of karma. However, biblical goodness is defined as the fullness of being. A worm, although a lowly creature, has a positive good because it has exactly the fullness of being that God designed it to have.

Third, the same impersonal law of karma that shuts the door on impartiality must, by the same token, slam the door on divine grace. Yet our lives are enriched and ennobled not only by strict justice, but also by undeserved mercy. The separation view ultimately cannot accept any acts of divine grace breaking into the created order as being significant. Indeed, grace is not even necessary. The presence of evil in the world is, as with the identity view, not taken seriously, though in the advaitin view it is because evil is part of saguṇa and is therefore another misperception of reality.

Finally, the law of karma makes righteous living, as defined by the *Laws of Manu* (which set forth the karmic consequences of various actions), something that can be humanly attained through the gaining of knowledge or the utilization of proper meditation techniques.[33] There are countless

33. See Wendy Doniger, trans., *The Laws of Manu* (New Delhi: Penguin India, 1991).

Brahmins whose rank on the Hindu chain of being attests that they have satisfied or nearly satisfied the burdensome debt of karma and are on the very cusp of liberation. However, biblical righteousness is humanly unattainable and is found only in God. Through Christ and his abundant grace, we become partakers of his unmerited and undeserved righteousness. Yes, people do have different endowments that, from our point of view, may be traced to both God's design and human response. However, the great thinker and the common laborer, although their endowments are different, have the same capacity to know and love God. There is no difference in their worth or in their capacity to receive God's grace or fulfill his calling. This only becomes a problem when one presupposes a hierarchical chain of being that makes a common laborer more evil than a great philosopher. This view has already been demonstrated to be a fundamental misunderstanding of the goodness of the entire created order.

Conclusion

The identity and separation views of creation incur different but equally serious problems. The identity view confuses the creation with God and, despite the intricacies of the doctrines of līlā and karma, fails to preserve God's independence from creation as well as the separate, but dependent, character of the created order. The results are a creation that is not fully distinct from the Creator and a Creator who is unnecessarily associated with change and evil. The separation view, while maintaining the independence of God, does so only at the expense of denying the full reality of the world (even if it is a lesser reality than God). Creation is not viewed as a positive good, and the created order is unnecessarily linked to various expressions of evil because creation, with all of its diversity, is not embraced as a positive expression and purposeful design of a personal, omnipotent Creator. In the end, neither view adequately accounts for the presence of evil in the world.

PART 2

Christianity and Buddhism

4

Doctrine of God

Dharma-kāya (Śunyatā/Citta)

"By faith we understand that the universe was formed at God's command, so that what is seen was not made out of what was visible."

Hebrews 11:3

"When this is, that is;
This arising, that arises;
When this is not, that is not.
This ceasing, that ceases."

Saṃyutta-Nikāya 2.28

Engaging in genuine dialogue with Buddhists concerning the nature of God or ultimate reality is not an easy task. Roger Corless has correctly observed that "the Buddhas and the Christian God function in their own universes and it is not at all clear whether these universes relate to each other at all, and, if they do, in what way or ways."[1] Debate concerning the nature of ultimate reality is central to the entire history of Buddhist thought, and that discussion has influenced every strand of Buddhism in one way or another. Despite the obstacles, we do not have the luxury of avoiding this central question when Christians and Buddhists sit down at the table of dialogue. Furthermore, the related tension between the one and the many that

1. R. Corless and P. Knitter, eds., *Buddhist Emptiness and Christian Trinity* (New York: Paulist, 1990), 1.

we observed in Hinduism is also a problem in Buddhism, but as we shall see in due course, Buddhists resolve this tension of theism in decidedly different ways than Śaṅkara and Rāmānuja.

Effective dialogue cannot begin until we trace the basic outlines of the rise of Buddhism and the key schools of thought concerning ultimate reality. Therefore, we will begin with a brief overview of the rise of Buddhism as a reform movement within Hinduism and of several great traditions that today mark the contours of this worldwide movement.

Historical Reflection

Buddhism traces its origin to a dissent movement started by Siddhartha Gautama in the sixth century B.C. Siddhartha Gautama (563–483 B.C.) was born into a life of wealth and privilege as a child of the powerful Sakya clan in a region located on the border of modern-day Nepal and northeast India. After being shielded from suffering and pain for many years in the opulence of his surroundings, Gautama went on a chariot ride and encountered the realities of old age, sickness, and death. According to Buddhist tradition, he was so moved by these inevitable realities that he forsook the wealth and privilege of his father's house, exchanged his clothes with a beggar, and at twenty-nine years of age went out into the world in search of the cause of human suffering and the path to liberation.

Over the next six years, Gautama studied under two high-caste Brahmins, Āḷāra and Uddaka, who taught him meditative techniques. Later, he explored various forms of extreme asceticism. However, even though he had brought himself to the point of death through asceticism, neither he nor any of his teachers had discovered how to break the cycle of birth, suffering, death, and rebirth. He then saw the futility of both his earlier life of extreme indulgence and his current state of extreme asceticism. Gautama decided to take the middle path between indulgence and asceticism. This point in his life would serve as the central paradigm for the entire Buddhist religion, which is known as the "Middle Way." Gautama took enough food to strengthen his body, and then he began to meditate under what would become known as the Bodhi tree ("tree of enlightenment"). On the forty-ninth day of his meditation as he sat under a full moon, he received enlightenment and triumphantly declared,

> I wandered through saṃsāra, with its many births,
> Searching for, but not finding, the builder of the house.
> How miserable to be born again and again.
> House-builder, you are seen!
> You shall build no house again!
> All your rafters are broken,
> Your roof beam is destroyed.

My mind has attained the unconditioned.
The end of cravings has come.[2]

Dhammapada 153–54

From this point on, Siddhartha Gautama is known as the Buddha, meaning "Enlightened One," and over the next forty-five years he traveled across the northern part of the subcontinent of India spreading his teaching. After attracting a wide range of followers whom he organized into an effective community known as a *saṇgha,* he died of food poisoning at the age of eighty, declaring in his dying breath the impermanence of all created things.

Teachings of the Buddha

Traditionally, the Buddha's teaching is known as the *dharma.* It sets forth a middle way free from extremes but open to all and leading to enlightenment. The dharma includes the four noble truths, the Eightfold Path, and the doctrines of dependent arising *(pratītya-samutpāda)* and no-self *(anātman).* Numerous other doctrines were later attributed to the Buddha by members of the community as they sought to bring the teachings of Buddha into a coherent system of thought and practice. When Buddha preached his first sermon outlining these core doctrines, it became known as "turning the wheel of dharma."

The first of the four noble truths asserts that all of life is suffering *(duḥkha).* This first truth affirms the cycle of birth, suffering, death, and rebirth with which we are already familiar in the Hindu tradition. The effects of karma have trapped all of life in this endless cycle of suffering and rebirth. The second noble truth explains the cause of this suffering, which is desire and craving *(taṇhā).* Our lives are driven by desires and cravings, but in the end anything we have attained is impermanent. The third noble truth declares that the solution is to blow out or extinguish the flame of desire that burns in each of us. The fourth noble truth declares there is a path that leads to the extinguishing of desire. This path is known as the Eightfold Path because it describes eight areas in a person's life that must be brought under complete control in order to extinguish all desire.[3]

The doctrine of dependent arising (pratītya-samutpāda), sometimes called the theory of dependent origination,[4] is the way the Buddha ex-

2. The *Dhammapada* is an ancient collection of poems and is thought to be drawn directly from the Buddha's teachings. The word *dhammapada* means "path of doctrine." For an English translation of the *Dhammapada* in paperback, see John Carter, trans., *The Dhammapada* (Oxford: Oxford University Press, 2000).

3. The eight areas are: right views, right thought, right speech, right conduct, right livelihood, right effort, right mindfulness, and right meditation.

4. See, for example, S. Chatterjee and D. Datta, *An Introduction to Indian Philosophy* (Calcutta: University of Calcutta, 1984), 133. The doctrine is also known as the "conditional existence of things."

plained how we experience the world—both joy and suffering—as reality. The doctrine is often explained by picturing a wheel with twelve spokes or a circular chain with twelve links. Simply put, the doctrine states that everything in the entire phenomenal world arises because it is linked with something else. The wheel of saṃsāra is constantly turning, but it is sustained by the twelve spokes of (1) ignorance, (2) karmic predispositions, (3) consciousness, (4) name and form, (5) the five senses and mind, (6) contact, (7) feeling and response, (8) craving, (9) grasping for an object, (10) action toward life, (11) birth, and (12) old age and death.[5] Each of these elements arises because of its dependence on the other link. Because the chain or wheel is circular, there is no end to it, and it is, to use the words of the Buddha, "the origin of this whole mass of suffering."[6] Pratītya-samutpāda doctrine is often summarized by the simple formula:

> When this is, that is;
> This arising, that arises;
> When this is not, that is not.
> This ceasing, that ceases.[7]

This doctrine is intended to demonstrate how everything has a cause and is conditional. Nothing exists that can be appropriately called a first or external cause because nothing is independent of this chain of causality. It is a circular chain of cause and effect. Liberation is achieved by breaking one of the links in this chain. The Buddha's Eightfold Path indicates that the two weakest links are the first (ignorance) and the eighth (craving). This aspect of the Buddha's teaching has been explained in some detail because, as we shall see in our dialogue, it continues to have a tremendous influence in any discussion concerning the existence and nature of an Absolute Being.

A second core doctrine of Buddhist thought is known as anātman (no-soul). This is a vigorous denunciation of the two central insights of the Hindu Upanishads, namely, that there is an ātman (soul) that serves as the ground of all being, and that ultimately ātman is Brāhman as reflected in the famous formula found in the Upanishads, "tat twam asi" (thou art that). In contrast, the Buddha denies the existence of both ātman and Brāhman, because both represent a source of permanence.

Buddhism thus emerged as a religion distinctive from Hinduism for two main reasons. First, it gave voice to a growing desire to challenge the dominance of the high-caste Brahmins in India. The Eightfold Path of liberation was not caste specific but rather opened the path of liberation to all, though

5. For the full text of the Buddha's discourse on this doctrine, see *Saṃyutta-Nikaya,* in *The Connected Discourses of the Buddha,* vol. 1 (Boston: Wisdom Publications, 2000), 533f.

6. *Saṃyutta-Nikāya,* 533.

7. *Saṃyutta-Nikāya* 2.26 (12.3.21) as found in R. Davids, trans., *Saṃyutta-Nikāya* (London: Oxford University Press, 1922), 23.

final liberation was only possible by becoming a Buddhist monk *(arhat)*. Thus, the dharma itself, rather than the high-caste Brahmins, represents the focal point of authority in Buddhism. Second, at the heart of Buddhist thought is a denial of the ultimate reality of both ātman and Brāhman, which are the most important and influential insights of the Upanishads.

Developments in Buddhist Thought: The Emergence of Mahāyāna Buddhism

Shortly after the Buddha's death in 483 B.C., his disciples met together in what is known as the First Council, followed later by a Second Council (383 B.C.). Through these councils, the process began of establishing the official canon of the Buddha's teachings, known today as the Pali canon. The Pali canon is divided into three major divisions known as the *tripiṭaka*, or "three baskets," and it represents the earliest corpus of Buddhist teaching. However, after the Second Council, there emerged separate schools of thought, each with authoritative texts that differed from the others.[8]

By the time of Christ, another major tradition was clearly rising that represents the vast majority of Buddhists today. This new movement emerged as a protest against more conservative Buddhism. It called itself *Mahāyāna*, meaning "Great Vehicle," as opposed to the older form of Buddhism which it pejoratively labeled *Hīnayāna*, or "Little Vehicle." Today, only the school of Therevāda (Way of the Elders) remains of this ancient, more conservative, form of Buddhism that insists enlightenment is an individual journey requiring a monastic life and a devotion to the historic Buddha and his original teachings.

In contrast, Mahāyāna Buddhism challenges two of the central elements in Therevāda Buddhism. First, Mahāyāna emphasizes the role of the laity and stresses that anyone can become enlightened. The emphasis on monastic life and the individual pursuit of liberation is replaced by a lay movement that focuses on becoming a *bodhisattva* ("enlightened being") who refuses nirvāṇa and liberation from the wheel of saṃsāra, compassionately remaining in the cycle of rebirth, suffering, and death to assist others in their path toward enlightenment. Mahayanists claim that the arhat emphasis in Hīnayāna is too self-focused and lacks compassion. Now the cosmos is filled with countless bodhisattvas, both here on earth and in various heavenly realms, who can also assist an earthly spiritual pilgrim toward enlightenment. This development in Mahāyāna, as we saw with Rāmānuja's break with advaitism, breaks the strict application of individualized karma

8. The most important of these early splits is a group known as the Mahāsāṇghika (Great Assembly-ites), which is the earliest known group to challenge the dominance of the arhats as a new kind of Brahmin-like threat to the community. Furthermore, the Mahāsāṇghikas are probably responsible for the exaltation of the Buddha and for an articulation of the bhodisattva ideal.

and opens Buddhism to grace because bodhisattvas can transfer their merit onto another and can assist the follower along the Eightfold Path.

The second major development is in the innovative ways the Buddha comes to be viewed by the Mahāyāna. This is particularly evident in their doctrine of *trikāya* ("three bodies"). Trikāya refers to the three ways the Buddha can be manifested or known. The idea that the concept of Buddha transcends the earthly historical Buddha is not new to Mahāyāna, but may be traced to a fourth-century B.C. dissenting group known as the Mahāsāṇghikas (Great Assembly-ites). However, it is under Mahāyāna that the doctrine flourished into the form we are familiar with today. First, there is the historical body known as the *nirmāṇa-kāya,* which refers to those times in history when a Buddha appears in physical form, as in the sixth century B.C. when Siddhartha Gautama received enlightenment and taught the dharma. However, the Mahāyāna do not limit the historical manifestations to Gautama alone, but acknowledge additional Buddhas who have appeared in history or who may appear at some future point. Most Buddhists, for example, are looking forward to a final Buddha named Maitreya who will appear in bodily form at the end of this age.

The second body of Buddha is known as the *sambhoga-kāya* or heavenly Buddha, sometimes called the "body of bliss." This refers to transcendent Buddhas who dwell in heavenly realms and are responsible for teaching the bodhisattvas, ruling over various paradises in the cosmos, and when necessary projecting themselves into the world in the form of historical Buddhas. It should be noted that when Buddhists refer to these Buddhas as "transcendent," it simply means that they are beyond the realm of sight, not that they are ontologically transcendent in the way the term is sometimes used in Western or Christian discussions. The most widely known transcendent Buddha is known as Amitābha (Unlimited Light) or simply Amitā. This Buddha is especially prominent in Chinese and Japanese Buddhism.

The third and final body of Buddha is known as *dharma-kāya* or "body of essence." Dharma-kāya is an all-pervading principle, both transcendent and immanent. It is the highest, ultimate principle in Mahāyāna and represents the essence of the entire universe, though the precise nature of this reality is a matter of great debate within Buddhism. The two major schools of Mahāyāna are largely split over the precise way to interpret the dharma-kāya.

The Mahāyāna justify these significant developments in Buddhist thought by asserting that the early core teaching of the Buddha represents only the more elementary aspects of the Buddha's full teaching. Mahāyāna claims that the Buddha secretly gave additional, more profound teaching to his intimate disciples that is only now fully coming to light through the preaching of Mahāyāna.

Discussions Concerning Ultimate Reality in Mahāyāna Buddhism

The discussion concerning the precise nature of dharma-kāya gave rise to two major schools of thought within Mahāyāna Buddhism. These schools clarified what they believed to be the parameters of dharma-kāya, and in the process they introduced additional themes that will be essential to review before we can engage in a serious dialogue with Buddhists concerning the nature of ultimate reality because (as with Hinduism) Buddhists do not speak with one voice regarding this issue.

School of Mādhyamika

The first major school of thought is known as the *Mādhyamika* or "Middle Way" school. It arose in the second century A.D. and is based on a group of texts (sūtras) known as *The Perfection of Wisdom,* which includes several famous Buddhist texts such as the *Diamond Sūtra.* Two brilliant thinkers, Nāgārjuna and his disciple Aryadeva, are given credit for founding Mādhyamika. Nāgārjuna was the first great teacher after Siddhartha Gautama and is often referred to as the second Buddha.[9] He is the expositor of the *Prajñāpāramitā Sūtras,* which he claimed represented the actual teaching of Buddha that was only now being made known. He also wrote six other works, the most important being the *Madhyamikakarika* (Middle Way verses).

In these works Nāgārjuna develops and applies his famous *tetralemma* in which he was able to logically reduce all propositional statements to one of the following options:

A
not A
both A and not A
neither A nor not A

Once a philosophical system was reduced to propositions that were, by definition, either true or false, Nāgārjuna would show how this had an inner inconsistency with the Buddha's teachings, especially as found in the *Prajñāpāramitā Sūtras* which, he declared, freed the mind from all dualistic thought formations. Philosophy assumes there is a truth that can be recognized or proved, and through philosophical inquiry one can learn to distinguish between the real and the illusory. Nāgārjuna rejected such an assumption and instead claimed that the universe is devoid of all reality. In short, everything is void *(śunya).* This is why the Mādhyamika school is sometimes known as the school of *śūnya-vāda* (all is void) and is often

9. Some scholars believe that the figure Nāgārjuna is actually a composite of two figures, a philosopher and a later tantric alchemist.

thought of as the philosophy of the Middle Way designed to root out all other philosophies. It is known as the nonphilosophy philosophy.

For Nāgārjuna, this view of the universe is the only way to be true to the Buddha's doctrine of dependent arising (pratītya-samutpāda), which removes all permanence and first causes and places everything within the realm of an infinite series of interdependent causes and effects. Rather than set this chain of causation within some transcendent, absolute framework like the dharma-kāya, Nāgārjuna relates everything to what he calls *śunyatā* (emptiness), of which even dharma-kāya must be identified. He reasons that if everything is dependent, then all things lack inherent existence. We perceive and behave as if the objects of our senses were real. This creates cravings and desires that cause suffering in our lives. The answer is not to reach out to an objective ultimate truth like dharma-kāya, but to recognize that everything, including dharma-kāya, lacks inherent existence and is empty. Thus, in the Mādhyamika system, śunyatā becomes the ultimate truth.

The doctrine of emptiness has been subjected to much misunderstanding both inside and outside of Buddhism. On the one hand, it is not an ultimate truth in the sense that it is an objective thing that can be identified or that has inherent existence. On the other hand, it is not a term for ultimate nonexistence. Instead, Nāgārjuna says there is a middle way between the extremes of existence and nonexistence, and it is the Buddha's doctrine of pratītya-samutpāda. Nāgārjuna identifies emptiness with the doctrine of dependent arising: śunyatā *is* pratītya-samutpāda because all dualities have finally collapsed. Even the distinction between nirvāṇa and saṃsāra has collapsed. One can only imagine the shock to many traditional Buddhists when Nāgārjuna declared that saṃsāra is nirvāṇa.

There is a famous story in the *Lotus Sūtra* (A.D. 255) that illustrates the possibilities in Buddhism when dualities are transcended. Traditionally, it was taught that a person's path toward enlightenment would take many thousand lifetimes performing various austerities and accumulating good deeds. It is therefore a shock when the *Lotus Sūtra* tells the story of an eight-year-old daughter of a dragon, King Sagara, who achieves Buddhahood instantly. She has everything against her: she is a nonhuman, she is a female, she is young. But to everyone's amazement, she achieves perfect Buddhahood because she realizes that all of these distinctions between male and female, young and old, human and nonhuman were meaningless.[10]

School of Yogācāra

The second major school of thought within Mahāyāna is known as *Yogācāra*, sometimes called the school of *Cittamātra* ("mind only") or *Vijnañavāda* ("way of consciousness").[11] The first traditional expounder of

10. Burton Watson, trans., *Lotus Sūtra* (New York: Columbia University Press, 1993), 187–89.

11. For the purpose of this dialogue, we will only use the term *Yogācāra*, meaning "practice of Yoga" after one of its key texts.

Yogācāra is a figure named Maitreyanatha, though it is unclear whether this figure represents the actual human teacher or if he is regarded as the transcendent bodhisattva who inspired two fourth-century brothers, Asaṅga and Vasubandhu, to fully articulate the distinctive doctrines of this school.[12]

Yogācāra claims that the Buddha turned the wheel of dharma three times. The first represents the core doctrines of the Buddha symbolized best by the four noble truths and the Eightfold Path. The second turn of the wheel of dharma is represented by the teachings of Nāgārjuna, who taught that "all dharmas lack inherent existence" and that there is no permanent reality in the universe.[13] However, Yogācāra claims that the Buddha turned the wheel of dharma a third and final time, giving the truth that all reality is ultimately located in the mind or consciousness *(citta)*. Everything in the universe, including the Buddha and the dharma, is produced and projected by the mind.[14] Fixing reality in the mind is not to be confused with attributing reality to the human brain. The concept of *mind* is meant to signify the storehouse of consciousness. Consciousness is ultimate reality, not the brain itself nor any information stored in one's memory. The only true focal point of consciousness is known as *tathatā* or "suchness."

Therefore, the Yogācāra agree with the Mādhyamika that there is no reality to external objects. However, in their view, the Mādhyamika fail to recognize that this could not possibly apply to the human mind. Indeed, if even the human mind is illusory and void, then all reasoning must likewise fall to the ground and be declared illusory. Thus, for the Yogācāra, ultimate reality is located only in the mind. All apparent realities are drawn from an illusory "storehouse of consciousness" caused by past karma and desires and projected as objects. This Buddhist articulation of what in the West is called philosophical idealism is attributed to the Buddha's own teaching in the *Dhammapada*, where he declared,

> They who will restrain the mind,
> Far-ranging, roaming alone,
> Incorporeal, lying ahiding—
> They are released from Mara's bonds.[15]
>
> *Dhammapada* 3.37

12. R. Robinson and W. Johnson, *The Buddhist Religion*, 2d ed. (Belmont, Calif.: Dickenson, 1977), 93.

13. Paul Williams, *Mahāyāna Buddhism: The Doctrinal Foundations* (London: Routledge, 1989), 79.

14. I am aware of the Tathagatagarbha tradition in Buddhism, which claims that the Buddha turned the wheel a fourth time. This tradition suggests that each person is a womb containing the embryo of Buddhahood. Every person contains a Buddha within. This embryonic seed of Buddha in every person is quite close to the Hindu view of ātman. Since this tradition never developed into a major school of thought, it will not be included in this dialogue, which focuses only on the dominant strands within each tradition.

15. Carter, *Dhammapada*, 8. Mara is the demon-god who tempted Buddha as he sat under the Bhodi tree prior to his enlightenment.

In reply, the Mādhyamika cite a text they attribute to the Buddha in which he compares thought and consciousness to a bolt of lightning. Lightning, like human thought, is powerful and energetic, but "it breaks up in a moment and does not stay on."[16]

Summary

We have now surveyed the dominant strands of thought within Buddhism regarding ultimate reality. Let me briefly summarize the various positions before us. In the earliest form of Buddhism, today represented by Therevāda Buddhism, the doctrines of no-soul and dependent arising clearly reject any first cause, since everything is placed within an interminable cycle of cause and effect. However, later followers of the Buddha thought that perhaps this observation only applied to the phenomenal world and was not necessarily a denial of an Absolute. Yet whatever Absolute was identified must be consistent with the Buddha's basic vision. The result, as seen in an early group of Buddhists known as Mahāsāṇghika, was an expansion of the Buddha's teachings and the emergence of an Ultimate, which is identified as dharma-kāya. Later, the two schools of Mādhyamika and Yogācāra provided further discussion and development to explain what is meant by dharma-kāya. The school of Mādhyamika suggested that śunyatā is ultimate reality, and therefore dharma-kāya must be seen as emptiness. The Yogācāra school, in contrast, insisted that ultimate reality is consciousness (citta). Therefore, dharma-kāya must be seen as a projection of the mind. Our roundtable discussion will revolve around how Christians and Buddhists from the Mādhyamika and Yogācāra traditions understand and respond to these perspectives of ultimate reality.

Religious Roundtable

I now have the privilege of sitting down with my two Buddhist friends and engaging in conversation concerning the Ultimate in Buddhism. Are there meaningful areas of agreement? Where are the major differences between Buddhist and Christian views of ultimate reality?

Let me begin by commending the proponents of both the Mādhyamika and the Yogācāra schools for their unflinching willingness to pursue the full implications of their convictions. Concessions are not made simply because it would make the intellectual or popular burden light. One senses a deep

16. Edward Conze, ed., *Buddhist Texts* (New York: Philosophical Library, 1954), 162.

commitment to take the Buddha's teaching seriously and to follow that line of thinking to its final conclusion. Both systems represent well thought-out philosophies with consistency and coherence that are almost without parallel in the history of intellectual thought. Yet proponents of both systems are not unaware of the popular and religious implications of their teaching. These systems of thought ultimately must provide the philosophical framework for invocational forms of Buddhism, such as Pure Land Buddhism which extols the splendor of Amitābha Buddha, as well as popular meditative forms of Buddhism, such as Zen. Therefore, despite the intricacy and subtlety of the arguments, one cannot accuse either system of being religiously irrelevant for modern-day popular Buddhism, though we will need to explore this connection during our dialogue.

In the discussion with Hindus in chapters 2 and 3, we found it helpful to engage with advaitism and viśiṣṭādvaitism separately, due to the vast differences in their perspectives. In this dialogue, I would like to keep the representatives of both Mādhyamika and Yogācāra at the table throughout the discussion. This seems prudent since both schools are trying to explicate the meaning of the one dharma-kāya, and there is no fundamental disagreement at this level. The differences, while significant, are not as vast as what we encountered with Śaṅkara and Rāmānuja. Before I offer any objections to either of the Buddhist positions, however, I would like to pose a simple question for the sake of clarity. I would like the proponents of Mādhyamika and Yogācāra to define dharma-kāya. What, in your view, is dharma-kāya? This, it seems, is the most fruitful place to begin our dialogue concerning ultimate reality in Christianity and Buddhism.

Yogācāra Explanation of Dharma-kāya

From the beginning, Buddha said that he as a physical being in the world would not lead the community forever. Instead, his dharma, the mental qualities which he embodied, continue to guide the Buddhist community. Dharma-kāya represents the mental qualities, the transcendent stream of consciousness, that is the ground of everything. In Buddhism we explain deep truths not through static propositions, but through simple stories pointing to truths that finally elude technical explanations. I will therefore use illustrations from two different Buddhist traditions that share a common devotion to Yogācāra: Tibetan Buddhism and Zen Buddhism.

Zen Buddhists have a well-known saying that if one meets the Buddha on the road, one should kill him. The idea is not to encourage killing, but to point out that the Buddha who appeared in history is not the Buddha who is to be revered; rather, the truths and mental qualities that he embodied and which the sword cannot extinguish are to be revered. The dharma-kāya helps to focus our minds away from historical (nirmāṇa-kāya) or heavenly beings (sambhoga-kāya) and on the ultimate reality of the mind and human consciousness (citta).

Tibetans tell the story of a saint named Asaṅga whose greatest goal in life was to have a vision of the transcendent bodhisattva Maitreya who, according to Buddhists, will someday be projected onto earth as the next historical Buddha. After meditating for many years, Asaṅga was on the verge of complete despair, fearing that he would never catch a glimpse of Maitreya. One day as he walked along, he stopped by the roadside to help a suffering dog. To the amazement of Asaṅga, the dog became Maitreya himself. The point, of course, is that Maitreya was always there but had to be seen through the eyes of compassion, one of the mental disciplines.[17]

Both stories are deeply rooted in the doctrine of trikāya (three bodies of Buddha). The first story contrasts the historical Buddha (nirmāṇa-kāya) with the ultimate reality of dharma-kāya. The second story teaches us to look beyond both the dog and even the transcendent Maitreya who is a heavenly Buddha (sambhoga-kāya) to the ultimate reality of our own mental disciplines. Thus, the dharma-kāya is not a static entity located objectively "out there" like some Creator God sitting on a throne any more than the Buddha who walked on the earth in a saffron robe was, at one time, objectively "here." Ultimately, these are all projections of mind or consciousness, which the principle of dharma-kāya exemplifies. Thus, dharma-kāya is not an entity with substance but is a descriptive principle of the absolute reality of the mind.

It is true, however, that on the popular level the dharma-kāya becomes manifest in various bodhisattvas and Buddhas who can serve as a "principle of awakening"[18] to assist those seeking true enlightenment by pointing them to the true reality of the mind, just as a thirsty man in a desert must be awakened to the reality that a mirage of water has no actual existence outside his own mind.

Mādhyamika Explanation of Dharma-kāya

From its very inception, Buddhism has been known as the Middle Way. This designation is descriptive both religiously as seen in the Buddha's rejection of materialism and extreme asceticism and philosophically in the doctrine of dependent arising, a middle position that transcends the dualistic language of being and nonbeing. Thus, in the view of our esteemed teacher Nāgārjuna, all theories of ultimate reality, including the doctrine of dharma-kāya, must first and foremost be consistent with the doctrine of dependent arising. Dharma-kāya, therefore, cannot be viewed as a first cause or external cause of the universe. Furthermore, it cannot be viewed as independent in any way, whether internally in the mind (as in Yogācāra) or externally in some objective realm (as in Christianity), as any of these theories

17. Williams, *Mahāyāna Buddhism*, 80.

18. C. W. Huntington Jr. *The Emptiness of Emptiness: An Introduction to Early Indian Mādhyamika* (Honolulu: University of Hawaii Press, 1989), 224.

would clearly violate the doctrine of dependent arising. In our view, the doctrine of dependent arising was the Buddha's way of forestalling anyone from introducing a first cause or Ultimate Being that would cause or create the universe. Let me illustrate by applying Nāgārjuna's famous *tetralema* to the doctrine of causation.

If you examine all philosophies of causation, they would fall into one of four categories:

1. Self-causation
2. External causation
3. Both self- and external causation
4. Arising out of a noncause

The great insight of Mādhyamika is that our nonphilosophy philosophy rejects these four positions in favor of a nonposition that denies any form of causation (either self or external) or noncausation. Instead, we hold to a middle way between causation and noncausation, which we call emptiness. Dharma-kāya is one way of expressing this emptiness and is, in fact, the only thing that can be said with certainty about dharma-kāya.

Neither dharma-kāya nor emptiness can be distinguished or defined, but it can be illustrated. As you may recall from your dialogue with the Hindus, they tell the famous story of the rope-snake illusion. The man comes into his tent at dusk and mistakes a curl of rope for a snake. Hindus contrast the reality of the rope with the illusion of the snake. Ultimately, the story is about recognizing the illusion of the world and the reality of ātman. In the Mādhyamika view, the whole dichotomy between a real rope and an unreal snake is fundamentally flawed. In fact, neither the snake nor the rope has any substantial reality: there is no rope, there is no snake, and there is not even a tent or a man. Furthermore, none of this sequence of effects and causes that the story describes is being projected objectively from someone's mind. The only reality is that of emptiness. Dharma-kāya is ultimately another example of that emptiness. In short, I would define the dharma body as a state of positive freedom beyond all contraries and opposites, form and nonform, being and nonbeing, objectivity and subjectivity. It is emptiness.[19]

Objection #1: Buddhism does not embrace a personal, absolute being who transcends the universe.

These expanded explanations of dharma-kāya have been helpful to clarify how the two major schools of thought within Mahāyāna understand ultimate reality. From a Christian point of view, it is difficult to accept either the

19. A. Verdu, *The Philosophy of Buddhism* (The Hague: Martinus Nijhoff, 1981), 147. This final definition is largely derived from Verdu's discussion of the dharma-kāya in chapter 4.

Yogācāra or the Mādhyamika views as even vaguely theistic, which brings me to my first serious objection. Both branches of Mahāyāna explicitly reject any notion of an objective, personal Creator who represents the first and sustaining cause of the universe. In Christianity, while God is fully immanent in his creation, he transcends the universe. Everything is dependent upon him for its existence, and yet he is self-existent, without a cause. The Hebrew name for God—Yahweh—is derived from the simple expression "I Am" and is a classic affirmation of the independent, self-existence of God. Everything in the universe ultimately derives its existence and being from God who stands as the first cause and who created everything out of nothing *(ex nihilo)*.

My central objection to Yogācāra is that to locate ultimate reality in the human mind not only confuses the Creator with the creation, but it actually makes God's very existence and reality dependent upon us and our perception of him. This is precisely the opposite of the Christian view. Rather than our existence being an expression of God's free act of creation, the Yogācāra view makes God's existence nothing more than a projection of human consciousness onto the heavens, though they do not use the term *God,* but citta (mind) or *tathatā* (suchness) about which nothing definite can be known.

My central objection to the Mādhyamika view is that this school of thought denies any and all concepts of objective reality. Even the reality of human consciousness, which the Yogācāra claim represents the great insight of Buddha's third turning of the wheel of dharma, is denied. The result is the denial of any objective reality. There is no first cause. There are not even any effects, since cause-effect and objective-subjective dualities are transcended. We cannot say with Rene Descartes, "I think, therefore I am," because ultimately there is no thinker who can think. While the Yogācāra equate the perceiver with the perceived, the Mādhyamika deny both the perceiver and the perceived. With one blow, the Mādhyamika have struck down the Creator and his creation. By denying all objective reality, we become lost in this sea of emptiness and pushed to the brink of nihilism. If nothing has inherent existence, then nothing can have any inherent meaning. That is nihilism.

In short, it seems that when it comes to ultimate reality, Buddhism offers us a meager choice between philosophical idealism (all reality is in the mind) and philosophical nihilism (there is no reality or meaning at all).

Mādhyamika reply:

We are accustomed to Westerners accusing us of being nihilistic. Even in the East, great thinkers like Śaṅkara made a similar accusation. However, our position is not nihilistic. When the Buddha was first turning the wheel of dharma, he was seeking to chart a middle path between two extreme views that were present in his day and are still with us today. The first view is that which affirms some kind of permanent, independent existence. In the

Upanishads, this is identified as ātman and Brāhman. In Christianity, this is identified as a Triune God. In Islam this is identified as Allah. The second view is that which affirms nihilistic nonexistence. This was a view advanced by a group known as the *Carvakas* (Materialists) and has been advocated in the West by such luminaries as Jean-Paul Sartre and Friedrich Nietzsche as well as in much of postmodernism. However, the Buddha rejected both the permanence of the Christian God and the nihilism of Neitzche's nothingness. Buddhism is the Middle Way between existence and nonexistence. Emptiness lies between "the extremes of externalism and annihiliationism, of strict determinism and chaotic indeterminism, of absolute reality and nihilistic unreality, of permanent identity and absolute difference."[20] The whole point of śunyatā (emptiness) and pratītya-samutpāda (dependent arising) is to repudiate all such dualities. But the repudiation of all dualities is not, like the Hindus, an affirmation of monism or the one reality of Brāhman, but a middle path of emptiness that transcends both the reality of Brāhman and the unreality of the nihilists.

Yogācāra reply:

Before I respond to my Christian friend's objection of the Yogācāra position, let me briefly say something to my Buddhist colleague who adheres to the teachings of Nāgārjuna. I find the Mādhyamika view of emptiness self-refuting because the entire nonphilosophy philosophy is argued using careful reasoning and logical methodology. The proponents of Mādhyamika take understandable pride in their reasoning abilities. Yet they claim that the mind is illusory and in the end has no reality. How can we become convinced of a rational argument, the acceptance of which involves a denial of the reality of reason? This seems to undercut the very basis of this dialogue. All educated debate, however well reasoned, and all exposition of sacred texts, however faithfully done, are ultimately cast to the ground as empty, illusory, and untrustworthy. The Mādhyamika "void" is a void about which one cannot speak intelligently.

Now, let me remind my Christian friend of one of your own great scholastic theologians who, in my view, affirms the basic premise of reality held by the Yogācāra. Anselm (1033–1109) argues in his *Proslogium* that God is "that than which nothing greater can be conceived."[21] It is known as the ontological argument for God's existence. He argues that God exists because we have the idea of an absolutely perfect God. This is essentially the Buddhist viewpoint held by the Yogācāra. We have an *idea* of God or ultimate reality or dharma-kāya which we recognize as a projection from the stream of consciousness we call citta (mind). This is the locus of all reality.

20. David Kalupahana, *Nāgārjuna: The Philosophy of the Middle Way* (New York: SUNY Press, 1986), 16.

21. S. N. Deane, trans., *Anselm: Basic Writings* (LaSalle, Ill.: Open Court, 1966), 8.

To use an analogy, ultimate reality (or the Christian term *God*) is like an echo that bounces off a canyon wall. We shout out across the canyon, and a few moments later we hear the echo. At that moment we experience it as an "other," a reality that seems separate from us. Nevertheless, the echo originates in us, and the sound is merely a projection from us. Christians talk about and experience God as an other and as a separate, distinct reality. However, you are only experiencing the echo of your own consciousness, your own idea of God, which is "that than which nothing greater can be conceived."

Evangelical reply to Yogācāra:

I will begin by responding to the Yogācāra position. I must say that you have not properly understood Anselm. Anselm is the most famous proponent of the ontological argument for the existence of God, and he did define God precisely as you quoted. However, the argument Anselm makes in the *Proslogium* is to compare the two notions of God as an idea only (the Yogācāra view) and God as existing in reality (the Christian view). He asks the reader which is greater: an idea that exists only in the mind, or an idea in our minds that also exists in reality? He opts for the latter and uses that as the basis for a rational argument for God's existence. The Yogācāra are right in saying that the human race does have an idea about God or ultimate reality. However, Anselm's whole point is that the idea of God does not only exist in our minds; it actually exists in objective reality.[22] To apply his argument to the Yogācāra view, Anselm would say that the objective existence of perfection is greater than any projection of perfection. God, for Anselm, is not merely an echo of human consciousness; he is the eternal, self-existent God. The evangelical view is that God exists from all eternity prior to any act of creation. Therefore, the reality of God precedes any mind that subsequently conceives of him. In an act of his free will, God created us in his image and implanted the idea of himself within us as part of that image. To turn that around and make God's existence dependent on the human idea of God is a gross misunderstanding of Anselm.

The Yogācāra will find more of an ally in the philosopher Ludwig Feuerbach than they will in Anselm of Canterbury. Indeed, it was Feuerbach, in *The Essence of Christianity,* who claimed that "the qualities of God are nothing else than the essential qualities of man" and that "only in the realm of human senses does there exist a being of really infinite qualities." Feuer-

22. Anselm's argument is quite effective in dealing with the philosophical idealism of the Yogācāra if we agree that existence itself is a perfection expressed in the completeness of being whereby all possibilities (in the mind) are actualized in reality. It is not clear how effective this argument might be against the monism of either Śaṅkara or Rāmānuja. The nondualists could offer their own proposition: "Whatever exists necessarily is a unity more encompassing than whatever cannot exist at all or whatever exists contingently." For a full discussion of this, see L. Howe, "The Ambiguity of 'Perfection' in the Ontological Argument," in *The Existence of God,* ed. George McLean (Washington, D.C.: Catholic University of America, 1972), 58–69.

bach also declares that all of "the fundamental dogmas of Christianity are only realized wishes of the human heart," meaning God is an idea in the human mind that has been projected into the heavens. Indeed, he argued, "There is no essential distinction whatever between God and man."[23] It is Feuerbach, not Anselm, who shares a common cause with Yogācāra, although even Western philosophers like Feuerbach, G. Hegel (1770–1831), and George Berkeley (1685–1753) at least believed in the self of the perceiver.[24] For Yogācāra, both perceiver and perceived are illusory.

As for the Mādhyamika position, I agree with the Yogācāra's assessment that their unwillingness to provide an objective foundation renders rational debate futile before it even begins. However, I still have difficulty understanding how the middle way of emptiness is different from nihilism. You made it quite clear when you first addressed this that your position is not nihilistic because it rejects the nonexistence as fervently as it rejects existence. Nevertheless, how does this middle nonposition protect from the despair of nihilism since you still have no objective foundation upon which to build your life, thought, and society?

Mādhyamika clarification:

You should not confuse our unwillingness to provide an objective foundation with the lack of foundation. We reject the objective-subjective dualism so prominent in Christian thought because Buddha has shown us a path that transcends these types of categories. Our problem with so-called objective starting points is that they are inherently contradictory. Let me illustrate with the central topic of this discussion. Christians assert that God is real and objectively exists. However, all existence involves change. Since God by definition cannot change (for all change is either to improve or to decline, neither of which is possible for God), then God must not exist. It is logically inconsistent to relate an objective, unchanging God to a subjective, changing world in a meaningful way. In short, it is impossible for a subjective world to build a foundation of reality on an objective God without violating God's immutability.

The alternative is the foundation of the middle way of emptiness, which avoids both extremes. On the one hand, we do not affirm that emptiness is real, that is, we do not claim that emptiness is some objective thing that has any true being, existence, or essence. On the other hand, we do not claim that emptiness is nonexistent. We use the analogy of seeing one's reflection in a mirror. It would be a grave error to mistake the image for the real thing. Likewise, the fact that it is merely a reflection does not mean we should de-

23. Ludwig Feuerbach, *The Essence of Christianity* (New York: Harper and Brothers, 1957), 19, 23, 140.

24. Technically, Feuerbach was an empiricist and not a philosophical idealist like Hegel or Berkeley. Nevertheless, Yogācāra could agree with arguments found in both empiricism and idealism.

spair because the reflection is unreal. This is the real difference between emptiness and nihilism. We have been liberated to see the image in the mirror for what it really is, namely, a dependent condition. We believe that the entire cosmos as we know and experience it is built on this ceaseless chain of cause and effect. The Buddha said this truth is as hard to grasp as it would be to believe a young man of twenty-five pointing to someone a hundred years old and saying, "This is my son" and the hundred-year-old man saying of the young man, "This is my father who sired and raised me."[25] Nevertheless, to grasp it is true enlightenment.

Emptiness is the medicine for the human disease of grasping, clinging, and desiring. It is only regarded as a negative reality when forced into the mold of a particular view of an objective, transcendent deity. This is the error of Christianity. This is why it is impossible to compare the Christian God with Buddhist emptiness. Indeed, the doctrine of emptiness is not an agent that acts and makes things empty (which is nihilism); it is simply that they *are* empty. The Buddha himself made clear that it is a grave error to adhere to emptiness as a central plank of a philosophical position. Instead, it exhausts all philosophical views—both theism and atheism—just as medicine given to a sick man must itself be purged from the body, or the man will become even sicker than before.[26]

Evangelical reply to Mādhyamika:

I remain unconvinced that meaning and values can be supported within an endless series of causes and effects. It seems that the Mādhyamika attempt to take refuge in a nonposition is like seeking to take a pound of flesh without shedding a drop of blood. It is difficult to see how a nonposition is not a position any more than a nonphilosophy is not a particular philosophy. Nevertheless, for the sake of argument, let us set that aside for the moment since that will be a focal point of a future dialogue (see chapter 5 on ethics in Buddhism). Even if we grant that the Mādhyamika position is not nihilistic, it does not alter the central observation that Buddhism will not affirm a personal God who transcends the universe he made. None of the responses from either Yogācāra or Mādhyamika have challenged this basic point. Evangelicals would not consider either position as theistic, but as atheistic or passively nontheistic, since the ultimate reference point is either internally subjective (Yogācāra's citta) or an impersonal principle (Mādhyamika's śunyatā). Neither view is compatible with Christian theism, which by definition declares that God is a "self-determining, conscious, feeling, willing Self who has relationships with other personal beings."[27] The

25. Watson, *Lotus Sūtra,* 221.

26. This final metaphor is taken from Buddha's exposition to Kasyapa. See Huntington, *Emptiness of Emptiness,* 58.

27. Thomas Oden, *The Living God,* vol. 1 of *Systematic Theology* (San Francisco: Harper and Row, 1987), 84.

Buddhist Reality cannot speak, see, or hear. There is no possibility of an I-thou relationship. This Ultimate may be meditated upon, but it cannot be prayed to or addressed personally in petition or supplication. In contrast, the Christian revelation concerning God is not about emptiness (śunyatā), but fullness *(pleroma)*. As we enter into communion with God, we realize that he is more than a part of the infinite chain of cause and effect. Rather, through Jesus Christ we are brought into a personal knowledge of and relationship with the living God who created the heavens and the earth and who enables us to share in his fullness. We are not being purged; we are being filled.

An additional point that the Mādhyamika used twice in their argument requires a response. They opened their clarification with a syllogism used to show that belief in an objective God is illogical and self-refuting. Their reasoning was based on the indisputable fact that existence involves change. Since God cannot change, he must not exist. Later in their argument, a similar point was made when the Mādhyamika insisted it is contradictory for an unchanging God to relate to a changing world and that bringing him into a meaningful relationship with the world would certainly violate his immutability.

Even though I have insisted that the Mādhyamika are nontheistic, I must commend them for knowing enough about Christian theism to know that God, by nature, is immutable. This doctrine has been misunderstood throughout the history of the church. Whenever the doctrine of immutability is misunderstood, it tends to cause theologians to either distance God from the world to preserve his immutability (as with deism or advaitism) or to dismiss the doctrine as unbefitting God's character and therefore to boldly state that God does change (as with the modern-day process theologians). I agree with the Mādhyamika that we cannot abandon the doctrine of immutability.

However, the Mādhyamika have not properly understood three points about the Christian view of immutability. First, this attribute of God cannot be understood in isolation from God's other attributes without creating the impression that immutability is a static, wooden term lacking the vitality of the actual biblical position. God's immutability does not violate either his love or his justice, both of which have caused him to act in the world. Second, no Christian denies the basic premise that "to exist is to change" as it applies to the created order. Our objection is that this maxim cannot, by extension, be applied to God's existence because he exists in perfection apart from the created order. His existence is necessary, ours is dependent; therefore, his existence does not imply or require change as ours does. Third, the doctrine of immutability refers to God's essence and nature only and does not necessitate a separation of God from the world or a relinquishing of God's immutability in order to be in contact with the world. Immutability affirms that God's essential nature cannot change but is fully active and alive with his other attributes through which he has chosen to interact with changing, faithless humanity. In short, divine immutability "does not mean that God is unresponsive or incapable of interaction,"[28] but only that his character, purpose, and essence remain unchanged despite his flexible and varied dealings within the ebb and flow of human history. As an illustration, Scripture teaches that God's wisdom is complete and therefore remains unchanging since God cannot learn new things or gain new insights to increase his wisdom (see Jer. 10:12, Rom. 11:33, and Col. 2:3). Nevertheless, God's wisdom is constantly addressing itself to changing situations and the ever-changing circumstances of human history. Scripture declares that the world is, indeed, constantly changing, comparing it with clothes that grow old and perish, but it goes on to proclaim that "you [God] remain the same, and your years will never end" (Ps. 102:26–27; Heb. 1:12). Thus, God's relationship with a changing world in no way violates his unchanging character, purpose, or essence.

Objection #2: The actual objects of worship and adoration in Buddhism are illusory and superseded by true enlightenment.

As noted above, one of the distinguishing marks of all branches of Mahāyāna Buddhism is an emphasis on the laity and the presence of transcendent bodhisattvas and Buddhas in various heavenly realms who are available to assist earthly pilgrims toward enlightenment. Much of our discussion has focused on various ways ultimate reality has been abstracted within Buddhist thought in the Mahāyāna tradition. At one point, the proponent of Mādhyamika said that God and emptiness cannot be compared. Indeed, it has often been observed that when Buddha gave his famous Eightfold Path, there was no mention of God anywhere along the path or as the goal of the path. So, let us shift the discussion away from abstract concepts and talk about the worship practices of ordinary Buddhists around the world.

Anyone who has ever traveled in areas of the world dominated by Mahāyāna Buddhism, which represents the vast majority of worldwide Buddhists, does not find Buddhists worshipping either śunyatā (emptiness) or citta (mind). What we find are countless shrines and temples to bodhisattvas and Buddhas with a steady stream of Buddhist worshippers. These are not abstract concepts but the living faith of millions of Buddhists. Prominent examples include the bodhisattvas of compassion, Maitreya and Avalokitseśvara, to whom Buddhists offer worship, veneration, and petition. The *Lotus Sūtra* mentions twenty-three such transcendent bodhisattvas. Others include the ever-youthful Manjusri of which even the hearing of his name can grant relief from thousands of births on the wheel of saṃsāra. Whoever worships Manjusri is promised to be born into the heavenly realm and protected by his power. What ultimate meaning do we grant to these figures? What do we say to the Buddhist devotee who claims, as many have,

28. Ibid., 113.

that Manjusri has appeared to him or her in a dream? Why do Buddhist women invoke the name of Avalokiteśvara in the hope of successful childbirths? How does this worship relate to śunyatā and citta?

In addition to these transcendent bodhisattvas, there are many transcendent Buddhas who, as we examined earlier, dwell in the sambhoga-kāya or second body of the Buddha. One cannot travel far in Buddhist lands without encountering the worship and invocation of Amitā or Amitābha Buddha (Buddha of Unlimited Light), who enjoys the most widespread devotion in all of Mahāyāna. In fact, some have observed that the worship of Amitābha is so dominant in China and Japan that it "most nearly approaches a devotional monotheism."[29] According to Pure Land Buddhists, before Amitābha received his final enlightenment, he lived as a prince named Dharmakara. He took forty-eight bodhisattva vows and declared that if any of these vows were not fulfilled, then he was prepared to forfeit his final enlightenment as a transcendent Buddha. Since Dharmakara is now exalted as Amitābha, it is believed that he kept all his vows. This is important because the eighteenth vow declares that anyone who thinks about him and recites his name ten times will be reborn to the Pure Land. In that famous vow, Dharmakara declared,

> If, after my obtaining Buddhahood, all beings in the ten quarters should not desire in sincerity and trustfulness to be born in my country, and if they should not be born by only thinking of me for ten times . . . may I not attain the Highest Enlightenment.[30]

After invoking Amitābha's name ten times, a person is not only reborn into the Pure Land but is given the assurance of never being reborn into a lower realm and, if he or she wishes, of living there forever.[31] The functional monotheism of Pure Land Buddhism is even more evident in the belief that by worshipping Amitābha, one is worshipping every god in the entire cosmos because all gods are contained within him.

The significance of this functional theism in popular Buddhism seems difficult to overestimate in light of our preceding discussion. If ultimate reality never rises above impersonal principles such as śunyatā and citta, then how do we respond to the vibrant worship of Buddhas and bodhisattvas in Buddhism? I do not think we can have an honest discussion about God or ultimate truth in Buddhism without the leading thinkers within Mahāyāna clearly addressing this basic question.

29. Williams, *Mahāyāna Buddhism*, 251.

30. As quoted in Willard Oxtoby, ed., *World Religions: Eastern Traditions* (Oxford: Oxford University Press, 1996), 274–75.

31. Some, as we shall see in chapter 5, may choose out of compassion to be reborn to help others toward enlightenment.

Yogācāra reply:

Your question is a good one, but I think it is incorrectly posed. You presuppose that an objective reality exists outside the universe. You call this reality "God." Given this assumption, it is only natural to inquire how the worship of various bodhisattvas and Buddhas corresponds to this objective God. It is not unusual for Christians who visit Buddhist lands to be shocked when they see men, women, and children bowing down before a bronze statue of Maitreya or Amitābha. They walk away shaking their heads and saying, "Do these poor Buddhists really believe that God is only *that?*" The real question is not whether there is an objective being who is worshipped in statues, but how the mind conceptualizes an ultimate reality and translates that into daily experience. There is a big difference between a conceptualized reality that is experienced and an experienced reality that is conceptualized.[32] Buddhism is about the former; Christianity is about the latter. To Buddhists it is a visual aid for meditation and concentration; for Christians it is an idolatrous offense.

However, when you teach Christianity to your children, don't you use visual aids to help them conceptualize God? Most Christians, even adults, probably visualize God as a larger-than-life man sitting on a massive throne in some heavenly realm, surrounded by winged angels in white robes and holding scrolls or harps in their hands. Reality, however, is always deeper than our visualizations. In the same way, Buddhists on the road to enlightenment use various images—including the Buddhas and bodhisattvas you alluded to, numerous maṇḍalas (drawings which depict or symbolize the cosmos), and the famous *than ka* (painted visualization scrolls) of the Tibetans—to assist in the development of the right mental attitude.[33] People are at different stages along the path. In the final analysis, it is childish for someone to bow before a statue of Maitreya, and enlightenment will finally demand the abandonment of such acts. Even the objects of meditation must eventually be emptied from the mind until one discovers pure consciousness.

You will recall that earlier in this dialogue, I referred to the famous saying shared among more enlightened Buddhists that if they see the Buddha on the road, they should kill him. The same saying would apply to Maitreya or Amitābha or any other form of visualization. It might anger a Pure Land Buddhist if you told him to kill Amitābha if he met him on the road, but his anger is based on an ignorance of ultimate reality. A bronze statue of Amitā-

32. I am indebted to Antony Fernando who points out this distinction in a different context in *Buddhism Made Plain,* rev. ed. (Maryknoll, N.Y.: Orbis, 1985), 115.

33. These depictions are known as cosmical homologies. The cosmos is reduced to a small diagram that represents the whole universe. The governing idea of a cosmical homology is that the macrocosm corresponds to the microcosm. For example, if you can understand the human body or a sacrifice or a maṇḍala diagram, you can gain insight into the entire cosmos.

bha is not a thing to be worshipped; rather, it must become a pointer to a reality that transcends the statue. Ultimately, popular worship of bodhisattvas and Buddhas must lead to the reality of the mind (citta), the great temple of consciousness, which leads to a more enlightened mental attitude toward life and the universe. A statue is like a raft that leads to a distant shore, but one should not confuse the raft with the shore. Once you arrive on the distant shore, the raft is no longer necessary.

Mādhyamika reply:

I do not think the question of the relationship between popular Buddhist worship and śunyatā is incorrectly posed. Rather, the question is irrelevant in light of more pressing issues. There is a well-known dialogue that took place between the Buddha and a monk named Malunkyaputta. The monk was concerned because the Buddha would not answer basic questions such as whether there is life after death or whether the world is eternal. The Buddha responded by saying that he did not answer because those kinds of questions were not of immediate concern to him. He illustrated his point by telling the following story:

> Imagine a man traveling through a thick jungle. Deep into the jungle he is shot by a poisoned arrow. If the poisoned arrow remains in his body for very long, he will die. But the injured person says, "I will not pull out this arrow until I know who shot it, whether he is tall or short, fat or lean, young or old, or a high caste or a low caste." I tell you, Malunkyaputta, the Buddha concludes, that man will die before he knows the right answers.[34]

The story illustrates the irrelevance of throwing up false dichotomies, as with the question about how the worship of a Buddha or bodhisattva in popular Buddhism relates to some concept of ultimate reality.

The whole scene of a Buddhist worshipper bowing before a bronze image of Maitreya is a manifestation of saṃsāra, the illusory, karma-driven cycle of cause and effect. There is no statue of Maitreya nor any worshipper bowing before it. There is no tongue to offer prayers nor body to bow down. There is not even a stream of consciousness but only emptiness. Only on the plane of conditional existence do such dichotomies as worshipper and object of worship appear. Everything we would like to hold on to as objective is nothing more than a magical illusion, as it says in the *Aṣṭasāhasrikā Sūtra:*

> All objective facts are like a magical illusion, like a dream. . . . The various classes of saints, from "Streamwinner" to Buddhahood are all like a magi-

34. *Majjhima nikāya,* Sutta 63. As quoted in Fernando, *Buddhism Made Plain,* 105.

cal illusion . . . even Nirvāṇa, I say, is like a magical illusion. How much more so anything else.[35]

Christians assume that a Buddhist bowing before an image is worshipping that image as God. The Yogācāra speak as if there is a traveler on the Eightfold Path who is at a certain childlike stage moving toward the enlightenment of true mind (citta). In fact, there are no travelers on the Eightfold Path and no person bowing before any god. As the Buddha said,

> There is suffering, but no sufferer found;
> There is the deed, but no doer is there,
> Extinction is, but none who is extinct,
> The Eightfold Path is there, but no traveler on it.[36]

Therefore, the whole question about the existence of a so-called objective God and the experience of subjective worshippers falling prostrate before a statue of a Buddha is to evade the heart of true Buddhism. We should quit debating about who shot the arrow of karma and ignorance into the human condition and focus on pulling the arrow out.

Evangelical reply:

Both replies have only confirmed the reason why the Buddhist conceptions of ultimate reality are, in the end, vastly different from the Christian view of the Triune God as revealed in Scripture. Neither of you are willing to concede that there is any ultimate reality present in the worship of millions of Buddhists who daily visit shrines. The Yogācāra concede that these acts of worship may provide a temporary, childish stepping-stone or raft to a deeper enlightenment. But in the end (like Feuerbach), these acts of worship are nothing more than mental projections thrown up against a sky that is called the Pure Land. We must ultimately empty ourselves of these objects. From the vantage point of Yogācāra, a heavy blanket of temporary delusion rests over millions of Buddhist worshippers around the world. These acts of worship may, like a raft, someday lead to a distant shore, but all they have previously believed to be true must be abandoned. Indeed, the "enlightened" shore on which they arrive is bereft of the footprints of God.

For the Mādhyamika, the whole temple scene and gathering of sincere worshippers is nothing more than a horrible illusion, just another point on the wheel of saṃsāra. After all, Nāgārjuna claimed that saṃsāra *is* nirvāṇa, that there is no ultimate distinction between the two. Thus, the whole matrix of life and worship, of devotion and prayer is summarily dismissed.

35. *Aṣṭasāhasrikā* 2.38–40. A "streamwinner" (*srotāpanna*) refers to a Buddhist who has progressed sufficiently toward enlightenment to merit only happy future births.

36. *Visuddhimagga* (of Buddhaghosa) 16, II. See also Hans Schumann, *Buddhism* (Wheaton: Theosophical Publishing House, 1974), 90.

From my vantage point, it seems that the only thing keeping Buddhists from being pushed toward nihilism is this functional theism in which they live, work, and worship.

The whole of Christianity revolves around the central fact of Jesus Christ. The true and living God who created the universe and called everything into existence through his spoken word becomes incarnate in the person of Jesus Christ. This means that, in the Christian view, the eternal God has actually stepped into the pages of human history. Those who gazed into the face of Jesus were not seeing a mirage nor were they experiencing a mental projection. Rather, the eternal God was fully and completely actualized into real human history. John declares, "The Word became flesh and made his dwelling among us . . . full of grace and truth" (John 1:14).

Our hazy mental images and childlike perceptions were all brought into sharp focus in the life and ministry of Jesus of Nazareth. The fact of Jesus Christ is not something we will one day discard for a greater truth. Jesus did not just give us a path to follow. He declared that he is the path: "I am the way, and the truth and the life" (John 14:6). To see Christ is to see the fullness of the Father (John 14:9). The human race was mortally struck with a poisonous arrow called sin. However, through his death on the cross, Jesus has removed the arrow, taking the poison into himself. The Scriptures declare, "He himself bore our sins in his body on the tree, so that we might die to sins and live for righteousness; by his wounds you have been healed" (1 Pet. 2:24). Through the bodily resurrection of Jesus Christ, a path has been opened for the human race to enter into a living relationship with a God who is there. He is not silent but has chosen to enter into a relationship with his creation and to reveal the abundance of his character.

Conclusion

This chapter has sought to engage in an honest dialogue with Buddhists concerning the nature of ultimate reality and how it compares or contrasts with the Christian understanding of the Triune God of Scripture. The dialogue began with an honest admission that many observers have noted that the Christian God and the Buddhas seem to "function in their own separate universes." This testimony is not far off the mark, for although Buddhism may be functionally theistic, even at times functionally monotheistic, at its deepest level it is clearly nontheistic. Popular Buddhist worship and experience may give the appearance of some continuity with Christianity, but the actual gap between emptiness or mind and the God and Father of our Lord Jesus Christ is indeed great. Only the naïve join in the common refrain that declares all religions are basically the same. In fact, while Buddhism and Christianity both claim the ardent allegiance of millions around the world, we must candidly admit that these two religions are fundamentally different. To use religious language to mask this difference is to be unfaithful to both the history of Buddhist thought and the integrity of Christian revelation.

5

Doctrine of Ethics

Karuṇā, Maitrī, and Dāna

"So in everything, do to others what you would have them do to you, for this sums up the Law and the Prophets."

Matthew 7:12

"I take upon myself the burden of all suffering, I am resolved to do so, I will endure it . . . I have made the vow to save all beings."

Sikshasamuccaya 280–81

The role of ethics is central in both the Christian and Buddhist worldviews. In fact, many advocates of interreligious dialogue claim that ethics is the common denominator of world religions. It is, therefore, a compelling place to engage in a serious dialogue between the two religions and to explore whether ethics is indeed a place where Buddhists and Christians can find common ground.

Buddhist training traditionally cultivates three key areas in the life of a Buddhist known as the threefold training: meditation leading to proper mental discipline *(samādhi)*; knowledge leading to true wisdom *(prajña)*; and compassion leading to ethical conduct *(śīla)*. The dialogue with Buddhism in chapter 4 focused largely on areas related to knowledge and the mental disciplines. It is, therefore, appropriate that this next dialogue focus on a thorough examination of Christian and Buddhist perspectives concerning ethics. We will begin with a general survey of the basis, goals, and distinctive features of Buddhist ethics.

The Basis for Buddhist Ethics: Cardinal Virtues

One of the key paradigms in understanding Buddhism is, as explored in chapter 4, its self-designation as the Middle Way. Buddhism seeks the middle path between such dichotomies as affluence and asceticism, existence and nonexistence, action and nonaction. It is not surprising, therefore, that the Buddha sought to balance the disciplines of the mind with the qualities of the heart. Buddhism is the middle way between the intellectual and the emotional streams in humanity. A close examination of the Buddha's Eightfold Path clearly reflects this balance. On the one hand, the Eightfold Path emphasizes mental disciplines such as right thought, right mindfulness, and right concentration. On the other hand, the path also emphasizes ethical responsibilities such as right speech, right action, and right livelihood. This ethical emphasis merits closer scrutiny so that we will be able to engage in a meaningful dialogue.

The ethical emphasis in Buddhism is rooted in a trio of virtues known as the three cardinal virtues: compassion *(karuṇā)*, loving-kindness *(maitrī)*, and giving/charity *(dāna)*. This emphasis on ethics does not emerge with Mahāyāna, as is sometimes believed, but is ultimately derived from two major sources: pre-Buddhist conceptions of ethics that were prevalent on the Indian subcontinent and the Buddha himself who remains the supreme ethical example for all Buddhists.

Pre-Buddhist Source of Ethics

The most prominent basis for ethics on the subcontinent prior to the dharma of Siddhartha Gautama was the concept of *ahimsā* or noninjury. Although derived from Hinduism, ahimsā became a major emphasis in the thought of Jainism. Jainism is a religion slightly older than Buddhism and, like Buddhism, was founded as a dissent movement against Hinduism. This movement, which continues today with several million adherents, was flourishing at the time of the Buddha. The ethics of Jainism is rooted in a strict application of ahimsā in the lives of Jains, especially in the areas of occupation and diet. All devout Jains, for example, are strict vegetarians because eating meat involves the killing of animals. Jains are prohibited from even touching a dead animal, which precludes them, for example, from having an occupation that involves working with leather or from wearing leather belts. By extension the doctrine of ahimsā is applied to social and ethical relationships within society, and in that context is better translated as "nonviolence." Indeed, the doctrine of ahimsā applied as nonviolence has been influential in the ethical framework of several major world leaders. Emperor Aśoka (273–232 B.C.) made ahimsā the central theme of his famous "dharma conquest." Aśoka erected hundreds of stones and pillars throughout his kingdom, encouraging his subjects to live by ahimsā and to become vegetarians. Another prominent example is Mohandas Gandhi (1869–1948) who made ahimsā the key theme in his successful drive toward Indian independence.

The doctrine of ahimsā was especially important for the Buddha. It provided an ethical foundation that was not rooted in theism, but was a "nonaction action" which would reduce the load of karma. In short, ahimsā was already conducive to the Buddhist worldview because it could easily be inserted into the causal theory of dependent origination (pratītya-samutpāda). The three cardinal virtues of Buddhist ethics—compassion (karuṇā), loving-kindness (maitrī), and giving/charity (dāna)—are all built on the foundation of ahimsā.

The Buddha As a Source of Ethics

The second major source of Buddhist ethics must be recognized as the Buddha himself, who is portrayed as the epitome of compassion, loving-kindness, and charity.

The Buddha once declared,

> Monks, there is one person whose birth in the world is for the welfare of many folk, for the happiness of many folk, who is born out of compassion for the world, for the benefit, welfare and happiness of gods and mankind. Who is that one person? It is Tathagata,[1] who is Arhat, a fully Enlightened One. This, monks, is that person.[2]

The third noble truth of the Buddha declares that the key to liberation from the wheel of saṃsāra is to extinguish all desires or "thirst" (taṇhā). This involves the abandonment of the ego by no longer clinging to the concept of "I." Once the ego has been extinguished, this allows for the blossoming of true selflessness toward others. The Buddha has led the way by precept and example, and the giving of the Eightfold Path is to be understood and received in the context of the Buddha's compassion for every person.

There is a well-known story among Buddhists about a time when the Buddha, out of compassion, used his powers to cure a fatal disease that had afflicted Devadatta, a man who hated the Buddha and had conspired against him. Even though the Buddha had saved Devadatta's life, he later mortally wounded the Buddha. The bleeding was so profuse that none of the doctors were able to prevent the Buddha's death. However, one of the disciples of the Buddha, Kassapa, declared the following: "O Blessed One, if it is true that you harbor in your heart the same feelings for both your friends and your enemies, may the flow of blood cease." The moment these words were uttered, the blood ceased to flow from the Buddha's wounds.[3] This story, along with many similar ones, is told to emphasize

1. A well-known title for the Buddha. It means "one who has gone thus," meaning that Siddhartha Gautama became enlightened and completely achieved all the qualities of Buddhahood.

2. *Majjhima nikāya* 1.10.

3. Moti Lal Pandit, *Transcendence and Negation* (New Delhi: Munshiram Manoharlal, 1999), 73–74.

the Buddha's compassion for others and to encourage all Buddhists to follow in his footsteps.

Despite the influence of ahimsā and the example of the Buddha, the overall focus of early Buddhism was on the personal or private ethics of the arhat, rather than a full-orbed public or societal ethic. Undoubtedly, the monastic emphasis in Therevāda tended to privatize ethics. The public ethic that did emerge tended to be negative, focusing mainly on what the monks were forbidden to do in their everyday interactions. The Buddha outlined five ethical prohibitions known as the five precepts: (1) do not injure another sentient being; (2) do not steal; (3) do not lie; (4) do not have illicit sex; and (5) do not cause discord among the people. When a monk receives full ordination, his head is shaved, he is vested with a saffron robe, and he takes additional vows, known as the ten precepts, that largely overlap the five precepts but also include special prohibitions such as watching dancing, adorning oneself with garlands, and sleeping on a high bed.[4] To violate any one of these would warrant punishment or even permanent expulsion from the monastic community (saṇgha). These ethical guidelines are primarily designed to assist in the individual purification and ultimate liberation of the monk.

The Goal of Ethics in Mahāyāna Buddhism

In the first century B.C., with the emergence of Mahāyāna and its emphasis on the bodhisattva ideal, ethical action on behalf of others became the centerpiece of Buddhism. Mahāyāna turned the narrow self focus of the arhat, idealized in the so-called Hīnayāna (Therevāda) tradition, into the broad others focus of the bodhisattva. In short, Mahāyāna transforms the religious goal of Buddhism from saving oneself to saving all sentient beings. This transformation is achieved through a momentous new concept of ethical responsibility within Buddhism. All of sentient life is divided into three categories: the lesser, the middling, and the superior. The lesser are those who simply live for their own pleasures and, under the weight of karma, are bound tightly to the wheel of saṃsāra. The middling refers to those who have turned their backs on the pleasures of this world and are acting to bring about their own purification. The superior are those who seek to bring an end to the suffering of all sentient beings.[5] Thus, in Mahāyāna, a bodhisattva on the verge of achieving enlightenment, out of compassion for those who are not yet enlightened, returns to the wheel of saṃsāra and vows to not enter into final release (nirvāṇa) until all other sentient beings have been liberated. This is the Buddhist equivalent of the great prayer of Moses

4. Richard H. Robinson and Willard L. Johnson, *The Buddhist Religion: A Historical Introduction*, 3d ed. (Belmont, Calif.: Wadsworth, 1982), 53.

5. Paul Williams, *Mahāyāna Buddhism: The Doctrinal Foundations* (London: Routledge, 1989), 197.

on behalf of Israel, "Please forgive their sin—but if not, then blot me out of the book you have written" (Exod. 32:32) or the apostle Paul's famous declaration, "For I could wish that I myself were cursed and cut off from Christ for the sake of my brothers, those of my own race, the people of Israel" (Rom. 9:3–4). Out of compassion, the bodhisattva is willing to enter once again into the full range of human experiences, including pain, suffering, and death, for the sake of liberating others. The goal of ethics is no longer personal liberation only, but the liberation of all sentient beings. In the *Diamond Sūtra,* a text revered by Mahāyāna, the Buddha taught this dramatic ethical action:

> The Buddha said to Subhuti, "All the bodhisattva-mahāsattvas, who undertake the practice of meditation, should cherish one thought only: 'When I attain perfect wisdom, I will liberate all sentient beings in every realm of the universe, whether they be egg-born, womb-born, moisture-born, or miraculously born; those with form, those without form . . . so long as any form of being is conceived, I must allow it to pass into the eternal peace of nirvāṇa, that leaves nothing behind.'"[6]

This doctrine exemplifies how the differences between Mahāyāna, which emerged from a debate within Therevāda over the role of the laity and the authority of various textual traditions, has evolved into a whole new way of acting in the world and a dramatic expansion of the Buddhist worldview.

Hīnayāna (Therevāda) only teaches the path of ascent, where a person gradually travels along the Eightfold Path from ignorance to enlightenment. Mahāyāna introduces another path, one of descent, whereby a bodhisattva on the verge of final enlightenment chooses to descend back onto the wheel of saṃsāra to assist other sentient beings. This places the whole of Mahāyāna thought and practice into a new ethical framework, leaving nothing untouched. Most notable is that salvation itself is no longer based solely on a person's own efforts. Now, the compassionate grace of an unlimited number of bodhisattvas is available to assist believers along the path.

Distinctive Features of Ethics in Mahāyāna Buddhism

The heart of Mahāyāna ethics is publicly expressed through the three cardinal virtues of compassion (karuṇā), loving-kindness (maitrī), and giving/charity (dāna). Each of these three virtues will now be examined.

Compassion (karuṇā)

Two important aspects of Buddhist compassion (karuṇā) are important to note in light of the upcoming dialogue. First, in Mahāyāna the doctrine of compassion is linked directly to the bodhisattva ideal, just as Hīnayāna

6. Mu Soeng, trans., *The Diamond Sūtra* (Boston: Wisdom Publications, 2000), 141–42.

links compassion to the arhat ideal. This is important because it not only opens Buddhism to the concept of grace in general, but also clearly establishes the specific concept of vicarious suffering. Karma is no longer individualized. One bodhisattva can take on the suffering of many. Indeed, suffering and pain are prominent themes in Buddhist literature, and the bodhisattvas' hardships are portrayed as acts of compassionate selflessness on behalf of others. For example, this aspect of compassion is celebrated by the Buddhist poet Santideva when he declares, "If the suffering of many is brought to an end by the suffering of one, the one should foster this suffering in himself by means of compassion . . . you must exchange your well-being for the miseries of others."[7]

Second, compassion in Mahāyāna refers primarily to the tragedy of sentient beings who are held in bondage to the wheel of saṃsāra. A Buddhist should long for the liberation of *all* sentient beings. This is important because compassion is not just directed to certain groups or classes of people as might be assumed in the West. With Buddhism, every living creature, regardless of its economic state or physical health, is an object of pity and compassion, for all are trapped on the wheel of saṃsāra. Indeed, a healthy, comfortable, wealthy person is as much an object of compassion as a poor, destitute person, since both are trapped by the illusion of the world. The entire world is, to borrow the words of the Third Dalai Lama, "Like members in a drunken procession staggering towards a cliff, they are stumbling over the precipice of evil into the suffering of cyclic existence."[8] True compassion, therefore, should extend toward all beings, including those on other worlds throughout the entire cosmos:

> We should have this compassion from the depths of our hearts, as if it were nailed there. Such compassion is not merely concerned with a few sentient beings such as friends and relatives, but extends up to the limits of the cosmos, in all directions and towards all beings throughout space.[9]

Loving-Kindness (maitrī)

The second cardinal virtue is loving-kindness (maitrī). This virtue is so powerful that it can dispel the effects of karma and liberate one from such vices as hatred, anger, and envy. One early Buddhist text describes maitrī as such an important virtue that it absorbs all others:

> None of the means employed to acquire religious merit, O monks, has a sixteenth part of the value of loving-kindness. Loving-kindness, which is freedom of the heart, absorbs them all: it glows, it shines, it blazes forth.[10]

7. As quoted in Pandit, *Transcendence and Negation,* 82–83.
8. As quoted in Williams, *Mahāyāna Buddhism,* 200–201.
9. Williams, *Mahāyāna Buddhism,* 199.
10. *Itivuttaka* 27, as quoted in Pandit, *Transcendence and Negation,* 63–64.

Indeed, maitrī enables Buddhists to experience this "freedom of heart" to such an extent that even as assailants are cutting them limb from limb, they feel no anger, and their hearts are full of compassion:

> O monks, the many would not be fulfilling my commands who, even while ruffians were cutting him limb from limb with a saw, allowed hatred to fill his heart. Even then he should say, "This will not change my heart . . . I shall remain kindly and compassionate, with my heart full of loving-kindness [maitrī] and no hatred within me."[11]

It is important to notice that descriptions of maitrī are often expressed in positive rather than negative terms. In other words, it expresses what someone should do, not just the suppression of a negative impulse. It is more than the mere absence of anger; it is this "freedom of heart" which is directed toward all sentient beings. This is a notable difference from the concept of ethics generally observed in the Hīnayāna tradition, which focuses on the development of the five negatively stated moral precepts and defines morality (śīla) as the individual attainment of a cloistered monk who has ceased sinning.

Giving/Charity (dāna)

The third cardinal virtue is giving or charity (dāna). The meaning of *dāna* cannot be fully captured by the English translation "giving" or "charity," for it involves aspects of both. The concept of giving in Buddhism goes beyond providing alms for the poor and needy. Rather, dāna is an outgrowth of intense meditation whereby one is able to give oneself in exchange for another being. In other words, as meditators visualize the various realms of suffering in the cosmos, they begin to focus on the suffering of specific sentient beings. In the process of the meditation, the suffering of the sentient being is breathed in, and the joy of release and peace is breathed out or given to the one in need. It is the supreme example that the one who gives has emptied himself or herself of the illusory concept of self. This kind of giving is not just for bodhisattvas transferring merit to those who are suffering, but it is also a way to become a bodhisattva, especially if one gives his or her life for another. Mahāyāna literature is filled with stories of Buddhists who have given their lives for the sake of others in need and thereby become bodhisattvas. Furthermore, the stories of Buddhists giving up their lives rather than allowing animals to be killed show the close relationship between dāna and ahimsā. One well-known story, for example, recounts how a powerful king gave up his life for a dove. The depth of this charity has the effect of lifting both the giver and the receiver out of the endless stream of saṃsāra. This is, of course, the ultimate goal common to all Mahāyāna Buddhists—to produce an inner purging of self, resulting in the realization of emptiness or oneness with mind (citta) or consciousness.

11. *Majjhima nikāya,* 1.

Ethics and the Buddhist Worldview

Two qualifications need to be made in order to reconcile this new ethical emphasis in Mahāyāna with the overall worldview of Buddhism. First, when a bodhisattva refuses nirvāṇa and vows to return to the wheel of saṃsāra to save all sentient beings, this should not be interpreted as a presumptuous belief that by returning he becomes a super-savior and single-handedly is able to save the entire cosmos. That reading of the bodhisattva vow inserts a form of I-thou dualism that could not possibly be present in a true bodhisattva. There can be no bodhisattva "I" acting to save the lost and entrapped "thou" of the world. Instead, the vow should be taken to indicate that the truly enlightened bodhisattva realizes his oneness with the entire mass of the suffering world. By becoming one with the suffering world, he is able to finally assist the sentient world toward enlightenment.

Second, the bodhisattva vow must be heard in the context of the nondifference between saṃsāra and nirvāṇa. It would be a mistake to hear the vow as one leaving an objective place of ultimate freedom called nirvāṇa and returning to a place of bondage and suffering called saṃsāra. The earliest form of Buddhism attributed our suffering existence to the attachments we have to the world fueled by our desires and karma driven actions. Nirvāṇa was seen to be the goal of Buddhism. Later, in his exposition of the *Prajñāpāramitā Sūtras,* Nāgārjuna pointed out that "not only attachment to saṃsāra but also attachment to nirvāṇa" must be rejected. One of the major themes of the sūtra is the call to abide in neither saṃsāra nor nirvāṇa: "One should not abide in saṃsāra in order to awaken to wisdom: One should not abide in nirvāṇa in order to fulfill compassion."[12]

Thus, the forsaking of nirvāṇa by a bodhisattva is actually a testimony to his lack of attachment to anything, even to the so-called goal of enlightenment. The bodhisattva becomes yet another example of the Middle Way, dwelling fully in neither nirvāṇa nor saṃsāra. The path of ascent and the path of descent are both transcended, as the following text makes clear:

> Here a Bodhisattva, a great being, thinks thus: "Countless beings, I should lead to nirvāṇa, and yet there are none who lead to nirvāṇa, there are none who should be led to it." However many beings he may lead to nirvāṇa, yet there is not any being that has been led to nirvāṇa, nor that has led others to it.[13]

For the bodhisattva, nirvāṇa becomes the starting point of the journey of compassion and the manifestation of ethics in a suffering world. This new dimension is opened up because a true bodhisattva could not remain in

12. As quoted by Masao Abe in S. Heine, ed., *Buddhism and Interfaith Dialogue* (London: MacMillan, 1995) 91.

13. *Aṣṭasāhasrikā Prajñāpāramitā Sutra,* 1.20–21.

nirvāṇa, enjoying his own salvation while other beings are trapped in suffering. Thus, the bodhisattva vow must be seen primarily as an expression of an enlightened being's oneness with the entire universe and the lack of attachment to anything, even nirvāṇa.

Religious Roundtable

Positive Reflections on Ethics in Mahāyāna Buddhism

One cannot help admiring the deep and abiding emphasis on ethics in Buddhism, especially in its Mahāyāna forms. I find two aspects of Buddhist ethics particularly noteworthy. First, Buddhist ethics are entirely nondiscriminatory. Indeed, emphasis on the universal application of ethics was the focal point of the Buddhist dissent against Hinduism, which had largely ignored the lower castes and those outside the caste system. It would be inconceivable, for example, for a Hindu Brahmin to give up his life for the sake of a *dalit* (outcaste Hindu). The Mahāyāna democratization of ethics serves not only as a rebuke against the disenfranchisement of the lower or scheduled castes and the untouchables but, by extension, as an ongoing challenge to similar exclusive tendencies that had developed in the Hīnayāna monastic tradition.

One of the most dramatic conversions to Buddhism in modern times is the story of B. D. Ambedkar, a dalit who championed the rights of the lower castes and the noncaste untouchables during the period when India was emerging as an independent nation. Ambedkar was an outspoken critic of Gandhi's desire to reform, not abolish, the caste system. He played a key role in the emergence of the Indian nation and had the privilege of writing the Indian constitution. In one of the most dramatic events of modern Indian history, Ambedkar declared at a public meeting that although he was born a Hindu, he would not die a Hindu. He proceeded to study the religious and ethical tenets of Islam, Christianity, and Buddhism to decide which religion to convert to. Meanwhile, tens of thousands of low-caste Hindus pledged that the religion Ambedkar converted to would be the religion they would adopt as well. Finally, on October 14, 1956, in a massive public ceremony in Nagpur, Ambedkar converted to Buddhism, followed shortly by over four million Indians.[14] Even though he died only two months after his famous conversion, he had set up a new political party in India

14. Stephen Hay, ed., *Sources of Indian Tradition*, vol. 2, 2d ed. (New York: Columbia University Press, 1988), 339.

based, in part, on Buddhist ethics, which would serve Indians from all religious groups and castes. Undoubtedly, Ambedkar was drawn to this universal application of Buddhist ethics.

Second, Buddhist ethics embraces the concept of vicarious suffering, which is central to Christianity but is virtually absent from the traditional Hindu understanding of karma. The Hindu view of karma permits neither the transfer of merit nor the sharing of spiritual burdens. Mahāyāna Buddhism joyfully embraces both. The functional monotheism of Amitābha Buddha in Pure Land Buddhism, for example, provides a compelling paradigm that can serve as a bridge for the Christian gospel. Many Christians have found it nearly impossible to communicate key concepts such as grace and vicarious suffering to the Hindu worldview. Buddhism has provided plentiful paradigms for both. This must be applauded, for it reveals the universal realization of our inability to save ourselves as well as a deep longing for a savior outside of ourselves, both crucial concepts for any serious attempt to share the Christian gospel with a Buddhist.

The purpose of this dialogue, however, is not only to grow in our understanding of and respect for other religions, but also to be open and honest about the serious differences. As I pointed out in chapter 1, asking Christians and sincere followers of other religions to suspend their genuine faith and religious convictions when approaching the table of dialogue is neither honest nor helpful. Therefore, the upcoming dialogue will focus on ethics as it finds its fullest expression in Mahāyāna Buddhism. I have two serious objections that I wish to pose to my Mahāyāna colleague. I invite his response and, wherever necessary, his clarification in areas where I may have misunderstood the Buddhist concept of ethics.

Objection #1: Buddhism denies the reality of both the agent and recipient of any ethical actions.

Ethical actions necessitate some kind of relationship between the one who acts with compassion or kindness and the one who is the recipient of these actions. It is nonsensical to speak about activating the impulse to love or show compassion if in reality there is no one to act and no one to receive the action. If such a relationship does not exist, then the entire structure of ethics collapses. Yet this is precisely the Buddhist position. Fundamental to the entire Buddhist religion, including ancient Buddhism (exemplified today by Therevāda) and the entire spectrum of Mahāyāna, is the absolute denial of the self. The Buddhist doctrine of anātman (no-self) asserts that the whole notion of self is illusory and imaginary. According to Buddhism, the widespread belief in the self is attributed to the depth of human ignorance due to the blinding effects of karma, which causes us to falsely project a self and to live with an insatiable desire for self-preservation. The great thrust of Buddhism is to break this false notion of a permanent self. Indeed, the doctrine of anātman stands as one of the fundamental lines of demarcation between Buddhism and all other major world religions.

As noted in chapter 4, in place of the concept of self, Buddhists have inserted the doctrine of dependent arising (pratītya-samutpāda), which views all existence as a never-ending chain of cause and effect, none of which has any substance or ontological reality. How does one reconcile an ethical system that calls for compassion toward all sentient beings with the doctrine that no being actually exists? How can ethics exist when there is no real suffering and no one who actually suffers? This denial of self coupled with the bodhisattva ideal of acting ethically on behalf of every suffering being in the cosmos explains the paradoxical words of the Buddha when he said that the bodhisattvas were "saving all beings, knowing full well that there is no one to save."[15] Any serious Christian-Buddhist dialogue will need to address this apparent contradiction. In short, how can Buddhists build a system of ethics on the foundational doctrine of anātman?

Mahāyāna reply:

I do not want to appear to be avoiding a direct answer to your question, but I think it is only right that any Buddhist answer to this tension between ethical actions and the doctrine of anātman be expressed in a way that is true to the Buddhist vision. Therefore, I want to begin by explaining more fully how Buddhists regard such a question in the first place, and then I will address the question you have posed.

I am convinced that if the Buddha himself were sitting at this table of dialogue and this question had been posed to him, he would have remained silent and would not have ventured to answer. A story in the *Saṃyutta-Nikāya* (The Book of Kindred Sayings) recounts how the Buddha was sitting in a grove of trees while his disciples gathered in a circle around him and asked him various metaphysical questions. All the questions were met only with the Buddha's silence. Finally, he took a handful of leaves in his hand and asked which were more numerous—the leaves in his hand or the leaves in the forest. His disciples replied that there were more leaves in the forest. The Buddha said that the leaves in the forest represented all of the insights and answers that he knew but chose not to reveal. He had only revealed a handful of truths because they were truths that promoted liberation and enlightenment; the rest were only theoretical questions and were of little use to Buddhists.

Let me explain the implications of this simple story. Western Christians steeped in Enlightenment assumptions approach questions such as this from a rational and logical point of view. Your doctrines are generally taught in your seminaries and explained in your Christian churches in a systematic and logical manner. These doctrines and beliefs are based on narratives, poetry, and teaching found in a body of clearly defined scriptural texts that

15. Soeng, *Diamond Sūtra*, 31.

you call the Bible. The Bible serves as the chief document for setting forth and safeguarding Christian life and practice. It is the standard of orthodoxy. The word *orthodoxy* literally means "correct doctrines" or "correct beliefs." This, in turn, becomes the framework for your attempt to discuss any question, including how the doctrine of anātman can be logically reconciled with a system of ethics.

However, Buddhism is not primarily oriented toward the concept of orthodoxy. We do not recite creeds the way Christians do, and we do not have a single set of texts that all Mahāyāna accept as final, authoritative revelation. It is true that most of us accept the original tripiṭaka (three baskets) that forms the earliest corpus of the Buddha's teaching, but we also believe that those baskets did not have lids on them. Over the centuries, other equally important texts have been added to the tripiṭaka. This, in our view, is not an embarrassment but a testimony to how the Buddha's teaching has remained vibrant across the centuries and among many distinctive cultural groups. To use Christian terminology, we do not have a closed canon. Some Japanese Mahāyāna Buddhists, for example, adhere to the teachings of the *Lotus Sūtra* and exclude all other texts in the entire Buddhist tradition. Other groups go to great lengths to show how the *Prajñāpāramitā Sūtras,* including the later textual summaries such as the *Diamond Sutra* and the *Heart Sūtra,* are in continuity with the earliest tripiṭaka collection.

While we have heated discussions about the value of various texts, it is not because of our interest in promoting orthodoxy in the Christian sense, but in promoting orthopraxy, that is, right practice. Mahāyāna Buddhists view the Buddha as extremely pragmatic. His concern was not to impose a rigid textual or doctrinal tradition on his followers nor to answer theoretical questions but to encourage the practice of Buddhism leading to enlightenment. Therefore, we are not particularly concerned with reconciling all Buddhists texts into a unified or systematic doctrinal scheme that excludes all contradictions. Rather, the various textual traditions should be seen as independent models of enlightenment that have served and continue to serve Buddhists around the world in the practice of Buddhism and the pursuit of enlightenment.

This is the backdrop against which doctrinal discussions about Buddhism must be viewed. In short, it is not always easy to see how the various components of Buddhism fit together, since these insights are not rationally understood but are seen only through the eye of enlightenment. However, in keeping with the mutuality of this dialogue, I will not sit in silence but will now seek to address the question that has been raised.

You are correct in pointing out how the doctrine of anātman is central to all Buddhist thought. In the Buddhist view, to build an ethical system on the basis of a self who acts ethically and a self who receives these acts of compassion is wrong and misses the benefit of the Buddha's enlightenment entirely. It is only because Christian thinking is so deeply immersed in a framework of I-thou dualism that it seems so shocking, even scandalizing, to see Buddhists discard both the compassionate "I" who acts as well as the needy "thou" who receives the action. We are accustomed to this reaction. The Buddha himself acknowledged that his teaching was "against the current" *(paṭisotagāmi)*[16] and difficult to understand. According to early accounts of the Buddha during the period immediately following his enlightenment, he almost decided not to turn the wheel of dharma and offer his teaching to the world, because he knew how few would understand the radical implications of anātman. The sense of "I" and "thou" is so deeply ingrained in the human race that it takes many kalpas of lifetimes and the assistance of tens of millions of bodhisattvas to break free from it.

Although the doctrine of anātman is true, it is not yet recognized by the great mass of suffering humanity. Therefore, ethics arises in a provisional way until the full attainment of this truth is realized. In your question, you asked how we build a structure of ethics on the foundation of the doctrine of anātman. Buddhism is not about building a structure but going on a journey. We do not see anātman as a foundation for ethics; rather, we see ethics as a temporary guide to the destination of anātman. We prefer the metaphor of the raft and the distant shore. In this case, ethics represents the raft and the doctrine of anātman is the distant shore to which we are headed. Once the realization of anātman occurs, then the raft of ethics can be discarded.

In the *Lotus Sūtra,* the most influential Mahāyāna text in the Far East, we find the parable of the burning house. It is the story of a wealthy father who lives in a beautiful mansion with many rooms. Inside the house, his children are completely engrossed in playing with their toys. Tragically, the house catches on fire and is burning to the ground while the children, unaware of the imminent catastrophe, are still inside playing. The father, recognizing the danger, knows he must quickly get the children's attention or they will perish. He stands outside and calls each child by name, promising each one a special toy that he knows will bring delight to that particular child. He promises the child the toy if he or she will come out immediately. Using this technique, the father is able to rescue all his children.[17] Like the wise father, the Buddha understands the particular needs of each person, and his teaching or dharma calls out to each one in its own way. The toys are symbolic of the various ethical acts of compassion that are necessary to lead each of us out of our illusory play into the safety of enlightenment. Thus, even though the bodhisattva knows that there is no self who is compassionate and no self who receives compassion, the bodhisattva is willing to reenter this illusion for the sake of rescuing all sentient beings.

16. Walpola Rahula, *What the Buddha Taught* (New York: Grove Weidenfeld, 1974), 52.

17. Burton Watson, trans., *The Lotus Sūtra* (New York: Columbia University Press, 1993), 56–57.

Evangelical reply:

The metaphors comparing ethics to a raft that is to be discarded and to nonexistent toys that the father promises his children, as well as your reference to ethics as a temporary guide, clearly demote Buddhist ethics to a functional level. Ethical actions do not actually exist but are temporarily useful in the illusion of the world for the sake of a higher goal. Thus, by your own admission, Buddhist ethics is not about alleviating human suffering, since there is no one who is suffering. The goal of Buddhist ethics is not to *assist* humanity, but to *transcend* it. This inevitably mires Buddhist ethics in a negative assessment of humanity. Ethics are not directed toward a real person who has innate worth and dignity. If there is no self, then there is no one who can be valued. Indeed, there is no ethical act, however great, that is not swallowed up in the ontological void of Buddhist emptiness. From a child's simplest act of kindness to the vicarious suffering and death of Jesus Christ, all are declared to be as illusory as a dream, having no ultimate substance or reality. Suppose you go to sleep one night and dream that you are performing charitable deeds such as feeding the hungry, tending the sick, or building homes for the homeless. When you wake up, you might be inspired to go out and perform such deeds, but you certainly could not declare that you had performed them. Yet in Buddhism the whole of life is nothing more than an insubstantial dream of aggregate causes and effects that arise and cease.

In contrast, the Christian ethic is rooted in God who created and fashioned the whole of humanity in his own image (Gen. 1:26–27). Therefore, love and compassion arise not simply because of the *conditions* in which people find themselves, but because the objects of our compassion are men and women created in the image of God. Christ did not come to transcend or extinguish humanity but to ignite it to be even more fully alive and fully human than before. Buddhist compassion can never rise above pity, because the focus is not on real human sufferers, only on the causal chain of conditions that gives the illusory experience of a self who suffers and is trapped on the wheel of saṃsāra. In contrast, Christian compassion can soar to the heights of sacrificial love because a genuine relationship is possible between real people who are bound by their common dignity as beings created in the image of God. To the Buddhist, there can be no eternal relationships, because we are nothing more than temporary aggregates of various components. For the Christian, love reflects a genuine relationship and carries an absolute value because God is love (1 John 4:16). All ethical acts of charity ultimately reflect God's nature. Love is never discarded like a raft, because it is essential to God's eternal being. He is the eternal source of all acts of compassion and loving-kindness. The Scriptures declare, "We love because he first loved us" (1 John 4:19). Our ethical actions, therefore, are joyful responses to his prior action in our lives and in the world. Christian ethics is rooted in the nature and love of the God who created us in his own image and bestowed his dignity on the whole of creation. Our relationship with a world in need is linked directly to our love for and our relationship with God himself, as 1 John 4:20–21 continues to make clear:

> If anyone says, "I love God," yet hates his brother, he is a liar. For anyone who does not love his brother, whom he has seen, cannot love God, whom he has not seen. And he has given us this command: Whoever loves God must also love his brother.

Christian ethics, therefore, finds its source and orientation in God and has been most profoundly demonstrated by God's action in the incarnation of Jesus Christ. Through the incarnation, the concrete nature of Christian ethics has been affirmed in a final sense. A bodhisattva, who out of compassion descends to alleviate suffering humanity, has often been compared to the incarnate Jesus Christ who comes to redeem the human race from sin and suffering.[18] However, they are comparable only on the most superficial level. Although there are many differences, I will highlight two to demonstrate my point.

First, the compassionate bodhisattva is part of a causal nexus with no substantial reality. The compassionate Christ is the embodiment of the eternal God and is the fullest expression of reality. This lack of substantial reality in Buddhism influences the whole framework of the Buddhist idea of the descent of the bodhisattva. For the enlightened Mahāyāna, there is not even a nirvāṇa for the bodhisattva to forsake because ultimately there is no difference between nirvāṇa and saṃsāra. How different this is from the Christian proclamation! At the incarnation, the Son of God, who from all eternity dwelled in the perfect bliss of the Trinity, actually stepped into the pages of human history. The traversing of the Son from the presence of the Father to the manger in Bethlehem is steeped in mystery but is a real event in history.

Second, because of the ontological nondualism in Buddhism, a bodhisattva's acts of compassion are part and parcel of his or her own salvation and purgation of self. The bodhisattva who acts compassionately and the recipient of the action are really one. The advantage of the bodhisattva is simply the realization that the doctrine of dependent arising means none are saved until all are saved. In contrast, Christ does not need to be saved and has no share in the fallenness of the human race. The biblical passage often quoted by Buddhists about Christ "emptying himself *[kenosis]*" (Phil. 2:1–11) has nothing to do with Christ purging himself of the notion of self.[19]

18. See, for example, Donald Lopez Jr. and Steve Rockefeller, *The Christ and the Bodhisattva* (Albany, N.Y.: SUNY Press, 1987).

19. Masao Abe in S. Heine, *Buddhism and Interfaith Dialogue*, 127–150. Note Abe's insistence that he is not engaging in Buddhist eisegesis of Christian texts in relation to Philippians 2:1–11. For a fuller treatment of this theme, see Abe's discussion of this passage with seven theologians in John B. Cobb and Christopher Ives, eds., *The Emptying God: A Buddhist-Jewish-Christian Conversation* (Maryknoll, N.Y.: Orbis, 1990).

Rather, the passage celebrates how Christ, in an act of unfathomable humiliation, laid aside his divine prerogatives to the point of dying on the cross for the sake of our salvation.

To sum up, Christian ethics reflect absolute truths rooted in the eternal, unchanging nature of God. The very expression of ethics serves to underscore the dignity of the entire human race as created in the image of God. The greatest expression and supreme example of ethics is the incarnation of Jesus Christ who enables us to enter into a genuine I-thou relationship with the living God and who calls, empowers, and sends us into the world as his ambassadors. As his ambassadors, we are called to lives of complete ethical integrity in all our relationships. Despite remarkable similarities in the ethical language used to describe Christ and the bodhisattvas, there is an unbridgeable gulf between the two communities.[20]

Mahāyāna rejoinder:

I would like to offer two brief responses to your statement about Christian ethics and to pose a few questions. First, as a Mahāyāna Buddhist I do not see why clinging to the notion of an independent self makes the exercise of ethics more valuable. We often compare the idea of self to a wheel. At the level of daily life and experience, the wheel has a certain kind of reality. But once the spokes are removed from the wheel and the rim and hub are dismantled, the "wheel-ness" of the wheel is gone. The fact that the wheel or self no longer exists does not devalue ethics, but actually empowers it because the whole purpose of ethics is to assist a person in the realization that there is no self. Nonexistence of self is the goal and reward of ethics, not an embarrassment that renders ethics futile and useless.

Second, you are quite right that Buddhist ethics functions on a practical, functional level; ethics is merely a raft to get to the distant shore. However, couldn't Christian ethics function equally well on the same functional level? Why is it so important to relate ethics to a supreme, personal God? A suffering person who receives your assistance and compassion does not care if you are a Christian or an atheist. Didn't Jesus himself make this point in the parable of the Good Samaritan? The Samaritan was commended for his ethical actions, despite the fact that he was clearly identified by the audience as an unbeliever. In contrast, the two men who were devout believers in God were condemned because they had failed to act ethically.[21] Thus, ethical actions can function apart from God or faith in God. All that matters is that they become embodied and activated for the sake of the one who is suffering.

20. Many scholars have pointed out the likelihood that the Buddhist doctrine of a suffering bodhisattva has been influenced and shaped substantially by Christian theology, which was, of course, vigorously present in Persia from the third century.

21. See A. Fernando, *Buddhism Made Plain* (Maryknoll, N.Y.: Orbis, 1985) 107–8.

Finally, while I admire Christian ethics very much, I believe that Buddhist ethics are more suitable in light of the current environmental crisis. I noticed that you made several references to the value of humanity because we are created in the image of God and how this should influence our actions toward others. Yet you never mentioned any ethical responsibilities we have to animals and other forms of life. You pointed out how you admire the nondiscriminatory nature of Buddhist ethics, which embraces high-caste Brahmins as well as outcaste dalits. However, Buddhist compassion extends even further than that. The word *compassion* literally means "passion for all." A true bodhisattva maintains compassion for all sentient life in every region of the cosmos. Buddhist ethics, as you noted in the introduction to this dialogue, arises out of the doctrine of ahimsā or noninjury, which applies to all life in the entire ecosystem, not just to human life. Christian ethics, in contrast, assumes that humans hold a moral priority over all other forms of life. God is above, nature is below. This seems to give humans the right to dominate and exploit nature because animals and other nonhuman forms of life have no moral worth or, at least, are not the recipients of ethical actions. Therefore, a Buddhist ethic would seem to provide the basis for a more holistic, environmentally friendly ethic.

Evangelical rejoinder:

You have raised three important issues, all of which I will seek to respond to. First, you insist that the exercise of ethics is not compromised even though there is no substantial reality to the self. Indeed, the goal of Buddhist ethics is the extinguishing of self. However, I find this view untenable for two reasons. To begin with, those who affirm this view must face the inevitable fact that once the self who acts compassionately and the self who receives the act of compassion realize there was no self who acted nor any self who received an action, then all ethical acts are likewise nonexistent. You cannot value or devalue something that does not exist, never has existed, and never will exist. You contrasted the building metaphor of Christianity with the more dynamic road or path metaphor of Buddhism, but in Mahāyāna even the road does not really exist. Indeed, Buddhist ethics are part of the world's karma-driven illusion and lack any intrinsic value. In short, how can one speak of the value of ethics when, in fact, there is nothing to be valued? As in the well-known story about the emperor with no clothes, continuing to place value on ethics would be like continuing to value the emperor's beautiful clothes, even after you realize that there never were any clothes. In fact, the Buddhist situation is even more grim, because not only are the clothes nonexistent, so is the emperor and the adoring crowds. Even the little girl, who like a compassionate bodhisattva speaks the truth in the midst of a self-deluded crowd, does not exist.

The other reason I find this view troubling is that denying the reality of self means that there are times when unethical actions and even cruelty may be justified for the sake of the dharma. This is justified because, although a person may be mistreated, we know that there is no real person being mistreated. A certain action may be evil, but we justify it because we know that this action never really existed. Several Buddhist sūtras give surprising examples of how even the Buddha in his previous lives acted unethically for the sake of the greater good of the dharma. For example, the *Upāyakauśalya Sūtra* recounts how under a vow of celibacy he once had sexual intercourse with a girl because she threatened to kill herself unless he requited her great love for him. In another instance, he murdered a man to prevent him from killing five hundred others.[22]

Admittedly, all ethical systems face difficult choices in complex situations where conflicting values are present or when the choice is only between the lesser of two evils. However, in the Christian view, the knowledge that every person is created in the image of God and is therefore a person of infinite worth created for eternity, helps to strengthen and stabilize our moral resolve in the world. To exchange our belief in the infinite value of the self for a belief in the nonexistence of the self would certainly have a negative impact on the structure of Christian ethics.

Second, you have said that ethics can exist on a functional level quite apart from God or faith in God. However, Christian ethics cannot exist apart from God because he represents the moral grounding for our entire ethical system. This is best summarized in Leviticus 19:2, where God declares to Israel, "Be holy because I, the LORD your God, am holy." Our ethical actions are rooted in his ethical nature. The moment ethics becomes separated from the living person of God, we lose our footing and can no longer speak with moral certainty. Indeed, we are incapable of ethical action apart from God because it is his work through us, for he said, "I am the LORD, who *makes you holy*" (Lev. 20:8; 22:32, emphasis added). Buddhist ethics, in contrast, are attainable through human actions, either ours or the bodhisattvas. In either case, there is no truly transcendent source or foundation of ethics.

The self-revelation of God's person, nature, and character that began at the dawn of creation became fully manifested in the incarnation of Jesus Christ. The compassionate and sacrificial life of Christ is the ultimate standard for us to imitate and to learn how best to love God and our neighbor. Christ took the ethical commandments off the tablets of stone and supremely demonstrated how to live them out in real relationships. The Scriptures declare that the Holy Spirit actually writes his law on our hearts, demonstrating that the whole thrust of Christian ethics is to internalize them into the lives of real people (John 14:17; 16:13; Heb. 8:10). For Christians, ethics cannot be abstractly separated from either God or people. Indeed, the parable of the Good Samaritan is set in the context of verses about the two greatest commandments—love God and love your neighbor (Luke

22. Williams, *Mahāyāna Buddhism*, 145.

10:25–37). The point of the parable is to expose the tragedy of a person who spends his or her life trying to love God and yet fails to see the vital connection between loving God and loving one's neighbor. This was precisely the state of the lawyer in Luke 10 who wanted to love God but was not prepared to embrace the implications this had for how he treated others. Only by extracting the parable from the larger context of Jesus' encounter with the lawyer could someone say that the parable is commending ethical action apart from God or faith in God. The intent is actually the opposite: to reinforce the connection between love of God and love of neighbor.

Finally, I want to thank my Buddhist friend for raising the difficult question about the ability of Christian ethics to address modern environmental issues. This dialogue encourages this kind of challenging question because only then can the actual boundary lines between Christianity and Buddhism be fully known. Your position, as I understand it, is that an ahimsā-based compassion ("passion for all") that embraces all sentient life may be a more suitable ethic in which to address many of the environmental issues we face today.

I freely admit that some Christians have not properly understood biblical teaching regarding the proper relationship we should have with the larger created order. Regaining a proper biblical attitude must begin by going back to the creation account as found in the first chapter of Genesis, which teaches that men and women, unlike the rest of creation, were created in the image of God and were given authority and dominion over the creation:

> So God created man in his own image, in the image of God he created him; male and female he created them. God blessed them and said to them, "Be fruitful and increase in number; fill the earth and subdue it. Rule over the fish of the sea and the birds of the air and over every living creature that moves on the ground." (Gen. 1:27–28)

This text upholds two principles that must be kept in proper balance. On the one hand, as the unique bearers of God's image, humans are clearly given authority over the created order. We were commissioned by God to fill and subdue the earth. This gives humanity legal and moral priority over the creation. On the other hand, since our authority is not independent but derived from God, we must be careful and wise stewards of the earth and its resources, including nonhuman life. When the text says we are to rule over every living thing, this does not mean unbridled, autonomous dominance, but wise and sensitive stewardship. We sometimes mistakenly associate the phrase "rule over" as a negative, abusive authority. However, the phrase refers to the wise extension of God's gracious authority and rule. The ownership of the earth still belongs to God (Ps. 24:1). Our role is a special appointment to fulfill his plans for the earth. Thus, despite the important privileges and responsibilities God gives us, the Bible remains unequivocally God centered, not man centered.

This stewardship emphasis is further reinforced when we realize that creation is innately good apart from us. Before humans were created, God created plant and animal life and called them good (Gen. 1:11, 21, 24). Creation has intrinsic value, not just instrumental value. The Psalms repeatedly declare that the whole of creation gives praise, honor, and glory to God (e.g., Ps. 19 and 148). The very presence of God in the incarnation of Jesus Christ is a further testimony to the inherent goodness of creation. Indeed, as Jesus institutes the Lord's Supper, the sacramentalization of the common elements of bread and wine assumes that "the natural [order] has the capacity to be made sacred."[23]

This brief overview demonstrates how the Christian model, which balances unique human authority with wise stewardship, is quite different from the Buddhist model, where there is no fundamental separation or substantial difference between humans and nature. Everything is the result of an endless chain of dependent arising and ceasing. The Buddhist view clearly ties humanity much closer to nature than does the Christian view, but this does not necessarily provide the basis for a more responsible, environmentally friendly ethic.

Objection #2: Ethical choices are relative, since ultimately there is no difference between good and evil in Mahāyāna Buddhism.

This objection will be stated with more brevity because it shares the same root as the previous objection. In both objections, I am pointing out various implications when all permanent absolutes are denied.

The Buddhist worldview (as with most of Hinduism) rejects a dualistic concept of the world in favor of a nondualistic or monistic one. Dualistic distinctions are present only in a provisional way during the illusion of life. True enlightenment will jettison all such dualistic distinctions. Dichotomies familiar to Christians, such as saved and lost, heaven and hell, God and Satan, are merely psychological props that must be dissolved by true knowledge. The implications this has for ethics cannot be easily ignored. How can compassion (karuṇā) and loving-kindness (maitrī) and giving/charity (dāna) be recognized or measured when there can be no ultimate distinction between good and evil? Once the enlightened bodhisattva has realized that saṃsāra is nirvāṇa, how can any subsequent act be declared an act of compassion? To speak of an act as compassionate must involve contrasting reference points to be intelligible. To declare that any given deed is an act of compassion assumes that compassion is a beneficial virtue. It also assumes possible negative scenarios should the act of compassion be withheld. But these kinds of distinctions are impossible in the world of pratītya-samutpāda (dependent arising) because everything is linked together in a never-ending monistic chain. Life cannot be accorded any better status than

23. Ronald Massanari, "A Problematic in Environmental Ethics: Western and Eastern Styles," *Buddhist-Christian Studies* 18 (1998): 42.

death, because everything is dependent and would not arise if not for the other. Pratītya-samutpāda is the great leveler in Buddhism. By reducing everything to an insubstantial chain of cause and effect and by tightly closing the door against anything that is ontologically transcendent (Brāhman, ātman, God), Buddhism loses all ethical reference points. Once ultimate distinctions are gone, ethical distinctions become temporary psychological props. Health and vitality cannot be accorded any more favorable status than sickness and disease because, according to the first noble truth, *all* life is suffering. Existence itself is suffering. A healthy self needs to be extinguished every bit as much as a sick self, for both are trapped by the illusion of the world and remain bound to the wheel of saṃsāra. How can meaningful ethical choices be made in light of this monistic ontology?

Mahāyāna reply:

Buddhist spirituality is linked to six perfections *(pāramitās)*, beginning with virtues like dāna (giving) and śīla (morality) at the lower rungs of the spiritual ladder and culminating in prajña (wisdom). Therefore, true knowledge *is* higher than ethical virtues like dāna (giving/charity). Our whole religious worldview is based on the pilgrimage model whereby a devotee travels the Eightfold Path to final nirvāṇa. Along the way there are many stages and levels. At any given level certain things will be true that may not be true at a different level. But would you insist that a baby who can only take milk be given meat? Would you chastise a child who is crawling because he or she cannot run? In the same way, Buddhists are sensitive to the particular needs each person has at a given stage. The bodhisattva realizes that all duality is ultimately transcended, but descends back onto the wheel of saṃsāra and into the world of apparent duality in order to assist sentient beings.

A story recorded in the *Lotus Sūtra* is the Buddhist version of the parable of the Prodigal Son. The son left the comfort of his home for a distant country but eventually fell into dire poverty and desperation. Meanwhile, his father moved to a different city where he prospered greatly and lived in a fabulous mansion. One day, the son arrived in that city and was standing outside the gates of his father's home. The father instantly recognized the son, but the son had experienced so much hardship that the memory of his earlier life had grown dim, and he failed to recognize his father. In fact, the son was frightened by the father and was about to run away. The father realized that he must help his son to recognize his status in gradual stages even though the son was the heir to all of his father's wealth. The father offered his son a dirty, menial job. After the son performed each job well, the father promoted him to a better job, eventually awarding him a role at his side and treating him as his own son. As the father's death grew near, he announced to all that this man was really his son and heir. The son was overjoyed at the realization and took his place as head of his father's household.[24] The para-

24. Watson, *Lotus Sūtra*, 81–85.

ble demonstrates the importance of working with devotees at each stage in a way that is appropriate to their levels of knowledge. In this way, Buddhism can embrace a whole range of ethical absolutes that serve us provisionally until the time when true awakening occurs. This, in fact, is the central role of the bodhisattva.

Evangelical reply:

Christianity has no disagreement with Buddhism regarding the observation that men, women, and children may be at different stages in their spiritual growth and development. Jesus' parable of the sower (Mark 4:1–20) acknowledges that although the same seed is sown in the hearts and lives of people, they receive it differently, depending on the condition of their hearts. Likewise, the apostle Paul refers to the first-century Christians in Corinth as "mere infants in Christ" to whom he had to give "milk, not solid food" (1 Cor. 3:1–2). What makes the Christian position distinctive is that Christianity rejects the concept of various levels or stages of knowledge that negate earlier levels. In the first century, a group known as the Gnostics taught that they possessed a higher level of knowledge. In a clear reference to gnosticism, Paul wrote to his disciple Timothy and warned him to "turn away from . . . the opposing ideas of what is falsely called knowledge, which some have professed and in so doing have wandered from the faith" (1 Tim. 6:20–21). In contrast to this view of superior knowledge, Paul declared that he came not with "superior wisdom as I proclaimed to you the testimony about God. For I resolved to know nothing while I was with you except Jesus Christ and him crucified" (1 Cor. 2:1–2). The youngest believer reads the same Bible and worships the same Christ as the most mature believer. This point is illustrated by an experience in the life of Karl Barth, the Swiss theologian who is widely regarded as one of the most learned, mature theologians of the twentieth century. At the end of a public lecture, he was fielding questions from the audience when someone asked him what was the greatest and highest truth he had ever learned. He replied by quoting the simple song, "Jesus loves me, this I know, for the Bible tells me so." His many years of study, prayer, and reflection had never negated the first truth he ever learned about the Christian gospel.

Conclusion

This dialogue has highlighted several key differences between Christian and Buddhist ethics. Each of the central points was related to how Buddhist ethics operate apart from any absolute reality and why Christian ethics are so closely linked to an absolute reality. From a Christian point of view, the Mahāyāna denial of self and ethical deeds places the whole framework of Buddhist ethics in jeopardy, because ethics necessitate relationships and an ultimate differentiation between good and evil. The Buddhist ethical system is like an onion that, after peeling back all of the layers, has no substantive core. The result is that ethics function on a temporary, provisional level as concessions to human ignorance and lack of true spiritual knowledge. In the final analysis, true knowledge will trump all ethical actions, however noble they may be, as well as the givers and receivers of compassion, loving-kindness, and giving.

An appreciation of the profound differences between Christian and Buddhist ethics serves to expose a false assumption frequently made by those who engage in interreligious dialogue. In order to demonstrate the continuity and common ground between world religions, it is believed that one should avoid contentious theological topics and focus on ethics as the great common denominator of all world religions. What students of religion must come to see is that when two religions diverge on ultimate questions like the nature and existence of God or the reality of the world and self, it reverberates through the entire structure of the religion. Indeed, one of the reasons the major non-Christian religions have become world religions is they have a certain rigorous consistency in their worldviews that millions have found compelling. There are no gaps where those who want to seriously dialogue can step into a convenient neutral zone where differences magically disappear. This dialogue has demonstrated how Christianity and Buddhism are fundamentally different, even when analyzing ethics.

PART 3

Christianity and Islam

6

Doctrine of God

Allah

"Hear, O Israel: The Lord our God, the Lord is one."

Deuteronomy 6:4

Say: "Allah is One, the Eternal God."

sūrah 112:1–3

Allāhu Akbar! Allāhu Akbar! [God is most great! God is most great!] So begins the famous Islamic call to prayer that goes out five times a day to over one billion Muslims around the world. In response to the muezzin's call from minarets that are found on every continent, hundreds of millions of Muslims fall prostrate before Allah. In that great act of solidarity, the central article of the Islamic faith is reaffirmed: "There is no God but Allah." The entire Islamic faith is centered on this truth. Indeed, the very word *Islam* is an Arabic word meaning "to surrender," and the word *Muslim* is derived from the same root, meaning "one who has surrendered to God." The Muslim faith is seen as a response of obedience to the will and unrivaled power and majesty of the one true God, whom Muslims call Allah. Since Islam is the only major world religion to emerge after Christianity[1] and is today the second largest and the fastest growing religion in the world,[2] it is fitting that we conclude with a fo-

1. Sikhism emerged in the seventeenth century but remains at only 1.2 percent of world population and is, therefore, not considered a major world religion.

2. Because of the exponential growth of world population, the best way to measure which religion is growing the fastest is not by comparing numerical growth but growth as a percent of total world population. Using this measurement, according to David Barrett, Islam grew from 12.5 percent of the population at the dawn of the twentieth century to 17

cus on Islam and a dialogue with Muslims. As with the other dialogues, I will begin with an introduction to the doctrine that will be the focus of the dialogue. It is not our purpose here to survey the entire historical development of Islam but to highlight those features in the rise of Islam that are particularly relevant to a cogent discussion concerning the doctrine of God.

Historical Perspectives on the Rise of Islamic Monotheism

Arabia is the cradle and center of Islam. The religion of seventh-century Arabia was a mixture of polytheism and animism. Nomadic groups scattered across the Arabian Peninsula worshipped a wide range of tribal deities and sacred stones associated with the earth, the sky, and abstract concepts like fate and time. Muhammad would later refer to this period as the *Jāhilīyah,* or "time of ignorance." Many images of these gods and goddesses were kept in a central shrine known as the *Kaᶜbah* (meaning "cube") in the principal city of the peninsula, Mecca. According to tradition, the Kaᶜbah contained 360 images of various gods and goddesses. By the time Muhammad was born in Mecca, the principal deities were al-ᵓUzzah (power), al-Lāt (the goddess), and Manah (fate), all female deities who were considered the daughters of a high god known as Allah. Some groups combined these three goddesses into a single goddess figure who served as a partner to Allah. These beliefs were particularly strong among the tribe to which Muhammad and his family belonged, known as the Quraysh, who were the guardians of the Kaᶜbah and its images.

In addition to the indigenous Bedouins, there were also a large number of Jews living in Arabia. While the Jewish presence on the peninsula dates back to 1200 B.C., a much larger influx of Jews occurred in the wake of the second failed uprising against the Romans (A.D. 132–135).[3] There were also Christians on the peninsula, although they were significantly fewer in number and influence than the Jews. The Christian settlements were quite diverse, including Nestorians, Monophysites, and other groups who were influenced by Christologies that lay outside the parameters of orthodoxy as articulated by the Council of Chalcedon in A.D. 451.[4] There were also a number of Christian ascetics who had come to the desert of Arabia for meditation and contemplation. Undoubtedly, Jewish and Christian monotheism, which stood in such contrast to the surrounding religious milieu, made a significant impact on the early formation of Islam.

percent at the close of the century, compared to a decline of Christianity from 34.5 percent to 33 percent. See "Annual Statistical Table," *International Bulletin of Missionary Research* 25, no. 1 (January 2001): 25.

3. Caesar Farah, *Islam,* 6th ed. (Hauppauge, N.Y.: Barron's Educational Services, 2000), 28.

4. Monophysites believed that the divine nature of Christ subsumed the human nature of Christ. The Nestorians accepted the two natures of Christ but denied that they were truly united in one person. This will be discussed in more detail in chapter 7.

By the time of Muhammad's birth in A.D. 570, there had existed for over a century a group of Arabs who had forsaken polytheism and belonged to a monotheistic movement known as the *Ḥanīfs,* meaning the "pure ones." They believed that the Kaᶜbah was originally a shrine to the one true God and that a certain stone within the shrine, known as the Black Stone, was the central stone Abraham used in building an altar to the one God. Furthermore, they believed that someday a prophet would come to restore the Kaᶜbah to its original, monotheistic purity. The emergence of the Ḥanīfs represents a movement independent of Judaism, but may be regarded as a neo-Abrahamic movement since it affirms many elements that could also be affirmed by Jews, such as monotheism, the centrality of Abraham, the importance of a central place of worship, and a messianic hope.

This is the context into which Muhammad was born. Muhammad's early life in Mecca appears interesting, though not extraordinary. Orphaned by age six, he was raised by his paternal uncle, Abū Ṭālib. At age twenty-five, he married a wealthy woman from his tribe named Khadījah who owned a caravan operation that promoted trade between Arabia and Syria. Muhammad worked in the caravan trade for the next fifteen years. In the year 610, on the twenty-seventh day of the Arab month of Ramaḍān, Muhammad's life took a surprising turn that would, in time, dramatically influence the course of human history. According to Muhammad, he was meditating one night in a cave on Mt. Hira outside Mecca when he received a vision of the angel Gabriel who commanded him to "recite in the Name of thy Lord!"[5] This night, later referred to by Muslims as the night of power and excellence, began a series of revelations to Muhammad that continued sporadically over the next twenty-two years and today comprise the sacred scriptures of Islam known as the Qurʾān. The word *Qurʾān* means "recitation," referring to the Muslim belief that Gabriel recited to Muhammad the exact words of Allah and called Muhammad to recite them without error to the people. The central message in these revelations was the absolute, uncompromising oneness of God: "Say: 'Allah is One, the Eternal God. He begot none, nor was he begotten. None is equal to him!'"[6]

Later, as Muhammad was again meditating in the cave with his cloak wrapped around him, he received his call from Gabriel to be a prophet *(nabī),* a messenger *(rasūl),* and a warner *(nadhir)* to the peoples of Arabia: "You that are wrapped up in your vestment, arise and give warning!"[7] After some initial success, Muhammad began to face stiff opposition from the Meccans because his monotheistic message threatened their understanding of tribal and economic identity, which was closely tied to the wide array of tribal deities. Even Muhammad's own tribe, the Quraysh, fiercely opposed him because they were the guardians of the images in the Kaᶜbah. Thus, Mu-

5. Sūrah 96:1.
6. Sūrah 112:1–4.
7. Sūrah 74:1

hammad sought out allies among Jews and Christians who were already monotheistic. He was able to secure a temporary pact with the Jewish community in Yathrib (modern-day Medina), who comprised nearly one half of the entire population of the city. However, by 615 opposition was so great in Mecca that Muhammad had to flee across the Red Sea to Abyssinia (modern-day Ethiopia) and was granted protection by the Christian king, Negus.

In 622, Muhammad received a formal invitation from Yathrib to relocate the entire besieged Islamic community there. Muhammad's departure from Mecca to Yathrib, known as the *Hejira,* marks the beginning of the Islamic calendar and parallels in theological significance the Hebrews' exodus from Egypt. The city of Yathrib was renamed Medina, which means the city of the Prophet, and the Islamic movement began to grow in strength and numbers until the year 630 when the Muslims were able to march victoriously back into Mecca. Muhammad entered the Kaʿbah, destroying all 360 idols except for the Black Stone because, as noted above, tradition held that this stone represented monotheism. The Qurʾān teaches that Abraham and Ishmael originally built the Kaʿbah to house the Black Stone.[8] The Black Stone has remained in the southeast corner of the Kaʿbah until the present time. With the destruction of the idols in the Kaʿbah, the tide of polytheism was turned back, and monotheism was on the rise in Arabia.

Two years after his return to Mecca, Muhammad died. Although he left no clear successor to lead the community, he left behind what Muslims regard as the only miracle in the life of Muhammad—the gift of the Qurʾān.

The Doctrine of God in the Qurʾān

The Qurʾān, which began as an oral recitation, was officially written down and codified in 657, twenty-five years after Muhammad's death. It is composed of 114 chapters, called sūrahs, totaling six thousand verses of rhymed prose written in what is widely regarded as the most beautiful Arabic ever composed.[9] It is comparable in length to the New Testament, although each sūrah may be read as a separate unit because the arrangement of the Qurʾān is essentially by the length of the sūrah, not by any particular thematic or

8. According to the Qurʾān, Abraham and Ishmael sojourned into Arabia, erected the Kaʿbah, and used the Black Stone to build an altar to the one true God. Then Abraham prayed that God would send to Arabia an "apostle of their own who shall declare to them your revelations and instruct them in the Scriptures and in wisdom and purify them of sin." This apostle is believed to be Muhammad. See sūrah 2:124–29.

9. The unique quality of the Arabic in the Qurʾān is cited as a testimony to its inspiration. If someone challenged Muhammad by saying that he invented the Qurʾān himself, he was to refute them by challenging anyone to "invent ten chapters like it" (sūrah 11:13). In another passage, the Qurʾān acknowledges its superior literary quality when it states, "Allah has now revealed the best of scriptures, a book uniform in style proclaiming promises and warnings. . . . We have revealed it in the Arabic tongue, a Qurʾān free from all faults, that they may guard themselves against evil" (sūrah 39:23, 28).

chronological arrangement. For the purposes of the upcoming dialogue, I will limit the following survey to five key themes in the Qurʾān concerning the doctrine of God.

Allah Is One, with No Partners

First, the Qurʾān teaches a doctrine of absolute monotheism. Absolute (sometimes called radical) monotheism is distinct from the Trinitarian monotheism of Christianity in that the Qurʾān permits no eternal distinctions within God. Allah is an absolute unity, with no distinctions or associations. This is known as the doctrine of *tawḥīd.* Allah is one and, to use the language of the Qurʾān, he has "no partners." The doctrine of tawḥīd is believed by Muslims to represent the purest form of monotheism.

This strict, uncompromising emphasis on the simplest expression of God's unity becomes understandable in light of the particular challenges Muhammad faced in seventh-century Arabia. The citizens of Mecca were prepared to worship Allah, as long as other subordinate gods or goddesses could be included alongside him. The pressure was so great that on one occasion, while Muhammad was meditating in the Kaʿbah, he acknowledged the existence of the three female deities (al-Lāt, al-ʿUzzah, and Manah) and conceded that "their intercession is hoped for."[10] Later, Gabriel rebuked Muhammad and commanded him to renounce the utterance as a satanic verse and expunge it from the Qurʾān. Muhammad did so, replacing the verses with new ones and declaring that "Allah abrogates the interjections of Satan and confirms his own revelations."[11] This remarkable event in Muhammad's life gained worldwide attention with the publication of *The Satanic Verses* by Salman Rushdie.[12]

Thus, the Qurʾān, responding to both internal pressures of Arab polytheism as well as Christian Trinitarianism, firmly shuts the door on any conception of monotheism that might compromise God's absolute unity:

> Say, "People of the Book, let us come to an agreement: that we will worship none but Allah, that we will associate none with him, and that none of us shall set up mortals as gods besides him."[13]

10. The pressure on Muhammad from the citizens of Mecca is acknowledged in sūrah 17:72–77. The so-called "Satanic Verses" came after 53:19–20 and were proclaimed in public at the Kaʿbah in Mecca as follows: "Have you considered al-Lāt, al-ʿUzzah and Manat, the third, the other? These are the intermediaries exalted, whose intercession is hoped for. Such as they do not forget."

11. Sūrah 22:52–54. The so-called "Satanic Verses" were replaced by sūrah 53:19–23: "Have you thought on al-Lāt and al-ʿUzzah, and thirdly, on Manat? Is he to have daughters and you sons? This is indeed an unfair distinction! They are but names which you and your fathers have invented: Allah has vested no authority in them." Muhammad defended the change in sūrah 16:101–2.

12. Salman Rushdie, *The Satanic Verses* (London: Viking, 1988).

13. Sūrah 3:64. The expression "People of the Book" is a frequent way in which Muhammad refers to Jews and Christians.

To associate partners with Allah is to commit *shirk* (idolatry or setting other gods alongside Allah as partners) and is regarded by Muslims as the unpardonable sin *(kabirah)*. This prohibition clearly includes Christian Trinitarian monotheism, because to identify Jesus Christ as God or as the Son of God is, in the Islamic view, to commit shirk. The Qurʾān declares, in an obvious reference to Christian teaching regarding Christ, "Never has Allah begotten a son, nor is there any other god besides him. . . . He that invokes another god besides Allah—a god of whose divinity he has no proof—his Lord will bring him to account."[14] Jesus is revered as a great prophet, but it is considered blasphemous to ascribe deity to him because, in the Muslim view, this violates Allah's oneness (tawḥīd). Muhammad openly rebukes the Christian position when he declares,

> People of the Book, do not transgress the bounds of your religion. Speak nothing but the truth about Allah. The Messiah, Jesus the son of Mary, was no more than Allah's apostle and his Word which he conveyed to Mary: a spirit from him. So believe in Allah and his apostles and do not say: "Three." Forbear, and it shall be better for you. Allah is but one God. Allah forbid that he should have a son![15]

The Qurʾān clearly sees the Christian doctrine of the Trinity as no different than the Arab belief in the three daughters of Allah. Both, according to the Qurʾān, represent a compromise to Allah's oneness.

Faith in Allah and His Prophet

Second, faith in Allah's oneness (tawḥīd) is linked to an acceptance of Muhammad as the final prophet. The Qurʾān affirms a wide range of prophets, including Noah, Job, Abraham, Joshua, Joseph, Moses, Elijah, and Jesus. However, Muhammad is the final prophet and is considered the "seal" *(khatimah)* of all the prophets. While it is considered blasphemous to worship Muhammad, it is proper to honor and revere him as the one who restored Arabs to monotheistic faith, received the revelation of the Qurʾān, and provided the greatest example of how to live as a Muslim. In fact, the example *(sunna)* of the Prophet has been codified into several collections known as the *Ḥadīth*, which serves as a second source of authority for Muslims.[16] Thus, the full confession of faith that ushers someone into the Islamic faith is the *shahādah:* "There is no God but Allah and Muhammad is the Messenger of Allah." To affirm faith in God is to affirm faith in Muhammad's prophethood.

14. Sūrah 23:91, 117.

15. Sūrah 4:171. See also sūrah 2:116; 9:30; 10:68; 17:111; 18:15; 19:35; 19:88–90; 21:26; 23:91; 25:2; 39:4; 43:81; 51:51; 72:2–3; and 112:1–4.

16. It is beyond the scope of this dialogue to pursue the fact that Muhammad, while not being worshipped, is undoubtedly more than a source of revelation but an actual object of faith and belief in many respects. See Abrahim H. Khan, "Muhammad as Object and Subject," *Studies in Religion* 7, no. 4 (fall 1978): 373–85.

One cannot accept the one without the other and still remain a true Muslim. The Qurʾān declares not only that "Muhammad is Allah's Apostle,"[17] but that "he that obeys the Apostle, obeys Allah himself."[18] Faith in Allah and faith in the Prophet are directly linked as the Qurʾān repeatedly makes clear: "The true believers are those that have faith in Allah and his Apostle and never doubt."[19] The great Islamic theologian from Iran, al-Ghazālī (1058–1111), once wrote that the entire Christian religion could be accepted by Muslims if Christians would only forsake their belief that God is "three" and that "Muhammad is not a prophet of God."[20]

Islam As a Restoration of Ancient, Pure Monotheism

Third, the absolute monotheism of the Qurʾān is not understood as a new or novel revelation to Muhammad. Rather, Muhammad was convinced that his role was merely to confirm what had been originally taught in the Jewish and Christian Scriptures, but which had become distorted, especially in the Christian doctrine of the Trinity. Muhammad sought to restore the doctrine of monotheism to its original purity. The Qurʾān was being given by Allah to confirm what had already been revealed to the Jews and Christians but was now being revealed to the Arabs: "This Qurʾān could not have been composed by any but Allah. It *confirms what was revealed before it,* and fully explains the Scriptures."[21]

The common source of all true revelation has important implications for the Islamic doctrine of God. According to Muslims, no distinction can be made between the true God of Islam and the true God of Christianity and Judaism. We all are worshipping the same God.[22] When Abraham built an altar near Bethel and "called on the name of the LORD" (Gen. 12:8), when Jesus knelt in the Garden of Gethsemane and cried out to God (Matt. 26:39), and when Muhammad prostrated himself and cried out, "Allāhu Akbar," according to Muslims, they were all crying out to the same God. There is only one God. The failure of Jews and Christians to accept Allah as the one true God is only because they have misunderstood the teaching of their own Scriptures or they are relying on corrupted texts that have been altered, just as Muhammad himself almost succumbed to permitting impure verses to become in-

17. Sūrah 48:29.

18. Sūrah 4:80. See also sūrah 8:1 ("Obey Allah and his Apostle if you are true believers") and sūrah 48:9.

19. Sūrah 49:15.

20. *Al Qistas* (Cairo, 1909), 60, as quoted in Samuel Zwemer, "The Allah of Islam and the God Revealed in Jesus Christ," *The Muslim World* 36 (October 1946): 310.

21. Sūrah 10:37, emphasis added.

22. The question of whether Christians and Muslims worship the same God is a more complex issue than may be apparent at first and cannot be addressed adequately in the context of this particular conversation. However, this issue will be revisited in the first case study located in chapter 8. See also Timothy George, *Is the Father of Jesus the God of Muhammad?* (Grand Rapids: Zondervan, 2002).

terjected into the Qurʾān. However, if the original purity of the revelation could be seen, we would recognize that the message is the same. Gabriel told Muhammad that he should emphasize the original unity of the world's three great monotheistic religions because all trace their roots back to Abraham: "Be courteous when you argue with the People of the Book. . . . Say, 'We believe in that which is revealed to us and which was revealed to you. Our God and your God is one. To him we surrender ourselves.'"[23] In the view of Muslims, Jesus and Muhammad were merely following the faith of Abraham. This is why Muhammad told his compatriots, "Allah has declared the truth: Follow the faith of Abraham. He was an upright man, no idolater."[24]

The Attributes and Essence of Allah

Fourth, the Qurʾān extols the attributes of Allah by celebrating his many names. In one widely quoted passage, the Qurʾān declares,

> He is Allah, beside whom there is no other god. He is the Sovereign Lord, the Holy One, the Giver of Peace, the Keeper of Faith; the Guardian, the Mighty One, the All-powerful, the Most High! Exalted be he above their idols! He is Allah, the Creator, the Originator, the Modeler. His are the most gracious names.[25]

Although the tradition encouraging Muslims to recite the ninety-nine beautiful names of Allah goes back to Muhammad, the practice did not become widespread until the writings of al-Ghazālī.[26] Today Muslims around the world can be observed using a rosary-like prayer aid with thirty-three beads on it known as a *subḥa.* A person uses it to keep track as each name is recited. Three times around the subḥa, and you will have recited all ninety-nine of the beautiful names. Thus, the public declaration of the many attributes and qualities of Allah is commonplace throughout the Islamic world.

However, behind the popular expressions of Islam, the emphasis in the Qurʾān on the pure unity or simplicity of the divine essence (tawḥīd) has created a theological challenge for serious students of Islam trying to reconcile the doctrine of tawḥīd with Allah's many attributes. Describing and extolling the many attributes of Allah has made Islamic theologians influenced by the

23. Sūrah 29:46.
24. Sūrah 3:95.
25. Sūrah 5:23–24. See also sūrah 17:110.
26. Sūrah 7:180 declares that "the most beautiful names belong to Allah: So call on him by them." According to the Ḥadīth, as passed down by Abu Huraira, Muhammad said, "Allah has ninety-nine names, i.e., one hundred minus one, and whoever knows them will go to Paradise" (Sahih Al-Bukhārī 3.894). For a full list and discussion of the ninety-nine names, see Samuel Zwemer, *The Moslem Doctrine of God* (New York: American Tract Society, 1905), 33–46. For an English translation of the Ḥadīth, see Muhammad Muhsin Khan, trans., *The Translation of the Meanings of Sahih Al-Bukhārī,* vol. 1–9 (Dar Ahya: Us-Sunnah, Al Nabawiya, n.d.).

early Muʿtazila school of theology uncomfortable for three main reasons. First, it implies divisions or distinctions within the essence of God, which would violate the divine simplicity. Second, attributes are difficult to conceive apart from perceptions of corporeality. To think of a judge, for example, conjures up the physical image of a judge sitting in a courtroom. This kind of corporeality is, in their view, contrary to the proper understanding of the divine essence. Finally, it implies a knowability and self-revelation of God, which may convey the mistaken notion that we can perceive the inner life of Allah.[27]

These theologians insist that tawḥīd means you cannot distinguish between God's essence and his attributes. Therefore, all descriptions of Allah's attributes are merely the result of our own inability to find an adequate way to express the full singularity of Allah's oneness. In their view, when Muhammad said, "Do not speculate on the Creator," he was forbidding speculation concerning both God's essence *(dhāt)* as well as his attributes *(ṣifāt)*. Instead, Muslims should "meditate on the blessings and mighty power of God."[28] This school of theology continues to influence the branch of Islam known as Shiʿite, which comprises approximately 14 percent of the religion and is the majority in Iran and Iraq.

Other theologians, influenced by the Asharite school of theology, affirm that the attributes of Allah are not to be identified with his essence. Furthermore, they believe that the attributes of Allah can be understood apart from the ways they are embodied in men and women. These theologians point out that the Qurʾān is filled with declarations of Allah's attributes. Indeed, virtually every sūrah of the Qurʾān begins with the phrase, "Allah the compassionate, the merciful." If the words in the Qurʾān are not part of Allah's self-revelation, then the Qurʾān must also be a part of Allah's eternal essence, which means that there would be two eternal realities—Allah and the Qurʾān—rather than one, and this would abrogate the doctrine of tawḥīd. This school of theology tends to dominate the perspective of the main body of Islamic practice, known as Sunni, which comprises approximately 86 percent of worldwide Muslims. Thus, any discussion concerning the doctrine of God in Islam must be clear how the attributes accorded Allah in the Qurʾān relate to the knowability of Allah and the rigorous application of tawḥīd.

Allah's Personableness and Knowability

This discussion concerning the attributes of Allah leads naturally to the fifth and final theme to be explored, the knowability and personableness of Allah. Islamicist Kenneth Cragg has pointed out the vast difference between the confession, "There is no God but Allah," and the confession, "There is no God but You."[29] The former is a declaration to an unbelieving, polytheistic

27. Fadlou Shehadi, *Ghazali's Unique Unknowable God* (Leiden: E. J. Brill, 1964), 47–49.

28. J. M. S. Baljon, *Religion and Thought of Shah Wālī Allah Dihlawi, 1703–1762* (Leiden: E. J. Brill, 1986), 36.

29. Kenneth Cragg, *The Mind of the Qurʾān* (London: George Allen and Unwin, 1973), 130.

world of the reality of God. The latter is a confession of the believer in the very presence of Allah. Both phrases are found in the Qurʾān. In sūrah 37:35 we encounter the first:

> Thus We [Allah] shall deal with the evil-doers, for when it was said to them: "There is no God but Allah," they replied with scorn: "Are we to renounce our gods for the sake of a mad poet?"[30]

The second expression is found in sūrah 21:87 on the lips of the Israelite Jonah when he realized it was impossible to flee from God: "He cried out, 'There is no God but You. Glory be to You! I have done wrong.'" On the one hand, there is no question that the tone of the Qurʾān as a whole falls decisively on the side of a warning to an unbelieving world that has placed other gods alongside the one true God and does not emphasize the relationship of the believer to Allah. This is why Islam has been accused of advocating a harsh monotheism with excessive austerity and no possibility of a vibrant, intimate I-thou relationship between God and man. On the other hand, the Qurʾān declares that God is nearer to us "than the vein of our neck."[31] The Qurʾān speaks of Allah's presence with Muhammad and his followers in the victorious battle at Badr in A.D. 624, revealing a striking sense of Allah's immanence:

> It was not you, but Allah, who slew them. It was not you who smote them: Allah smote them so that he might richly reward the faithful.[32]

Within the two main branches of Islam, Sunni and Shiʿite, there arose a mystical movement known as Ṣūfism, which advocates the possibility of an intimate relationship leading to final union with Allah. The Ṣūfi claim that there are two paths to Allah: the external path of law *(sharīʿa)* and the internal path of mystical purification *(taṣawwuf)*. The Ṣūfis often read esoteric meanings into the Qurʾān, particularly the metaphorically rich Light Verse in sūrah 24:35 and the frequent refrain, "To him we shall return." The movement is organized into a wide variety of sects, advocating a wide range of paths *(ṭarīqas)* to Allah. Ṣūfism is actually an umbrella term for a spectrum of smaller movements within Islam, ranging from groups who are fully orthodox but emphasize the importance of the believer's heart condition, all the way to heterodox groups who advocate monism and use the word *Allah* as a mantra similar to the Hindu use of om. One well-known Ṣūfi saint, al-Hallaj, advocated the ability to enter mystical union with God to the point that the distinction between Creator and creation disappeared. It is in this context that he once declared, "I

30. The Qurʾān routinely has Allah speaking in the majestic plural "We," but this is a convention of respect in the Arabic and is not in any way a compromise of tawḥīd.

31. Sūrah 50:15.

32. Sūrah 8:17.

am the Truth," resulting in his execution by orthodox Muslims.[33] However, much of the Ṣūfī literature is devotional in its orientation and focuses on the ecstatic relationship of love and intimacy between Allah and the believer, as seen in this well-known prayer from the female Ṣūfī saint, Rabia:

> O God! If I worship Thee in fear of Hell, burn me in Hell; and if I worship Thee in hope of paradise, exclude me from paradise; but if I worship Thee for Thine own sake, withhold not Thine everlasting Beauty.[34]

Conclusion

We have examined the rise of Islamic monotheism among seventh-century Arabs and have surveyed five major themes about the doctrine of God in the Qurʾān. These themes have stimulated a wide variety of theological and religious responses while still affirming the absolute authority of the Qurʾān, the prophethood and example (sunna) of Muhammad, and a firm commitment to tawḥīd. It is now our privilege to invite several Muslims to the table of dialogue to discuss the doctrine of God in Islam and Christianity. In order to have a broad, inclusive representation of Islam, I have invited Muslims from three distinct traditions: a representative from mainstream Sunni Islam, a representative of Shiʿa Islam as practiced in Iran, and a devout member of a Ṣūfī order. Since all three share a commitment to the basic core of Islam, there will be times when all three may be in perfect accord on an issue, whereas in other instances there may be a variety of perspectives given within Islam. This is not unlike our dialogue with Hinduism, which included followers of both Śaṅkara and Rāmānuja, and our dialogue with Buddhism, which included those who affirmed the ultimate reality of mind versus those who could affirm nothing beyond the mystery of emptiness.

Religious Roundtable

In the year 615, seven years before the Hejira, several dozen families of Muhammad's embattled followers fled across the Red Sea to Abyssinia and

33. David Waines, *An Introduction to Islam* (Cambridge: Cambridge University Press, 1995), 143. For a full treament of the life and theology of al-Hallaj, see Louis Massignon, *The Passion of al-Hallaj*, vol. 1–4, trans. Herbert Mason (Princeton: Princeton University Press, 1982).

34. As quoted in Jacob Dharmaraj and Glory Dharmaraj, *Christianity and Islam: A Missiological Encounter* (Delhi: ISPCK, 1998), 77. Some Ṣūfīs describe the movement as a path (ṭarīqa) leading off the main highway (sharīʿa).

were granted refuge under the protection of the Christian king, Negus. This is the earliest example of an open dialogue between Islam and Christianity.[35] During that time, Muhammad's uncle, Abū Ṭālib, gave an exposition of Islam based on a passage in the Qurʾān known as "Mary" (after the mother of Jesus) and explained to the king why they were being persecuted. After hearing him, Negus reportedly picked up a stick, drew a line in the sand and said, "As God is my witness, the difference between your position and ours is not as wide as this line."[36] Contrarily, in *Christianity and World Religions,* Catholic scholar Hans Küng acknowledges that most Muslims and Christians who have entered into serious conversation have found the doctrines of the Trinity and the incarnation to be what he calls the "dead end" on the road of dialogue. Chapters 6 and 7 are dedicated to these two great themes. The upcoming dialogue will reveal whether King Negus or Hans Küng more accurately described the relationship between Islam and Christianity.

Areas of Agreement

Even a cursory reading of Islam reveals that there are vast areas of agreement between the Islamic view of Allah and the Christian view of God. Both Islam and Christianity affirm the absolute reality of God as the center of everything that is. Islam does not debate the existence of God; it is taken for granted as an undeniable reality. Allah is the creator, the Lord of history and the one to whom everyone must give an account on judgment day. Both Islam and Christianity affirm that God sends prophets, that he calls us to worship him, and that he is the central reality of our existence.

The similarities between Yahweh of the Old Testament and Allah of the Qurʾān are striking. Hundreds of examples could be explored, but for our purposes a few will suffice. Allah creates the earth in six days (sūrah 25:59), culminating in the creation of the first man, Adam. He and his wife eat the forbidden fruit and become aware of their nakedness (20:115–22). Allah sends Moses to confront Pharaoh, inflict the plagues on Egypt, and lead the Israelites out of Egypt by parting the Red Sea (26:9–75). Allah gives Moses the Ten Commandments on two tablets of stone which, as in the biblical account, are subsequently broken (7:143–50). Throughout the Qurʾān, many of the Ten Commandments are repeated, including the command to "serve no other gods" (24:55), the prohibition against making idols (4:116), the commands to not covet (4:32) or murder (6:151), and the command to honor your father and mother (6:151). In the Qurʾān, one can read about familiar

35. Muhammad is also reputed to have received a delegation of sixty Christians from Narajan, which included a long theological discussion. The Christians did not convert to Islam but acknowledged that Muhammad was a prophet. However, the chronology of this meeting and the delegation to Negus of Abyssinia is unclear. See Geoffrey Parrinder, *Jesus in the Qurʾān* (London: Faber and Faber, 1965; reprint, Oxford: One World, 1995), 163.

36. Suwar min Hayat Muhammad, *Images from the Life of Muhammad* (Dar al-Ma'arif, Egypt: Amin Duwaidar, n.d.), 185.

Old Testament stories such as Noah building the ark (11:25–49), King David's adultery with Bathsheba (28:21–25), the Queen of Sheba's visit to Solomon (27:22–44), and Jonah being swallowed by the great fish (37:139–48). These, along with many others, give the Qurʾān a sense of familiarity to the Christian or Jewish reader, though at times the Qurʾānic version has surprising departures from the biblical account.[37] Nevertheless, Allah is clearly identified with Yahweh of the Old Testament, and one cannot read the Qurʾān without being impressed by the all-encompassing reality of Allah so central to Islamic life and thought and the deliberate attempt to identify Allah with the monotheistic God of Christianity and Judaism.

In addition to specific references to God, Islam shares common theological categories with Christianity, including concepts such as sin, righteousness, divine judgment, heaven, hell, forgiveness, and mercy. All these categories have tremendous influence on how Muslims understand the nature of God and how he acts in the world. Over the centuries, Islamic theological discussions have mirrored many of the great discussions within Christianity, including the relationship of faith and good works, the role of human freewill versus divine sovereignty and predestination, and the trustworthiness of God's revelatory disclosures. These categories, most of which reveal our common embrace of the Abrahamic heritage, will certainly shift our dialogue away from the general theistic discussion with which we engaged Hinduism and Buddhism and closer to the inner life of Christian thought, because that is where the real differences between Christianity and Islam begin to emerge. Therefore, this discussion will focus primarily on the boundary between the Islamic doctrine of tawḥīd and the Christian doctrine of the Trinity. Because of the particular complexities of the doctrine of the Trinity coupled with the number of participants in this dialogue, I will offer only one central objection to the doctrine of tawḥīd.

Objection: The Muslim doctrine of monotheism (tawḥīd) protects God's otherness at the high cost of sacrificing the relational aspect of God's nature as expressed in the Trinity. In this respect, the two doctrines are utterly incompatible.

It is no secret that Muslims from the days of Muhammad to the present have emphatically rejected the concept of a Triune God. However, it is important to explore the basis for this rejection and the implications it has for the Muslim concept of monotheism.

Islam's rejection of the Trinity is based on a wide range of reasons that fall into two general categories. First, some objections are based on a fun-

37. The most important departure is Abraham's sacrifice of Ishmael rather than Isaac. However, there are many others, including Potiphar accusing his wife of seducing Joseph (12:21–30) and Satan's fall resulting from his refusal to prostrate himself before Adam at the dawn of creation (20:115–22). Chapter 7 will point out many glaring omissions in the Qurʾān. Nevertheless, the parallels are significant.

damental misunderstanding of what the Christian doctrine actually teaches. In other words, the Muslim is not rejecting the doctrine itself but a caricature of the doctrine. Among serious students of Islam and Christianity, this is the simplest kind of disagreement to resolve. Nevertheless, one should never underestimate the power these kinds of misunderstandings have in shaping popular attitudes toward Islam or Christianity. Some of these misunderstandings are blatant and can be quickly recognized when a Christian and a Muslim begin to dialogue. Other misunderstandings are rooted in semantic confusion that sometimes arises when English nomenclature is translated into Arabic. For example, English words like *person* and *nature* that are often used in discussing the Trinity are based on precise Greek and Latin formulations meant to clarify the doctrine. However, these very words can carry unintended nuances when translated into Arabic, resulting in a misunderstanding of what Christians actually teach regarding the Trinity.

The second category consists of more difficult objections that are not linked to any confusion or misunderstanding but are objections to the genuine Christian doctrine, which Muslims believe violates pure monotheism. During the course of this dialogue, we will inevitably encounter objections from both categories. It is, therefore, imperative that everyone state their positions with absolute clarity.

In the early days of the Islamic-Christian encounter, Muhammad rejected a mere caricature of the Trinity, not the genuine doctrine. Later Islamic scholars developed arguments against the actual Christian doctrine. In the Qur'ān, Muhammad clearly confuses the doctrine of the Trinity with the shocking notion that the Trinity implies some form of divine cohabitation with a deified Mary from which Christ was born:

> Then Allah will say: "Jesus, son of Mary, did you ever say to mankind: 'Worship me and my mother as gods beside Allah?'"[38]

Indeed, it is in that same sūrah that Muhammad says, "Unbelievers are those who say: 'Allah is one of three.'" He then goes on to say that the "Messiah, son of Mary, was no more than an apostle . . . and his mother was a saintly woman. They both ate earthly food."[39]

The clear implication in these texts is that Muhammad understands the doctrine of the Trinity to include Mary as one of its members. Muhammad condemns the Trinity, at least in part, because it is wrong to elevate Mary to the status of a god and to advocate that Christians worship her. Muhammad's confusion is largely due to the fact that most Christians living in Arabia during his lifetime were Nestorians or Monophysites who themselves had deficient views of the Trinity. Furthermore, this is precisely the kind of

38. Sūrah 5:116.
39. Sūrah 5:73, 75.

idea being espoused by the Meccans who worshipped the three female deities in the Kaᶜbah as daughters of Allah. If by the term *Trinity* Muhammad means divine cohabitation with a deified Mary, then I find myself in happy agreement with his forceful rejection of this blasphemy. However, this is not the historic Christian doctrine of the Trinity.

The word *Trinity* is shorthand for "tri-unity" or "three-in-one" and refers to the mystery of God the Father, God the Son, and God the Holy Spirit who are one and indivisible in essence *(homoiusios)* and yet are known through three eternal distinctions *(hypostases)*. When Christians use the word *God*, they are not referring to the Father only, but to the Father, Son, and Holy Spirit. These three are eternal distinctions, not temporary modes or spheres of action or operation, but inner relations within the one Godhead.

The doctrine of the Trinity is fully monotheistic because it affirms only one God and emphatically rejects the belief that there are three Gods. Thus, the doctrine is not understood as a third position in contrast to monotheism and polytheism. The earliest Christian community was made up of Jews who were rigorously monotheistic and regularly recited as the central creed of their faith, the *shema:* "Hear, O Israel, the LORD our God, the LORD is One" (Deut. 6:4). The doctrine of the Trinity does not violate this ancient Jewish creed because Christians have historically affirmed that God is one in essence *(ousia)*, even though he has three personal distinctions known as hypostases. The precise articulation of this balance between God's essence and his hypostases (persons) did not fully emerge until the Council of Constantinople in 381, but was accepted by the church as accurately reflecting the apostolic witness as revealed in the biblical record. Trinitarianism reveals that, even apart from creation, God's very nature is relational. To abandon the doctrine of the Trinity risks a form of monotheism that can easily drift toward cold austerity and a legalistic relationship with the living God, because God is not regarded as being relational.

Sunni reply:

As a Muslim scholar interested in Islamic-Christian dialogue, I have carefully studied Christian writings about the Trinity and am aware that the vast majority of Muslims could not explain the doctrine in a way you would find acceptable. However, only rarely do I meet Christians who understand the doctrine either. The doctrine strikes Muslims and many Christians as contradictory and confusing, and unless you are armed with a basketful of technical vocabulary, you can easily find yourself articulating some version of modalism or blatant tritheism.[40] How can anybody negotiate through the Christian conglomeration of hypostases, persons, processions, and rela-

40. Modalism affirms the unity of God but reconciles it with the Trinity by declaring that Jesus and the Holy Spirit are only modes of the Father. These are three names for God, not three eternal distinctions. The Father, Son, and Holy Spirit are successive revelations of the one person.

tions? Muhammad, may peace be upon him,[41] was given specific revelations by Allah to respond to the actual position of Christians he encountered in Arabia at the time. The Islamic view of monotheism, in contrast, is simple enough for the youngest child to understand. We believe in one God, not three gods. Not a God who is somehow one and three at the same time. Not a God who became man or, as some Christians have affirmed in history, a man who became God.[42] We do not understand how God can proceed from God. We simply believe in one God.

However, putting aside the way the doctrine has been misunderstood by Muslims and Christians alike, I would like to demonstrate why we find the doctrine to be in error, even when your best theologians articulate it. In your opening statement, you pointed out how Muhammad (PBUH) equated the Meccan's belief that Allah had daughters with the Christian belief that God had a son. You agreed wholeheartedly that Muhammad (PBUH) was right in condemning the Meccan blasphemy against God. However, in your own statement of the Trinity, you refer to God by such designations as *Father* and *Son.* This is the error of the early Meccans. There are two major reasons why such terms are wholly inappropriate ways to refer to God. First, the word *father* undeniably conveys the idea of physical generation or procreation linked with a concept of corporeality, and this is an unacceptable way to speak about Allah. The Qurʾān teaches that "He begot none, nor was he begotten."[43] Second, the terms *father* and *son* involve the idea of temporal sequence. Fathers exist and then, in the fullness of time, they beget a son. This notion of temporal sequence, which is inherently bound up with terms like *father* and *son,* should be abandoned because the Qurʾān teaches that Allah is the eternal God.[44]

Evangelical reply:

I completely agree that the idea of procreation and temporal sequence cannot be properly applied to God. However, the doctrine of the

41. When Muslims refer to Muhammad, it is considered proper to add the blessing, "Peace be upon him" after his name ("ṣalla ʾllāh àlayi wa sallam"). For the remainder of this dialogue, whenever Muhammad's name is mentioned by a Muslim, out of respect for their tradition, the four letters PBUH will appear representing the full blessing. Islamic writings use the four-letter Arabic abbreviation (SAWS).

42. This is an allusion to Arius. Arianism gained considerable ground among some early Christians but was eventually defeated in lieu of the orthodox position.

43. Sūrah 112:3. In an officially sanctioned English version of the Qurʾān with accompanying commentary, a modern-day Islamic scholar makes the following comment: "Begetting a son is a physical act depending on the needs of men's animal nature. Allah Most High is independent of all needs, and it is derogatory to attribute such an act to him. It is merely a relic of pagan and anthropomorphic materialist superstitions." From Mushaf Al-Madinah and an-Nabawiyah, trans., *The Holy Qur-an: English Translation and the Meanings and Commentary* (Saudia Arabia: King Fahd Complex for the Printing of the Holy Qurʾān, n.d.), 862 n. 2487.

44. Sūrah 112:2.

Trinity denotes neither of these. Let me explain. First, it is essential to understand that fatherhood and procreation are two separate ideas. An adopted child may refer to his or her parents as 'father' and 'mother' even though there is absolutely no genetic, procreative link between them. It is an expression of a relationship. This is because procreation and fatherhood are separate.

In Christianity, the terms *father* and *son* refer to a spiritual, not a physical, relationship. The ideal father is related to his son through love, tenderness, and communion, and it is these relational qualities that the words convey. Unfortunately, in Arabic the connotations associated with the word for son *(ibn)* are hardly distinguishable from the connotations for the word for child *(walad)*. However, in many other languages the semantic range of the terms *father* and *son* are much broader. In Judaism, for example, it is normal to address someone as father as an expression of respect or as son to reflect a relationship of affection, even though they are completely unrelated in a physical or genetic sense. These terms refer to a spiritual and moral relationship and do not imply either physical corporeality or physical procreation. Christians affirm that God is incorporeal, infinite, and omnipresent, all of which would be contradicted if we also affirmed a doctrine of corporeality. The New Testament declares that "God is spirit" (John 4:24). I will not address in this current dialogue how the Son of God, at a certain point in human history, took on physical corporeality in an act we call the incarnation, since our next dialogue is dedicated to addressing this particular question.

As for temporality, it is impossible for a father to temporally precede his son. The two terms are completely reciprocal. A man does not become a father until the precise moment when the son is born. Indeed, one cannot occur without the other precisely because the terms are inherently relational. In reference to God, however, it refers to an eternal relationship without any temporal beginning, which is why Jesus prayed in the Garden of Gethsemane, "Father, glorify me in your presence with the glory I had with you before the world began" (John 17:5). Thus, the terms signify an eternal, coequal relationship, "that all may honor the Son just as they honor the Father" (John 5:23).

Of course, as my Muslim friend pointed out, there are those who have misunderstood this. The alternative is to abandon relational terms altogether, resulting in a metaphysically unified God who is closer to Pascal's distant "God of the Philosophers" than to the God and Father of our Lord Jesus Christ with whom we may enter into a personal relationship. God is no abstract unmoved mover. On the contrary, he has revealed himself as a conscious, feeling, willing self who may be called by name. It is this personal relationship with God that the prophet Isaiah celebrates when he declares, "O LORD, our God, other lords besides you have ruled over us, but your name alone do we honor" (Isa. 26:13).

Shiʿite reply:

I agree with the points made by my Sunni friend in objecting to the designations *father* and *son,* but there are additional reasons why I find the terms objectionable. First, all such designations—whether names like Father and Son or the so-called ninety-nine beautiful names of Allah—are mistakenly used to ascribe attributes to Allah that directly contradict the doctrine of tawḥīd. The doctrine of tawḥīd allows no compromise in the absolute unity of Allah. Therefore, it is impossible to distinguish between Allah's essence (dhāt) and his attributes (ṣifāt). All such terms, whether found on the lips of Muslims or Christians, serve to divide the essence of God into smaller, identifiable bits rather than to worship the indivisible singularity of Allah's oneness. Thus, it would be better to abandon all such descriptions of God.

Second, terms like *father* and *son* strike at the unity of God, because they introduce an idea of plurality. Either God is plural or God is one; he cannot be both without contradiction. To affirm that God is one is to affirm tawḥīd. To say that God is plural or three is to commit shirk; there is no middle ground.

Evangelical reply:

Both of your objections stem from the same root. You interpret the doctrine of tawḥīd as either absolute, indivisible unity that cannot permit either descriptive attributes to break down God's oneness into individual parts or as the personal distinctions inherent in the Christian doctrine of the Trinity. However, all unity contains plurality. The idea of undifferentiated unity is only a theoretical construct of the mind or a mathematical abstraction. Ultimately, it is no different from nonbeing.[45] In nature we discover that the lower the degree of differentiation something has, the less unity it has, meaning it is divisible or lacks the quality of indivisibility. For example, a stone has little internal differentiation. If you split a stone into two pieces, you have not destroyed the essence of the stone; you have only created two smaller stones. However, as you go up the chain of being and take, for example, a tiger and cut it into two pieces, you do not get two smaller tigers. In the act of dividing the tiger, you destroy the very essence of the tiger. A tiger, although a complex and internally differentiated creature, has an indivisible essence because it cannot be separated into parts without destroying that essence. Some creatures lower on the chain (like a praying mantis) can be severed into two parts and still live and move independently for some time. Because their differentiation is low, their unity is low. The more conscious and intelligent a being is, the greater the differentiation and the more pro-

45. This is based on the reasoning of Plotinus, who argued that God's oneness could not even allow for self-knowledge, because that would imply a distinction between the knower and the known. God, Plotinus concluded, must be beyond knowing or consciousness or even being itself. Thus, God must be nonbeing. See also W. H. T. Gairdner, *God as Triune, Creator, Incarnate, Atoner* (Madras: CLS, 1916), 9.

found the unity. A person possesses a mind, thoughts, and speech. He or she functions as a unity despite internal distinctions. The same point could be made about the body, soul, and spirit of a person. The fact that God himself has internal differentiation does not contradict his indivisibility. In fact, we observe this harmony of plurality and unity in all higher life. When Muslims discuss tawḥīd, they often seem to confuse internal differentiation with external divisibility. This is a grave error.[46] In short, unity does not necessitate singularity.

Ṣūfi reply:

Al-hamdu li'Llah! [Praise be to Allah!] My Christian and Muslim friends seem to be preoccupied with some mental concept of a being called God or Allah. The doctrine of tawḥīd is not about this kind of abstract oneness nor is it about any intellectual exercise regarding the internal differentiations within the being of God. Tawḥīd refers to the experience or tasting *(dhawq)* of God's being by becoming one with Allah in a way that supersedes all discussion or debate about him. Jesus Christ said, "I and the Father are one" (John 10:30). From the Ṣūfi perspective, Jesus was not speaking about the Trinity but was giving his disciples a remarkable glimpse into the advanced state of his spiritual journey. Jesus had realized a mystical oneness with Allah. To reduce the Christian or Islamic doctrine of God to a set of formulas—whether the Nicene Creed of Christianity or the tawḥīd doctrine of Islam—is to miss the joyful realization that God must be encountered not in the mind but in the heart.

In the Qur᾿ān, Muhammad (PBUH) rebuked those who had not experienced Islam in their hearts: "Arabs in the desert say, 'we are true believers' . . . say, 'you are not,' rather say, 'we profess Islam,' because faith has not yet found its way into your hearts'"[47] Islam can only find its way into your heart by practicing *dhikr* (remembrance of Allah), meditating on Allah, and invoking his name. For Allah said to Muhammad (PBUH), "I am with my servant when he thinks of me."[48]

To debate whether God has made himself present in one mode or three modes misses the more profound truth that God has made himself present in an infinite number of modes. The Qur᾿ān declares,

> Allah is the light of the heavens and the earth. His light may be compared to a niche that enshrines a lamp, the lamp within a crystal of star-like brilliance. It is lit from a blessed olive tree neither eastern nor western. Its very

46. When referring to the Trinity in Arabic, the intensive adjective *talut* should be used ("Allah talut") to indicate internal distinctions rather than *tatlit,* which tends to communicate the division of something into three parts. See Robert Caspar, *Trying to Answer Questions* (Rome: PISAI, 1989), 17.

47. Sūrah 49:14.

48. This is found in the Ḥadīth (ḥadīth *qudsi*), not the Qur᾿ān. See Waines, *Introduction to Islam,* 140.

oil would almost shine forth, though no fire touched it. Light upon light; Allah guides to his light whom he will.[49]

Even though the light of the sun is one, its radiant brilliance is refracted and reflected into innumerable rays of light. Likewise, Allah is one, but the ninety-nine beautiful names are symbolic of the dozens of ways his all-comprehensive name can be experienced. In fact, all the books in the world could not contain the many names of Allah. To my Christian friend I say, Jesus is one of the names of Allah. To my Muslim friends I say that even the Qurʾān does not exhaust the brilliance of Allah's light. As the Qurʾān declares, "Even if all the trees in the earth were pens, and the sea, with seven seas to replenish it, were ink, the writing of Allah's words could never be finished."[50]

God is not just known in Jesus; he is also known in the whole of creation. His power is revealed in the volcanoes. His sweetness is in the morning chirp of a sparrow. His judgment is in the thunderstorm. You will never truly experience tawḥīd until you experience Allah's oneness in the whole creation. Once tawḥīd is experienced, you will see that its truth transcends the confining man-made boundaries of all religions, including Islam and Christianity. For example, during the Middle Ages there arose a Ṣūfi-like movement among the Jews, known as Kabbalah. The central text of the movement was the Zohar, a commentary on the Pentateuch by Moses de Leon (1250–1305).[51] In that text, he declares that the Torah is but the outer garment of an inner mystery. That testimony is true for the Qurʾān as well as the Bible. Ṣūfism focuses on the inner mystery of this spiritual journey. It cannot be captured in the pages of the Qurʾān or on a pilgrimage to Mecca. It is a journey of the heart. When you experience tawḥīd, you will cry out, "I am the Kaʿbah," because in the temple of your heart the real Black Stone resides. Pure monotheism, tawḥīd, will have finally found its way into your heart.

Evangelical reply:

You are right in pointing out that God cannot be reduced to a mere abstraction but must be encountered personally. Indeed, this is underscored by the emphasis I have placed on the relational aspect of the Trinity. The Ṣufi movement arose, as many of your own writings testify, as a bold countermovement to the nonrelational austerity of Allah in mainstream Islam. Indeed, it was the great Egyptian Ṣūfi saint Dhu-'l-Nun al-Misri who introduced into Islam the distinction between *ʿilm* and *maʾrifa,* that is, outward knowledge about God and inner knowledge based on a direct experience of God.[52] However, it is vital that an experience of God be properly grounded in

49. Sūrah 24:35.

50. Sūrah 31:27.

51. Robert K. C. Forman, ed., *Religions of the World,* 3d ed. (New York: St. Martin's, 1993), 323.

52. P. J. Stewart, *Unfolding Islam* (Reading, England: Garnet, 1994), 178.

God's self-revelation as contained in Scripture. If we reduce Christianity to bare propositions, church councils, or creedal formulations, then we can slip into a dry legalism that is not true to the dynamic, Spirit-filled reality of the kingdom of God (Rom. 14:17). However, if we do not allow our experience of God to be informed by the steady hand of revelation as received in Scripture, we can easily slip into distortions and abuses that would hinder us from faithfully defending the historic Christian faith (Jude 3–4).

The history of Ṣūfism is replete with examples of Ṣūfī saints who advocated novel, experience-based doctrines that were not consistent with the historic Islamic message. There were those who advocated the annihilation *(fanāʾ)* of self in order to receive the full indwelling of Allah. When fanāʾ is experienced, the Ṣūfī loses all awareness of self and enters into a mystical union with Allah. Others advocated a mystical incarnation *(ḥulūl)* whereby a person leaves his or her own attributes and becomes incarnate into the attributes of Allah and shares in his deity. This notion of incarnating oneself into the attributes of Allah led Mansur al-Hallaj to make his famous declaration, "I am the Truth." Even within Ṣūfism, figures such as Abu Nasr al-Sarrah (d. 988) produced manuals to warn Ṣūfīs of the potential dangers inherent in the movement.[53]

Thus, the idea that Scripture is but a stepping-stone to a more profound experience with God puts an unwarranted tension between the experience of God and the propositional content of the Christian message. Take Abraham, for example, who is revered in both of our traditions. The Bible refers to Abraham as the "friend of God" (wālī Allah) which, interestingly, is also one of the most popular expressions by which Ṣūfīs refer to themselves. Certainly, Abraham is called the friend of God because of his personal experience with God, but that experience cannot be separated from the content of the revelation that God gave to Abraham. Christians, Jews, and Muslims are not merely the recipients of Abraham's experience; we are all, in our own way, seeking to be faithful to the content of the monotheistic revelation given to Abraham.

Sunni rejoinder:

I certainly agree that there are potential dangers in Ṣūfism if the movement engages in novel interpretations of the Qurʾān and drifts too far from historic Islam, but many members of the Ṣūfī order have inspired us by their devotion to Allah and their selfless assistance to those in need. However, in this rejoinder I want to go back to the Christian response to my reply and clarify a few points.

First, you argued about the distinction between internal differentiation and external divisibility but supported it through analogies based on nature and the created order (a stone, a tiger, a human). We consider it misleading, even blasphemous, to make such comparisons, since Allah is wholly other

---

53. Waines, *Introduction to Islam,* 143–44.

than the creation. Therefore, such comparisons are unreliable because Allah is in a different class than anything in the created order.

Second, you claimed that Christian Trinitarianism is not a "third option" between monotheism and polytheism. If that is true, I must conclude that Christianity is, indeed, tritheistic because the doctrine, as outlined in this dialogue, is vulnerable to serious logical fallacies. On the one hand, you claim that the distinctions or hypostases of the Trinity are eternally distinct. This means that the Father must be distinguished by certain qualities that differentiate him from the Son, the Son must be distinguishable from the Spirit, and so forth. If such distinctions *cannot* be made, then the three would merely be different names for the same reality, which is modalism, long condemned as a heresy of Christian orthodoxy. If these distinctions *can* be made—such as identifying the Father with election, the Son with incarnation, the Spirit with indwelling—then it means there are qualities in one person of the Trinity that cannot be applied to other members of the Trinity. Yet all three are called God, which by definition means the fullness of being, lacking nothing. It is a logical fallacy, for example, to say that God did and did not become incarnate. If the Father is God and he has not, nor ever will, become incarnate, and the Son is God and he did become incarnate, then how can God simultaneously be the one who became incarnate and the one who has never become incarnate? It is a contradiction that can only be reconciled if Christians give up trying to reconcile Trinitarianism with monotheism and acknowledge that Christianity is tritheistic.

Evangelical reply:

When using any analogies from nature and applying them to God, it should be noted that his reality is undoubtedly higher than our highest conception, just as the builder of a house is worthy of greater honor than the house itself (Heb. 3:3). As the creator of the natural order, God transcends all things. However, this does not mean that all analogous reasoning falls to the ground. Precisely because God is the author of creation, everything in creation reflects his glory (Ps. 19:1; Isa. 6:3). Indeed, since we live in the created order, it is only natural that analogies from creation be used to communicate truths that transcend nature. Even the Qurʾān is filled with analogies from creation in reference to Allah. After Allah created the world, he is said to "ascend" his throne (sūrah 32:4), even though we all know that to ascend implies relocation from one place to one another, which would contradict God's omnipresence. In a beautiful passage declaring Allah's omnipresence, the Qurʾān declares that "wherever you turn, there is Allah's Face," even though his incorporeality assures us that Allah has no face.[54] The Qurʾān refers to Allah speaking, hearing, and even breathing,[55] though we know Allah's incorporeality means that he has neither vocal chords nor ears nor lungs.

54. Sūrah 2:115.

55. For hearing, see sūrah 49:1. For speaking and breathing, see sūrah 38:71–72.

Your objection, if carried to its logical conclusion, would end in our inability to say anything meaningful about God at all, because the same objection could be made to central teachings of the Qurʾān, such as Allah's knowledge or compassion. Are we really prepared to say that there are no similarities whatsoever between Allah's knowing and our knowing or our compassion and his compassion? If our compassion has no relationship, however feeble, to his compassion, then the word becomes meaningless when used of Allah. Although God's reality transcends us, God has chosen to reveal himself in terms we can comprehend; therefore, it is no disgrace to make analogies based on the created order. The alternative is to surrender all knowledge of God or to give up speaking about him in a meaningful way. We would be left with an Ultimate Being like the Hindu's nirguṇa Brāhman or "belief in the great whatever," not the Allah of the Qurʾān or the God of the Bible.

Your second objection, which insists it is a logical fallacy for Christians to maintain both monotheism and Trinitarianism, fails to appreciate the distinction between God's essence and God's actions. God is a spiritual, incorporeal being whose essence is fully present in the action of all three members without violating the particular work of each. As explored earlier, the human body shares a unified essence, although it has differentiation, including specific tasks that each member performs as part of the whole. Both the eye and the ear are fully part of the body, yet the eye sees and the ear does not, the ear hears and the eye does not. Since both share fully in my essence, it could be said at any given time that I see and I don't see. But this is not a contradiction, because we distinguish between the essence of the body that is present in the whole and the actions or functions of the particular members. The sun is one in essence, but it shines forth as heat and light. Heat and light are distinct, but both share in the one essence of the sun.

A further illustration can be drawn from Islam itself. The Sunni tradition claims that the Qurʾān is eternal and uncreated. Gabriel's recitation to Muhammad was merely reciting the "transcript of the Eternal Book" (sūrah 43:1). Yet no Muslim claims that the Qurʾān *is* Allah or that the uncreated eternality of the Qurʾān compromises tawḥīd. They are both considered eternal, albeit distinct. Thus, it cannot be a logical fallacy to suggest God's essence is fully present in each person of the Trinity. This is why the doctrine of the three hypostases is linked to the doctrine of God's indivisibility. God's indivisibility means that every member of the Trinity is wholly present in essence in every other member. The Council of Florence declared that the indivisible unity of God meant that "the Father is wholly in the Son, wholly in the Holy Spirit; the Son wholly in the Father, wholly in the Holy Spirit; the Holy Spirit wholly in the Father and wholly in the Son."[56]

56. As quoted in Don Mark Pontifex, *Belief in the Trinity* (New York: Longmans, Green, 1954), 26.

Shiᶜite rejoinder:

The doctrine of tawḥīd, when properly understood, will not make a distinction between Allah's essence (dhāt) and Allah's attributes (ṣifāt). From the Shiᶜite point of view, there are two main reasons why we avoid speaking of Allah's attributes. First, to do so creates divisions within Allah's essence, which is a clear violation of tawḥīd. Second, it seems to imply that God reveals himself to us in a personal way, a claim made repeatedly by my Christian friend during this dialogue. To think of God only in personal terms encourages making analogies between Allah and humans, which leads to corporeal images of God. Allah does not reveal himself to anyone; he only reveals his will. Our task is to obey him, not to know him. Even to speak of God as knowing himself is a violation of tawḥīd since it implies an internal differentiation between the God who knows and the God who is known. This is why we reject the Sunni notion of an uncreated Qurʾān mentioned earlier. The idea of an eternal Qurʾān, in our view, compromises the indivisibility of Allah's oneness.

Christianity is a striking example, as well as a warning, to all Muslims of what can happen when an emphasis on the attributes of Allah go awry. Early Christians, influenced by Greek culture, focused on God's attributes of reason *(logos)* and power *(dunamis)*. Eventually, they hypostatized these attributes and made them into persons sharing in the same essence as God. This is a clear violation of tawḥīd and is, in fact, to commit shirk.

Evangelical reply:

Several important issues have been raised. First, what is the relationship between God's essence and his attributes? Second, how can Christians claim that the infinite, eternal God is knowable? Third, is the Trinity merely the hypostasizing of three attributes that were particularly prominent in the minds of the earliest Christians?

I agree with the vast majority of Sunni Muslims that it is entirely permissible to speak about the many wonderful attributes of God, but I would insist that the attributes of God are only revealed or exercised in a way consistent with his nature. This is why the Shiᶜites are also right in their view that the attributes of God cannot be separated from his nature. Nevertheless, they must come to see that this does not mean we cannot speak meaningfully about God. These two viewpoints are reconciled in Christian theology because we believe that his attributes reveal his nature. Our knowledge and experience of God's attributes give us reliable knowledge of God. But it is important to remember that genuine knowledge of God should not be taken to mean we can know God in the fullness of his essence.

In this regard, Christians make an important distinction between the knowledge of God and the comprehension of God. On the one hand, the Bible speaks of God "who alone is immortal and who lives in unapproachable light, whom no one has seen or can see" (1 Tim. 6:16). On the other hand, the apostle John declares that even though "no one has ever seen God," it is "God the One and Only, who is at the Father's side, who has made him known" (John 1:18). The former verse teaches that we can never have a full comprehension of God in his essence. The latter verse assures us that in Jesus Christ we have been given a true and reliable (though incomplete) knowledge of God. Jesus Christ is the ultimate expression of the personal nature of God. To assert that God is absolute Will and therefore cannot be known personally is an expression of nominalism[57] and leaves us with an unknowable God about whom we can say nothing with confidence. In contrast, we believe that the essence and attributes of God can only be separated academically. In an actual relationship with the living God, all his attributes are self-revealing of his inner nature.

The early church did not hypostatize certain divine names or attributes *(al-asma wālī ṣifāt)* into persons of the Trinity. The deity of Jesus Christ and the Holy Spirit is revealed in Scripture itself. Let me demonstrate by citing one of the examples you gave. You charge that the early church hypostatized the attribute *Logos* and by the fourth and fifth centuries made that attribute into the second person of the Trinity. In fact, in John's Gospel he refers to Jesus as the Word *(Logos)*, a title that is also given to Jesus in the Qurʾān (sūrah 3:45). John says that "in the beginning was the Word, and the Word was with God, and the Word was God" (John 1:1). Jesus himself claimed to preexist Abraham, identifying with the name of the sacred revelation of God to Moses, "I Am" (Exod. 3:14). Jesus said, "Before Abraham was born, I am" (John 8:58). From Jesus' own lips, we hear that he not only applies to himself the titles of deity, but he regularly exercises privileges unique to God, such as creating the world, forgiving sins, and presiding over final judgment. There is no question that Jesus taught these truths about himself. They were not imposed on him by later Christians. Even Jesus' contemporary opponents understood all too well the extent of his claims. They sought to stone him because he was making himself out to be God (John 10:33). Thus, the deity of Christ is based on Christ's own revelation about himself and the testimony of the apostles who were eyewitnesses of his life and ministry, not subsequent Christians who hypostatized certain attributes into a person of the Trinity.

Ṣūfī rejoinder:

Al-hamdu li'Llah! [Praise be to Allah!] You have given considerable attention to the distinction between Allah's essence and Allah's acts. In our view, his acts are the extension of the eternal light of his being. Union with that light is the goal of every Ṣūfī. We are guided by a spiritual guide known as a *shaykh* (Arabic) or *pīr* (Persian). Through many years of meditation, we learn

57. Nominalists hold that God's will to act is what defines what is right (as opposed to, for example, the intrinsic good in kindness or the inherent evil in cruelty) and that the manifestation of his attributes is to be carefully distinguished from his nature, which remains unknown. Thus, we can have no assurance that our encounters with God's attributes enable us to know him, even partially, in his essence.

to abandon trust in everything except for Allah. A Ṣūfi will pass through many stages until he or she achieves the inner knowledge of God that transcends the mind and scholarly debates. We become lost in his light, and eventually we hear his cry, "To us you shall return." We then enter into a state of complete union with Allah. I would like to know whether Christians believe in a state of final union with God.

Evangelical reply:

Union with God in Christianity is linked to our views regarding salvation, which are outside the scope of these conversations. Nevertheless, I will say in passing that we also affirm the goal of the believer's union with God but regard it as a spiritual union facilitated by Christ. It is a union that does not involve annihilation of self or an altered state of consciousness nor will we ever independently possess any incommunicable attributes of God. Nevertheless, we participate in and become partakers of the divine life. This final state is not a technique that can be learned nor is it a state that can be achieved by human effort any more than a turtle could learn to fly. The apostle Paul gives us a glimpse of this final union when he says that "now we see but a poor reflection as in a mirror; then we shall see face to face. Now I know in part; then I shall know fully, even as I am fully known" (1 Cor. 13:12). It is a union and a beatific vision made possible only through our relationship with Jesus Christ.

Conclusion

This dialogue has helped us gain a clearer picture of the boundary lines separating the Islamic doctrine of tawḥīd and the Christian doctrine of the Trinity. Important questions have been raised such as whether or not God personally reveals himself, whether fatherhood is synonymous with procreation, and whether internal differentiation violates the firm commitment to God's indivisibility that we all share. These are fundamental questions that should not be glossed over if genuine dialogue is to occur.

In my introduction to the conversation, I referred to two very different assessments of the Islamic and Christian views concerning God. King Negus said that the difference between the two religions was not as wide as a line he had drawn with a stick, whereas some modern writers have referred to the Trinity in particular as the dead end on the road to dialogue. I say that both assessments need considerable qualification. King Negus is right in pointing out the considerable continuity between the two religions, especially when compared to Hinduism, Buddhism, or the idolatry of seventh-century Arabia (with which King Negus would have certainly been familiar). Yet, although the number of differences between Christianity and Islam may not seem *wider* than the line drawn by King Negus, the theological significance stemming from those few issues is *deeper* than the Red Sea that separated Arabia from Abyssinia. To those who regard dialogue with Muslims about the Trinity as a dead end, I would acknowledge, on the one hand, that this assessment gravely recognizes what a fundamental dividing line our differences on this doctrine produce. On the other hand, an ongoing dialogue is never a dead end. It is, like the famous road to Emmaus, a place where our paradigms can be challenged and where we can continue to grow and learn. Even Muhammad once said, "If the Lord of Mercy had a son, I would be the first to worship him" (sūrah 43:81).

7

Doctrine of Christ and the Incarnation

ʿĪsā, Ḥulūl

"In the beginning was the Word, and the Word was with God, and the Word was God. . . . The Word became flesh and made his dwelling among us."

John 1:1, 14

"Allah is but one God.

Allah forbid that he should have a Son!"

sūrah 4:171

John 3:16 is probably the most recognizable reference to a passage in any sacred text in the world. Martin Luther called John 3:16 "the gospel in miniature" because he believed that one verse summed up the essence of the entire Christian message. In our own day, Rollen Stewart has devoted his life to displaying the simple reference "JOHN 3:16" at every major sporting event in the country. Stewart claims that millions of television viewers from around the world have seen this reference. The famous text begins by declaring the mystery of the incarnation: "For God so loved the world that he gave his one and only Son." This one phrase symbolizes the theological point of departure whereby Christianity emerges from the swaddling clothes of Judaism with its own distinctive message. The doctrine of the Trinity is presupposed in the verse, and the incarnation and our response to it is at the heart of the verse.

Contrast the opening phrase of John 3:16 with a verse from the Qur᾿ān that is familiar to Muslims all over the world—"God forbid that he should have a Son!" (sūrah 4:171). Our first Muslim dialogue focused specifically on how Islamic monotheism as expressed in tawḥīd contrasts with Christian monotheism as expressed in the Trinity. Christology, including a focus on the incarnation, is an extension of this discussion. Indeed, it is the profound mystery of the incarnation that, for the Christian, exemplifies the oneness of essence and plurality of persons that is such a distinctive feature of Christian theology. However, Islam and Christianity have long disagreed about the person of Jesus Christ, and, apart from the particular claims of Christ, Muslims have questioned whether the very idea of incarnation is not itself a violation of the doctrine of God. It is one thing to discuss the possibility of internal distinctions within the Godhead. It is entirely another to assert that one of the hypostases of the Trinity took on the limitations of humanity and suffered. For the Christian, this is the greatest example of God's love for us. For the Muslim, this doctrine is so shocking that one well-known commentator on the Qur᾿ān has called the incarnation "merely a relic of pagan and anthropomorphic materialist superstitions."[1] This dialogue will seek to explore the basis for these divergent assessments of the incarnation of God in Jesus Christ. We will begin with a brief survey of the nature of the Christian doctrine followed by a more extensive survey of what the Qur᾿ān actually teaches about Christ.

The Nature of the Incarnation in Historic Christianity

As explored in chapter 6, the unique stature of Christ is evidenced by his earthly exercise of prerogatives normally associated with deity (judgment, forgiveness, etc.) as well as titles that Jesus used of himself or allowed others to use of him (God, Lord, Word, Son of God). While these references to Christ's deity are present throughout the Gospels, the Gospel of John has a particular focus on the deity of Christ and the miracle of the incarnation. John's Gospel has forty-two references to Jesus as the "sent one." This title is particularly interesting because Muhammad is also referred to in the Qur᾿ān as the *rasūl* or "sent one." In Muhammad's case, it refers to his being the bearer of a message that came from Allah through the mediation of the angel Gabriel. Jesus, in contrast, claims to have preexisted eternally with the Father (John 8:42, 58; 17:8) and yet to have been sent into the world. Jesus did not merely receive a message, but he embodied the message. He claims to have left the Father's presence to come into the world (John 6:62; 8:42; 10:36). He calls himself the "one and only Son" *(monogenes)*, referring not to any sexual

1. Mushaf Al-Madinah and an-Nabawiyah, trans., *The Holy Qur-an: English Translation and the Meanings and Commentary* (Saudi Arabia: King Fahd Complex for the Printing of the Holy Qur᾿ān, n.d.), 862 n. 2487.

act of procreation but to his eternal, unique stature in relationship with the Father.

However, the doctrine of the incarnation involves much more than establishing the deity of Christ. It also calls us to affirm the full humanity of Christ. John's Gospel focuses on the real humanity of Jesus Christ. The Word who was eternally with the Father (John 1:1) became flesh and lived among us (John 1:14). John pictures Jesus as expressing the full range of human experiences, including thirst (4:6; 19:28), fatigue (4:6), anger (11:33, 38), joy (15:11), tears (11:35), and love (13:34; 15:9–13). The humanity of Jesus is also evidenced as he worships in the synagogue, participates in the Feast of Tabernacles, and prays regularly as an observant Jew (7:14; 17:1–26). The earliest Christians were in awe at the way the divine and the human coincided in the person of Jesus Christ. On the one hand, the Book of Hebrews affirms that Jesus Christ is "the radiance of God's glory and the exact representation of his being" (Heb. 1:3). The text commands that all the angels worship him (Heb. 1:6). Yet this same Jesus, in the mystery of the incarnation, suffered (Heb. 5:8), was tempted (Heb. 2:18), and cried out to God with human tears.

These twin truths of Scripture are reconciled through the incarnation, which declares that the second person of the Trinity, the Son, took on human flesh and walked among us as Jesus Christ. The historic Christian position is that the incarnation does not violate the full integrity of either the human or the divine nature, but that these natures *(phusis)* became fully united in one person *(hypostasis)*, Jesus Christ. The Son fully shares in the nature or essence *(homoousion)* of the Father, and that nature was expressed in a concrete way *(enhypostatic)* in the full humanity of Jesus Christ, who was born as a Jew in first-century Palestine. The two natures are fully and indivisibly united in the one person without any confusion or dilution of the two natures *(communicatio idiomatum)*. In short, the properties of the two natures are in no way suppressed or destroyed by their union but find full expression in the single hypostasis. The historic formulations describing the nature of the incarnation that emerged in the third and fourth centuries were not viewed as establishing a new doctrine, but articulating a position that was true to the full spectrum of biblical teaching regarding the person of Jesus Christ.

The Qurʾānic View of Christ and the Incarnation

In the Qurʾān, no such picture of Jesus Christ emerges, although the specific details of Christ's birth and life may surprise many first-time Christian readers of the Qurʾān. On the one hand, the Qurʾān affirms that Jesus was born without sin to the Virgin Mary (sūrah 19:15–22). His ministry is foretold by John the Baptist, and he is a worker of many miracles (3:49–50; 43:63). He is given several honorific titles, including the Word of God (3:39; 4:171), a Spirit from God (4:171), a sign (19:21; 21:91), a messenger (2:87), and the Messiah (3:45). Several of these titles could be interpreted as consistent with Christian claims about Christ. On the other hand, several sūrahs seem to denounce any view of Christ that would elevate him beyond the level of a prophet. In several places, the Qurʾān specifically rejects any assertion that Jesus should be considered a member of the eternal Godhead, though the reason for this rejection seems to be based on a false understanding of the doctrine. Therefore, it is essential that this dialogue begin with a clear and careful development of what the Qurʾān actually teaches about Christ with an eye to how the Qurʾānic rejection of Christ's deity may be shaped by misunderstandings of the actual Christian position.

Muhammad recorded the Qurʾān over a period of twenty-two years. Because the received text is not arranged in chronological order, it is not always easy to determine when a particular sūrah was written, although it is clear that the Qurʾān (by its own testimony) contains a progressive development of certain ideas.[2] The most basic division is between those sūrahs revealed in Mecca and those revealed in Medina, although Muslim scholars agree that many sūrahs traditionally identified with a particular period often contain verses collated from another period. Many of these sūrahs can be dated because of historical allusions to important battles, treaties, marriages, or other events. Furthermore, as noted in chapter 6, the Qurʾān contains several examples of abrogation where an earlier sūrah is cancelled out by a later one.[3] These provide valuable clues as to the relative dating of various sūrahs. Finally, many of the 114 sūrahs contain a superscription stating explicitly when they were revealed.[4] This chronological perspective reflecting different locations and stages in the Islamic movement is particularly significant when seeking to understand what the Qurʾān teaches about Christ. There is an evolution in Muhammad's interaction with and response to Christian claims about Christ that is apparent as the Qurʾān unfolds.

Early Passages in the Qurʾān concerning Christ

The sūrahs that emerged early in Muhammad's career often feature stories shaped around a central theme. The theme is about various messengers or prophets who were sent by God but were met with rejection. They were later vindicated by God, who intervened to punish those who doubted.[5] Thus, figures like Noah and Abraham become important models for Muhammad's own prophetic ministry, which during this early Meccan period was widely rejected. Interestingly, Mary the mother of Jesus is also an exam-

2. See sūrah 87:6; 2:106; 18:24; 13:39; 16:101; and 17:41, 86. The official English translation and notes of the Qurʾān authorized by King Fahd of Saudi Arabia state that changes and abrogation in the Qurʾān are not a problem "if we believe in progressive revelation." See Al-Madinah and an-Nabawiyah, *The Holy Qur-an,* 44 n. 107.

3. Sūrah 2:106 and 13:39 clearly establish the principle of abrogation in the Qurʾān itself. The most well-known example is the changing of the *qiblah* (direction of prayer) from Jerusalem to Mecca (sūrah 2:142).

4. H. S. Stanton, *The Teaching of the Qurʾān* (London: SPCK, 1969), 15.

5. See, for example, sūrahs 7, 11, and 26.

ple Muhammad uses to reinforce this theme. Like Muhammad, Mary was given a divine message by Gabriel. People did not believe that she, a virgin, was carrying a holy child. Even Joseph did not believe Mary at first. In the Qur'ān, the infant Jesus speaks from the cradle and vindicates his mother in the presence of those who were accusing her of sexual immorality. The infant Jesus tells the disbelievers, "I am the servant of Allah. He has given me the Gospel and ordained me a prophet. . . . I was blessed on the day I was born, and blessed I shall be on the day of my death; and may peace be upon me on the day when I shall be raised to life."[6] Thus, the earliest mention of Jesus in the Qur'ān is in connection with the vindication of Mary. Muhammad clearly draws a parallel between himself and Mary. Both were common people who unexpectedly received visions, both believed that the angel Gabriel had spoken to them, and both believed that God had called them to be his chosen servants.

This same sūrah which refers to Jesus as a "sign to mankind" and a "blessing" from Allah[7] goes on to warn against anyone who blasphemes Allah by stating that Jesus was begotten by Allah:

> Those who say: "The Lord of Mercy has begotten a son," preach a monstrous falsehood, at which the very heavens might crack, the earth break asunder, and the mountains crumble to dust. That they should ascribe a son to the Merciful, when it does not become him to beget one![8]

The warning seems to indicate a clear misunderstanding of the Christian position, either because of confusion among the Christians with whom Muhammad interacted or because of Muhammad's own assumption that Christianity had been unduly influenced by pagan ideas of sexual procreation among the gods which were so dominant in the beliefs of the indigenous people.

In these early passages, the words attributed to Jesus could easily be put into the mouth of Muhammad as a vindication of his own mission. During the early days of Muhammad's mission, there is little doubt that he uses the prophetic ministry of Jesus as a common reference point in attacking Meccan polytheism and paganism. At this stage, Muhammad may have been optimistic that Christians and Jews would eventually rally behind him and

6. Sūrah 19:30, 33. The phrase "raised to life" is a reference to the general resurrection at the end of time.

7. Sūrah 19:21.

8. Sūrah 19:88–91. The fact that the Muslims interpret this as a statement of sexuality is clear in the following commentary on this passage: "The belief in Allah begetting a son is not a question merely of words or of speculative thought. It is a stupendous blasphemy against Allah. It lowers Allah to the level of an animal. If combined with the doctrine of vicarious atonement, it amounts to a negation of Allah's justice and man's personal responsibility. It is destructive of all moral and spiritual order, and is condemned in the strongest possible terms." See Al-Madinah and an-Nabawiyah, *The Holy Qur-an,* 875 n. 2529.

support his monotheistic initiative on the Arabian Peninsula. God gave Moses the Torah, Christians the Gospel, and now he is giving Arabs the Qurʾān. The peoples of Arabia are going to join the ranks of the People of the Book *(ahl al-kitāb)*.

Later Passages in the Qurʾān concerning Christ

Muhammad's relocation from Mecca to Medina in 622 (Hejira) transformed him from a position of being constantly embroiled in opposition and controversy to becoming the leader of a newly emerging religious and political community, which in the decades following his death would conquer an astonishing portion of the globe. Unlike Mecca, there were many more settled Jewish and Christian communities in Medina. The Jewish community composed nearly one-half of the entire population. For the first time, Muhammad enjoyed sustained contact and interaction with Jews and Christians.

The longer Muhammad was in Medina, the more his hostility toward the Jews grew, leading to several early battles in 627 and 629 involving the slaughter of hundreds of Jews. The Jews, particularly after the Battle of Badr (624), began to resist Muhammad's claim to prophethood and, because of their numbers in Medina, posed a political threat to Muhammad. In this context, Muhammad speaks favorably of Jesus as an example of another prophet who, like him, had been shown hostility and was rejected by the Jews. Jesus is portrayed as a true messenger of God who, like Muhammad, came to confirm the Torah and call for "helpers" *(anṣār)*, a term Muhammad also uses for those who became his followers in Medina. At this juncture, Muhammad quotes Jesus as announcing that a future prophet or messenger will come after him "whose name is Ahmed" (sūrah 61:6). Many Islamic scholars believe the name Ahmed (meaning "praised one") is actually a title for Muhammad. It certainly demonstrates that Muhammad saw himself in continuity with, not in opposition to, Jesus Christ.

During this Medinan period, the Qurʾān discusses many crucial issues surrounding the life of Jesus, particularly his death on the cross. The proper understanding of these verses will be discussed in more detail in the upcoming dialogue. However, it is clear that in the early period, Jewish opposition actually occasions several positive references to Christ.

Toward the end of the Medinan period, as well as in the closing years of the Prophet's life, the Qurʾān finally begins to address Christian views regarding the status of Jesus. It claims that Christian views regarding Christ are based on either a misunderstanding of the actual teachings of their Scriptures or a deliberate attempt to distort and exceed the bounds *(ghuluw)* of the received revelations in the gospel *(injīl)*. Essentially, the Qurʾānic perspective is that Jesus is a true messenger of God, but his followers have drifted into idolatrous worship without any scriptural warrant. The Qurʾān affirms a long list of honorific titles for Jesus as the servant of Allah. But it also points out several references to Jesus' real humanity (5:75), which is why, in the Qurʾānic view, Christians should not call him the Son of God, for that would make Jesus out to be "another god besides Allah" (5:116).

Taken as a whole, the Qurʾān seeks to strike a balance between what it regards as two extreme views concerning Jesus. There were some who regarded Jesus as a deluded man and a deceiver. Others viewed him as a manifestation of a divine being or as God in the flesh, the result of an act of divine sexual procreation. The Qurʾān avoids both extremes by affirming that Jesus was a great prophet, but no more than that. Muhammad was careful not to label Jesus as a deluded preacher, because this is precisely the designation he himself was trying to avoid. When he told the Quraysh tribe about the one true God, they responded, "Are we to renounce our gods for the sake of a mad poet?"[9] Yet to exalt Jesus to the status of a divine being would, in his view, sacrifice the very monotheistic message he had come to deliver.

The tension between these two views of Christ influences virtually everything that is said in the thirty-five references to Jesus in the Qurʾān. In the birth narrative found in sūrah 19, we have already noted how Muhammad records Jesus speaking prophetically from the cradle (19:30–34). However, the exalted nature of the passage is blunted somewhat by the fact that the passage is immediately followed by a condemnation of those who would say that Allah has begotten a son (19:35). Thus, Muhammad preserves the balance between what he regards as two extremes. The desire to preserve this balance helps to explain how Jesus is granted honorific titles not even accorded to Muhammad, yet Muhammad strongly denounces those who refer to Jesus with a title such as Son of God. For example, in sūrah 3 Jesus is referred to as "the Word of Allah" (3:39) and as a "Word from him" (3:45). The text explicitly parallels Jesus' miraculous appearance in the womb of Mary with the word of Allah that created the world *ex nihilo* (out of nothing). The Qurʾān teaches that Allah spoke Jesus directly into the womb of Mary by divine fiat! It is one of the most remarkable testimonies to the stature of Christ found anywhere in the Qurʾān. On the other hand, in sūrah 9 Muhammad denounces the title Son of God in the strongest possible terms:

> The Jews say Ezra is the son of Allah, while the Christians say the Messiah is the Son of Allah. Such are their assertions, by which they imitate the infidels of old. Allah confound them! How perverse they are! They worship their rabbis and their monks, and the Messiah the son of Mary, as gods besides Allah; though they were ordered to serve one God only. There is no god but him. Exalted be he above those whom they deify beside him![10]

9. Sūrah 37:35–36.

10. Sūrah 9:30–31. There is no known historical evidence that any sect of Judaism ever regarded Ezra as the Son of God.

Thus, the titles given to Jesus in the Qurʾān serve to safeguard both Muhammad as a prophetic messenger and his monotheistic message.

This same tension is found in the Qurʾānic explanation of the passion of Christ. Christ's rejection by the Jews is parallel to the rejection of all the prophets who preceded him. His very rejection is a testimony to his prophetic message. Yet, precisely because he was a true prophet, most Muslims believe that God would never allow him to suffer the cruel agony of crucifixion. This is based on a passage in sūrah 4 that says,

> They denied the truth and uttered a monstrous falsehood against Mary. They declared, "We have put to death the Messiah, Jesus the son of Mary, the apostle of Allah." They did not kill him, nor did they crucify him, but they thought they did.[11]

The passage goes on to declare that Allah "lifted him [Jesus] up to his presence." While this passage deserves closer scrutiny in our upcoming dialogue, it is clear that the strikingly different assessments of Jesus found in the Qurʾān are not due to blatant contradictions in the text but are a careful attempt to avoid theological tendencies Muhammad regarded as dangerous to the doctrine of tawḥīd.

The upcoming dialogue will seek to explore two main areas. First, does the view of Christ in the Qurʾān explicitly contradict any points of orthodox Christian theology? Second, does the biblical doctrine of Christ contradict or compromise the doctrine of monotheism (tawḥīd)? Specifically, is the concept of incarnation, which embraces the full humanity and the full deity of Christ, inconsistent with a vigorous commitment to the doctrine of monotheism?

Religious Roundtable

During our first dialogue with Muslims (chapter 6), I began by noting the remarkable number of parallels between the Qurʾān and the Bible. On the surface, this is undoubtedly true as many stories from the Bible found their way into the Qurʾān. From another perspective, one could also remark how little Muhammad seems to be aware of the Bible. This is not meant to criticize Muhammad. In fact, one of the charges against Muhammad is that the Qurʾān is largely a hodgepodge of borrowed and sometimes altered stories

11. Sūrah 4:157.

from the Bible. However, a closer examination reveals that the Qurʾān is far more original than it may first appear.

We must remember that in the seventh century the Bible had not yet been translated into Arabic. Thus, Muhammad's knowledge of the Bible is based on oral traditions that were relayed on the Arabian Peninsula at the time and that contained huge omissions. For example, Muhammad knows about Moses leading the people out of Egypt, but he gives no indication that he is aware of its significance in the history of Israel. The Qurʾān never even mentions the settlement of the promised land or the division of the kingdom. The Qurʾān is silent about Israel's exile and their return. Yet these are all crucial features in a proper understanding of Old Testament theology.

A similar observation can be made about the New Testament. The Qurʾān states that Jesus was a miracle worker who caused the blind to see, cleansed the lepers, and raised the dead; yet not a single specific account is recorded that would indicate Muhammad was familiar with any eyewitness accounts in the New Testament. In fact, the Qurʾān never even acknowledges that there are four Gospels but always refers to the injīl or Gospel in the singular. Furthermore, Muhammad never indicates any knowledge of the writings of Paul or other New Testament authors outside the Gospels.

Thus, despite numerous biblical allusions in the Qurʾān, a thorough knowledge of the Bible appears to be absent. This is important because unless a Muslim picks up a translation of the Bible in his or her own language, the main source of information about Christ is the Qurʾān, which fails to adequately reflect the Christian position. Therefore, one of the purposes of this roundtable is to promote a genuine understanding of the Christian and Muslim positions regarding Christ. As with the earlier dialogue, I have invited three representatives of the Islamic faith to participate in the dialogue. We welcome back the representatives of Sunni and Shiʿia, and we welcome a new participant from the Qadiri Order of Ṣūfism.

Areas of Mutual Agreement concerning Christ

I begin this dialogue by noting several areas where Christians and Muslims are in agreement about the person of Christ. First, we appreciate the respect shown to Jesus in the Qurʾān. Any Christian who takes the time to read the Qurʾān cannot help but be impressed by the honor accorded to Jesus. We have already alluded to several of the titles applied to Christ in its pages. Before we explore the points of departure, it is important for Christians to be aware that the Qurʾān does not contain a single negative reference to Jesus in any of its 114 sūrahs. Second, we need to be reminded once again that both Christians and Muslims are committed to monotheism. The Qurʾān is to be commended for its unwavering commitment to the oneness of Allah. While Christians do not believe that either the Trinity or the incarnation compromises this oneness, it is important to acknowledge that the doctrinal motivation that fuels Islamic opposition is, in the final analysis, a doctrine with which we are in agreement. Third, the negative references to Christian beliefs concerning Christ that are found in the Qur'ān are largely directed toward christological heresies that orthodox Christians also reject. In the previous dialogue, we pointed out how Islam and Christianity are both fundamentally opposed to tritheism, and therefore Muhammad's opposition to tritheism should not be taken as an opposition to the Trinity. In the same way, Muhammad's denunciation of christological positions we identify with Arianism or Monophysitism should not make us assume that the Qur'ān is rejecting the biblical doctrine of Christ. In other words, we should not read more negativism into the Qur'ān than is actually there.

Nevertheless, vital differences exist between the Islamic and Christian assessments of Jesus Christ. It does no service to Muslims to gloss over the differences and call them anonymous Christians. Nor is Christianity properly served by calling Jesus an anonymous Muslim.[12] This dialogue is dedicated to exploring the real boundary between the two religions as it relates to the doctrine of Christ. This theme is of particular interest since the Qur'ān has so many references to ʿĪsā or the son of Mary, names by which the Qur'ān refers to Jesus.[13] The doctrine of the incarnation is the closest any of these dialogues comes to a discussion of salvation, but in keeping with our agreement to postpone a full discussion of salvation, we will not delve into a discussion of the salvific ramifications of the life or death of Christ. As with the last conversation with Muslims, I will focus on one central objection to stimulate the conversation and allow plenty of time for interaction among all participants.

Objection: Muslims have improperly concluded that the Christian doctrine of the incarnation is a violation of monotheism.

The doctrine of the incarnation asserts without compromise the full humanity and deity of Jesus Christ. This is possible because the divine and human natures remain distinct although they are fully united in the person of Jesus Christ. The Qur'ānic picture of Christ is too monotone. The Christology of the Qur'ān undoubtedly portrays Jesus as a great prophet and messenger of God. However, in the process it mutes the full expression of his humanity and his deity. Jesus as both suffering servant and eternal Lord is simply not in view. The notion of a God who lives with and suffers with his creation seems blasphemous to the Muslim. However, this is precisely what occurs in the incarnation of Jesus Christ. In the Incarnate One, we experi-

12. Karl Rahner has called Muslims, among others, anonymous Christians. As noted in chapter 6, certain Islamic leaders such as Nurcholis Madjid in Indonesia have called Christians anonymous Muslims, and Vivekananda has called the followers of all religions anonymous Hindus. However, all such attempts to impose one's own religious designation upon another group are unwarranted.

13. ʿĪsā is probably a derivation of the Syriac *Yshua.* The expression "son of Mary" is the favorite way the Qur'ān refers to Jesus, numbering twenty-three times. It is an expression found only once in the New Testament.

ence the full expression of God's love for his creation. The depth of his love cannot be expressed adequately from a distance. It is not enough to hear the word of God's compassion and grace. In Christ, "the Word became flesh and made his dwelling among us" (John 1:14). In Jesus Christ, God entered human history, took on our humanity, and reconciled the world to himself. The God who for so many years remained distant or even unknown becomes known in Jesus Christ. Far from violating the doctrine of God, the incarnation is the greatest expression of God's self-revelation.

The Scriptures reveal not just a doctrine of God or a doctrine of God's will, but a revelation of God himself in the person of Jesus Christ. The incarnation bridges the metaphysical, moral, and spiritual gap which, as Islam itself testifies, separates the human race from God. In our view, this gap could only be closed through the union of the two natures in one person. Admittedly, this is a great mystery *(ghayb)* because the incarnation combines two incommensurate natures. God, for example, is infinite in knowledge and power. Humans are finite in knowledge and power. God is limitless and without beginning or end. Humans are finite and bound by time and space. How the two natures were united in Jesus Christ remains a great mystery, but it is clearly taught in Scripture. One of the earliest Christian creeds is found in the pages of the New Testament: "He appeared in a body, was vindicated by the Spirit, was seen by angels, was preached among the nations, was believed on in the world, was taken up in glory" (1 Tim. 3:16). The apostle John, considered Jesus' closest disciple, proclaimed about Christ, saying, "We have seen and testify that the Father has sent his Son to be the Savior of the world" (1 John 4:14). These verses both refer to the humanity and suffering of Christ as well as to his preexistence and eternal glory, and yet they both refer to the same person. This is the mystery that the incarnation seeks to describe.

Sunni reply:

Orthodox Muslims everywhere unequivocally affirm that Allah is immutable. He cannot change. He cannot suffer. He cannot in any way be affected by anything in this world. To state otherwise is to deny the very definition of God. This is the root of my objection to the incarnation. The statement found in your Scriptures which says, "The Word became flesh," surely cannot mean that Allah became something he previously was not, for that is a clear violation of his immutability. Allah cannot be subject to change, because all change must be for the better or for the worse, and that would violate God's perfection. Sūrah 112, which is quoted daily by Muslims during *ṣalāt* (ritual prayer), says that "Allah is One, the Eternal God. He begot none, nor was he begotten. None is equal to him." The idea of Allah being born to a human mother, growing up in Nazareth, being hungry and thirsty is so utterly inconsistent with the nature of Allah that you must be using the word

God in a symbolic way or in some other restricted sense when you apply it to Jesus.

Evangelical reply to Sunni:

The relationship between the immutability of God and the incarnation is an extremely important question. To answer it properly, I will need to explore in some length the way this issue was debated in Christian history and how this struggle may have shaped Muhammad's understanding of Christ.

The mystery of the incarnation is so profound that even early Christians struggled with the best way to describe what took place in the person of Jesus Christ. The many attempts to accurately describe the mystery fell into two broad perspectives on Christology. The first school of thought, originating in the city of Alexandria, produced what is known as Word-flesh Christologies. As with our Muslim friends, they did not want to blur the vast differences between God and the world. Therefore, this view emphasized the deity of Christ, sometimes without giving proper weight to his full humanity. The second school of thought, originating in the city of Antioch, produced what are known as Word-man Christologies. This view emphasized the humanity of Christ, sometimes without giving proper weight to his full deity. An appreciation of these schools of thought is important in understanding the view of Christ in the Qurʾān and the Islamic response to the doctrine of the incarnation. Several representative groups stemming from these schools of thought were present on the Arabian Peninsula during the time of Muhammad. Unfortunately, most of the groups who were there had adopted views that the church had already determined to be improper reflections of the biblical revelation. In short, they were not orthodox Christians; they were heretics. They were not espousing Christianity but a caricature of Christianity.

Two views that were present among Christians in seventh-century Arabia had arisen out of the Word-flesh camp. First, there were Christians who held to a Monophysite Christology, so named from the Greek phrase meaning "one nature." As their name indicates, the Monophysites have traditionally been understood as believing that in the incarnation the divinity of Christ absorbed or obliterated his humanity so that we can only speak of one nature of Christ—the divine nature.[14] In this view, Jesus only appeared to be human. This conclusion was reached through a process of theological reasoning that sounds similar to the language used by my Sunni friend in his response. He pointed out that because God is immutable, the incarnation cannot mean God took on humanity, for that would involve God in change. Thus, the humanity of Christ must be illusory.

14. Recent discussions between Greek Orthodox theologians and the so-called Monophysite or non-Chalcedonian churches have led to substantial doctrinal convergence in Christology. See Paulos Gregorios, William Lazareth, and Nikos Nissiotis, eds., *Does Chalcedon Divide or Unite?* (Geneva: World Council of Churches, 1981), 8.

A different view based on similar theological grounds was known as Arianism, named after Arius, the presbyter from Alexandria who vigorously promoted this view. Arians, like Muslims today, were deeply committed to protecting the oneness and immutability of God. They insisted that God cannot share his essence with anyone else, for that would make him divisible and subject to change. Because this view arose from the Word-flesh camp, there was also a tendency to separate God from creation because "the created order could not bear the weight of the direct action of the increate and eternal God."[15] God created the Son to act as the intermediate agent of creation. Thus, Jesus was believed to be a created being, though his origin reaches back to the dawn of creation.

Other views arising from the Word-man Christologies placed so much emphasis on the humanity of Jesus that they failed to faithfully treat the biblical witness to the deity of Christ. They argued that Jesus was born as an ordinary man but became God during the days of his earthly ministry. He was a man who, at his baptism, was adopted into the Godhead. In this view, sometimes called adoptionism, the incarnation is not about God becoming a man but a man becoming God. Adoptionism endorses an idea that Muhammad denounced and that every good Muslim knows is blasphemous, namely, that man could somehow become God.

Another group from the Word-man camp, the Nestorians, also proposed a solution that was eventually condemned.[16] The Nestorians were concerned about a christological issue that is also taken up by Muhammad in the Qurʾān. Nestorius opposed any reference to Mary as the mother of God and did not believe she should be referred to by the title *Theotokos* (God-bearer). To Nestorius, these references implied that God could somehow be contained in the womb of Mary or that Mary was some kind of goddess who gave birth to a god. Nestorius once asked, "How can God have a mother?" It is the same question Muhammad would ask two hundred years later.[17] Nestorius preferred to give Mary the title *Christotokos* (Christ-bearer) or to always link the title *Theotokos* with the title *anthropotokos* (human-bearer) so as not to confuse the two separate natures of Christ. Later Nestorians were so eager to defend the separateness of the two natures of Christ that they opposed the idea of the two natures united in one person. Many in the Christian church were not convinced that Nestorius and his followers were committed to expounding the full unity of the person of Jesus Christ. The result was that Nestorianism was condemned at the Council of Ephesus in 431.

This brief survey is important because it demonstrates that long before the rise of Islam, the Christian church was hammering out a christological position that affirmed the incarnation without violating the immutability,

15. J. N. D. Kelly, *Early Christian Creeds* (New York: Longmans, Green, 1950), 232.

16. It should be noted that Nestorianism was probably not held by Nestorius himself but by some of his followers.

17. Sūrah 5:116; 9:31. See also sūrah 3:43 and 4:171.

transcendence, or oneness of God. Indeed, it was because so many christological heresies arose in the third and fourth centuries that the church responded with such a carefully worded position as reflected in the Council of Chalcedon in 451. The orthodox position preserves the immutability of God by insisting that the two natures of Christ are in no way changed, merged, or suppressed by their union. The properties of each are safeguarded even when united in a single hypostasis.

In the incarnation, the Second Person of the Trinity (Tri-unity) took on human attributes without the inherent loss of any divine attributes. The beautiful hymn in the second chapter of Philippians describes this remarkable event. On the one hand, the hymn clearly says that Jesus was "in very nature God." He fully participated in the divine nature *(morphe)* of God. Yet in the incarnation he "made himself nothing, taking the very nature of a servant" (2:7). The reference to Jesus taking on human nature and emptying himself cannot possibly mean that Jesus emptied himself of the divine nature, for that would be an assault on the immutability of God. This is the question raised by my Muslim friend. Rather, it means that Jesus temporarily accepted the limitations of human nature and emptied himself of the free exercise of many of his divine prerogatives. The hymn declares that Jesus "did not consider equality with God something to be grasped" (2:6). Rather than cling to his prerogatives, he voluntarily suspended their free exercise for our benefit. They were suspended because, although the two natures remained separate, they functioned as one in the incarnation. This meant, for example, that the omnipresence of Christ would not violate the finite limitations of the human body lest his true humanity be destroyed. Thus, in the incarnation Jesus became functionally subordinate not only to God the Father, but even to those who crucified him. However, he never became ontologically subordinate. Indeed, Colossians 2:9 declares that "in Christ all the fullness of the Deity lives in bodily form." In the incarnation, we see that God is no longer an abstract concept but the living God who created us and loves us. Jesus allowed himself to become fully identified with our experience—including hunger, thirst, temptation, and even death—for the purpose of revealing God's love to humanity.

Shiʿite reply:

You are quite right in pointing out how Christians were hopelessly divided into a wide range of beliefs concerning Jesus. In sūrah 19:37, Muhammad (PBUH) declared that "the Sects are divided concerning Jesus." Undoubtedly, the various Christian councils were seeking to bring greater clarity to this state of confusion. Nonetheless, all the christological formulas in the world, however precise and orthodox, cannot change the testimony of the Qurʾān. As Muslims, we believe that the Qurʾān was composed by Allah and is, therefore, without error. The Qurʾān provides a twofold witness against the Christian elevation of Jesus Christ to divine status. First, the

Qur'ān clearly teaches that Allah cannot have a son, and yet you call Jesus the Son of God. The Qur'ān condemns this as shirk (idolatrous associations) because Allah is not begotten nor does he beget (sūrah 19:35). Second, in the Qur'ān Jesus himself prophesies about the coming of Muhammad (PBUH), whom he calls by the title Ahmed.[18] This peculiar title is used to call to mind the same prophesy in the original version of the Gospel of John, where Jesus tells his followers that he is going to send another who will witness to the truth. The Greek in your New Testament refers to this person as *paracletos* (comforter or counselor).[19] However, this is actually a distortion of the word *periclutos,* which is the Greek word for Muhammad's title Ahmad, meaning "praised one."[20] If Jesus is the final revelation of Allah, then why did Jesus himself tell his disciples that Muhammad (PBUH) was coming after him in order to "guide you into all truth" (John 16:13)?

Therefore, despite all of the precise language and fine distinctions established by the Christian councils, the Qur'ān condemns the Christian doctrine, and therefore Muslims should reject it on that ground alone.

Evangelical reply to Shiʿite:

I will first address your claim that Jesus prophesied the coming of Muhammad in the Gospel of John, followed by a more detailed analysis of the texts in the Qur'ān that, according to your view, reject the Christian claims about Christ.

There are three main reasons why your claim about the Gospel of John cannot be sustained. First, we have over five thousand Greek manuscripts of the New Testament. In all of those texts, there is not a single occurrence of the word *periclutos* as a variant to any of the places where John uses the word *paracletos.* The claim simply has no textual foundation whatsoever. Second, the context of the entire passage in John's Gospel is set in a Trinitarian framework whereby the Father sends the Spirit in order to bear witness to Jesus. There is no reference to a future prophet or any further revelation that would point away from Jesus. Our Lord says, "When the Counselor *[paracletos]* comes, whom I will send to you from the Father, the Spirit of truth who goes out from the Father, *he will testify about me*" (John 15:26, emphasis added). Later, he says the Counselor will bring glory to Jesus (John 16:14). Muhammad neither pointed to Jesus nor gave him glory. Third, the Comforter whom Jesus sends is promised to "be with you forever"

18. Sūrah 61:6.

19. See John 14:16; 15:26; and 16:7.

20. This argument continues to be made by Muslims. The footnote to sūrah 61:6 in the recently published official English translation and notes to the Qur'ān sponsored by King Fahd of Saudia Arabia states, "Our doctors contend that *Paracletos* is a corrupt reading for *Periclytos,* and that in their original saying of Jesus there was a prophecy of our holy Prophet Ahmad by name." See Al-Madinah and an-Nabawiyah, *The Holy Qur-an,* 1738–39 n. 5438. The origin of this idea is probably from the pen of Ibn Ishaq, a well-known biographer of Muhammad.

(John 14:16) and to dwell "in you" (John 14:17). Muhammad cannot fulfill either of these promises. Muhammad is buried in the Tomb of the Prophet in Medina. Furthermore, how could he dwell in the apostles hundreds of years before he was even born?

I will now address the first part of your statement. It is not easy to give you a complete response, since the scope of this dialogue does not permit a full discussion concerning the authority of the Qurʾān. Nevertheless, an examination of the major texts that refer to Jesus will be sufficient to demonstrate that it is not as easy as you may think to use the Qurʾān to refute Christian claims about Christ. I believe the negative christological statements in the Qurʾān are actually directed toward the heretical Christologies espoused by Arians, Adoptionists, Nestorians, and Monophysites, all of whom had already been censured by the church nearly two hundred years before Muhammad.

A survey of the Qurʾān reveals that the christological statements fall into five general groups. The first group contains those passages condemning the idea of Allah being begotten or begetting, as in sūrah 19:35 and 112:3. I would include in this group the negative references to the word *son* as applied to deity in sūrah 72:3. The second group includes all the shirk passages, which denounce the concept of associating partners with God as in sūrah 17:111. The third group contains references or allusions to the Christian belief in the Trinity as in sūrah 4:171. The fourth group contains texts that accuse Christians of elevating Jesus from the status of a prophet to divine status as in sūrah 9:30–31. The last group contains references condemning the notion that the son of Mary was divine because that would imply Mary also would be entitled to worship as in sūrah 5:116. In addition to these five groups of texts, there is a single enigmatic passage in sūrah 4:157 concerning the crucifixion of Christ that frequently is a focal point in Muslim-Christian dialogue.[21]

A closer examination of these texts reveals that all of them are attacking views which Christians likewise condemn. The passages about Allah begetting and having a son are all references to physical, sexual generation and sexual cohabitation. When Christians refer to Jesus as the "only begotten Son" (John 1:14; 3:16), they are referring to his unique status, which has nothing whatsoever to do with physical procreation.[22] In short, both Christians and Muslims find the notion of physical cohabitation by God to be offensive and blasphemous. At the fourth Lateran Council in 1215, the church stated that the divine nature "does not beget nor is it begotten," a word-for-word parallel of sūrah 112:3.[23]

21. This passage will be dealt with later in this chapter.

22. Modern English translations of John 1:14; 3:16; 3:18, and so forth render the phrase "one and only Son" rather than "only begotten Son" to avoid confusion.

23. Robert Caspar, *Trying to Answer Questions* (Rome: PISAI, 1989), 36. Compare the Latin, "illa res non est generans neque genita" with the Arabic "lam yalid wa lam yulad." While the context of the two statements is different, both are intended to emphasize God's oneness, and both condemn the idea of physical cohabitation in God.

The shirk passages, as well as the two passages that make reference to the Trinity, are either rebuking idolatry or some conception of polytheism (including tritheism) which Christians also reject in the most forceful terms. Those texts express horror at the idea that a mere prophet could be given divine status, the same horror orthodox Christians felt toward followers of adoptionism or Arianism who tried to advance the idea that a man could become God or that Christ was a created being.

Finally, the concerns Muhammad had regarding the status of Mary the mother of Jesus reflect the same reluctance many dedicated Christians have felt throughout church history at the unqualified or unrestricted use of the title *Theotokos* for Mary. Therefore, it is important to point out that the Qurʾān does not explicitly reject historic Christian Christology. I concede that subsequent Islamic interpretation of these texts has often been used against orthodox Christian positions, but I do not think that the Qurʾān itself explicitly rejects the historic view. Therefore, Muslims should not reject the proper Christian doctrine of Christ without a more thorough examination.[24]

Ṣūfi reply:

I come to this dialogue as a follower of shaykh Jili and a member of the Qadirite order of Ṣūfism.[25] The Christian doctrine of the incarnation is, in my view, an attempt to describe the ecstatic realization of Jesus that Allah was not a being utterly different from himself. As Qadirites, we affirm that through meditation one can come to experience the reality of Allah and the essence of Muhammad (PBUH) as the creative principle and ultimate ground of everything *(al-Ḥaqq)*. When the saint Hallaj declared, "I am the *Ḥaqq*" (I am the Truth), what he meant was that he had become a living and personal witness of Allah whose essence is love. His human nature *(násút)* was mystically united with the divine nature *(láhút)*. As Hallaj declared,

24. There are six passages (out of forty-one) in al-Bukhārī's *Ḥadīth* that might be interpreted as portraying Jesus in a negative light. See *Ḥadīth* 4:506; 4:644; 4:658; 6:105; 7:209; 8:817; and 9:601. Furthermore, there are an additional six passages that have clear negative reference to Christians in general. See *Ḥadīth* 1:749; 4:660; 4:654; 4:662; 6:105; and 9:461. (Several of these passages are repeated in other places in the *Ḥadīth*.) Some of these texts, like 9:601, are clear departures from historic Christian faith about Jesus, but most of these passages attack Christian heresies, not the actual Christian position regarding Christ. I am not seeking to minimize the vast differences between Islamic and Christian Christology, but I am pointing out the huge strategic advantage that falls to Christians if the focus of the conversation can remain on Christ and not be shifted to a debate over the authority of the Qurʾān versus the Bible. For a translation of the Ḥadīth, see Muhammad Muhsin Khan, trans., *The Translation of the Meanings of Sahih Al-Bukhārī*, vol. 1–9 (Dar Ahya: Us-Sunnah, Al Nabawiya, n.d.).

25. The full name for this shaykh or pīr is ʿAbdu ʿl-karim ibn Ibrahim al-Jili (1365–1417). The name Jili comes from Jilan or Gilan, the name of the province south of the Caspian Sea. Jili is a physical and spiritual descendent of the founder of the Qadirites, one of the four major Ṣūfi orders.

> I am he whom I love, and he whom I love is I.
> We are *two* spirits dwelling in one body,
> If thou seest me, thou seest him;
> And if thou seest him, thou seest us both.[26]

The great shaykh Jili taught that in every age there are perfect men who manifest the essence of Muhammad (PBUH) and who can take a wide variety of forms. Jili himself records the precise time and place when he had a personal meeting with Muhammad (PBUH), although the Prophet appeared to him in the guise of his own spiritual shaykh. Muhammad's essence can appear in many forms, including Jesus Christ. You noted how it was impossible for Muhammad (PBUH) to dwell in the apostles who lived hundreds of years before his birth or for the Prophet to be with you forever since he is buried in Medina. We believe in the preexistence of Muhammad (PBUH) as well as the ongoing vitality of his essence in the world today. Indeed, Christ is one of the most notable examples of the preexistence of Muhammad (PBUH). According to our Ṣūfi traditions, it was Muhammad (PBUH) himself who was speaking when Jesus said, "He who has seen me has seen the Father."[27] Even my Shiʿa friends believe in the intercessory power of the Imams and Karbala martyrs,[28] and they pray to saints like ʿAlī, Husayn, and Zainab.[29] We accept this practice because we see these saints as operating out of the essence of Muhammad (PBUH). This perspective enables the tension between Islam and Christianity to subside. The different creeds and practices in Islam and Christianity lose their meaning in the lives of those who have realized union with Allah. You are all discussing the outward peel of religion and missing its inner core.

A Ṣūfi shocked his followers when he declared, "I am neither Christian, nor Jew, nor Muslim." Jili taught that there are ten principal religions in the world, and God is the essence behind all of the different beliefs.[30] This truth enables us to look beyond our outward differences and to catch the image of our beloved. This image of God's love must be found, according to Jalal

26. As quoted by R. A. Nicholson in *Studies in Islamic Mysticism* (Cambridge: Cambridge University Press, 1921, reprinted, 1989), 80.

27. This quotation from John 14:9 does appear in the Ṣūfi *Ḥadīth* on the lips of Muhammad, but substitutes the word "Allah" for "Father." As quoted in Nicholson, *Studies in Islamic Mysticism,* 88.

28. In the Shiʾa tradition, an Imam is a successor of Muhammad. The Karbala martyrs refers to those who died at the famous battle of Karbala near Kufa on the tenth of Muharram A.H. 61 (A.D. 680).

29. Husayn is regarded as the first Islamic martyr in the Shiʾa tradition. His death in the Islamic civil war at Karbala has become symbolic for the suffering of the entire Shiʾa community. Each year the Shiʾa community celebrates the Ashura, which reenacts his passion and death.

30. Jili identified the ten religious sects as idolaters, physicists, philosophers, dualists, Magians, materialists, Brāhmins, Jews, Christians, and Muslims.

al-Din, whether it is in the temple of idols, in the Kaʿbah, or in the synagogue.[31] No theological disputes from the Bible or the Qurʾān should stand in the way of this union. It was al-Tilimsani, the follower of Ibn ʿArabi, who said that if the Qurʾān keeps you from experiencing true union with Allah, then the Qurʾān is shirk, that is, an unnecessary association with Allah.

All Muslims agree that Muhammad (PBUH) believed in the essential unity of all revelation. The faith that was revealed to Allah's messenger is the same faith that was revealed to Abraham and to Jesus. In sūrah 23:53, Allah revealed to his messenger that there is but one true religion and "yet men have divided themselves into different sects, each rejoicing in its own doctrines." I believe that both Christians and Muslims can accept the incarnation of Allah in Jesus Christ in the sense that incarnation or ḥulūl expresses the permeation of existence by essence, which is the kernel underlying all true religion.

Evangelical reply to Ṣūfī:

I see that these dialogues have come full circle. I began these dialogues in chapter 2 by discussing the nondualistic or monistic doctrine of God as expressed in the major sects of Vedantic Hinduism. Now, quite surprisingly, I am encountering it again within the fold of Islam. While I welcome the positive attitude toward the concept of incarnation in Ṣūfism, there are two major problems with the view as expressed here.

First, the unique status of Christ as the one and only incarnation of God is completely lost. In the Qadirite Ṣūfī view, everyone is a potential recipient of the reality of Allah and the essence of Muhammad. Figures like Christ, Hallaj, and Muhammad are all examples of people who were incarnated with the attributes of Allah. However, this is a serious departure from historic Christian teaching, regardless of how it is interpreted. If figures like Christ and Hallaj are mere humans who, through meditative discipline, became endowed with Allah's attributes, then it is a form of adoptionism which, as we noted earlier, is in violation of the Christian view of incarnation. If these figures are interpreted as genuine incarnations of Allah, the view must be rejected because Christianity denies the possibility of multiple, ongoing incarnations. This would detract from the unique stature of Christ and would be a de facto denial of Trinitarian monotheism, thus jeopardizing the oneness of God.

Second, your view ultimately subordinates all the expressions of incarnation to the essence of Muhammad, who is either anticipated or expressed in these figures. The very words of Christ, for example, become the words of a preexistent Muhammad. This is intended to illustrate the unity of all revelation. However, Christianity does not accept the unity of all revelation. In our view, Jesus Christ embodies the fullest and most complete expression of

31. As quoted by Ignaz Goldziher in *Introduction to Islamic Theology and Law* (Princeton: Princeton University Press, 1981), 152.

God's self-revelation. Any revelation that does not point to his unique stature must ultimately fall to the ground.

Sunni rejoinder:

In your response to my statement, you made a distinction between Jesus' functional subordination, which you accept, and his ontological subordination, which you deny. You noted that Jesus was functionally subordinate even to those who crucified him. It is unimaginable for us to accept that Allah would allow one of his prophets to be treated as an unbeliever and subjected to the horrors of crucifixion. The Qurʾān rebukes the Jews who claimed to have put him to death on the cross:

> They denied the truth and uttered a monstrous falsehood against Mary. They declared: "We have put to death the Messiah Jesus the son of Mary, the Apostle of Allah." They did not kill him, nor did they crucify him, but they thought they did.[32]

The last phrase of this *āya* (verse) is literally, "He was made *to resemble* another for them." ʿĪsā did not die on the cross, but an imposter who resembled him died in his place. It is my view that Simon of Cyrene, who carried his cross, was nailed to the cross instead of ʿĪsā.[33] Allah exalted ʿĪsā into his presence until the day when ʿĪsā will return and vindicate Allah's servant Muhammad (PBUH) as it says in sūrah 4:159. In that text we learn that Jesus will return and bear witness against the People of the Book (Jews and Christians) on the day of judgment.[34] According to the Ḥadīth, ʿĪsā will descend as judge and reign for forty years before he dies and is buried in Medina.[35]

We are shocked when we hear Christians affirm that ʿĪsā died on the cross and then portray this as part of Allah's sovereign plan before the creation of the world. Christians couple this with the assertion that ʿĪsā is actually Allah! You argue that ʿĪsā fully shares in the very nature of God, and yet you say that ʿĪsā suffered death on a cross. How can Allah suffer? How can God die? Allah is the ever-living one! He is eternally existent and cannot be subject to pain, suffering, or death. Even an uneducated Muslim can see how the contradiction of the Christian position is exposed in the following syllogism:

32. Sūrah 4:157.

33. Muslim commentators base this belief on the writings of the second-century Egyptian Gnostic Basilides. There is considerable scholarly debate about whether Basilides actually taught this, since none of his writings are extant and we only know of him through the writings of his opponents. See Geoffrey Parrinder, *Jesus in the Qurʾān* (London: Faber and Faber, 1965; reprint, Oxford: One World, 1995), 110.

34. Sūrah 4:159.

35. This is a belief based on a composite of several independent Ḥadīth, most notably, *al-Bukhārī*, vol. 3, 34, Ḥadīth 425; vol. 4, 55, Ḥadīth 657–58. See Khan, *Translation of the Meanings*, vol. 3, 233–34; vol. 4, 436–37.

God cannot die.
Jesus died on the cross.
Therefore, Jesus is not God.

If Christians accept the first two statements, they cannot deny the third. I admire your devotion to Jesus Christ, but I fear you have placed ʿĪsā on a pedestal which he never intended. Can you give me one example in the entire Gospels where ʿĪsā himself claims to be God or asks others to worship him? This doctrine is surely the creation of Paul who falsified Christ's original monotheistic message.

Shiʿite rejoinder:

Before you respond to my Sunni friend, I would like to add further weight to his argument against the Christian position regarding the crucifixion of Christ. In your response to my statement, you claimed that the Qurʾān never explicitly denies orthodox Christology but only attacks heretical positions that Christians also condemn. However, sūrah 4:157, which my Sunni friend just quoted, seems to explicitly deny that ʿĪsā died on the cross. The text says, "They did not kill him, nor did they crucify him, but they thought they did." Many Sunnis believe that he was never crucified at all. I believe that Jesus may have been crucified, but he did not die on the cross. He was taken down after only a few hours and hidden by his disciples.[36] In either scenario, Jesus did not die on the cross. Does that not cut to the heart of orthodox Christianity?

Ṣūfī rejoinder:

Since my Sunni and Shiʾa friends have both given their rejoinders and focused on the crucifixion and death of Christ, I will do the same. I do not accept the imposter theory but believe that the body of ʿĪsā was truly nailed to the cross where his body died. The passage in sūrah 4:157 is merely pointing out that they could not kill the essence of Jesus, which was, in fact, the essence of Muhammad (PBUH). A God-man like Jesus Christ can appear in a wide range of bodies over many centuries, and therefore nailing Jesus' body to the cross was a futile attempt by the authorities to snuff out that essence which is at the ground of the whole universe. Jesus' body underwent various cruelties and suffering, but Jesus himself was not subject to pain or suffering or death, for his essence was lifted up to Allah. The passage from sūrah 4 goes on to say, "Those that disagreed about him were in doubt concerning his death, for what they knew about it was sheer conjecture. They were not sure that they had slain him. *Allah lifted him up to his presence.*"[37]

All Muslims believe that Muhammad (PBUH) was miraculously transported from Mecca to Jerusalem on a winged steed in what is known as his

36. This is known as the swoon theory.
37. Sūrah 4:157–58, emphasis added.

night journey. Once in Jerusalem, the Prophet was caught up (Mi'raj) into the presence of Allah, where he received several revelations, including the ritual of fivefold daily prayer. However, this was a spiritual journey because in the Ḥadīth his wife ʿĀʾisha said that throughout the night journey the Prophet's body remained in the bed.[38] Likewise, according to the Acts of John, Jesus appeared to the apostle John during the actual crucifixion while John was hiding in a cave. Jesus said to John, "To the multitude in Jerusalem I am right now being crucified and pierced . . . and given vinegar and gall to drink, but unto you I am speaking."[39] This is consistent with our view that it is a mistake to focus on the historical Jesus and give him divine stature, rather than the essence Jesus embodied that transcends his earthly sojourn.

Evangelical reply to all:

The humiliation that the eternal Word took on in the incarnation finds its greatest expression in the death of Christ on the cross. It is fitting, therefore, that we bring our dialogue to a close with a discussion concerning this central feature of the Christian message. A number of important questions have been raised by all three of you. The first issue to be addressed is whether the Qurʾān actually teaches that Jesus did not die on the cross, but only someone who resembled him. A survey of the scholarly discussion among Islamic commentators concerning sūrah 4:157 demonstrates that the precise meaning of the passage is unclear. It is important, therefore, to let passages in the Qurʾān that are clear assist in understanding this passage. Sūrah 19:33 unambiguously records Jesus prophesying about "the day of my death." This is confirmed by sūrah 19:15 as well as 3:55.[40] The passages cannot be construed as speaking either symbolically or of some future eschatological death without violating the plain meaning of these texts. The Qurʾān even refers to the institution of the Eucharist or Lord's Supper, which is unintelligible apart from the death of Christ.[41] It is, therefore, difficult to see how an exaltation or resurrection of Jesus can be inserted in a way that completely circumvents the real death of Jesus. We must now examine the passage in sūrah 4.

All are in agreement that the passage is a quotation of a Jewish boast designed to blaspheme Mary the mother of Jesus. The passage is preceded by several references to key points in Jewish history, leading up to the declaration that the Jews "denied the truth and uttered a monstrous falsehood against Mary" (4:156). The boast that follows in the next verse (āya) is the

38. J. A. Williams, *The Word of Islam* (Austin: University of Texas Press, 1994), 44.

39. R. M. Wilson, ed., *The New Testament Apocrypha*, vol. 2 (Philadelphia: Westminster, 1964), 232.

40. Some Muslim translators do not translate this latter verse with a clear reference to physical death. However, it should be noted that the word *mutawaffika* in 3:55 refers to physical death just the way it does in 2:240, which no one disputes as referring to physical death. It should be rendered "cause Thee to die," as translated by N. J. Dawood.

41. See sūrah 5:112–14.

Jewish claim that "we have put to death the Messiah Jesus the son of Mary, the apostle of Allah" (4:157). The verse goes on to point out that "they" (i.e., the Jews) did not kill him, nor did they crucify him. This does not necessarily indicate that an imposter was crucified in Jesus' place. Islamicist Geoffrey Parrinder points out that the phrase "mā ṣalabū-hu" may be translated as either "they did not crucify him" or "they did not cause his death on the cross."[42] It merely points out that the Jews were wrong in boasting that they were responsible for the death of Christ on the cross. The last part of the verse, the phrase "shubbiha la-hum," is ambiguous and has been translated in a wide variety of ways, including,

> "it appeared to them as such" (Massignon, M. Pickthall)
> "they thought they did" (Dawood)
> "only a likeness of that was shown to them" (Arberry)[43]

While Arberry does render the verse in a way that could be interpreted as supporting the imposter theory, it is more likely a phrase that simply reinforces the falseness of the Jewish boast. If an entirely new idea that so profoundly contradicts the Christian Scriptures was being inserted at this point, one would expect greater clarity. Taken as a whole, the passage makes sense if it is read in light of the passages that affirm the actual death of Christ along with a passage in sūrah 5:17, where Muhammad is instructed to ask, "Who could prevent Allah from destroying the Messiah, the son of Mary, together with his mother and all the people of the earth?" The point of the verse is to emphasize the power and sovereignty of Allah. Allah alone held the power to put Jesus to death. The Jews could not put Jesus to death, for no one dies apart from Allah's sovereign will. Though it may be difficult to understand why Jesus had to die, the Qurʾān indicates that this is within the power of Allah.

Understanding sūrah 4:156–57 in this way harmonizes the passages that teach the real death of Jesus as well as the verse where Allah declares that he would cause Jesus to die. The main point of the passage, therefore, is to rebuke the Jews for taking credit for something that was actually a sovereign act of Allah. It is even consistent with the general theme of John 19:11, where Jesus says to Pilate, "You would have no power over me if it were not given to you from above." Thus, while many Muslims claim that an imposter died in place of Jesus, I am convinced that the Qurʾān itself does not teach this.[44] Therefore, to also respond to the question raised by my Shiʾa friend, I

42. Parrinder, *Jesus in the Qurʾan,* 108.
43. Ibid., 109.
44. Many Muslim scholars agree with me. For example, modern Muslim writer Dr. Kamel Hussein says in his *City of Wrong* (Oxford: One World, 1995) that "the idea of a substitute for Christ is a very crude way of explaining the Quranic text" (p. 222), as quoted in Parrinder, *Jesus in the Qurʾān,* 112. It is also highly unlikely that the differences in the passage can be explained through the abrogation principle since that applies to commands, not historical narratives.

do not believe that the Qurʾān explicitly contradicts the historic Christian position concerning the historicity of the death of Jesus Christ on a cross.

The second question concerns the apparent contradiction in the Christian claim that Jesus died on the cross and yet he is the eternal God. The syllogism quoted by my Sunni friend is designed to put Christians in a position where we are forced to admit that we cannot affirm both the full deity of Christ and the real death of Christ. The two claims are made out to be mutually exclusive since God cannot die. However, the Christian position is not trapped in a logical contradiction because of the two natures–one person doctrine. The two natures remained ontologically distinct in the incarnation, although they functioned in harmony as they were united in the one person. The divine nature of Christ was expressed within the finite limitations of the human body so as not to violate the true humanity of Christ. The result is that Jesus as the incarnate God-man was subject to pain, suffering, and even death on the cross. The death of Jesus Christ on the cross refers to the death of the person, not the divine nature. Jesus truly died, as is evidenced by the biblical account. When the soldiers came to break his legs in order to speed up death, they found he was already dead (John 19:33). One of the soldiers pierced his side with a spear, and it brought forth a "sudden flow of blood and water" (19:34), which doctors say is a sure sign of death. Yet, although the death of Christ was real, it in no way affected or destroyed the divine nature.

The third question does not deal specifically with the crucifixion but with the larger issue of the deity of Christ, which I already addressed in the last conversation (chapter 6) and earlier in this dialogue. However, the specific question was raised whether Jesus himself ever claimed to be God or asked others to worship him. The Christian response to this question is twofold. First, it is a violation of Christian theology to isolate the words of Jesus from their Gospel context or to separate the Gospel accounts from the larger apostolic witness recorded in the whole New Testament. To ask us to arbitrarily separate the words of Jesus from the words of the apostles, who were eyewitnesses of his incarnation, would be like a Christian questioning a Muslim but insisting that the Muslim could only quote from early Meccan sūrahs. The restriction is unfair.

Second, even allowing for this unfair restriction, Jesus did claim to be God and received worship as God. In John 8:58, the Jews were shocked that Jesus claimed to have seen Abraham, even though he was not yet fifty years old. Jesus replied, "I tell you the truth, before Abraham was born, I am!" This was an unmistakable identification with the sacred name of God revealed to Moses at the burning bush (Exod. 3:14). The claim to deity was so blatant that his opponents picked up stones to stone him for blasphemy (John 8:54–59). Furthermore, the most common self-designation Jesus ever used for himself was the title Son of Man. Far from being a reference to his humanity, the title refers to the exalted Son of Man passage in the prophecy of

Daniel. That text declares that the Son of Man "was given authority, glory and sovereign power; all peoples, nations and men of every language worshipped him."[45] This is the context in which Jesus testified before the chief priests and teachers of the law, saying of himself, "From now on, the Son of Man will be seated at the right hand of the mighty God" (Luke 22:66–71). His opponents clearly understood it to be a claim to deity, and they condemned him to die on the basis of this perceived blasphemy.

Jesus also received worship after his resurrection. Thomas fell down at the feet of Jesus and declared, "My Lord and my God!" (John 20:28). And when Jesus met the women at the empty tomb, Matthew records that the "women fell at his feet and worshipped him" (Matt. 28:9). The Gospels also record that the disciples worshipped him.[46] If anyone tried to worship an upright observant Jew, he would have torn his garments and declared it a blasphemy. Jesus, however, received these many acts of worship because it was due him as the risen Lord.

The fourth and final point, as raised by my Ṣūfi friend, accepts the fact that Jesus Christ died on the cross but applies it only to his outward body. I have no major quarrel with the Ṣūfi claim that the enemies of Jesus could kill his body but could not extinguish his essence. All Christians would accept the basic truth of that statement. However, we cannot accept that the essence of Christ is so loosely connected with his body that it has appeared in countless other bodies in a way that undermines the unique stature of the historical Jesus of Nazareth, the one and only incarnation of God in human history. Attempts to separate the Christ of faith from the Jesus of history are as ancient as the Docetists and Gnostics and as legendary and modern as Rudolph Bultmann. Nevertheless, evangelical Christians who affirm historic Christianity have rejected this repeatedly. The Jesus who was exalted and raised from the dead was not the disembodied inner essence of Jesus. He was not raised symbolically in the experience or preaching of the apostles. His was a bodily resurrection (1 Cor. 15:12–20). He was seen by the women (Matt. 28:9), by the apostles (Matt. 28:16–17), and by over five hundred followers (1 Cor. 15:6). He could be touched (Luke 24:38). He even ate with his disciples after the resurrection (John 21:12–13). These are all clear testimonies to the bodily resurrection.

Conclusion

This dialogue has focused on the doctrine of the incarnation as understood and expressed by historic, evangelical Christianity. Our conversations

45. Daniel 7:13–14. Jesus' Son of Man sayings are frequently associated with his glory, not his humiliation (see, for example, Matthew 16:27f; 19:28; 24:27; 24:30; 25:31; and 26:64). Therefore, the title is more likely an allusion to the exalted Son of Man in Daniel 7 than the more humble connotations associated with Yahweh's address to Ezekiel.

46. See Luke 24:52 and Matthew 28:17.

have focused largely on how the full humanity of Christ can be affirmed without violating the very definition of God. This is the most important issue for Muslims when discussing the nature of Christ and the incarnation. Issues such as the virgin birth and the sinlessness of Christ, which have dominated discussions in the West, are not as prevalent in the Christian-Muslim exchange since Islam accepts both the virgin birth and the sinlessness of Christ.[47] The precise formula of two natures–one person is essential to ward off a whole range of misunderstandings that err on one side or the other, compromising either his full humanity or his full deity. The formula agreed upon at Chalcedon safeguards with equal vigilance both his full humanity and his full deity without dividing or confusing either.

Confusion concerning the precise relationship between deity and humanity in the incarnation spawned a wide range of views, several of which the church ultimately determined to be heretical. We examined how Muhammad seems to have been aware of several christological heresies that were present in small numbers in seventh-century Arabia. The Qurʾān attacks these heresies—including Monophysitism, Arianism, Adoptionism, and Nestorianism—while remaining largely silent in responding to the orthodox position per se. The result is that although the Qurʾān does not launch any sustained attack against the Christ of Scripture, it does fail to acknowledge his true stature. This, in my view, is the central problem with the Qurʾānic view of Christ. We are left with a monotone, middle-of-the-road view of Christ. The pulse rate of the Qurʾān only quickens when attacking christological positions that we reject with equal vehemence. The Qurʾān does not actually engage with the Christ of the New Testament. However, this fact may provide a window of opportunity to engage Muslims with renewed energy in serious, prayerful encounters about Jesus Christ. This may yield fruit in the Muslim heart that the doctrine of Christ's incarnation, when properly understood, does not violate the doctrine of God.

47. Sūrah 3:47 affirms the virgin birth, and Ḥadīth 4:506 (al-Bukhārī) and sūrah 3:47 affirm the sinlessness of Christ.

PART 4

Case Studies and Conclusion

Christianity is the only world religion whose primary source documents are in a language other than that of the religion's founder. The New Testament is written in Koine Greek, not in Aramaic, which was the language of Jesus. This is unique among all world religions, and it is a remarkable testimony to the translatability of the Christian message that has been enshrined in our most sacred texts. This linguistic translatability of the Christian message has been the inspiration for translating the New Testament into thousands of languages. However, the gospel is not only linguistically translatable, it is culturally translatable. The gospel is not only delivered to us in the enscripturated text, but also in the proclamation and witness of a believing community belonging to a particular culture at a particular time in history. Andrew Walls has observed that the doctrine of the incarnation is not just that God became a man, but that God became a particular man. He lived in a particular place and belonged to a particular ethnic group.[1] The gospel must be made intelligible as it is proclaimed in specific, local contexts. Today the gospel is growing in areas that have long been dominated by the presence of non-Christian religions. This underscores the need for Christians around the world to become more familiar not only with

1. Andrew Walls, *The Missionary Movement in Christian History: Studies in the Transmission of Faith* (Maryknoll, N.Y.: Orbis, 1996), 27.

the beliefs and practices of those who belong to other religions, but also to become more familiar with Christians throughout the ages who have already thought deeply about many of the issues we face today.

The purpose of these final chapters is to teach the reader some lessons from church history (both ancient and modern) and to reflect on many of the pressing issues that have arisen when Christianity has seriously encountered other religions and philosophies. These case studies have been carefully chosen as representative of both the complex challenges the church has faced as well as the creative solutions that have been offered as Christians have tried to explore how the gospel can best address itself to the particular challenges posed by a religiously and culturally diverse world.

The three case studies in this section are based on four Christians who lived in different times and on different continents yet shared a common desire to be faithful to the Christian gospel in the midst of the unique challenges they faced. The scope of this study makes it impossible to give even a scant survey of the full scope of the work and writings of any of these figures. Rather, one relevant theme from their writings has been selected for discussion and reflection. Each case study is also designed to shed further light on relevant issues that emerged in the conversations in chapters 2 through 7.

The first case study is from the life and work of Justin Martyr, the second-century apologist from Syria who creatively used the *logos* concept in John's Gospel to better communicate the gospel in his philosophically rich Hellenistic culture. This case study will go on to reflect on whether Justin's use of *logos* is applicable in a specific setting in modern-day Africa. The writings of Kwame Bediako, a contemporary theologian from Ghana, will highlight the particular challenge of trying to find vernacular dynamic equivalents to the titles of Jesus in the Akan culture of Ghana the same way Justin did in the context of second-century Hellenism. While ancient Hellenism and modern-day Christians in Ghana seem far removed from Islam, this discussion will actually shed light, as we shall see, on a similar issue that continues to surface in Islamic-Christian dialogues.

The second case study focuses on the writings of the nineteenth-century Hindu convert to Christianity, Brahmabandhav Upadhyay (1861–1907). He was a journalist, a theologian, and at the end of his life an imprisoned leader of India's nationalistic movement. He earnestly sought to use the language of advaitic Hinduism as an interpretive bridge or hermeneutic to better communicate Christianity to inquiring Hindus. This case study will focus on his use of the advaitic doctrine of *saccidānanda (sat-cit-ānanda)* to explain the doctrine of the Trinity. The conversation in chapter 2 concerning the nature of ultimate reality in Hinduism and Christianity left a sense of the tremendous gulf that separates the two religions. This discussion will open up the possibility of an interpretive bridge that might provide some kind of border crossing over the vast frontier separating Hinduism and Christianity.

The third case study highlights the work of A. G. Hogg, a scholar from Western Europe who worked as a missionary in the East in the early decades of the twentieth century. Hogg challenged the prevailing ideas of fulfillment theology and offered a different, though controversial, solution to the tension between the uniqueness of Jesus Christ and the plurality of religions. This case study will contribute to the ongoing conversation between Christians and Buddhists about the meaning of faith.

Taken together, all of these case studies serve as another expression of interreligious dialogue. Archbishop Marcello Zago, secretary of the Congregation for the Evangelization of Peoples (formerly *Propaganda Fide*), makes the helpful distinction between interreligious dialogue and ecumenical dialogue.[2] The former refers to dialogue between Christianity and non-Christian religions. This has been the focus of this book. Ecumenical dialogue refers to dialogue between Christians, such as Pentecostals talking with Baptists or Roman Catholics talking with Presbyterians. I would like to suggest a third form of dialogue, which I call *historical dialogue*. In some ways, it is similar to ecumenical dialogue in that it is an intramural conversation between Christians. However, it is distinctive because it encourages contemporary Christians to engage in dialogue with Christians who have lived at different times throughout the history of the church. This is a historical engagement with men and women throughout the history of the church who have struggled with similar issues. Obviously, since these figures belong to history, we cannot get direct answers to our questions. But it is remarkable how much insight we can gain by understanding the problems they wrestled with. Actually, there are few new problems that the church faces. Most of the problems that we think are new are really just old problems with a slightly different look to them. Furthermore, when we realize that every generation—including our own—has its blind spots, we can be forgiving of issues that are important to us which they completely missed, and we can also gain tremendous insight into ways of looking at issues that have escaped us. By listening to history, we always come back to our own context enriched.

Chapters 8–10 draw us into historical dialogue with several figures out of the variegated chapters of church history. We will be listening to a Syrian, an Indian, a European, and an African whose lives collectively span the entire history of the church.

Each of these Christians faced different challenges, yet each sought to address the gospel faithfully. I have purposely chosen three case studies

2. Marcello Zago, "Mission and Interreligious Dialogue," *International Bulletin of Missionary Research* 22, no. 3 (July 1998): 98. Zago also regards Christian dialogue with Judaism as a separate endeavor having so many unique features that it should not be regarded like dialogue with the other non-Christian religions.

that, on the surface, are not part of any of the major contemporary discussions in interreligious dialogue. Yet, as will become clear, each of these case studies sheds tremendous light on many of the current discussions. Furthermore, it is likely that you may disagree sharply with some of the proposals made by these figures. However, a fair and thorough discussion of their views is vital in developing our ability to critique modern trends in interreligious dialogue. If we are attentive, we will learn a great deal from these historical dialogues, and we will also be able to understand and respond to the challenges we face in our own time. Indeed, we neglect the past at our own peril.

At the conclusion of each case study, there will be a brief application of the study to issues raised during the conversations with world religions in chapters 2–7. Finally, each case study concludes with questions for discussion and further reflection in the hope that this book will be the beginning of an increased awareness of and an intelligent engagement with peoples from around the world who have not yet heard the gospel of Jesus Christ in a way they can understand.

8

Was Socrates a Christian before Christ?

A Study of Justin Martyr's Use of Logos Spermatikos

Justin Martyr (110–165) was raised in a Gentile household in Syria-Palestine. He was well trained in the major schools of Greek philosophy, including Stoicism and Platonism, but he had little firsthand knowledge of Judaism. Justin's search for true philosophy led him to study Socrates and Plato and eventually led to his conversion to Christianity. Subsequent to his conversion, he began to study the Hebrew prophets, and he became fascinated with how they had predicted and prepared the way for the coming of Christ and the gospel.[1] Justin also became well acquainted with Hellenistic Judaism, a school of Greek-speaking diaspora Jews who sought to reconcile Judaism with certain features of Greek philosophy. As a convinced Christian, Justin spent the rest of his life defending the Christian faith, culminating in his martyrdom.

Three works form the corpus of what remains of Justin's writings: his First and Second Apologies addressed to Emperor Antoninus Pius and his more extensive and well-known *Dialogue with Trypho,* which is yet another precedent for the kind of apologetic dialogue in this book.[2] The *Dialogue* is a

1. *First Apology,* 53–59 (*ANF* 1:180–83).

2. It is beyond the scope of this case study to examine a wide range of other works attributed to Justin, such as the *Discourse to the Greeks* and *The Admonition to the Greeks.* However, the vast majority of scholars reject that these additional works are genuine writings of Justin.

fictional conversation between Justin and a Jew named Trypho, and it was probably based on actual discussions Justin had with Jewish leaders.[3]

Use of *Logos* and *Logos Spermatikos* in the Second Century

This case study focuses on Justin's use of the concept of *logos spermatikos* or "seed of the word" in his apologetic writings. The general concept of *logos* was well known in the ancient world, and it is used in a variety of ways in the writings of Platonists, Stoics, Hellenistic Jews, and of course in the prologue to John's Gospel. There is a fierce debate among scholars about which of these groups had the biggest influence on Justin, but most agree that even if he were influenced by others, he developed the concept in his own way. The specific expression *logos spermatikos* also appears in writings from several strands of thought in the ancient world. For the Middle Platonists, the concept of *logos spermatikos* was an ethical principle that sowed the foundational seeds for human ethics. In contrast to the ethical emphasis among Platonists, the Stoics interpreted *logos spermatikos* as reason. They frequently use the expression in the plural, *logoi spermatikoi* ("seeds of reason"), referring to a rational capacity that pervades the entire universe and allows humans to reason and ultimately to participate in divinity. The Hellenistic Jew Philo also uses the expression in his disputes with the Stoics. He seems to use the expression vaguely to refer to a "governing faculty" or "generative principle" that is present in all of nature. The exact words *logos spermatikos* never appear in the New Testament, although Jesus' parable of the sower depicts the Word *(logos)* being sown broadly in the world, leading many to argue that this theological usage, rather than the more philosophical orientation of the Stoics and Platonists, is the primary reference for Justin. Indeed, Justin even uses the expression "sowing of the implanted word *[logos]*" in his *Second Apology*.[4]

The most explicit connection between the general philosophical usage and the more biblical and theological imagery appears in the prologue to John's Gospel. John, addressing a Greek audience, uses the familiar philosophical term *logos* as his starting point, but connects it with the divine, spoken word which in the Book of Genesis brings the whole created order into being. Genesis begins, "In the beginning God" (Gen. 1:1). John's Gospel begins, "In the beginning was the Word" (John 1:1). Genesis goes on to picture God bringing forth the entire creation through his word *(logos)*.[5] John's prologue continues to resonate with this theme as he describes Christ's presence at the creation: "Through him all things were made; without him noth-

3. L. W. Barnard argues that the *Dialogue with Trypho* is based on an actual dialogue that took place in A.D. 132 and was later expanded and elaborated for apologetic purposes. See L. W. Barnard, *Justin Martyr* (Cambridge: Cambridge University Press, 1967), 24.

4. *Second Apology*, 13 (*ANF* 1:193).

5. The word *logos* is the word used in the Septuagint, the Greek version of the Old Testament. The Septuagint is probably the only version of the Old Testament read by Justin.

ing was made that has been made" (1:3). John then declares that God has spoken another Word into the world. Not the original word of creation, but the Word of redemption, Jesus Christ, the Word *[logos]* made flesh: "The Word *[logos]* became flesh and made his dwelling among us . . . full of grace and truth" (1:14). With this background, we now turn to Justin's use of *logos spermatikos.*

Use of *Logos* and *Logos Spermatikos* in the Writings of Justin Martyr

While Justin does not use the full expression *logos spermatikos* in his *First Apology,* he makes several references to *logos* that are important for this study. In this first apologetic work, Justin seeks to expose errors in the false worship associated with the Greek gods and goddesses. He declares that these Olympian deities are nothing more than demons, which form the basis of all such pagan religions. He goes on to praise Socrates who "endeavored *by true logos* and examination, to bring these things to light, and deliver men from the demons."[6] He then makes a remarkable parallel between the things condemned by Socrates (470–399 B.C.), who lived over four hundred years before Christ, and the current practices of the "barbarians" of his own time who, he argues, were "condemned by Reason, or the Word, the *Logos* himself who took shape, and became man, and was called Jesus Christ."[7] Justin is clearly identifying the *logos* that became flesh in Jesus Christ with the *logos* by which Socrates perceived and denounced the perverse worship of the gods and goddesses in the Greek pantheon. In other passages, Justin identifies the *logos* as operating in the Hebrew prophets of the Old Testament, who not only predicted the coming of Christ but through their writings also influenced the formulation of philosophy throughout the world. Justin specifically cites insights from Plato that he believed were drawn directly from Moses.[8]

Justin also utilizes the *logos* principle as a way to demonstrate to the emperor the antiquity of the Christian faith which, through *logos,* was able to actually precede the incarnation of Christ. He writes,

> We have been taught that Christ is the first-born of God, and we have declared above that he is the *logos* of whom every race of men were partakers; and those who lived reasonably (by *logos*) are Christians, even though they have been thought atheists; as among the Greeks, Socrates and Hera-

6. *First Apology,* 5, emphasis added (*ANF* 1:164).

7. Ibid.

8. *First Apology,* 32, 44 (*ANF* 1:173, 177). Justin says that "whatever both philosophers and poets have said concerning immortality of the soul, or punishments after death, or contemplation of things heavenly, or doctrines of the like kind, they have received such suggestions from the prophets as have enabled them to understand and interpret these things."

> clitus, and men like them; . . . and among the barbarians, Abraham, and Ananias, and Azarias, and Misael, and Elias and many others whose actions and names we now decline to recount.[9]

Thus, Abraham, Moses, and Socrates are considered by Justin to be Christians before Christ. This is vital to Justin's theology because the Christian faith was rejected in large part because it seemed to be such a recent and novel development. Viewed from Justin's perspective, Christianity was actually ancient because of the universal access to the *logos* of God throughout history. This does not, however, diminish the significance of the emergence of Christianity in history because, as we shall see, the *logos* of God was only completely and fully manifested in the historic incarnation. All previous manifestations were only shadows of what was to come. Justin refers to these pre-Christian manifestations as fragments or seeds *(spermatikos)* of the *logos.*

In his *Second Apology,* Justin introduces the concept of *logos spermatikos.* In chapter 8 Justin attributes the insights of Platonist and Stoic philosophers as well as poets like Heraclitus to the "seed of the Word" *(sperma tou logou),* which was "implanted" within them and is present "in every race of men."[10] What makes Christians distinct from the other non-Christian peoples of the world is that they do not have merely the seed of the *logos,* but they have "the knowledge and contemplation of the *whole logos,* which is Christ."[11] According to Justin, this explains the particular severity of Christian persecution when compared with the relatively scant persecution of the philosophers. This is because the latter "lived according to only part of the *logos spermatikos,*" whereas Christians live by the knowledge of the "whole *logos,* which is Christ."[12]

This distinction between the seed of the Word and the whole Word is also used to explain the various contradictions within philosophy. Whenever the philosophers contradicted themselves, it is because "they did not know the whole of the Word (*logos*)." If they spoke accurately, it was because they had found and properly contemplated some part of the Word.[13] Thus, Justin maintains a firm distinction between the seed and the whole, the former being a mere imitation and shadow of the whole. Nevertheless, from Justin's perspective, Greek philosophy became a tool to turn people away from the worship of false gods and to prepare them to receive the gospel of Jesus Christ, who alone is the fullness of *logos.*

9. *First Apology,* 46 (*ANF* 1:178).
10. *Second Apology,* 8 (*ANF* 1:191).
11. Ibid.
12. Ibid.
13. *First Apology,* 10 (*ANF* 1:191).

Application of Justin Martyr's *Logos Spermatikos* in Modern-Day Africa

Moving to the twenty-first century, we will now examine a contemporary African theologian who, like Justin in the second century, is struggling to communicate Christ in his particular context. Justin, as we have seen, followed the lead of the apostle John in utilizing and exploring a title for Jesus that arises not from the traditional vocabulary of Judaism, such as Messiah, but from the dominant philosophical thinking of the day, namely, *logos*. Justin broke new ground by seeing continuity not only between Christ and the Hebrew prophets, but between Christ and the pre-Christian philosophers and poets of Hellenism. All Christians accept that the Hebrew prophets served as a *preparatio evangelica*, but it is Justin who explored the possibility that other cultural and historical movements unconnected with Judaism (as in the rise of Greek philosophy) might also serve in this capacity.

Likewise, Ghanian theologian Kwame Bediako has explored how to relate Jesus Christ to dominant pre-Christian ideas in sub-Saharan African culture such as chief and ancestor. Despite their many differences, ancient Greeks and contemporary Africans both come to the Christian faith apart from a prehistory in Judaism. A declaration that the Messiah has finally arrived and that Jesus has fulfilled the hope of the prophets is largely unintelligible to someone who has not previously been schooled in the expectations of Judaism prior to the coming of Christ. A more indigenous title would not be Jesus the Messiah, but Jesus the Ancestor or Jesus the Chief. Does Justin Martyr provide a precedent for this kind of application in the African context?

In Ghana, the word in the Akan language for ancestor is *nana* and the word for Jesus is *Yesu*. Kwame Bediako has frequently heard Ghanians praying to *Nana Yesu*. After reflecting on this, he raises several points that shed further light on our study of Justin Martyr. First, Bediako asks if *Nana Yesu* is a modern equivalent to the apostle John's or Justin Martyr's reference to Jesus the *logos*. He asks, "Can the reality and actuality of Jesus as intended in the Christian affirmation inhabit the Akan world of *nana* in the same way that it could inhabit the Greek world of *logos*?"[14] In other words, was the apostle John inspired to utilize the *logos* concept not only in order to communicate the reality of Jesus to the Greek world, but also to model a hermeneutic or interpretive method that can, by extension, be applied to other languages and cultures as the church spreads around the world? If so, John's use of the *logos* is not only a sign of the cultural translatability of the gospel in its own right, but it is actually helping to train Christians to be better missionaries and communicators as they seek to bring the gospel to every ethnic group in the world. In short, does John's imaginative use of *logos* provide

14. Kwame Bediako, "The Doctrine of Christ and the Significance of Vernacular Terminology," *International Bulletin of Missionary Research* 22, no. 3 (July 1998): 110. Bediako's book comparing issues in the second century with issues in contemporary Africa is titled *Theology and Identity: The Impact of Culture upon Christian Thought in the Second Century and in Modern Africa* (Oxford: Regnum, 1992).

the theological support for Bediako's encouragement for Ghanians to pray to *Nana Yesu?*

Bediako compares titles such as Word *(logos),* which in John and Justin's usage have at least a partially secular origin, with titles such as Messiah, which are rooted fully within the historic revelation of God in the Old Testament. He asks if the titles in this latter category are "more biblical in view of the prehistory of the first in Greek philosophy?"[15] If they are, does that restrict the application of these titles to an explicitly Christian context? For example, Christians widely accept that Jesus fulfills the Jewish expectation for a coming Messiah, and therefore it is appropriate to refer to Jesus as the Christ, which means Messiah. However, can Christians also refer to him as Jesus *logos* because he fulfills the highest ethical aspirations of Middle Platonism's use of *logos* as well as the ethical application of *logos* by the Stoics? If John's use of *logos* makes this acceptable, then can we also refer to Jesus as Ancestor Jesus? And then, following Justin, can we take the next step and declare that present in African ancestor worship are the seeds of the *logos* that Christ completes and fulfills? Is the term *ancestor* just another fragment of the many truths that are shadows of the fulfillment in the whole *logos,* Christ? Can Christ be spoken of as the true Ancestor who alone guards his people and who alone finally speaks words of guidance to the community, thereby fulfilling the noblest aspirations of the ancestors?

Second, Bediako observed that although many Ghanians prayed to *Nana Yesu,* rarely, if ever, would that same Ghanian pray in English to Ancestor Jesus or Chief Jesus.[16] This is because even though the term *nana* does correspond to the English category expressed by the term *ancestor,* it is also a personal name. It functions as both a name and a title in the Akan language. The designation Jesus Christ is, of course, a combination of a personal name, Jesus, and a Jewish title, Messiah. Thus, the Jews were joining together the name of Jesus with a particular title, Messiah. Likewise, John and Justin were linking the name of Jesus to another title, *Logos.* However, is it appropriate to link the name of Jesus not only to a title, which expresses his fulfillment of some category of human thought like the salvific concept Messiah or the philosophical concept of *logos,* but also with a personal name? The Ghanians transferred the name Nana to Jesus, not just the title. There are important differences between the connotations surrounding a name versus those associated with a title.

Application to World Religions: Islam

This conversation with the apostle John, Justin Martyr, and Kwame Bediako is far more than a historical and exegetical debate. It has specific appli-

15. Kwame Bediako, "The Doctrine of Christ," 110.
16. Ibid.

cation to our ongoing contemporary conversations with the major non-Christian religions. Christians are frequently asked if Muslims and Christians worship the same God. Put another way, are the words *Allah* and *God* interchangeable? The word *God* is a title or concept but not a personal name.[17] The word *Allah,* on the other hand, functions among Muslims as both a title and a personal name. Therefore, the question, if it is to be answered thoughtfully, must be addressed at three distinct levels: linguistic, revelational, and positional.

Linguistic Level

First, speaking linguistically, the terms are semantically identical and are therefore completely interchangeable. The etymological origin of *Allah* is the same as *el,* the Hebrew word for God.[18] Thus, if someone asks whether the Arabic word *Allah* properly corresponds to the English word *God,* the answer is yes. In other words, *Allah* is the Arabic translation of the English word *God.* This is why it is not surprising to find Christians throughout the Arabic-speaking countries of the world addressing God as Allah. Indeed, the word *Allah* as a divine designation in Arabic precedes the rise of the Islamic faith in the seventh century.

Revelational Level

However, there is a second level on which this question functions. Frequently, a person who asks about the relationship of the terms *Allah* and *God* is asking with specific reference to Allah as understood by Islam and God as understood by Christians. This is undoubtedly more than a linguistic question; it is a question about the corresponding attributes of the Allah of the Qurʾān and the God of the Bible. This addresses the question revelationally. This question should not be addressed to linguists, but to theologians. From this perspective, a careful study of the Qurʾān and the Bible will reveal that there are considerable areas of overlap between the Allah of the Qurʾān and the God of the Bible. For example, both Allah and God are compassionate and merciful. Both Allah and God created the world and continue to sustain it.

Nevertheless, speaking revelationally, it must be said that the terms are not completely interchangeable. Indeed, the specifics of revelation are at times completely incompatible. For example, Allah did not and cannot become incarnate, whereas in the New Testament God did become incarnate in Jesus Christ. In the New Testament, God is by nature triune; in the Qurʾān, Allah is not. In this respect, how can one identify the God who be-

17. Moses knew the Hebrew word for God—*el*—before his encounter at the burning bush. It was at the burning bush that God revealed his name, YHWH.

18. The word *Allah* is probably derived from *illah,* the past-participle of the verb *ilaho,* "to worship." See Norman Geisler and Abdul Saleeb, *Answering Islam: The Crescent in the Light of the Cross* (Grand Rapids: Baker, 1993), 14.

came incarnate with the God who did not and cannot become incarnate? Robert Jenson has correctly pointed out that the doctrine of the Trinity is the Christian attempt to spell out the identity of God in order to avoid confusion with rival claims to the title.[19] Attempts to identify God with Allah at the revelational level are made only when religious and theological language is reduced to convey human expressions about the meaning of the words to us without any assurance that they correspond to ultimate reality. If revelation in the Bible and in the Qurʾān is taken seriously by the adherents of Christianity and Islam respectively, then we cannot gloss over the important differences in revelation, even as we affirm those areas where there is agreement.

Positional Level

Finally, the question about God and Allah can, at times, operate at a positional level. From this perspective, it is not a question of linguistics or revelation per se, but a question about the Islamic person who worships Allah and the Christian person who worships God. I have heard both Muslims and Christians say with regularity that we all worship the same God. Do these two worshippers stand equally before God/Allah as reconciled, forgiven people? When a Muslim cries out "Allāhu Akbar!" (God is Great!) or a Christian cries out, "Praise God!" what is his or her relative position before God/Allah?

Both Islam and Christianity insist that a person outside the realm of true revelation stands in a position of discontinuity. From the Islamic point of view, a Christian who cries out (even in Arabic) "Allāhu Akbar!" is still a member of a community that has "gone astray" (sūrah 1:7).[20] From the Christian point of view, God (or in the mouth of an Arabic-speaking Christian, Allah) is the "Father of our Lord Jesus Christ." The positional discontinuity is further confirmed in the New Testament when John says that "no one who denies the Son has the Father" (1 John 2:23). In this sense, because the Muslim does not know the Father and, from the Islamic point of view, the Christian does not know the true revelation of Allah, they each regard the other as standing in a position of profound discontinuity. One worshipper is experiencing God's favor, the other stands in need of reconciliation.

19. Robert Jenson, *The Triune Identity* (Philadelphia: Fortress, 1982), 1–20.

20. This is taken from the famous *Al-Fatihah* or "the Opening," which forms the first sūrah of the Qurʾān and is referred to as the seven often repeated verses. The seventh āya is widely believed to express the division of humanity into three groups: "those whom Thou hast favored" (Muslims); "those who earn Thine anger" (people without revelation or infidels who have rejected Islam); and "those who go astray" (People of the Book, namely Jews and Christians, who have received revelation but have not yet accepted the straight path of Islam). The Qurʾān clearly rejects the exclusivity of the Christian message. See, for example, sūrah 2:105f.

Allah As Concept, Title, and Personal Name

Despite these differences, it is normal even in evangelical literature to identify, without qualification, God and Allah. For example, in *Answering Islam* by Norman Geisler and Abdul Saleeb, the authors state, "Allah is the personal name for God in Islam. We make no distinction in this book, as some do, between the word 'Allah' and the English word 'God'."[21] After stating that Allah is the personal name for God in Islam (revelational level) and that we all worship the God of Abraham (positional level), they go on to support their position with a discussion on the etymology of the word Allah (linguistic level). The linguistic evidence is important, but remember that it does not address the word *Allah* as a personal name within a particular religion known as Islam nor does it take into account the relative position of the worshipper who stands before Allah.[22] After all, the linguistic point applies equally to those Christians who have used the word *Allah* for centuries quite apart from it being a personal name for God in Islam.

Geisler and Saleeb offer further support by quoting the respected Islamicist Kenneth Cragg, who states that Muslims and Christians "are obviously referring when they speak of him, *under whatever terms,* to the same Being."[23] The phrase "under whatever terms" causes me to wonder if the case for total identity is being overstated. Cragg points out that the common reference is based on the fact that both Islam and Christianity "believe in one, Supreme, Sovereign, Creator-God."[24] This is a clear reference to revelation, not to etymology or linguistics. Cragg has pointed out the areas of continuity within the revelation, but he has been silent about other equally important areas of revelation—such as the Trinity, the incarnation, and the atonement—where there is discontinuity. Thus, even if we agree with the conclusion of Geisler and Saleeb, we must be certain that we are clearly defending the position without confusing the scope and intent of the question from the actual meaning of our answer.

Undoubtedly, this issue deserves more careful scrutiny. In order to stimulate ongoing discussion in this area, a few more points should be noted. First, the association of a particular designation for God within a language group dominated by a world religion makes it nearly impossible to restrict discussion to the linguistic level. This is why Muhammad Pickthall's English translation of the Qurʾān makes the following point

21. Geisler and Saleeb, *Answering Islam,* 13.

22. Geisler and Saleeb quote Ajijola, a Muslim author, who states that the difference between *illah* and *Allah* is that the latter is the "essential *personal name* of God" (emphasis added). This is the intent of the confession of faith that says, "There is no god but Allah." Geisler and Saleeb, *Answering Islam,* 14–15.

23. Ibid., 14, emphasis added.

24. Ibid.

about his retaining the word *Allah:* "I have retained the word Allah throughout, because there is *no corresponding word in English.*"[25]

Second, the difference between Allah as a title or concept and Allah as a personal name is an important distinction that must be addressed. Indeed, Pickthall and other Islamic authors will not identify the English word *God* with the Arabic word *Allah* because for them, Allah is not just a concept, but a personal name. The term is associated with the revelation of the Qur'ān and Islamic worshippers (revelational and positional levels). In short, the Arabic use of the word *Allah* is actually quite similar to what Bediako observed among the people of Ghana in reference to *nana.* For those who see the Arabic word *Allah* as a concept or title, the word poses no difficulty for usage in the life of prayer, worship, and liturgy. However, those who identify the term *Allah* with the particular theology of the Qur'ān and with Muslim views of Allah find identification with the English word *God* very difficult, indeed.

Finally, when Muslims come to faith in Christ, the vast majority continue to pray to and worship Allah. However, the Allah who is the object of their worship is now the "God and Father of our Lord Jesus Christ." Allah is a Triune God. This is, perhaps, the most important argument for identifying Allah with God. From the perspective of Muslim converts to Christianity, it is not so much that Islamic revelation must be rejected as supplemented by the truths of the Christian gospel. For them, the case for identity seems axiomatic. By accepting Christ, the Muslim views Allah with no less continuity than the first-century Jews who worshipped Yahweh as the Father of our Lord Jesus Christ, whom he sent into the world. However, this identity has little to do with the etymology of the words but with the newly enhanced revelation which removes the tension that previously existed at the revelational and positional levels.

Conclusion

It is clear that our dialogue with figures from church history has opened up new vistas of discussion and areas of much-neglected dialogue. The study of Justin Martyr raises vital questions about the presence of God working among and preparing peoples to receive the gospel. The possible application of Justin's *logos* theology to contemporary Africa or to a major world religion like Islam should continue to demand our attention and reflection. We need to continue our dialogue to further clarify our positions in areas of both identity and discontinuity. This case study has provided historical dialogue that has opened up an important theme for discussion. The following questions may help to further stimulate discussion and reflection on this case study.

25. Muhammad Marmaduke Pickthall, trans., *The Glorious Qur'ān* (Mecca: Muslim World League, 1977), 1, emphasis added.

Questions for Further Discussion and Reflection

1. How is Justin Martyr's view of the *logos*'s activity in the life of Socrates similar to and/or different from the kind of anonymous Christianity advocated by many modern-day inclusivists influenced by Karl Rahner? (See chapter 1 for the discussion and critique of inclusivism and anonymous Christianity.)
2. What is the difference between Justin Martyr's view of *logos spermatikos* and the concept of general revelation?
3. How important is it for people groups who do not have any background in Judaism to become acquainted with Jewish expectations that are fulfilled in Jesus? Does Jesus the Messiah, for example, have priority over Jesus the *logos?* If so, should Bible translators working in a new language group start with the Old Testament before they translate the New Testament? In your view, is Justin utilizing the Greek word *logos* primarily to connect his non-Jewish readers to the Jewish background of the all-pervading presence and power of God's Word as is seen in Genesis 1, or is he directly linking the Greek concept of *logos* to Christ without a significant reference to the Jewish context?
4. Is the apostle John's use of *logos* in the prologue to his Gospel merely an inspired demonstration of Christ's fulfillment of both Jewish and Greek expectations, or is he also providing a hermeneutical tool that can, by extension, be applied to aspirations in non-Jewish cultures? Could, for example, John's hermeneutic be applied to Islam, which like Greek philosophy, has led thousands of people out of idolatry and idol worship and oriented them toward monotheism? Could Islam serve as a massive *preparatio evangelica* for the gospel? Rather than opposing Islam, should we be thankful to God for it and merely try to complete what is lacking in that faith?
5. How important is it to relate Christ to a culture's past? The mission historian Andrew Walls has reminded us of how important it is to demonstrate that the gospel relates to someone's past, not just his or her future. Early Jewish missionaries understood the continuity of their Jewish past with their Christian future. Those of us who have grown up as second-, third-, or even fourth-generation Christians understand our present Christian life in the context of our past. But what about Africans from a traditional African background or Muslims who come to Christ in a family that has been Muslim for many generations? They face what Andrew Walls calls a "religious identity crisis." Walls goes on to explain: "It is our past which tells us who we are; without our past we are lost. The man with amnesia is lost, unsure of relationships, incapable of crucial decisions, precisely because all the time he has amnesia he is without his past."[26] Justin Mar-

26. Andrew Walls, *The Missionary Movement in Christian History: Studies in the Transmission of Faith,* (Maryknoll, N.Y.: Orbis, 1996), 13.

tyr was trying to help non-Jews with a Greek background to find Christ in their past as they embraced the fullness of the *logos* for their future. Can Christ likewise be found in the African past or the Islamic past? In your view, how important is this kind of theological reflection? Is this theological attempt to find continuity with the past actually robbing the gospel of its distinctive claim as a radical rescue "from the dominion of darkness" into the kingdom of Jesus Christ (Col. 1:13), or is it a bridge by which unbelievers can cross over into Christ's kingdom?

6. Is there an important difference between identifying Christ with a title that reflects a noble human category and a name of a non-Christian deity? In other words, is there an important distinction between the affirmation that Christ fulfills the noblest aspirations of concepts like justice and mercy (e.g., Christ the judge; Christ the merciful one) and the affirmation that Christ fulfills the worship of a particular deity in an African pantheon who may embody or exemplify some of those same attributes?

9

Can the Hindu Upanishads Help Us Explain the Trinity?

A Study of Brahmabandhav Upadhyay's Use of Saccidānanda

This second case study focuses on the work of Brahmabandhav Upadhyay, the nineteenth-century convert from Hinduism who has been called the father of Indian Christian theology. Since many readers will be unfamiliar with Brahmabandhav Upadhyay, I will begin with a brief overview of his life and work, followed by a case study focusing on Upadhyay's attempt to communicate the doctrine of the Trinity to Hindus using the language and thought forms of the Upanishads.[1]

Overview of the Life of Brahmabandhav Upadhyay

Brahmabandhav Upadhyay (1861–1907) was born Bhavani Charan Banerjea into a Bengali Brahmin family. In 1887, he was formally initiated into the Brāhmo Samāj, a Hindu reform movement founded by Ram Mohan Roy (1772–1833). In keeping with the vision of the society, Upadhyay worked hard during his years with the Brāhmo Samāj to promote a version of Hinduism that was more consistent with monotheism. However, during this pe-

1. For a comprehensive study of the theology of Brahmabandhav Upadhyay, see Timothy Tennent, *Building Christianity on Indian Foundations: The Legacy of Brahmabandhav Upadhyay* (Delhi: ISPCK, 2000).

riod he became increasingly attracted to the uniqueness of Christ, and on February 26, 1891, he received Christian baptism, though he did not formally unite with the Catholic Church until September 1891. In 1894, he declared himself a *sannyāsin* (world renouncer)[2], and thereafter he was known as Brahmabandhav Upadhyay.[3] Upadhyay's conversion to Christianity marks the beginning of a series of journalistic efforts to demonstrate how Christian theology, particularly neo-Thomist thought, was compatible with indigenous thought forms in India. His writings are contained in several journals he founded, including *Sophia, The Twentieth Century,* and *Sandhya.*

Upadhyay was dismayed at the inability of Christianity to flourish in India. He once described Christianity in India as "standing in the corner, like an exotic stunted plant with poor foliage, showing little or no promise of blossom."[4] He decided to dedicate his life to a non-Western expression of Christianity that was fully Indian. Over the course of his life, he made three major attempts to discover an appropriate foundation upon which the gospel could effectively take root and flourish in India. First, he attempted to construct a Christian proclamation on the foundation of natural theology based on general revelation and the universal knowledge of God that is present among all people. However, deficiencies in this foundation led him to reexamine the possibility of using the language and thought forms of Hindu philosophy as a more appropriate foundation for establishing Christian thought in India.

Upadhyay observed how Thomas Aquinas had boldly adopted the Aristotelian system of philosophy and effectively used it as the basis for constructing a Christian theology and philosophy which, in time, came to dominate the Middle Ages. Why, he reasoned, "should we Catholics of India now wage a destructive warfare with Hindu philosophy?" Alternatively, he argued, we should "look upon it in the same way as St. Thomas looked upon the Aristotelian system." He then declared,

> We are of the opinion that attempts should be made to win over Hindu philosophy to the service of Christianity just as Greek philosophy was won over in the Middle Ages. . . . The task is beset with many dangers. But we have a conviction and it is growing day by day, that the Catholic church will find it hard to conquer India unless she makes Hindu philosophy hew wood and draw water for her.[5]

2. In traditional Hinduism, life has four idealized stages: student, householder, meditating forest dweller, and world renouncer.

3. It was customary for Brahmin teachers to take a new name consistent with their life work. The word *Brahmabandhav* is the Sanskrit equivalent of the Greek name Theophilus, meaning "lover of God." His surname, Upadhyay, means "teacher."

4. As quoted in B. Animanada, *The Blade* (Calcutta: Roy and Son, 1947), appendix 1, i.

5. *Sophia: A Monthly Catholic Journal* 4, no. 7 (July 1897): 8–9.

Upadhyay was convinced that the eighth-century Hindu philosopher Śaṅkara (discussed in chapters 2 and 3) could serve Christianity in India the way Aristotle served Aquinas. This project consumes much of Upadhyay's writing during the next four years. His writings concerning the Trinity that emerge during this period will be the focus of this case study.

While Upadhyay never abandoned his desire to establish a philosophical foundation for Christianity in India, he did come to realize that many Indians who were committed to popular, village Hinduism did not respond to the sublime philosophy of the Upanishads. Thus, in his later years he attempted to find ways to build Christianity on a third foundation of Indian culture through a Christian interpretation of such common cultural practices as the caste system, idol worship, and the four life stages. His attempt to affirm the value of India's cultural heritage eventually placed him as a leader of India's nationalistic movement. He has the distinction of being the first Indian to call publicly for complete independence from Britain. In fact, his writings were considered sufficiently seditious by the British to warrant his arrest and imprisonment. He continued his protest from prison. However, while his trial was still going on, Upadhyay fell ill and was rushed to the hospital where he received a successful hernia operation. Tragically, he developed a tetanus infection and died on October 27, 1907. Despite his untimely death, he left behind a remarkable collection of journalistic writings that continue to influence the debate concerning the relationship between Hinduism and Christianity. This case study will focus on only one aspect of his work, namely, his attempt to communicate the doctrine of the Trinity by using the language of the Upanishads and the advaitic philosophy of Vedantic Hinduism.

Understanding the Problem: The Classic Trinitarian Formulation and the Indian Context

The orthodox doctrine of the Trinity was formulated in response to heretical ideas such as modalism and Arianism. The Council of Constantinople in 381 issued an explicit statement of the Trinity to articulate the beliefs that had been implicitly held by the church until that time. As discussed several times in the course of our dialogues, the key formula is the affirmation that there is "one essence *(ousia)* in three eternal distinctions/persons *(hypostasis)*." All Western formulations that emerged in the centuries that followed were based on the Constantinople statement. Perhaps the most famous is the Westminster Confession, formulated in the seventeenth century to provide doctrinal guidance for the church in the newly united kingdom of England and Scotland. The following statement concerning the Trinity was issued, clearly reflecting the orthodoxy of Constantinople:

> In the unity of the Godhead there be three persons, of one substance, power, and eternity; God the Father, God the Son, and God the Holy

> Ghost. The Father is of none, neither begotten nor proceeding; the Son is eternally begotten of the Father; the Holy Ghost eternally proceeding from the Father and the Son.[6]

There are four technical terms in this brief statement: *person, substance, begotten,* and *proceeding.* All these terms are immensely difficult to translate into Indian languages with the necessary precision. The word *person,* for example, is often translated as "individual," which it cannot mean in the orthodox statement. The word *begotten* will invariably utilize a word with sexual connotations. The word *substance* is often translated as something solid and material, which is not what was meant by the Greek word *ousia.*[7] The word *proceeding* is invoked because of a longstanding theological and philosophical debate between the Eastern and Western branches of the church. It is an important debate, but one in which the Indian church has not participated, so the terminology seems alien to them. In short, the orthodox formulations can be translated into Indian languages, but truly capturing the essence and heart of the formulation is exceedingly difficult.

Brahmabandhav Upadhyay recognizes this problem and attempts to restate the same truths, capturing the essence of the Constantinople formulation but using language and thought forms more familiar to Indians. For Westerners, many of the terms and concepts utilized by Upadhyay may be strange. Nevertheless, Upadhyay is writing as an Indian for other Indians, and he is seeking to convey the Trinity in language and terms they will understand. He does this through a restatement of Trinitarianism, using as his starting point the Upanishadic and philosophic doctrine of *saccidānanda.*

God As Saccidānanda: A Restatement of Trinitarianism

In the later Upanishads, it is not uncommon to find Brāhman described as *sat* (being or reality), *cit* (intelligence or consciousness), and *ānanda* (bliss).[8] Thus, sat, cit, and ānanda—often designated by the term *saccidānanda*—are widely regarded as the most complete description of Brāhman in all of Hindu sacred literature.[9] In light of our conversation in chapter 2, it

6. Westminster Confession 2.3. For a full text of the Westminster Confession, see Robert L. Dabney, *The Westminster Confession and Creeds* (Dallas: Presbyterian Heritage, 1983).

7. For a full exposition of the problems of translating Latin doctrinal formulations into the Indian context, see the excellent book by Robin Boyd, *India and the Latin Captivity of the Church* (Cambridge: Cambridge University Press, 1974).

8. *Vajrasucika Upanishad,* 9, in S. Radhakrishnan, ed., *The Principal Upanishads* (Delhi: Harper Collins, 1996), 937–38.

9. Saccidānanda is a religious formula similar to an *ādeśa,* a compact presentation of truth often contained in a single word or phrase that summarizes the essence of a teaching. The formula saccidānanda does not appear in the earlier Upanishads, but it was used by later Vedantists to summarize the essence of Upanishadic teaching regarding the Absolute as sat, cit, and ānanda.

is significant that the saccidānanda formula is believed to apply even to nirguṇa Brāhman.

The first Indian theologian to identify saccidānanda with the Christian Trinity was Upadhyay's mentor, Keshab Chandra Sen. Sen used the picture of a triangle with Brāhman of the Vedas at the apex. Brāhman descends down as the Son, and moving along the base of the triangle represents his permeation of the world. Finally, by the power of the Holy Spirit, he returns to the apex carrying degenerated humanity with him: the Still God, the Journeying God, the Returning God; Truth, Intelligence, and Joy.[10] However, this is only a first step, a bare sketch in terms of any comprehensive identification of the two great doctrines of saccidānanda and Trinity. Sen's conception of the Trinity was modalistic and therefore could not serve as an effective model for the Christian Trinity.[11] It is Upadhyay who provided the first detailed analysis of how the two doctrines could relate to one another without compromising Christian orthodoxy. Upadhyay sought to restate the Trinity in a way that utilized the Upanishadic categories but was faithful to the historic Christian position regarding the Trinity. The various components Upadhyay uses to construct this doctrine will now be examined.

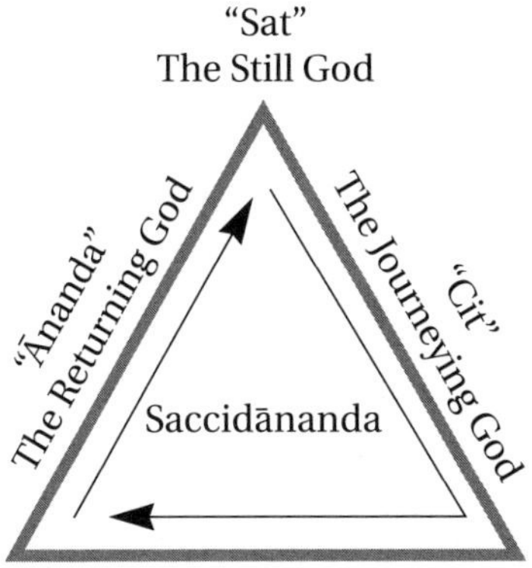

Internal Knowledge/Relationship within Sat, Cit, and Ānanda

Upadhyay begins by arguing that the threefold distinction within the Upanishads of sat, cit, and ānanda points to internal knowledge and relationships within the Godhead.

10. Peter May, "The Trinity and Saccidānanda," *Indian Journal of Theology* 7, no. 3 (July–September 1958), 94. See also David Scott, ed, *Keshub Chunder Sen* (Madras: CLS, 1979), 220–29.

11. Modalism refers to the ancient heresy of rejecting the three eternal distinctions in the Godhead and instead viewing the Father, Son, and Holy Spirit as three, successive manifestations of the one God. According to modalism, God has revealed himself in three names only. Sen also failed to relate the Trinity to nirguṇa Brāhman, only to precedents within Hindu literature identified with saguṇa Brāhman.

If, for example, God is cit (intelligence) as the Upanishads claim, then he must necessarily know himself. To this end, "He must form to himself an inward word or image through which this self-knowledge is effected." However, the difference between the inner images we form and that of the Supreme Being is that our images are "accidental and transitory." For God nothing can be accidental or transitory. Therefore,

> His eternal self-comprehension or word is to be conceived as identical with the divine nature and still as distinct from the Supreme Being in as far as he by comprehending himself generates his word. God, knowing himself by producing or generating his own image and word, is called Father; and God as known by himself by this inward generation of the word is called the Word or the Son.[12]

This inner relation must be carefully distinguished from any necessary relationship external to God. Upadhyay writes, "The Supreme Being is absolute; he is beyond all *necessary* relationship with any object external to himself."[13] Thus, God has an eternal, necessary relationship within himself; all relationships outside of himself are not necessary but contingent (*vyavahārika*).[14] The idea of relating the relationship between sat, cit, and ānanda to the internal mystery of the three persons of the Trinity is completely unique to Upadhyay and becomes the basic hermeneutic from which his whole argument proceeds.

This argument by Upadhyay is clearly an application of scholastic Thomism to the Indian context. However, Upadhyay is not trying to explain the doctrine of the Trinity through reason alone. He says that the doctrine of the Trinity is a truth "which man can never find out but [is] revealed by God himself or through his infallible messengers."[15] In other words, Upadhyay believes that the revelation of God extends beyond the Bible, because he sees fragments of divine revelation present in the indigenous scriptures of India. It is unclear whether Justin Martyr or Upadhyay himself would classify these as examples of general revelation or as more profound examples of the *logos spermatikos*. Nevertheless, Upadhyay does argue along lines similar to Justin Martyr in that whenever he finds the Upanishads agreeing

12. *Sophia Monthly* 2, no. 4 (April 1895): 11. This is a summary of the position of "the Editor of *Sophia*" (Upadhyay) as found in an article by A. Heglin titled "One God and Three Persons." Similar statements may be found in Upadhyay's own writings, but this gives some insight into the early support, encouragement, and written defense that he received in the early years from the Jesuit community in India.

13. *Sophia Monthly* 3, no. 2 (February 1896): 5, Upadhyay's emphasis.

14. *Sophia Monthly* 4, no. 8 (August 1897): 9.

15. *Sophia Monthly* 3, no. 3 (March 1896): 4. In another article, Upadhyay writes of "the wonderful fitness of the Christian doctrine of the Trinity [which] illumines the darkness of that abode where dwells the Absolute in light inaccessible, [and] where human reason gets dazzled and blinded." See *Sophia Monthly* 4, no. 8 (August 1897): 9.

with Christian theology, he credits it as a fragment of revelation. Whenever the text seems to contradict Christian theology, he argues it is because they did not have the full revelation. This becomes more evident as we explore the full development of his theology of the Trinity as expressed through the doctrine of saccidānanda.

God As Sat, Cit, and Ānanda

By December 1897, Upadhyay is convinced that seeds of the Trinity are present in the Upanishads. He credits the Vedantic philosophers with soaring so high as to "peep into the Essence of God [and] to contemplate His interior life."[16] What they realized is that God could not go outside himself to satisfy his infinite knowledge and bliss. If he did, he would not be absolute (asaṅga) and unrelated (nirguṇa). However, rather than recognize the internal relatedness of the Godhead, the philosophers either denied the reality of anything external to God or declared that it was a mystery too great for the "undeveloped intellects of the common people . . . who must be satisfied with stocks and stones."[17] For Upadhyay, this is the source of the idolatry that stands in stark contrast to the sublime heights the Vedantic philosophers scaled.

Upadhyay's understanding of advaitic Vedantism is profoundly influenced by his reading and study of the fourteenth-century neo-Vedantic teaching manual, *Pañcadaśī*, by Vidyaranya.[18] The *Pañcadaśī* contains fifteen chapters divided into three sections known as quintads. Broadly speaking, "The three quintads have for their theme the three aspects of Brāhman, *sat* (existence), *cit* (consciousness) and *ānanda* (bliss)."[19] Characteristic of Upadhyay's own theological approach, the *Pañcadaśī* builds Vedantic revelation on the foundation of human reason, including the insight of Brāhman as saccidānanda.

16. *Sophia Monthly* 4, no. 12 (December 1897): 2.

17. Ibid. This also sheds light on why Upadhyay was unwilling to move closer to Rāmānuja's position which, for his point of view, gives too much credence to the crude, exoteric worship of village Hinduism. *Stock* is a nineteenth-century term for a block of wood.

18. For a modern English translation of the *Pañcadaśī*, see T. M. P. Mahadevan, trans., *Pañcadaśī* (Madras: Sri Ramakrishna Math, 1967). Upadhyay even attempted his own translation and verse-by-verse exposition of the *Pañcadaśī*, a portion of which was published in 1902. It is not known for certain how much of the *Pañcadaśī* he completed, as only the first fourteen verses (with commentary) are found in the Goethal Library archives at St. Xavier's College in Calcutta. Unfortunately, the only extant copy stops in the middle of a sentence in his exposition of chapter 1, verse 14. However, even in the small selection that is available, Upadhyay clearly sets out his understanding that the three divisions of the *Pañcadaśī* correspond to the three aspects of being: sat, cit, and ānanda.

19. T. M. P. Mahadevan, *Pañcadaśī*, ix. This is an editorial comment by Mahadevan, who goes on to emphasize that though the three quintads carry these three themes, all three sections carry the essential teachings of Vedantism and reflect the common repetitious nature of this kind of teaching manual.

Adopting the *Pañcadaśī's* threefold framework of God as sat, cit, and ānanda, Upadhyay uses it as the basis for his Trinitarian theology. His application of this theology to each of the three persons of the Trinity will now be explored.

God the Father As Sat

In his journal *Sophia Weekly,* Upadhyay launched a five-week series to demonstrate the philosophical underpinnings of his thought. Upadhyay argues that Descartes' famous *cogito ergo sum* (I think, therefore I am) is "beset with innumerable dangers" because it makes "human thought the measure of existence." Instead, Upadhyay argues for *ens est ergo cogito* (Being is, therefore I think).[20] If Being is not posited first, then one risks falling into what Upadhyay called the abyss of nothingness and emptiness, an almost certain reference to Buddhism. For Upadhyay, "Being is the ultimate foundation of all certitude, the foundation of thinking." Only God can be truly called sat, that is, existence by itself that is eternal, immutable, and infinite. All other being has only a borrowed or contingent existence, enduring in time, and both mutable and limited. To deny that true Being is self-existent "is to affirm that being and non-being are identical."[21]

For Upadhyay, Being (sat) implies not only relatedness, as explored earlier, but it also implies action. Two questions arise: What does an infinite, self-existent, eternal being act upon? How does it act? First, any form of dualism or polytheism is self-destructive, argues Upadhyay, because "there can be only one self-existence; there is no room for a separate, co-eternal recipient of its influence," which is external to the self-existent being. Thus, the action must be necessarily inward, that is, within its own self-existent being, without ruling out the possibility of action with and upon contingently related finite beings. Second, the only way a self-existent being can act upon itself is through knowledge and intelligence. Its action is self-knowledge: "The result of its self-act is an eternal distinction between its knowing self and known self without any division in the substance."[22] Thus, the presence of sat necessarily involves a self-related cit.

God the Son As Cit

We have already demonstrated that, for Upadhyay, the object of God's knowledge is God. The consciousness (cit) of God must, of necessity, be distinguishable from the subject (sat) because, he reasons, "A being cannot stand in *relation* to its *identical* self."[23] Yet, as has also been demonstrated, God cannot go outside himself for any necessary relations. Thus, Upadhyay

20. *Sophia: A Weekly Review of Politics, Sociology, Literature and Comparative Theology,* n.s., 1, no. 2 (23 June 1900): 8.

21. Ibid.

22. *Sophia Weekly,* n.s., 1, no. 7 (28 July 1900): 7.

23. *The Twentieth Century: A Monthly Review* 1, no. 1 (January 1901): 6–7.

argues, there must be a "relation of reciprocity" without any division in the divine substance. This, according to revelation, is precisely what the Trinity provides: "God begets in thought his infinite Self-Image and reposes on it with infinite delight while the begotten Self acknowledges responsively his eternal thought-generation."[24] Without compromising the unity of the absolute, there is, nevertheless, a "variety of cognition and re-cognition, the subject and the object corresponding with each other in knowledge."[25] Upadhyay has now established the ontological basis for the Second Person of the Trinity in a way consistent with advaitic thought.[26]

God the Holy Spirit As Ānanda

The third radical making up the doctrine of saccidānanda is the term *ānanda,* translated as bliss or joy. Ānanda as joy or bliss sounds strange to the Western ear until we recognize that it seals the internal joy of the Triune Godhead apart from any external relationships, or, to use Upadhyay's phrase, it celebrates "the beatitude of triple colloquy."[27] All other sources of joy outside the Godhead must stand in a contingent relationship to his eternal joy, lest the doctrine erode the doctrine of God as asaṅga (absolute). Upadhyay's development of ānanda emphasizes three main areas. First, he seeks to demonstrate how ānanda confirms the unrelated nature of the Absolute.[28] Second, he seeks to make clear that ānanda is a person, a third eternal distinction within the Godhead. Third, ānanda protects the doctrine of God from slipping into a rationalistic abstraction, but it clarifies that the Christian God is one who, out of joy, does enter into direct, personal relations with humanity.

To begin with, Upadhyay defines bliss (ānanda) as "the complacent repose of a being upon its own self or its like."[29] He makes an important distinction between the Upanishadic use of ānanda as a description of the Absolute, as opposed to vijñāna. He argues that vijñāna "cognises [sic] self through not-self," which implies that the Supreme Being knows himself through relations outside his own eternal existence. The term *ānanda,* in contrast, implies that the infinite is "self-sufficient, self-satisfied and not de-

24. Ibid.

25. Ibid., 116.

26. Although space does not permit a full discussion of Upadhyay's development of the Son as cit, he seeks to establish it not only on epistemological grounds but also on religious grounds through the application of *logos* theology to the advaitic context and through a hymn of Christian worship to the Son of God using the language of Vedānta. For a full exposition and discussion of this advaitic hymn and the application of *logos* theology to the Indian context, see Tennent, *Building Christianity on Indian Foundations.*

27. *The Twentieth Century* 1, no. 1 (January 1901): 116.

28. As the discussion concerning ānanda will make clear, Upadhyay's initial emphasis on the unrelated nature of God only means that God is not related to his creation out of necessity.

29. *Sophia Weekly,* n.s., 1, no. 7 (28 July 1900): 6.

pendent upon relations which are not co-terminous with his substance."[30] For Upadhyay, any being that is "obliged to form alliance with something other than its own self cannot be *essentially* happy."[31]

Second, the three aspects of the Trinity are not qualities but eternal, personal distinctions within the one absolute Godhead. Indeed, as explored in chapter 2, one of the great mysteries of Hinduism is the relationship between the one and the many. Upadhyay seeks to demonstrate that this ānanda is distinct, yet one. The three eternal distinctions within the Godhead are not inconsistent with the unity of God. Upadhyay says, "*Sat, cit* and *ānanda* cannot be made to give up their distinctions though they are one in *Brāhman*."[32] Ānanda is distinct, yet it manifests "the infinitude of the Eternal Essence."[33]

Finally, Upadhyay is convinced that the Upanishadic summary of the essence of Brāhman as saccidānanda separates God from the mere abstraction of the rationalists. While Upadhyay repeatedly affirms God's self-sufficiency and independence, this does not mean that God is unknowable or unapproachable. In a review of a collection of sonnets titled *Naivedya*, Upadhyay writes:

> The keynote of the Sonnets is the direct, personal relation with the Infinite. There are some who argue that as the Infinite is not easily approachable, the finite should be worshipped tentatively as the Infinite by the less spiritually advanced. Is the Infinite really unapproachable? If it had been so, Reason would be an anomaly. The perception of the Infinite is the dawn of Reason.[34]

Upadhyay views creation itself as "an overflow of bliss *[ānanda]*." Vedānta teaches that "to know that the supreme being is bliss *[ānanda]* and that the creation of the world *[loka]* is an outflow of that bliss, is the culmination of divine science *[vidyā]*."[35] While it is not essential to God's nature, the multiplicity of personal relationships nevertheless occurs as an overflow

30. Julius Lipner and Gilbert Gispert-Sauch, eds., *The Writings of Brahmabāndhab Upādhyāy*, vol. 1 (Bangalore: UTC, 1991), 145. Upadhyay's identification of ānanda with reason is based on his study of the *Pañcadaśī*, which affirms that "inanimateness manifests his being, sentiency his intelligence and rationality his bliss" (Pañcadaśī 15:20–21). See *Sophia Weekly*, n.s., 1, no. 18:7. In *Sophia Monthly* 3, no. 2 (February 1896): 5. Upadhyay translates ānanda as "unalloyed joy" to reinforce that his joy is not related by necessity to any contingent being to make his joy complete or full.

31. *Sophia Monthly* 5, no. 8 (August 1898): 119. This clearly means that humans have no intrinsic or self-grounded ability to be joyful apart from a relationship with the living God.

32. *Twentieth Century* 1, no. 6 (June 1901): 12.

33. Ibid.

34. Animananda, *The Blade*, 101; see also Robin Boyd, *Introduction to Indian Christian Theology* (Delhi: ISPCK, 1994), 71.

35. As quoted in *Sophia Weekly*, n.s., 1, no. 7 (28 July 1900): 6.

or abundance. Upadhyay comments, "It is not a product of necessity, but of superabundance. But this overflow, this superabundance is a mystery which reason encounters at the very outset of religious enquiry."[36] God has endowed each person with a spiritual part or sheath *(ānandamāyā koṣa)*, which "enables him to become a passive recipient of Divine grace and joy."[37]

Upadhyay's development of God as sat, cit, and ānanda is one of the most significant of his theological contributions. It is a step toward a theological summary that, for Upadhyay, can harmonize a wide variety of theological strands, including Śaṅkara, Rāmānuja, and Aquinas. He considers the Vedantic concept of the Supreme Being to mark "the terminus of the flight of human reason into the eternal regions."[38] Its sublimity is the ultimate point where the great theological systems with which Upadhyay wrestles come together:

> Brāhman considered in himself is Being, Knowledge and Beatitude; but considered as *Īśvara* (Creator) he is Power, Wisdom and Love; and considered as the object of contemplation, he is Beauty, Truth and Goodness. . . . This is the teaching of the great St. Thomas. In it are harmonized the different schools of Vedantic philosophy. It is one with Śaṅkara in regard to the philosophy of the absolute being and its contingent relation to the finite; it agrees with Rāmānuja in enforcing the immortality of individual souls but avoids his error of making the infinite necessarily correlated to the finite.[39]

Ultimately, it is a mystery that can only be grasped via revelation. It is beyond human comprehension to understand how "God begets in thought his infinite Self-image and reposes on it with infinite delight," never losing "blissful communication and colloquy within the bosom of God-head" and without creating "any division in the divine Substance."[40]

Application to World Religions: Hinduism

Upadhyay's theology is explicitly and intentionally related to the particular demands of the Indian context, especially Hinduism. There is no better

36. *Sophia Weekly* n.s., 1, no. 8 (4 August 1900). A similar statement is found in Upadhyay's personal translation of a portion of the *Pañcadaśī*. He comments on verses 8 and 9 of the first chapter: "This eternal *Samvid* is bliss transcendent . . . it is its own object of supreme love. Its love of self is independent of its love of dependent objects; and its love for objects other than self proceed from super-abundance of its love of the self-object. It is not in need of being correlated with the finite for the purpose of maintaining its bliss. It is a pure self-act." See *Pañcadaśī*, translation with commentary by B. Upadhyay, 14, Goethal Library archives, St. Xavier's College, Calcutta.

37. *The Twentieth Century* 1, no. 1 (January 1901): 10.

38. *Sophia Monthly* 5, no. 1 (January 1898).

39. *Sophia Monthly* 6, no. 2 (February 1899): 228.

40. *Twentieth Century* 1, no. 1 (January 1901).

illustration of his application of Christian theology to the Indian context using the language of Vedānta than his Trinitarian hymn to saccidānanda.

Upadhyay's "Canticle to the Trinity" published in the pages of *Sophia Monthly* in October 1898, is widely regarded as a magnificent "gem of Christian hymnology."[41] It has also been cited as one of the most original contributions of Upadhyay to Indian Christian theology, combining ideas from the Christian Scriptures with Greek and Hindu sources in a unique work. Gispert-Sauch calls it the "best example of a deep adaptation of the Christian faith to the cultural patterns of Indian religious thought."[42] The hymn consists of a refrain and four stanzas. The first stanza develops the theme of the refrain, which is an adoration to the Trinity. The last three stanzas are dedicated to each of the three persons of the Trinity. The following is an English translation by Upadhyay that originally appeared in *Sophia Monthly:*

Refrain
(1) I adore:
The *Sat* (Being), *Cit* (Intelligence) and *Ānanda* (Bliss):
(2) The highest goal, which is despised by worldlings, which is desired by *yogis* (devotees).

Stanza One
(3) The supreme, ancient, higher than the highest, full, indivisible, transcendent and immanent.
(4) One having triple interior relationship, holy, unrelated, self-conscious, hard to realise.

Stanza Two
(5) The Father, Begetter, the highest Lord, unbegotten, the rootless principle of the tree of existence.
(6) The cause of the universe, one who createst intelligently, the preserver of the world.

Stanza Three
(7) The increate, infinite *Logos* or Word, supremely great.
(8) The Image of the Father, one whose form is intelligence, the giver of the highest freedom.

Stanza Four
(9) One who proceeds from the union of *Sat* and *Cit*, the blessed Spirit (breath), intense bliss.

41. G. Gispert-Sauch, "The Sanskrit Hymns of Brahmabandhav Upadhyay," *Religion and Society* 19, no. 4 (December 1972), 60.

42. G. Gispert-Sauch, "The Sanskrit Hymns of Brahmabandhav Upadhyay," *Religion and Society* 19, no. 4 (December 1972): 60. This hymn is also alluded to in Peter May, "The Trinity and *Saccidānanda*," *Indian Journal of Theology* 7, no. 3 (July–September 1958): 92–98.

(10) The sanctifier, one whose movements are swift, one who speaks of the Word, the life-giver.[43]

We will now carefully explore each stanza of the hymn in order to demonstrate how Upadhyay sought to contextualize the communication of the Trinity in the Indian context by using the language and thought forms of Vedānta.

The Refrain

Upadhyay's purpose is clearly to celebrate the Triune Godhead, using language that evokes an Indian (rather than a Greek or Latin) atmosphere. Indeed, the opening word of the hymn—*vande* ("I bow to" or "I adore")—would almost certainly evoke associations with the Indian nationalistic anthem, *Vande Mataram*. The word *vande* is the only verb in the entire hymn, the remainder of the hymn standing as the object of the verb "I adore." The rest of the refrain is the primary object of adoration, saccidānanda, the advaita equivalent to the Christian word *Trinity*. Neither word—*saccidānanda* or *Trinity*—appears in the primary documents of advaita (Classical Upanishads) or Christianity (New Testament) respectively. However, both serve as a *māhāvakya* (great utterance) or *ādeśa* (religious formula) summarizing the essence of advaitic or Christian teaching regarding the nature of God.

This summarizing utterance does not reflect qualities in the Absolute or composition of substance, but serves to "define . . . his very essence by an indirect signification *(lakṣaṇārtha)*" such that each term "completes the other" and "gives an aspect of the One Reality that remains without any internal division or composition."[44] Thus, the opening refrain is directed to the worship of God as he is in himself, pure, undifferentiated nirguṇa. The later stanzas explore, in part, how God has freely related himself to his creation.

The second line of the refrain tells us that he is "the highest goal" *(carama pada)*. The literal meaning of *carama pada* is "the last step." The language calls to mind one of the most well-known stories in Hindu literature, that of Viṣṇu and his three steps or *padas*. In the myth, Viṣṇu takes the form of a Brahmin dwarf during a time when all the world was controlled by demons. Viṣṇu approaches Bali, the lord of demons, and asks if he might give the dwarf the space he could cover in three strides. Bali grants the request only to watch as Viṣṇu assumes his cosmic form and in three strides steps over the earth, the sky, and the heaven, thus regaining the universe for the gods.[45]

43. *Sophia Monthly* 5, no. 10 (October 1898): 1–3. I am indebted to Father Gispert-Sauch in my analysis of this hymn. His publication "The Sanskrit Hymns of Brahmabandhav Upadhyay" and his willingness to meet with me in Delhi in the winter of 1997 to discuss Upadhyay's writings have helped me considerably.

44. Gispert-Sauch, "Sanskrit Hymns," 67.

45. Wendy O'Flaherty, ed., *Hindu Myths* (New York: Penguin, 1975), 175–79.

The expression *paramam padam* also appears in the *Kaṭha* Upanishad, which says, "He who has the understanding for the driver of the chariot and controls the rein of his mind, he reaches the *end of the journey,* that supreme abode of the all-pervading."[46] Thus, the verse celebrates that the Trinity or saccidānanda is the last step or end of the journey in one's understanding of the Godhead.

The second part of the last line of the refrain paradoxically declares that this last step is both despised and desired. The great unity of the Godhead nevertheless divides humanity because this truth is "despised by worldlings" *(bhogis)* who would rather follow sensuality and turn away from the last step, whereas "those who are for self-renunciation and self-control *(yogis)* accept it and yearn for it."[47] Upadhyay ingeniously brings out the division that the New Testament affirms is characteristic of the human response to God, yet he employs indigenous philosophical and mythological language to communicate the idea.

First Stanza to the Triune God

The first stanza develops the refrain and praises the Triune God in a way consistent with the Upanishadic tradition. Upadhyay uses adjectives and titles that are frequently given to Brāhman in the Upanishads, but here they refer to the Christian God. The alliteration of the description adds to the beauty as God is adored as *parama, purāṇa,* and *parātpara.* The first term means "supreme," the second means "Ancient of Days," and the third means "beyond the beyond" or "transcendent." All of these terms are found in the Upanishads as well as in popular Hindu literature.[48] This first line of the stanza celebrates the Triune transcendence. The second line underscores Christian and advaitic opposition to Buddhist śūnyā (emptiness) by emphasizing the fullness of the Triune God. The fullness of Brāhman is a recurring theme in the *Bṛhad-Āraṇyaka,* especially 5.1.1: "That is full, this is full. From fullness, fullness proceeds. If we take away the fullness of fullness, even fullness then

46. Radhakrishnan, *Principal Upanishads,* 624. Gispert-Sauch comments that Upadhyay ingeniously employs both philosophical language and mythological imagery in his hymn. The philosophical language gives the hymn lakṣaṇa power, that is, the power to imply meanings that are higher than the words designate, as well as *vyanjana* power, the power to touch religious attitudes and evoke resonances of popular meaning in the hearts of the devoted. See Gispert-Sauch, "Sanskrit Hymns," 69.

47. Gispert-Sauch, "Sanskrit Hymns," 69.

48. For *parama* see *Bṛhad-Āraṇyaka* 4.1.2–7; for *purāṇa* see *Śvetāśvatara* 3:21. See also *Bṛhad-Āraṇyaka* 4.4.8. This passage refers to the "ancient narrow path" that Rumi attributes to Jesus, the *Logos:* "For the true believers I become a bridge across the river." It is the Upanishadic equivalent of John 14:6. See also *Bhagavad-Gītā* 2:20. For *parātpara* see *Muṇḍaka Upanishad* 3.2.8, where Radhakrishnan translates "parat-param purusam" the same as Upadhyay, "higher than the high," 691. See also *Bhagavad-Gītā* 8:20.

remains."[49] The fullness that Upadhyay celebrates is both transcendent and immanent, a theme vital to orthodox Christianity.

The last line of the stanza explores the mystery of God's oneness, a oneness that has "triple interior relationship." Here we see one of Upadhyay's favorite themes, namely, that God is one and unrelated (nirguṇa), yet related internally within the Godhead in the mystery of tri-unity (trisaṇga). Gispert-Sauch appropriately quotes Abhishiktananda, who said that the "*sat* of God is in reality *sam-sat*," that is, a being with communion or internal relationships. Yet, "in all his inner relatedness, God remains pure, *śuddha,* the inner relations in no way compromising the inner purity of the divine essence, which remains one only without a second, free from any essential duality."[50] Thus, in the mystery of the Trinity, God is both trisaṇga and asaṅga, triple related within, yet unrelated (of necessity) to the world.

Upadhyay then balances the unrelated nature of God with the declaration that he is conscious, using the powerful Eastern word *buddha* ("awakened" or "enlightened"), asserting God's claim as the ultimate enlightened one and the source of all enlightenment and reflecting the words of John's Gospel, "He is the light which enlightens every man in the world" (John 1:9). The paradox and mystery of the Trinity has now been declared: triple related, yet unrelated; unrelated to the world, yet the source of the world's enlightenment. The mystery cannot be penetrated apart from revelation. Thus, Upadhyay ends by declaring this truth "hard to realize." Even the enlightenment of God is never completely separate from the mystery of the unfathomable, ineffable nature of the Trinity.

Second Stanza to the Father

The second stanza is dedicated to the adoration of the Father. It opens with the Sanskrit word for father, *pitṛ*. Upadhyay then uses a key word found in the first verse of the Vedas—*Savitṛ*. Gispert-Sauch comments that "*Savitṛ* is the designation of God . . . that is taught to the young Brahmin at the *upanayana* or initiation ceremony: the famous *gāyatrī mantra* which is revered as specially auspicious: *tat savituṛ vareṇyam / bhargo devasya dhīmahi / dhiyo ya no pracodayat:* 'May we meditate upon that splendour of the God *Savitṛ* and may he inspire our thoughts.'"[51] The word *Savitṛ* refers to a solar deity (or, as Upadhyay would prefer it, the God of the Sun) in the *Ṛg-Veda.* Thus, the word evokes images of the Father as the creative source of life and the power and energy that gives life to the whole earth.

49. Radhakrishnan, *Principal Upanishads,* 289.

50. Gispert-Sauch, "Sanskrit Hymns," 70. Upadhyay's reference to the Upanishadic formula that God is one without a second means, for him, that although God is triune and internally related, his nature is not divided.

51. Gispert-Sauch, "Sanskrit Hymns," 71. See *Ṛg-Veda* 3.62.10, *Bṛhad-Āraṇyaka* 6.3.6, *Maitrī* 6.7, and *Chāndogya* 5.2.7.

The Father is also called *parameśam,* the supreme or highest Lord, a title for Śiva. The mystery is again pressed as Upadhyay now calls the Begetter (Savitṛ) unbegotten. He who has brought all of creation into existence is himself uncaused, recalling not only the language of early Christian creeds but the language of the Upanishads, which assert that Brāhman is "not-engendered."[52] The idea of the unbegotten Begetter is reinforced by the next expression, which Gispert-Sauch has translated as "unsown seed of the tree of existence."[53] The Father is the seed *(bījam)* who is himself without seed *(abījam).* The tree metaphor is popular in Indian figurative religious language.[54]

In the last line of the second stanza, the Father is celebrated as the great Cause *(kāraṇam)* of the whole universe. Here we meet Aquinas's intelligent, personal, first cause, a declaration that separates Upadhyay from the Sāṃkhya school of Indian philosophy, which rejects a personal or intelligent cause of the universe. Creation in advaita, as understood by Upadhyay, is an "intelligent *(īkṣaṇa),* personal act, not an impersonal evolution."[55] The last description of the Father in this stanza is the word *govinda,* which translates as "preserver of the world," an expression resonating with Western theological formulations. However, the literal meaning of the expression is "cowherd of the universe," as Upadhyay boldly draws from popular mythological literature one of the most recognizable titles of Krishna. Here Upadhyay emphasizes the providential, shepherding care of the Father over the universe but does so while evoking language found in both the *Ṛg-Veda* and the *Bhagavad-Gītā.*[56]

Third Stanza to the Son

The third stanza is devoted to praise of the Son. The opening words declare the Son to be *anāhata śabda,* which means "nonstruck sound." It is a technical distinction in Indian philosophy that refers to the "transcendental cosmic Sound that is said to fill the universe."[57] The sound is said to be eternal, having no originating strike that produced it. This powerfully reflects

52. *Bṛhad-Āraṇyaka* 4.4.20–25. Brāhman is referred to repeatedly as "the great Unborn (*aja*) self." See also *Bhagavad-Gītā* 2:20. *Aja* also stands for the principle of *prakṛti,* which the Sāṃkhya philosophers considered to be a principle without beginning, that is, "unborn."

53. Gispert-Sauch, "Sanskrit Hymns," 76.

54. See, for example, *Bhagavad-Gītā* 15:3.

55. Gispert-Sauch, "Sanskrit Hymns," 71.

56. Gispert-Sauch points out that there is an ancient RigVedic myth of Indra symbolically "finding the cows." Here, God is shown to find the straying cows all over the universe, evoking Luke 15:3–6 and Psalm 23. The controversial choice of Upadhyay using *govinda* as a description of the Father is why, according to Gispert-Sauch, Father Antoine changed the word to *visvesam* (which makes *parameśam* redundant and does away with the rhyme) when it was used for public worship ("Sanskrit Hymns," 72 n. 19).

57. Gispert-Sauch, "Sanskrit Hymns," 72. The *Yoga Darsana* identifies this eternal sound with the sacred syllable *om* (pronounced AUM).

Christ as the Word that has eternally gone forth from the Father, the "infinite Logos" as the next phrase affirms. Calling the Son "infinite" *(ananta)* draws upon advaita's emphasis that the Supreme Being is infinite. It is also (when used adjectively) one of the names used to describe the gigantic mythological snake, Śeśa, who is the mount of Lord Viṣṇu. The last word of this line describes the Son as "supremely great," reminiscent of the *Śvetāśvatara* Upanishad, which regularly speaks of the *mahān puruṣa.*[58]

The last line of this stanza to the Son begins with an affirmation that the Son is consubstantial with the Father through the phrase *pitṛ-svarūpa,* translated by Upadhyay as "image of the Father." The word *svarūpa* denotes essence or inner form, reflecting the truth that the Son and the Father share the same essence. Also, in North India the word is widely used to refer to the image of a god.[59] The next phrase *(cinmāyā-rūpa)* reinforces the concept of the Son as *cit* and is translated "one whose form is intelligence" or as Gispert-Sauch renders it, "whose essence is made of Consciousness."[60] The last phrase of the stanza to the Son is the phrase *sumukunda,* which has mythological overtones associated with Viṣṇu. Mukunka is a name for Viṣṇu, but the *su* prefix makes it adjectival, distancing it from a direct identification with Viṣṇu and instead emphasizing the etymology of the root *muk,* from which come words such as *mukti* (liberation). Upadhyay translates it as "giver of the highest freedom,"[61] reflecting the redemptive, liberating work of Christ that is so central to the Christian message and celebrating him who liberates from the bonds of saṃsāra.

Fourth Stanza to the Holy Spirit

The fourth and final stanza begins by bridging traditional Latin filioque theology with the doctrine of saccidānanda. The Holy Spirit is pictured as "proceeding from the union of *Sat* and *Cit.*" This is followed by a concept as deeply imbedded in the Vedantic tradition as the filioque is in the Latin. The Holy Spirit is *ānandaghana* (literally, a "solid mass of bliss"), which Upadhyay translates as "intense bliss."[62] The expression seeks to convey the

58. *Śvetāśvatara* 3:8, 12, 19. Radhakrishnan translates the phrase as "Supreme Person" in verses 8 and 19, and as "Great Lord" in verse 12.

59. For example, child actors who play the role of gods are known as *svarups* or images of the gods they represent. Likewise, the Vallabha sect calls the image of Krishna by the term *svarūpa.*

60. Gispert-Sauch, "Sanskrit Hymns," 73.

61. Gispert-Sauch also points out that this phrase, like *govinda,* was omitted in the printed musical version and replaced with the more obvious Christian title *Jisu-Krishtam.* Gispert-Sauch seems to stretch the etymology of *sumukunda* too far to render it "good Savior," though it does conform to his overall structure by having each stanza conclude with a single summarizing affirmation: stanza one, the Mystery; stanza two, our Shepherd; stanza three, good Savior; and stanza four, our Life-giver.

62. Gispert-Sauch, "Sanskrit Hymns," 73. The word *ghana* also means "cloud," referring to the solid mass of monsoon clouds that bring nourishing rain to India.

purity of the supreme bliss, unmixed with anything unclean. Thus, it appropriately carries the idea of holiness, which proceeds from the Father and the Son as their pure and good *(śubha)* breath or spirits *(śvasita)*.

The second part of the final stanza celebrates the work of the Holy Spirit. He is called the *pavana,* a term that the Sanskrit tradition appropriately connects with both fire and wind, "the two great purifying agencies in nature,"[63] and consonant with the biblical description of the Holy Spirit as fire and wind. As the wind of God, his "movements are swift," recalling both the *Śvetāśvatara* Upanishad and John's Gospel.[64] In the final line of the stanza, the Holy Spirit is extolled as the one who "Speaks of the Word" (i.e., bears witness to Christ and the prophets), and as the "Life-giver," reflecting the task of regeneration while echoing the language of the *Bhagavad-Gītā.*[65]

Keep in mind that this is first and foremost a Christian hymn, seeking to worship and adore the Triune God. However, it is Christian worship grown from the seeds of Indian tradition and planted in the soil of India. For this reason, Gispert-Sauch says that in this hymn one finds "the most successful example of true adaptation or incarnation of faith in India."[66]

Conclusion

Brahmabandhav Upadhyay once said that the reason his Hindu friends could not understand "the subtlety and sanctity" of the Christian faith is "because of its hard coating of Europeanism."[67] This case study has focused on Upadhyay's attempt to restate the classic Trinitarian formulation in terms and thought forms that are alien to those of us in the West but are more familiar to Indians. Upadhyay never claims that his use of saccidānanda was able to capture the incomprehensible mystery of the Trinity. After all, every formulation must accept the limitations of human language. Nor did he believe that his restatement of the Trinity using the language of Vedānta could ever become normative for anyone outside the Indian context. Rather, he was pioneering an experiment in contextualization involving the restatement of doctrines that continue, for the most part, to be taught around the world using the Latin and Greek conceptual framework. The fact that the church is now predominantly non-Western makes the kind of work by Upadhyay and other non-Western Christians impossible to ignore. We need a more vigorous discussion concerning the viability of these efforts. Perhaps this case study will help to stimulate dialogue in the years ahead.

63. Ibid.
64. *Śvetāśvatara Upanishad* 3:19 and John 3:18.
65. *Bhagavad-Gītā* 7:9.
66. Gispert-Sauch, "Sanskrit Hymns," 74.
67. As quoted in Animananda, *The Blade,* 74.

Questions for Further Discussion and Reflection

1. What are the limits of general revelation? Can insights gained from general revelation or even fragments from Jewish or Christian sources of special revelation be incorporated into sacred texts of non-Christian religions? There are numerous instances of this, for example, in the Qurʾān. If the Qurʾān incorporates revelatory material from the Old or New Testaments, how should it be regarded by Christians? How do you respond to Brahmabandhav Upadhyay's claim that the seeds of the doctrine of the Trinity are found in the Upanishads?
2. How does Upadhyay's attitude toward Hindu philosophy parallel that of Justin Martyr's? Do both view philosophy as a *preparatio evangelica?* Since Greek philosophy is less overtly religious in its scope and tone than Hindu philosophy, is Upadhyay's attempt to use the language of Hindu philosophy the way Justin and others used the language of Greek philosophy viable?
3. Would you characterize Upadhyay's view of Hinduism as an expression of fulfillment theology? Is the Christian gospel the crown of Hindu thought, or is Brahmabandhav merely using the language of Hindu philosophy to communicate the Trinity within the thought forms of Hindus?
4. How important is the normative role of the traditional Latin formulations of orthodoxy? Can the growing non-Western church remain fully orthodox and yet restate the classic formulations in ways more intelligible in their own context? Is there such a thing as a dynamic equivalent of the Constantinople formulation? What would the impact be on the unity and long-term orthodoxy of a global church that no longer explicitly affirms the ancient, ecumenical councils but affirms countless smaller local formulations of orthodoxy?

10

Can *Sola Fide* Be Understood Apart from the Specific, Historic Revelation of Jesus Christ?

A Study of A. G. Hogg's Distinction between Faith and Faiths

The third case study focuses on a missionary to India named Alfred George Hogg (1875–1954) and his work in finding a new solution to preserve the uniqueness of Christ in the context of a religiously plural world. A. G. Hogg was born in Egypt to missionary parents. After his father's death, Hogg returned to his home in Scotland and eventually studied at the University of Edinburgh. In 1903, he accepted an invitation by the Madras Christian College to go to India as a professor of philosophy, and from 1928 to 1938 Hogg served as principal of the college. During his career, Hogg published regular articles in the Madras Christian College magazine, a number of pamphlets, and four books: *Karma and Redemption* (1909), *Christ's Message of the Kingdom* (1911), *Redemption from This World* (1922), and *The Christian Message to the Hindu* (1947). In these writings, Hogg articulates the distinction between faith and faiths or faith and beliefs, which is the focus of this case study.

Faith and Faiths

For Hogg, faith is not an intellectual assent to certain creedal formulations. Faith must be personal and existential. It reflects a dynamic, living trust in God. Faiths or beliefs, on the other hand, are those doctrines, creeds, and intellectual expressions that are constructed to protect and perpetuate faith. Our beliefs sustain, propagate, and nourish our faith. Hogg thought that the goal of all religions is to produce and nurture faith. The various beliefs that make religions so radically different arise because of the different ways cultures experience faith. If God is viewed as an impersonal and absolute self-sufficiency (Hinduism), then it is not surprising that "an order like Karma, which insists on mechanical retribution—a judicial system without a personal judge—is understandable."[1] On the other hand, if God is viewed as love, then the doctrine of the incarnation and God's personal intervention to redeem humanity is both necessary and understandable. As cultures and events shape the way we think and experience God, our beliefs must likewise be adapted to preserve and nurture our faith. As James Cox has observed about Hogg's distinction between faith and faiths, "New circumstances will make the old beliefs obsolete and transform what once provided an avenue for faith into a stumbling-block for faith."[2] If a person begins to regard his or her beliefs as false, then faith is imperiled until the beliefs are reexamined or changed.

Hogg used several analogies to illustrate his faith-faiths distinction. One of the most vivid is the analogy of the clouds and the moon. Hogg compared his view to a person standing in the middle of an open field and looking up at the moon. It is a partly cloudy night, so at times clouds obscure the view. When this occurs, the person must shift his or her position on the field until the beauty and radiance of the moon is visible once again.[3] In the analogy, the moonlight symbolizes faith. The clouds represent the ever-changing historical and cultural circumstances in which we live. The position on the field represents our beliefs at a given moment. The point of the analogy is that we must be prepared to alter and shift our beliefs if genuine faith is to be maintained.

Hogg's Missionary Method

Using this distinction, Hogg developed a missionary method that encouraged a careful study of how non-Christian beliefs contrast with Christian beliefs. His goal was to demonstrate how Christian beliefs are more cogent and consistent than those of other religions and are therefore better able to sustain faith. A presentation of the gospel to a Hindu or Muslim or Buddhist should arouse a keen awareness of a problem for which his or her own beliefs have no answer. The person becomes spiritually disoriented until he or she realizes that the tension "cannot be resolved except by the ac-

1. From Eric Sharpe's introduction to A. G. Hogg, *Karma and Redemption* (1909; reprint, Madras: Christian Literature Society, 1970), xv.

2. James Cox, "Faith and Faiths: The Significance of A. G. Hogg's Missionary Thought for a Theology of Dialogue," *Scottish Journal of Theology* 32 (1979): 242.

3. A. G. Hogg, "Notes of the Month," *Madras Christian College Magazine*, n.s., 7, no. 4 (1907): 202.

ceptance of the Christian position."[4] To use the analogy, the preaching of Christ will create clouds in the sky for non-Christians, and they will be forced to shift their ground. In Hinduism, for example, Hogg sought to demonstrate how the doctrine of karma could not properly sustain living faith and must ultimately be transformed and replaced by the Christian doctrine of redemption.

This method stands in stark contrast to the approach that was popular in Hogg's day (as well as ours), which seeks to downplay the differences and harmonize the various beliefs of the world's religions. The early-twentieth-century fulfillment theologians, in particular, were trying to demonstrate how Christ fulfilled aspirations within other religions by pointing to common nuggets of truth. Hogg believed that the task of the missionary should never be to draw out various parallels between systems of thought. He asked, "Why is it, that in drawing comparisons between Hindu and European philosophy we are so often willing to accentuate superficial parallelisms and ignore fundamental contrasts?"[5] Thus, in Hogg's view, the kind of theological effort made by Brahmabandhav Upadhyay is fundamentally flawed. In fact, he explicitly stated that it would be a mistake to "reformulate Christian thought in terms of Indian philosophy."[6] Such an attempt would only encourage syncretism and actually allow people to retain their Hindu beliefs longer because the inherent difficulties in their beliefs are not sufficiently exposed.

Hogg was not interested in theological systems per se, but in a personal encounter between an individual and God. Faiths are radically divergent, he argued, but "the innermost faith of all religions which are still, at any time, worthy of the name must be one and the same."[7] Doctrinal systems, in his view, only petrify God into dead dogma, rather than liberating someone into a living relationship with God. According to Hogg, the sole purpose of doctrine and theology is to produce in someone "an absolute trust in God."[8] Whether it be the Christian or the non-Christian, Hogg wrote, "God reveals himself; he does not reveal ready-made truths about himself. And the thought and language in which a man expresses to himself or others his apprehension of that supernatural self-disclosure has to be human thought, human language—always defective, sometimes gravely distorting."[9] Hogg was convinced that the incarnation was the greatest revelation of God. However, it is the experience of the incarnation, not the doctrine of the in-

4. Eric Sharpe, *The Theology of A. G. Hogg* (Madras: Christian Literature Society, 1971), 52.

5. A. G. Hogg, *Madras Christian College Magazine* (September 1904): 122.

6. A. G. Hogg, "The God That Must Needs Be Christ Jesus," *International Review of Missions* 6 (January 1917): 62.

7. Hogg, *Karma and Redemption*, xix.

8. Sharpe, *Theology of A. G. Hogg*, 45.

9. A. G. Hogg, *The Authority of Faith* (Madras: Christian Literature Society, 1939), 104.

carnation, that is important to Hogg. Indeed, all propositional revelation must submit to the personal revelation of Jesus Christ in an individual's life.

To the careful reader, it may already be evident that Hogg was deeply influenced by the German theologian Albrecht Ritschl. Ritschlian theology utilized a method of evaluating religion through the "judgment of value." This judgment was oriented toward one's own relationship with God rather than any theoretical system of doctrine. Ritschl made a sharp distinction between religious knowledge and theoretical knowledge, which is evident in Hogg's faith-faiths distinction.[10]

This brings us to another important distinction that is integral to understanding Hogg's conception of faith and faiths: the content of revelation versus the occurrence of revelation.

Content and Occurrence of Revelation

Viewed in context, Hogg was clearly seeking to steer a course between two extremes. On the one hand, Hogg rejected the harsh view of Hendrick Kraemer, who recognized no revelation of God in the world apart from that which has been self-disclosed in the Scriptures. On the other hand, Hogg was not prepared to travel down the path of the fulfillment theologians and an emerging group of pluralists who seemed to make no radical distinction between Christianity and other religions, except one of degrees. For the fulfillment theologians, the seed of Christianity is already present in all religions. For Kraemer, all religions represent failed, fallen attempts of humanity to reach out to God who, apart from his own initiative and self-disclosure, remains hidden. Fulfillment theologians like J. N. Farquhar emphasized the continuity between other religions and Christianity. Kraemer affirmed the discontinuity between Christianity and other religions. Hogg charted a middle path by affirming that the occurrence of revelation has happened over and over throughout the world and in all religions as God continues to reveal himself to people throughout history. The discontinuity that exists in world religions is because people have misperceived God's self-revelation. According to Hogg, Kraemer focused exclusively on the imperfect human responses to revelation, and therefore he saw only discontinuity. The fulfillment theologians had focused too much on the doctrinal content of revelation and missed the radical uniqueness of Jesus Christ. For Hogg, Jesus Christ is the unique content of revelation. The miracle is not that the Word became text but that the Word became flesh.

Hogg tried to look at revelation from God's view and discover how God has always been seeking to reveal himself to humanity. He affirmed the continuity argument of the fulfillment theologians by agreeing that the occurrence of revelation is universally present in all religions. He affirmed the dis-

10. For an overview of Ritschl's theology, see A. T. Swing, *The Theology of Albrecht Ritschl* (New York: Longmans, Green, 1901).

continuity argument of Kraemer by agreeing that the content of revelation is uniquely and finally present only in Jesus Christ. Jesus Christ is unique not because he is a set of beliefs or a doctrinal system, but because he is a living person who became incarnate in history. Focusing on the historical act, not the doctrinal response to the act, preserves the absolute uniqueness of Christianity without having to deny the occurrence of revelation in other religions. Thus, Hogg can affirm that all religions are a testimony to the "revealing initiative of God" while maintaining that the content of revelation in Jesus Christ is found uniquely in Christianity. Hogg believed that "by exposing other religions to the historic Jesus as the *content* of revelation, Jesus would disturb non-Christian beliefs sufficiently as to render them ineffective for faith."[11] The result is that the non-Christian will turn to Christ who alone enables a person to experience lasting faith without any fear of becoming spiritually disoriented.

Application to World Religions: Buddhism

How would A. G. Hogg's distinction between faith and faiths apply to Buddhism? In chapter 4 we examined the emphasis in Pure Land Buddhism on the worship and invocation of Amitā or Amitābha Buddha (Buddha of Unlimited Light). As noted, the devotional worship that is directed to Amitā or Amitābha Buddha became so focused, particularly after the great teacher Honen (1133–1212), that it is often referred to as a form of devotional monotheism. One of the distinctive features of Pure Land is the propagation of the Nembutsu or invocation of Amitā/Amitābha, whereby one is delivered from all sins and ushered into the heavenly realm known as the Pure Land. The faith of Pure Land Buddhists is expressed in the familiar cry, "Namu Amitā Butsu."[12]

Even a cursory reading of the Pure Land literature and popular songs about Amitā reveals that at the heart of the whole movement are a desire to eschew one's ability to save oneself through good works and a strong belief that the only hope is to have trusting faith in Amitā/Amitābha. This is what led one of the other great proponents of Pure Land and the Nembutsu doctrine, Shinran, the disciple of Honen, to declare that "wicked people might be more acceptable to Amitā than good people, since the former threw themselves entirely on the mercy of the Buddha, while the latter might be tempted to think that their chances of salvation were improved by their own meritorious conduct."[13] The obvious parallels between the faith of evangeli-

11. James Cox, "The Influence of A. G. Hogg over D. G. Moses: A Missionary Message for India," *Religion and Society* 27, no. 4 (December 1980): 74, emphasis added.

12. The Nembutsu doctrine is best summed up in the following invocation: "Hito tabi mo Namu Amitā bu to Yu hito no Hasu no utena ni Noboranu wa nashi" (He never fails to reach the Lotus Land of Bliss who calls, if only once, the name of Amitā).

13. William Theodore de Bary, *The Buddhist Tradition in India, China and Japan* (New York: Vintage, 1972), 332.

cals and the faith of Pure Land Buddhists make it an excellent choice to test and apply A. G. Hogg's views.

According to Hogg, there is no substantive difference between the faith of a Pure Land Buddhist and the faith of an evangelical Christian. The difference lies only in the respective faiths of Buddhism and Christianity and how the doctrines have developed to nurture their common faith. Both the Pure Land Buddhist and the Christian, according to Hogg, understand our utter inability to save ourselves and the need to trust and rely upon the power of another. Hogg's distinction downplays the differences in the philosophical and theological frameworks of Buddhism and Christianity respectively and focuses on the personal encounter of the believer with God. It is only as Pure Land Buddhists begin to encounter Christian beliefs that their own spiritual equilibrium might be thrown out of balance and they may see problems with the Pure Land doctrines. Hogg hopes that in time a Buddhist would shift his or her field position and finally realize that the faith which trusts not in oneself but in another is best expressed and understood in the Christian gospel.

To my knowledge, Hogg never articulated how his views might specifically apply to Pure Land Buddhism. Nevertheless, from his writings about how he relates his views to Hinduism as well as his comments about non-Christian religions in general, it is safe to conclude that Hogg would make the following two points when applying his perspective to Buddhism. First, Hogg would certainly affirm that Buddhist doctrines have emerged because of the universal occurrence of revelation whereby the Living God has truly sought to reveal himself to Buddhists. However, this revelation has been distorted, misunderstood, and eventually expressed in the defective system known as Pure Land Buddhism. Second, Hogg would acknowledge that, for many Buddhists, the doctrine of Nembutsu produces nurturing faith in the heart and life of the worshipper. According to Hogg, this is a saving faith, even though the Buddhist may be ignorant of the precise content of revelation in Jesus Christ. The preaching of the Christian gospel must finally demonstrate the problems with Pure Land and the need to shift from nontheism to faith in Jesus Christ, the final revelation of God.

Although there are differences, the parallels between Hogg's view and modern-day inclusivism are stunning. Hogg's emphasis is not so much on widening the scope of general revelation per se, but on expanding the scope of special revelation in non-Christian religions. Furthermore, Hogg consistently views revelation from God's perspective of revealing himself, rather than the human perspective which has tried to collate and codify these revelations into various defective systems of thought. Inclusivism focuses more on the sincere heart experience of the believer, Hogg more on the long-suffering acts of God's self-revelation. Nevertheless, like the inclusivists, Hogg is more concerned with the salvific experience of faith in the lives of believers than he is with any specific epistemological connection to the work of

Christ. I do not think Hogg would ever call a Pure Land Buddhist an anonymous Christian, because Hogg takes the occurrence of revelation within Pure Land far too seriously. Nevertheless, like the inclusivists, he affirms the primacy of the content of revelation in Christ without denying the presence of saving faith apart from any knowledge of the gospel. Thus, this case study highlights several keys issues, including the nature of faith apart from an explicit knowledge of Christ; the extent, purpose, and role of general revelation; and the relationship between propositional truth statements (what Hogg refers to as faiths or beliefs) and the personal revelation of God in the lives of believers designed to produce faith. The questions that follow will help to focus the discussion on these and other issues. Furthermore, these questions highlight themes that can be used to dialogue with both Christians and non-Christians.

Questions for Further Discussion and Reflection

1. Hogg's entire faith-faiths distinction is built on the premise that although beliefs in the world's faiths differ radically, faith in God is a universal constant. Is faith really the same in all religions? How does Hogg reconcile the faith of theistic religions like Islam and Christianity with faith in nontheistic religions like Buddhism and Taoism? How can Hogg defend the position that only intellectual differences separate Christianity from all other religions? If all the beliefs, creeds, doctrines, and theological systems were stripped away from every religion in the world, would there remain a common core?
2. What is Hogg's view of truth? In particular, how does Hogg regard propositional truth statements? What are the implications of his views? If all propositional truths are relative, how can we speak intelligently about Christ and his mission in the world? Can the personal revelation of Jesus in the world be separated from the content of his teaching? How, according to Hogg, does Jesus Christ reveal himself personally to us apart from propositional truths?
3. Hogg's emphasis on the importance of faith is undeniable. However, what are his actual views regarding the object of faith? In the application to Buddhism, we must remember, as was made clear in our conversations with both the Yogācāra and Mādhyamika representatives, there is no objective reality in which we put our faith. There is no one to receive any acts of worship and adoration. As the spokesperson for Mādhyamika put it, "Only on the plain of conditional existence do such dichotomies as 'worshipper' and 'object of worship' appear." Undoubtedly, Hogg would be willing to exploit problems in the Mahāyāna system that might create a "crisis of faith" for a Buddhist. But before the gospel is preached, upon what basis does this kind of faith save someone? At least the inclusivists objectify everything in Christ, even if it is being applied anonymously. Hogg believes that behind

Pure Land Buddhism is the seeking God, but given the massive discontinuity between Christianity and Pure Land Buddhism, can someone's faith be salvific, even if exercised on the basis of such a faulty and distorted system of beliefs?

4. Reflect critically on the following statement by A. G. Hogg: "Christianity is not any particular system of beliefs, but . . . essential Christianity is *whatever* system of beliefs, *whatever* play of emotions, *whatever* outgoings of the will, a man is led into by utter devotion and obedience to Jesus Christ."[14]
5. It has been said that the most important contribution of A. G. Hogg was his theory of disturbance. This is the view that the presentation of the gospel upsets or disturbs the spiritual equilibrium of non-Christians. To borrow from Hogg's moon-cloud analogy, the preaching of the gospel causes clouds to obscure the moon and forces the non-Christian to shift his or her ground closer to Christ. Does this, in your view, actually happen when the gospel is presented to non-Christians?
6. Compare and contrast the inclusivism of Karl Rahner with Justin Martyr's view of the preexisting *Logos* implanting the *logos spermatikos* in people and Hogg's view of the universal occurrence of revelation. How are Martyr's and Hogg's views similar to and distinct from the inclusivism of Rahner?
7. The Protestant reformer Martin Luther taught the importance of faith alone *(sola fide)* for salvation. On the basis of this case study, how do you think Hogg would understand the concept of *sola fide?* If Hogg were allowed to go back to the sixteenth century and present his ideas to Luther during one of the Reformer's famous table talks, how might Luther respond to the faith-faiths distinction?
8. How would you compare and contrast the attitudes of Justin Martyr, A. G. Hogg, and Brahmabandhav Upadhyay regarding the importance of relating the Christian gospel to the dominant systems of philosophy and thought? How would each understand the concept of *praeparatio evangelica?*

14. A. G. Hogg, "Some Fundamentals of Christianity," *Madras Christian College Magazine,* quarterly series, 3, no. 1 (1923): 15–26, as quoted by James Cox, "The Influence of A. G. Hogg over D. G. Moses," 75.

Epilogue

Closing Thoughts about Evangelicals and Interreligious Dialogue

This book is based on the premise that genuine dialogue can occur in a way that is faithful to historic Christianity and yet is willing to listen and respond to the honest objections of those who remain unconvinced. I have made no apology for either my commitment to dialogue or my belief that the Christian faith embodies revelatory truths rooted in historical events culminating in the life, death, and resurrection of Jesus Christ. I remain convinced that the unique and normative claims of the Christian gospel must be defended at the table of dialogue. Indeed, my convictions regarding the truthfulness of the Christian gospel do not relieve me of the responsibility to explain how Christianity relates to other faiths; rather, they make it imperative.

The world we live in no longer allows any of us to isolate our faith from those who belong to the other major world religions. Through these conversations and case studies, I have sought to encourage many more evangelicals to engage in interreligious dialogue to help assuage this neglected area of witness and faith. My own convictions concerning interreligious dialogue arise out of three fundamental commitments that can assist evangelicals in negotiating the sometimes turbulent waters of interreligious dialogue.

Just Say No to Pluralism

First, we must not succumb to the forces of religious pluralism that seek to bring to the table of dialogue a version of Christianity that has been robbed of its distinctiveness.[1] For too long interreligious dialogue has been

1. I am using the term *religious pluralism* to refer to the common pluralistic ideology that is so often advocated by liberals at the religious roundtable. This is not to be confused with the fact that we live in a pluralistic society that correctly respects and protects the rights of individual expression.

advanced and identified with a pluralist agenda that openly seeks to accommodate other world religions by discarding distinctive Christian doctrines such as the incarnation and the resurrection of Christ. The result, as Alister McGrath observes, is that "it is not Christianity that is being related to other world faiths; it is little more than a parody and caricature of this living faith, grounded in the presuppositions and agenda of western liberalism rather than in the self revelation of God."[2] Pluralism seeks to censure all truth claims as imperialistic, dogmatic, and divisive. Our desire to avoid such nasty labels has caused us all too often to avoid the table of dialogue and by our silence to acquiesce to the idea that all religions are fundamentally the same.

True interreligious dialogue acknowledges that all religions in one way or another seek to defend certain truth claims.[3] It is not fair to any religion to allow it to be ensnared in the swamp of religious pluralism, which concludes that we are all saying the same thing.

Dialogue As Persuasive Witness

Second, we must not view dialogue and witness as mutually exclusive. Evangelicals have sometimes been guilty of reducing Christian witness to a monologue of proclamation. Since dialogue necessarily involves a mutual give-and-take of ideas, it is often regarded as an unsuitable arena for genuine Christian witness. Many of the proponents of dialogue reinforce this idea by insisting that any desire to convert another person is a fundamental violation of the mutuality inherent in dialogue. The result is the advocacy of a dialogue without persuasion. However, the mutuality of dialogue is not sacrificed if everyone is permitted to speak with persuasion. As I stated in chapter 1, a Muslim who earnestly desires the entire world to acknowledge that "there is no God but Allah, and Muhammad is his Prophet" does not offend me. Indeed, I fully expect it and do not believe he would be a trustworthy representative of Islam if he said that such a confession did not really matter or that Christians and Muslims were really no different from each other.

This is why it is so important that the table of dialogue brings together actual adherents of the various faiths and not just those who are masking their postmodern notions of truth behind religious language. Indeed, we must learn to listen to and understand the actual claims of other religions in order to effectively bear witness to our faith. The New Testament does not just call us to preach the gospel, but to communicate the gospel. This means we cannot speak the gospel into thin air; rather, it must be effectively

2. Alister McGrath, "The Christian Church's Response to Pluralism," *JETS* 35, no. 4 (December 1992): 489.

3. Even the claim that there is no truth that can be known or apprehended is, in itself, a truth claim.

communicated to specific contexts, and we must be ready and willing to respond to real and specific objections and doubts, giving reasons for the hope that is within us (1 Pet. 3:15). To do this, we must be prepared to utilize the full range of communicative skills at our disposal, including dialogue. Of course, our witness should be conveyed with proper humility and sensitivity, but not lacking in conviction.

Dialogue Stimulates Our Own Understanding of Truth

Third, dialogue is always a two-way encounter. One danger in a forceful rejection of pluralism and a firm commitment to persuasiveness at the religious roundtable is the charge that Christians only come to the table of dialogue to give and not to receive. Thus, it is argued, Christians who dialogue are actually engaged in a monologue disguised as a mutual exchange. On the contrary, I have discovered over and over again that I am enriched by the mutual exchange. I constantly sense how much I am being given by my non-Christian friends. My dialogue with Hindus has helped me understand with far more clarity what Christians actually affirm regarding creation. Hindus have forced me on more than one occasion to search the Scriptures with more diligence. I do not think my own appreciation for the doctrine of the Trinity would be nearly as deep if the doctrine had not been challenged so often by my Islamic friends. It was the Buddhists, not my own Christian friends, who finally helped me see the momentous dangers of advocating faith without a clear connection to the historical Jesus of Nazareth.

Furthermore, I have been forced to greater reflection because of questions my non-Christian friends in other parts of the world have asked me such as, "Why do American Christians wear their shoes in church?"; "Is it true that you allow menstruating women to worship in church?" and "Do Christians believe in prayer? I have never actually seen a Christian pray." These are not the kinds of questions one is asked in a typical question-and-answer session with new seekers in a church in the West.

An additional benefit of the mutuality of exchange is that our own stereotypes and misunderstandings of other religions are exposed. I thought that Hindus were mostly polytheists until I talked to Hindus and discovered that the majority are not. I thought that Islam had advanced into sub-Saharan Africa mainly through the sword until I studied the history of the Islamic spread into Africa. I never understood the significance of translating the Buddhist doctrine of śunyatā as emptiness instead of nothingness until a Buddhist explained it to me. True witness to someone of another faith means that we must understand his or her actual position, not a caricature of it. We should be just as unwilling to allow a caricature of another religion to be presented at the table of dialogue as we would be to see Christianity presented in such a manner.

Postmodernism and the Gospel: The Opportunity of the Present

In conclusion, we stand at an opportune time in the history of the church. For centuries the Enlightenment worldview has exalted reason over faith and revelation. To be sure, there have been valiant attempts over the centuries to respond to this challenge. The finality of revelation has been posited with various forms of accommodation to the claims of human reason. However, the dawn of postmodernism, with all its challenges, has begun to reveal cracks in the seemingly unassailable walls of the Enlightenment. The vagueness of postmodern thought makes it difficult to define. Broadly speaking, however, it refers to the general perspective that no one can speak of truth in an absolute or final way. Certainly, the role of reason in providing a foundation for some body of universal knowledge of the world, including God, has all but collapsed. People are no longer certain that reason is the final arbiter of truth. The postmodern response has been to cast doubt on the ability of words and language to disclose any meaning at all. In short, if the Enlightenment symbolizes the overthrow of revelation and the enthronement of reason, postmodernism seeks to overthrow both reason and revelation.

The only remaining arbiter for truth is the sole perspective of an autonomous, vacillating individual.

Tragically, postmodernism has already begun to cast its shadow onto the church. The most obvious example is the new postmodern hermeneutic in approaching Scripture. Postmodernism claims that the original intent and meaning of the writers of Scripture cannot be known. Therefore, all personal interpretations of meaning are equally valid or, for some, equally meaningless. This kind of perspective renders most of the conversations found in this book meaningless, since all the participants rely on revelation and the original meaning of the text to make their cases. Yet the postmodern position is one that is intellectually vulnerable and difficult to sustain. To say that any person's view of truth, if sincerely held, is equally valid is ludicrous, because it would mean the end of all moral discrimination. The terrorists who attacked the World Trade Center on September 11, 2001, believed sincerely and passionately that they were serving Allah and making the world a better place for the spread of Islam. Hitler believed passionately that Europe would be better off by putting six million Jews into the gas chambers. Are these personal perspectives on truth to be regarded with equal validity as those of the person who believes we should live in harmony and peace with our friends and neighbors? The recent terrorist attacks have jolted many postmodernists into realizing that there must be standards of judgment and objective criteria that will allow certain viewpoints to be excluded and others to be embraced. Indeed, the fissures are already appearing in the postmodern worldview.

William Inge has wisely stated, "He who marries the spirit of the age today will be a widower tomorrow."[4] Many who so eagerly jumped onto the postmodern bandwagon are beginning to realize that the real struggle is not between tolerance and intolerance but between truth and falsehood. A new openness to revelation is emerging as well as a desire to reclaim the language of truth that has, until recently, been dropped into the abyss of relativism. This makes it an exciting and strategic time to sit down at the religious roundtable and bear witness to the good news of Jesus Christ.

4. As quoted in Alister McGrath, "The Christian Church's Response to Pluralism," 501. William Inge was the dean of St. Paul's Cathedral in London.

Glossary

ʿĀʾisha: The third and favorite wife of Muhammad and daughter of Abū-Bakr.

Abū Ṭālib: Uncle and guardian of Muhammad and father of ʿAlī.

Ādeśa: A religious formula used in Hinduism to summarize a body of teaching.

Adoptionism: A Christological heresy that emerged in the eighth century and held that Jesus as a human was adopted into the Godhead and thereby *became* the Son of God. The term "adoptionism" was later used retroactively to refer to any movement throughout church history which suggested that Jesus Christ was a man on whom divine qualities were conferred.

Advaita: Literally, "not-two." Refers to Hindu views of non-dualism. It is associated with one of the major branches of Vedanta, known as advaitism.

Agni: A fire god worshipped in Vedic religion.

Ahimsā: Principle of non-injury prominent in all Indian religions and often cited as the basis for vegetarianism.

ahl al-kitāb: Literally, "peoples of the book." Refers to followers of monotheistic religions with revealed scriptures, such as Christianity and Judaism.

Āḷāra: One of the two high-caste Brahmins under whom Siddhārtha Gautama studied prior to his enlightenment. *See* Uddaka.

al-Ghazālī: Influential Iranian philosopher, theologian, and mystic of the Shafi'ite school who helped to reconcile Ṣūfism with orthodox Islam.

al-Hallaj: Persian Ṣūfi poet who was executed as a heretic in 922. He is best known for his ecstatic utterance, "I am the truth."

ʿAlī: According to the Sunni, the fourth of the "Rightly Guided Caliphs." Shiʿite Muslims regard Ali as the first imām and the true successor of Muhammad.

Allāhu Akbar: A formula, known as the takbīr, which is used in the ritual prayers and means, "God is most Great."

Ambedkar, B.: (1891–1956) Prominent Indian Minister of Law from dalit background who led a movement of low-caste and non-caste Indians to convert to Buddhism.

Amitā: *See* Amitābha.

Amitābha: The Bhodisattva of "unlimited light" in Pure Land Buddhism; known in China as A-mi-t'o and in Japan as Amida (Amita). According to Pure Land texts, Amitābha was once a monk named Dharmakara who, after countless lifetimes of practice, achieved enlightenment and can rescue others through the repetition of his name. *See* Namu Amita Butsu, Nembutsu.

Anāhata śabda: Literally, "unstruck sound," referring to the transcendental cosmic sound that Hindus regard as resonating throughout the universe and frequently characterized by the sound *om* (pronounced AUM).

Ānalatva: In the viśiṣṭādvaitin philosophy of Rāmānuja, one of Brāhman's five defining attributes, meaning "purity."

Ānanda: Bliss; often referred to in conjunction with the three affirmations of Brāhman: Sat, Cit, and Ānanda. Also used by Rāmānuja as one of the five defining attributes of Brāhman.

Anantatva: In the viśiṣṭādvaitin philosophy of Rāmānuja, one of Brāhman's five defining attributes, meaning "infinitude."

Anātman: Literally, "no-self." In Buddhist thought, a denial of the Brahminical tradition which posited an eternal self (ātman). Clinging to the concept of self or ātman was, for the Buddha, an attachment which impeded true enlightenment.

Animism: A broad term which normally includes the belief in impersonal spiritual forces and in controlling deities and subordinate spirits.

Anonymous Christian: Term used to describe a theological perspective arising from the writings of Roman Catholic theologian Karl Rahner (1904–84). Rahner argued that the grace of God is at work implicitly in other religions such that many are saved by Christ apart from their explicit awareness of Christ. These 'implicit' Christians have been called anonymous Christians.

Anṣār: Literally, "helpers" referring particularly to those from Medina who assisted the Prophet in the Battle of Badr.

Antaryamin: One of the three ways in which God expresses His immanence, particularly in Vaiṣṇava literature, meaning "inner controller." The other two major ways are through icons and avatāra.

Arhat: Literally, "worthy one," referring to an enlightened person who has joined the monastic community.

Arianism: A Christological heresy named after its main advocate, Arius, who held that the Son of God was not eternal but was created by the Father before the creation. Arianism was condemned by the Council of Nicea in 325 CE.

Arundhatī: A hermeneutical principle in Hinduism which allows for indirect discourse in discussing truths which elude direct apprehension.

Āryadeva: The most famous disciple of Nāgārjuna, the founder of the Mādhyamika school of Buddhism.

Aryans: The name of the people-group which migrated into the northern plains of India from central Asia around 1500 BCE.

Asaṅga: Buddhist founder of the Yogācāra school of Buddhism.

Aseity: A reference to God's self-existence which separates God's being from all other being that is dependent upon him. In theology, aseity refers to the study of God's essence and nature as He is in Himself.

Ash'arite: School of theology founded by al-Ash'ari (873–935) which emphasized the superiority of revelation over reason. He taught that the Qur'ān was uncreated and eternal.

Aśoka: Third ruler in the Mauryan Dynasty, known for convening a Buddhist council as well as his Dharma Conquest which promoted Buddhism throughout his realm. His reign is traditionally held to be between 272 and 231 BCE.

Atharva Veda: The fourth of the four Saṃhitās after the Ṛg-Veda, Sāma-Veda, and Yajur-Veda. It was compiled approximately 900 BCE and contains collections of hymns as well as magical formulas. *See* Saṃhitās.

Ātman: Self or essence in Hinduism. Often cited as a form of pure consciousness within every being. In the Upanishads, the ātman is identified with Brāhman. *See* Brāhman.

Avalokitseśvara: Literally, "the Lord who looks down." One of the three most important bodhisattvas in Mahāyāna Buddhism. He is the chief attendant to Amitābha and is the embodiment of compassion.

Avatāra: Literally, "descent," referring to a corporeal form of a deity or superhuman being.

Āya: Literally, "signs," referring to the individual verses into which each of the 114 chapters (sūrahs) of the Qur'ān is divided.

Badr, Battle of: The first military victory of the Muslims in Medina against a superior force of Meccans (March, 624).

Bhagavad-Gītā: Literally, the "song of our Lord," widely regarded as the most famous of Hindu Scriptures. It was probably composed between 150 BCE and 250 CE and is actually part of a larger work known as the *Mahabhārata.*

Bhakti: Devotion, faith, and loving surrender to a deity in Hinduism. A bhakta is one who is devoted to a particular deity.

Bhasya: A commentary on a sacred Hindu text.

Black Stone: A venerated stone in Islam which represents monotheism and is located in the southeastern corner of the Kaʿbah.

Bodhi: Technical term meaning "enlightenment." In Buddhism, refers to those who have realized the Four Noble Truths and completed the eight-fold path.

Bodhisattva: Literally, an "enlightened being." Refers to someone who has refused liberation from the wheel of samsara, postponing their own salvation, and, out of compassion, returned to assist all sentient beings towards perfect enlightenment.

Body of bliss: *See* Saṃbhoga-kāya.

Body of essence: *See* Dharma-kāya.

Brahmā: In Hindu mythology, a particular deity who fashions the world.

Brāhman: The all-pervading Ultimate Essence or Reality in Hinduism.

Brahma Sūtra: Famous ancient commentary on the Upanishads by Bādarāyaṇa. The major Hindu philosophers introduce their philosophies through a careful commentary on the Brahma Sūtra.

Brahmin: The highest caste in Hinduism; a priestly caste.

Brāhmo Samāj: Hindu reform movement (Society of God), founded by Ram Mohan Roy in the nineteenth century, which sought to reconcile ancient Hinduism with unitarian theism.

Buddha: The title of one who has been awakened or enlightened. In Hinayana Buddhism there is only one historical Buddha per world-cycle. In Mahāyāna, there may be many buddhas. *See* Dharma-kāya.

Buddhaghosa: Late fourth- and early fifth-century Therevādin scholar. He is widely regarded as the greatest commentator in Therevāda Buddhism.

Buddhahood: The state of being a Buddha; attaining the goal of perfect enlightenment or the realization that all beings already contain a Buddha nature.

Cārvākas: Materialist school of thought in Hinduism which reduced the entire universe, including human intelligence, to the four elements of earth, water, fire, and air.

Caste: In Hinduism, a religiously sanctioned, stratified social order broadly associated with the four varṇas known as Brahmin, Kṣatriya, Vaiśya, and Śūdra.

Chalcedon, Council of: The fourth ecumenical council held in Asia Minor in 451 CE, most famous for repudiating errors in some expressions of Nestorianism and Eutychianism and establishing the orthodox Christological formula which declared Christ to be two natures united in one Person without confusion, change, division, or separation.

Christotokos: Literally, "Christ-bearer." A description of Mary which was preferred by Nestorius to the title Theotokos.

Citta: A technical term for "mind" or "thought," particularly important in Yogācārin thought. *See* Yogācāra.

Cogito ergo sum: Literally, "I think, therefore I am." Rene Descartes' (1596–1650) foundational statement to discover the basis of all philosophical thought.

Communicatio idiomatum: Literally, "the sharing of attributes," referring to a Christological expression to express the unity of Christ's person. Epithets appropriate for Christ's humanity or deity are applied to the unified person of Christ.

Constantinople, First Council of: The second ecumenical council, held in 381 CE, which reaffirmed the Council of Nicea's (325 CE) condemnation of Arianism and safeguarded Christ's humanity by condemning Apollinarianism, which, in part, denied that Christ had a human mind.

Council of Florence: Regarded by Roman Catholics as the seventeenth ecumenical council. It was held in various sessions between1438 and 1445 to discuss theological differences between the Roman and the Eastern Church.

Dalai Lama: Honorary title given to the successive reincarnations of Avaloiteśvara in Tibetan Buddhism. He is considered to be the political and religious leader of Tibet.

Dalit: Chosen self-designation by untouchables and other non-caste (scheduled caste) peoples of India.

Dāna: A term referring to the ethic of giving, originally associated with the laity providing assistance to Buddhist monks but in Mahāyāna, the first stage in the ethical path towards enlightenment.

Deism: Rational thought associated with the eighteenth century which believed that knowledge of God was attainable apart from revelation. Deism posited a God who, after creation, remained distant and uninvolved with His creation.

Dependent arising: *See* pratītya samutpāda.

Dependent origination: *See* pratītya samutpāda.

Deva: A god and/or personification of a deity in Hinduism (feminine, devī, is goddess).

Dhammapada: Literally, "sayings of the dhamma," referring to a collection of verses widely believed to be the utterances of the Buddha.

Dharma: In Hinduism, a broad conception of duty, particularly the importance of fulfilling caste obligations (varṇa) and life stages (aśrama). In Buddhism, the term is used to refer to the essential body of Buddhist teaching, including the Four Noble Truths, the eight-fold path, pratītya-samutpāda, and other key Buddhist doctrines.

Dharma conquest: *See* Aśoka.

Dharma-body: *See* dharma-kāya.

Dharmakara: Earthly name of a Buddhist follower who took on the 48 vows and who, upon enlightenment, became known as Amitābha. *See* Amitābha. It is his eighteenth vow which is the source of the Nembutsu doctrine. *See* Nembutsu.

Dharma-kāya: One of the bodies of Buddha in Mahayana referring to the essence of Buddha and the innate reality of Buddhahood. *See* Trikāya.

Dhāt: Essence of Allah in Sunni thought.

Dhawq: The "tasting" of God in Ṣūfism, associated with the experience of communion and, ultimately, union with Allah.

Dhikr: Literally, "remembrance," referring to the Ṣūfi practice of remembering God's commands through recitation of a litany that highlights the names of Allah and various passages from the Qur'ān.

Diamond Sūtra: A famous Mahāyāna sūtra written between 300 and 700 CE which, like the Heart Sūtra, is a condensed version of the famous Perfection of Wisdom Sūtras. *See* Prajñāparamitā Sūtras.

Docetism: A range of doctrinal positions which downplayed the real humanity and suffering of Christ.

Dualism: A philosophical doctrine that rejects monism and maintains a fundamental distinction between mind and matter.

Duḥkha: Literally, "suffering," referring to the first of the Four Noble Truths and describing the condition of transitory existence. *See* Four Noble Truths.

Durgā: Popular warrior goddess who slays the buffalo demon Mahiṣa and the most important manifestation of the Great Goddess in Hinduism. *See* Māhā Devī.

Eightfold Path: The spiritual path prescribed by the Buddha along which a devotee must travel to achieve enlightenment. The eight stages along the path are right understanding, right thought, right speech, right action, right livelihood, right effort, right mindfulness, and right concentration.

Ekam evādvītiyam: Literally, "one without a second," an important Upanishadic phrase supporting monism. *See* māhāvākya.

Emanation: In Hinduism, the cosmological principle that creation proceeds from and is identical in essence with God or Īśvara.

Engaged exclusivist: An exclusivist who nevertheless maintains optimism regarding God's preparatory activity through general revelation and the necessity of maintaining a missiological focus in all evangelical theologizing. *See* exclusivism.

Enhypostatic: The doctrine that the hypostasis of the Godhead who became incarnate (Christ) included perfected human attributes, allowing the one person of Christ to be fully human and fully divine without compromise. *See* hypostasis.

Ephesus, Council of: The third ecumenical council, held in 431 CE, which condemned tendencies in certain expressions of Nestorian theology that maintained that there were two separate Persons in the incarnate Christ. It is unlikely that Nestorius himself actually held to the view which, unfortunately, bears his name. *See* Theotokos.

Epistemology: The study of the source, nature, and limitations of knowledge.

Exclusivism: An evangelical soteriology which insists on the unique authority of Jesus Christ, the centrality and historicity of the death and resurrection of Jesus Christ, and the necessity of an explicit act of repentance and faith in Christ. *See* engaged exclusivist.

Ex-nihilo: Literally, "out of nothing," referring to God's creative acts apart from pre-existing materials.

Fanāʾ: Literally, "extinction," used in Islamic mysticism to refer to the final stage in the spiritual journey whereby the believer loses the "self" in union with Allah.

First Buddhist Council: Influential Buddhist council held in 483 BC which helped to promulgate Buddhist doctrines.

Five Aggregates: In Buddhism, the five constituent elements that make up human selfhood: form, sensation, perception, mental formations, and consciousness.

Four Noble Truths: Four truths promulgated by the Buddha which form the foundation of all Buddhist dharma. The giving of these four truths is generally referred to as "turning the wheel of dharma."

Gandhi, Mohandas: (1869–1948) Leader of the Indian independence movement and spiritual father of the modern Hindu nation; proponent of a form of non-violent resistance known as satyāgraha or truth-force.

Gaṇeśa: The elephant-headed son of the god Śiva and the goddess Parvati who was popularized in the Puranas.

Gautama, Siddhārtha: The historical founder of Buddhim who lived from 563–483 BCE. After enlightenment, he taught the Four Noble Truths and became known as the Buddha.

Gāyatrī mantra: A popular prayer appearing in the Ṛg-Veda: "Let us meditate on the desireable splendor of the Sun God, Savitri. May he stimulate our thoughts."

General revelation: Knowledge about God which is universally accessible to the human race. Frequently, the created order (Psalm 19:1–4) and the presence of human conscience (Rom. 2:14–16) are cited as examples.

God of the Philosophers: Theism as propounded through philosophic reasoning and speculation in contrast to the self-revelation of God through the Scriptures.

Great Assembly-ites: *See* Mahāsanghika.

Guṇa: In Hindu theism, a term used to mean "qualities" or "attributes." *See* nirguṇa, saguṇa.

Ḥadīth: A collection of oral traditions (sunna) related to things the Prophet said, did, or approved of which have been written down in a short narrative and verified through a reliable chain of oral transmitters (isnad). The most important collections of Ḥadīth are those by al-Bukhārī (d. 870) and al-Muslim (d. 875).

Hajj: The fifth pillar of Islam, which calls for a pilgrimage to Mecca sometime during the lifetime of all Muslim believers.

Ḥanīfs: Monotheists in pre-Islamic Arabia.

Hanumān: The monkey helper of Rāma in the Rāmāyana epic in Hindu literature.

Harappā: One of the principal cities of the ancient Indus Valley civilization, located in modern-day Pakistan.

Heart Sūtra: A famous Mahāyāna sūtra written between 300 and 700 CE which, like the Diamond Sūtra, is a condensed version of the famous Perfection of Wisdom Sūtras. *See* Prajñāparamitā Sūtras.

Hejira: Literally, "immigration," referring to the origin of the Islamic era when Muhammad and a group of followers left Mecca for Yathrib (Medina) on July 16, 622. *See* Yathrib.

Hīnayāna: Literally, "little vehicle." A pejorative term used by Mahāyāna (great vehicle) Buddhists to describe ancient Buddhism, which, in their view, was not privy to the full knowledge of the Buddha's revelations. *See* Therevāda.

Homoiousios: Expression found in the Trinitarian debate which declares the Son to be "of like substance" with the Father. The word is used to emphasize the full deity of Christ without denying distinctions within the Godhead. *See* homoousion.

Homoousion: Expression found in the Trinitarian debate which declares the Son to be "of one substance" with the Father. The word is used to emphasize the full deity of Christ and was a forceful rejection of Arianism. *See* homoiousios.

Hōnen: Founder of the Pure Land School of Japanese Buddhism. Hōnen's school is sometimes called the "single practice" school because of its emphasis on the exclusive practice of the Nembutsu. *See* Nembutsu.

Ḥulūl: Ṣūfī conception of the divine permeation into human life and existence.

Husayn: Second son of ʿAli and Fatimah and grandson of the Prophet. Shiʿites consider him an imām and mourn his death on the tenth of Muharram through passion plays which recall his death at Karbala. *See* Karbala.

Hypostasis: From the middle of the fourth century this term was contrasted with "ousia" to refer to the individual reality of each person of the Trinity. The orthodox position affirms that God is one in essence (ousia), yet existing eternally in three distinctions (hypostasis) known as Father, Son, and Holy Spirit.

Ilm: Islamic knowledge and learning, particularly Islamic traditions which produce theology and canon law. *See* 'ulama.'

Imām: For Sunni Muslims, the prayer leader in a mosque. Used in reference to the Four Rightly Guided Caliphs and the founders of the four schools of law. Among Shiʿites the term is used for special descendants of ʿAli and Fatimah who, they believe, are the true successors of Muhammad. Shiʿites are divided over how many Imāms are accepted as true imāms.

Imposter theory: Christological position which denies that Jesus Christ died on the cross, insisting that an imposter died in his place.

Inclusivism: Soteriological view which affirms the centrality of Christ and the historicity of His death and resurrection, but denies the necessity of explicit faith in Christ for salvation. In other words, Christ's death is ontologically necessary but not epistemologically necessary.

Indra: Warrior god in Vedic religion.

Indus Valley Civilization: Ancient Indian civilization, also known as Harappān, which developed between 1500 and 1800 BCE with important cities in Mohenjo-Daro and Harappā.

Injīl: Islamic term for the original, uncorrupted New Testament gospel, which does not correspond to any of the four gospels found in the Christian New Testament accepted by Christians today.

Inner Controller: *See* antaryamin.

ʿĪsā: Jesus' name in Arabic.

Īśvara: The name for the supreme, personal deity in Hinduism often associated with creation or *saguṇa* Brāhman.

Jāhilīyah: The period of ignorance prior to the revelation of the Qurʾān.

Jainism: Indian religion founded by Mahavira in the sixth century BCE which stresses the jīva or soul in every living thing.

Jili: Important Ṣūfi teacher. Jili is the descendent of the founder of the Qadirites, one of the four major Ṣūfi Orders.

Jñāna: Literally, "knowledge," used broadly to refer to the "path of knowledge" which is one of the three main paths or margas to liberation in Hinduism. The Hindu philosopher Rāmānuja also cites jñāna as one of Brāhman's five defining attributes.

Kaʿbah: Literally, "cube," referring to the holiest shrine in Islam located in the Grand Mosque in Mecca. The Ka`bah contains the sacred Black Stone.

Kālī: Hindu goddess who, in one of her most famous forms, is garlanded with severed heads and girdled with several arms and dances on the corpse of her husband Śiva.

Kalpas: Hindu cosmology of time which corresponds to a day and a night of Brahmā, comprising approximately 8.649 billion years.

Karbala: Iraqi town near Kufa where a famous Islamic battle took place on the tenth of Muharram 61 AH (680 CE). In this conflict, Husayn and other revered martyrs lost their lives.

Karma: Principle of cause and effect in Hinduism and Buddhism which asserts that all acts or deeds leave their influence on a future transmigration of the actor.

Karuṇā: Compassion in Buddhism and, along with loving-kindness and giving/charity, one of the Three Cardinal Virtues.

Khadījah: Muhammad's first wife and, traditionally, the first to affirm Muhammad's prophethood.

Krishna: Important deity in the Vaisnava tradition of Hinduism known primarily for his conversation with Arjuna, which is recorded in the Bhagavad-gītā, as is the climax of the Mahabhārata. In this passage Krishna presents himself as the Supreme God, identical or even superior to Brāhman.

Kṣatriya: The second highest caste in Hinduism, the warrior caste.

Lateran Council: A series of councils held in the Lateran Palace at Rome between the seventh and eighteenth centuries. Five of these councils are numbered and rank as ecumenical councils in the Western church.

Laws of Manu: *See* Manusmṛti.

Light Verse: A reference to a verse in the Qurʾān (sūrah 24:35) which is used metaphorically by Ṣūfi muslims.

Līlā: Cosmological term in Hinduism meaning "sport" or "play," used in both popular and philosophical traditions in Hinduism to describe the relationship of the Supreme Being to the created order.

Little Vehicle: *See* Mahāyāna.

Logos spermatikos: An expression meaning "seed of reason" or "seed of the word" which appears in both Middle Platonist and Stoic ethical writings and is a possible source for Justin Martyr's adaptation and application of the phrase in a Christian context referring to Christ's presence in pre-incarnate contexts.

Lotus Sūtra: Popular title of an important Mahāyāna sūtra which is particularly revered by the Tendai and Nichiren schools.

Mādhyamika: "Middle Way" school of Buddhist philosophy founded by Nāgārjuna and emphasizing emptiness and use of a system of logical analysis to render all propositions absurd which assume independent existence.

Mādhyamikakarika: Important writing of Nāgārjuna, meaning "middle-way" verses. A foundational text for Mādhyamika thought.

Māhā Devī: Literally, the "Great Goddess" of whom innumerable goddesses of local traditions in India are regarded as manifestations. Devotees of the Goddess are known as Śāktas. *See* Durgā.

Mahāsanghika: Literally, "great assemblyites." Refers to an early school of Buddhism which is one of the sources of the later emergence of Mahāyāna Buddhism.

Māhāvakya: Literally, "great utterance" referring to key sacred passages or religious formulas which summarize important bodies of doctrine, e.g., *tat twam asi. See* ādeśa.

Mahāyāna: Literally, "great vehicle," referring to the largest division of Buddhism which strives to become an enlightened being rather than a monk.

Mahiṣa: Buffalo demon slayed by Durgā in Hindu literature. *See* Durgā.

Maitreya: Well-known bodhisattva who many Mahayana Buddhists believe will be the next historical Buddha.

Maitreyanatha: First traditional expounder of Yogācāra. *See* Yogācāra.

Maitri: Buddhist ethical principle of loving-kindness.

Manah: Female deity worshipped in Mecca and, in pre-Islamic Arabia, one of the three daughters of Allah.

Maṇḍala: A geometric diagram in Hinduism and Buddhism which contains a picture of a deity or drawing of a celestial realm, allowing the worshipper to use the diagram to experience the reality or larger macrocosm it represents.

Mañjuśrī: One of the three most important bhodisattvas in Mahāyāna Buddhism, along with Maitreya and Avalokiteśvara. Mañjuśrī, or "sweet glory," is known to appear in dreams and visions and protects Buddhists in times of danger.

Manusmṛti: Laws of Manu; a Brahminical guidebook of dharma containing 2,685 verses addressing a wide range of social obligations and the duties of various castes and of individuals at different stages of life.

Māra: Buddhist deity in the sense-realm who uses sensuality to prevent people from gaining enlightenment.

Ma'rifa: In Ṣūfism, experiential knowledge which passes through several stages leading, ultimately, to complete union with Allah.

Materialists: *See* Cārvākas.

Māyā: In Hinduism and Buddhism, a false way of looking at the world by attributing reality to the world which it does not have.

Mecca: The holiest city in Islam, located in Saudi Arabia, and where the Ka'bah and Black Stone are located.

Medina: The City of the Prophet, formally known as Yathrib, in which Muhammad found refuge after the Hejira.

Minaret: The tower located near a mosque from which the muezzin issues the call to prayer.

Mi'raj: Muhammad's mystical journey from Mecca to Jerusalem on a white, winged animal and his ascent into heaven with the Angel Gabriel where he was granted special revelations for the Islamic community.

Modalism: Trinitarian heresy which emphasizes the unity of the Trinity at the expense of the plurality by arguing that the three persons of the Trinity are actually three descriptions of the one God. The view denies the essential nature of the Trinity.

Mohenjo-Daro: *See* Indus Valley Civilization.

Mokṣa: Release or liberation from the wheel of saṃsāra or rebirth in Hinduism.

Monism: A philosophic position that reduces all substances to a single, irreducible constituent.

Monophysitism: Literally, "one nature," referring to the heretical doctrine that in the Incarnate Christ there is only one nature, not two. This view, held by Eutyches (378–454 CE), was condemned by the Council of Chalcedon in 451 CE.

Muezzin: The name for the Muslim who issues the call to prayer from the minaret or, sometimes, from the doorway of a mosque.

Mukti: *See* mokṣa.

Mu'tazila: The rationalist school of Islamic theology which seeks to reconcile faith and reason.

Mysterium tremendum: Term referring to the ineffable reality of the inner life of God.

Nabī: In Islam, a prophet sent by Allah.

Nadhīr: Literally, "warner." Refers to Muhammad's role in conveying Allah's revelation to submit to Allah and calling people to prepare for the Day of Judgment. *See* rasūl.

Nāgārjuna: Founder of the Mādhyamika or "middle way" school of Mahāyāna Buddhism. He lived sometime between 150 and 250 CE and popularized the concept of emptiness. *See* Mādhyamika.

Nāma-rūpa: Literally, "name-form," referring to the mental and physical constituents of existence.

Namu Amida Butsu: Enlightenment formula which expresses homage to Amitābha Buddha. In China it is known as the Nien-fo-Namo A-mi-to' Fo. The repetition of this formula is regarded as a necessary component for rebirth in the Pure Land.

Nembutsu: Japanese Buddhist doctrine of repeating the name of Amida Buddha as a source of enlightenment. *See* Namu Amida Butsu.

Nestorianism: A Christological position which denied that the two natures of Christ were fully united into one Person. Nestorianism was condemned by the Council of Ephesus in 431 CE. *See* Ephesus, Council of.

Neti, neti: Literally, "not this—not this," referring to the inability to ascribe attributes or qualities to nirguṇa Brāhman in Hinduism.

Night Journey: *See* Mi'raj.

Night of Power: Sacred period of time when, according to Islamic tradition, the Qurʾān was first revealed to Muhammad and the Angel Gabriel first spoke to Muhammad.

Nihilism: A rejection of or loss of certainty in all religious and moral principles, sometimes leading to despair.

Ninety-nine beautiful names: The traditional number of names and titles of Allah found in the Qurʾān which are recited by faithful Muslims using a rosary known as a subḥa. *See* subḥa.

Nirguṇa: Literally, "without qualities," referring to the highest expression of Brāhman in Hindu thought, especially the *advaitic* branch of Vedāntism as espoused by Śaṅkara. *See* Śaṅkara.

Nirmāṇa-kāya: One of the three bodies of Buddha in Mahāyāna thought. Nirmāṇa-kāya refers to the historical body of a Buddha who takes on physical form to assist living beings and teach the Dharma.

Nirvana: The goal of Buddhism, which involves the extinguishing of self and release from the wheel of saṃsāra.

Ousia: being or essence.

Pali canon: Title of the sacred text collection of the Therevada school of Buddhism. *See* Tripiṭaka.

Pañcadaśī: Well-known fourteenth-century Vedāntic teaching manual attributed to Śrī Vidyāraṇya.

Panentheism: Belief that the universe is contained within God and is part and parcel of God, without denying that God's being may also transcend the universe.

Pantheism: A term which equates God with the substance of the universe, especially the natural forces and "laws" of nature.

Pāramitā: The six or ten ethical virtues a bodhisattva is supposed to attain.

People of the Book: *See* ahl al-kitāb.

Phenomenal world: The world as perceived by the senses.

Pīr: A Persian term for a special guide within a Ṣūfī order. In Arabic, the equivalent term is a murshid or shaykh. *See* Shaykh.

Platonism: Philosophical reasoning based on an idealist (rather than materialist) philosophy which conceives of the primary realities behind the visible world as consisting in Ideas or Forms, sometimes called universals, that are eternal and transcend time and space.

Pluralism: In Christian soteriology, a reference to the belief that non-Christian religions may provide independent salvific access to God.

Post-modernism: A broad term referring to a wide range of thinking which, at its core, denies the existence of any ultimate principles and is pessimistic about finding any scientific, philosophical, or religious truth that provides a coherent explanation of meaning for existence.

Prajñā: A technical term meaning "wisdom" which is cited throughout all strands of Buddhist literature as a primary goal.

Prajñāparamitā Sūtras: Term for a collection of Mahāyāna texts known as the "perfection of wisdom" sūtras dated around 100 BCE and later condensed in such influential texts as the Diamond Sūtra and the Heart Sūtra.

Prapatti: A term associated with bhakti Hinduism meaning "surrender" to a personal deity.

Pratītya-samutpāda: The Buddha's theory of causality. The term, often translated as "dependent arising," refers to a chain of dependent links used to describe the process by which something is given apparent existence. All existence is causally conditioned and there is no first cause. The doctrine is often illustrated with twelve links called nidānas.

Preparatio evangelica: Literally, "gospel preparation," referring to God's work in the pre-Christian heart which prepares a person to receive and respond to the gospel message.

Propositional truth: The content of revelation expressed in a statement of truth such as "God is just" or "Christ died on the cross."

Pūjā: Image worship in Hinduism, often involving the offering of flowers, incense, food, and acts of veneration.

Purāṇas: Important body of Hindu religious texts which highlights the exploits of various gods and goddesses, often used to support key sectarian beliefs and traditions in popular Hinduism.

Pure Land: Mahāyāna conception of a "Buddha-land" where a transcendent bodhisattva resides. It has no ultimate reality or existence.

Puruṣa: Cosmic figure who appears in the Ṛg-Veda and plays a prominent role in Vedic conceptions of cosmology. It is believed that one-quarter of the Puruṣa is manifest in creation. *See* panentheism.

Qadirite: Followers of a Ṣūfi Order named after Shaykh and ascetic preacher al-Jilani (1088–1166 CE). His tomb is located in Baghdad and is an important place of pilgrimage for Ṣūfis around the world.

Qiblah: Direction of prayer in Islam; facing Mecca.

Quraysh: The ruling tribe of Mecca and the guardians of the pre-Islamic Kaʿbah.

Ramaḍān: The ninth month of the Islamic lunar calendar, during which Muslims fast during the daylight hours. *See* sawm.

Rāmānuja: Hindu philosopher and theologian (traditionally, 1017–1137) who is the intellectual father of the *viśiṣṭād-vaitin* branch of Vedantism is and widely regarded as one of the most influential thinkers in the history of India. *See viśiṣṭādvaita.*

Rasūl: Literally, "messenger," referring to one of Muhammad's main titles as a messenger of Allah. *See* nadhīr.

Ṛg-Veda: The earliest and most important of the four Saṃhitās of Vedic religion. The Ṛg-Veda contains 1,028 hymns, arranged in ten books, to various Vedic deities, some dating as early as 1200 BCE.

Ṛta: Vedic term for the controlling principle and order of the universe.

Rudra: Destructive god in Vedic religion who foreshadows Śiva. *See* Śiva.

Sabellian Modalism: Trinitarian heresy propounded by Sabellius in the early third century which proposed that God is one hypostasis with three successive names. *See* hypostasis.

Saccidānanda: *See* Sat-Cit-Ānanda.

Saguṇa: In Hinduism, Brāhman with qualities or attributes. *See* Īśvara.

Sakya: One of the four major schools of Tibetan Buddhism.

Ṣalāt: Second pillar of Islam, which refers to ritual prayers performed five times daily by Muslims.

Sāma-Veda: The second of the four Saṃhitās of Vedic religion, a precursor religion to Hinduism. The Sāma-Veda is a book of chants based largely on the text of the Ṛg-Veda. *See* Ṛg-Veda.

Samādhi: Concentration or deep stage of meditation in Buddhism, associated with the eight-fold path.

Saṃbhoga-kāya: One of the bodies of Buddha in Mahayana thought, referring to the celestial or heavenly Buddha which is the destination or reward of devout Buddhists. *See* Trikāya.

Saṃhitās: A collection of the four earliest strands of the Vedas apart from the later additions of the Brāhmaṇas, Āraṇyakas, and Upanishads.

Saṃsāra: The cycle of life or existence in Hinduism and Buddhism, perpetuated by karma. Hindus and Buddhists advocate various paths through which a follower may escape this ever-turning "wheel of saṃsāra."

Saṃyutta-Nikāya: The third major portion of the Sutta Piṭaka of the Pali Canon, containing 56 groups of sūtras arranged according to subject and known as the "connected discourses."

Saṇgha: The monastic order or "assembly" founded by the Buddha. The members of the Saṇgha are known as bhikkus (monks) or bhikkhuṇī (nuns).

Śaṅkara: Hindu philosopher and theologian who lived from 788–820 and is widely regarded as one of the most influential thinkers in the history of India. He is the intellectual father of advaitism and his bhasya on the *Brahma Sūtra* continues to influence the formulation of Hindu thought today. *See* advaita.

Sannyāsin: Someone who renounces the world. According to many Hindus, it is the fourth and highest of the life-stages.

Śāntideva: Eighth-century Buddhist poet and philosopher who wrote *Undertaking the Way to Awakening*.

Sat: Being, which can be interpreted in Hinduism to be the opposite of non-being or a reference to that which lies beyond all duality.

Sat-Cit-Ānanda: Literally, "Being, Consciousness, and Bliss." A reference to nirguṇa Brāhman that has been used by some Indian Christian theologians as a bridge to communicate the doctrine of the Trinity.

Satya: Used to mean "truth" or "reality" and, in Hinduism, sometimes used to refer to ultimate being. Indeed, Rāmānuja cites satya as one of the five defining attributes of Brāhman. In Buddhism it can be a reference to the Four Noble Truths.

Savitri: Sun god in Vedic religion. *See* gāyatrī mantra.

Sawm: The fourth pillar of Islam, which requires abstaining from all food and drink during the daylight hours of the ninth month of the Islamic calendar. *See* Ramaḍān.

Scholasticism: A method of scholarly inquiry that examines authoritative texts such as the Bible to discover paradoxical statements that are subjected to careful logical scrutiny to reveal their inner consistency. Although the scholastic method has been used in all branches of scholarship, it is widely used to apply in particular to medieval theologizing.

Second Buddhist Council: Influential Buddhist council convened one hundred years following the Buddha's death to reform monastic practice which revealed important early divisions between the laity and the monks. *See* First Buddhist Council.

Second Vatican Council: Influential council convened by Pope John XXIII in 1961 and meeting in regular sessions between 1962 and 1965. Produced a wide range of documents which have influenced the life, theology, and doctrine of the Roman Catholic Church.

Semen religionis: Literally, the "germ or seed of religion," referring to knowledge of God which is universally latent in human hearts. *See* sensus divinitus.

Sensus divinitus: Literally, the "sense of the divine," used to describe the universal awareness of God's existence. *See* semen religionis.

Śeṣa: The name of the gigantic mythological snake in Hindu mythology who is the mount of Lord Viṣṇu.

Shahādah: The first of the five pillars of Islam, known as the Confession of faith: "I bear witness that there is no god but Allah, and Muhammad is the prophet of Allah."

Sharīʿa: Literally, "path." Refers to Islamic Law. *See* sunni.

Shaykh: Islamic title for a leading Islamic scholar or spiritual guide within a Ṣūfi order. *See* Pīr.

Shema: Important confession of faith in Judaism located in Deuteronomy 6:4 and affirming monotheistic theism in general and, more precisely, the unrivaled sovereignty of Yahweh.

Shiᶜite: The sect of ᶜAli which claims that the Caliphate belongs exclusively to members of ᶜAli's family and affirms the special role of an infallible imam. Eventually Shiᶜism developed three major branches based primarily on how many imams they officially recognize. The branches are known as the Zaydīs (also called Fivers), the Ismā`īlīs (also called Seveners), and the Imāmites (also called Twelvers).

Shinran: The most famous disciple of the Buddhist teacher Hōnen. Shinran (1173–1263) founded an influential school of Pure Land Buddhism known as *Jōdo Shinshū,* the True Pure Land School. *See* Hōnen.

Shirk: A grievous sin in Islam referring to polytheism or attributing "partners" to Allah.

Ṣifat: Literally, "attributes," referring to the Islamic sunni belief in seven attributes of Allah which are distinct from His essence: life, knowledge, power, will, hearing, sight, and speech.

Śīla: Morality or ethical conduct in Buddhist thought.

Śiva: Prominent Hindu deity associated with fertility and destruction. Many other deities such as Gaṅeśa or religious symbols such as Śiva's lingum and the Ganges River are associated with Siva, further heightening the important role of Śiva in Hinduism.

Śruti: Literally, "that which is heard," referring to the highest level of sacred literature in Hinduism, including the Vedas and the Upanishads. It is often contrasted with a lower level of literature, smṛti, meaning, "that which is remembered." *See* anāhata śabda.

Streamwinner: A Buddhist who has reached a sufficiently advanced stage to merit only happy rebirths and a speedy enlightenment. More advanced stages include becoming a "once-returner" and a "never-returner."

Subḥa: An Islamic rosary with 33 or 99 beads, used for reciting the 99 beautiful names of Allah. *See* Ninety-nine beautiful names.

Suchness: *See* tathatā.

Śūdras: The fourth, and lowest, of the four varnas or social castes in India. It refers to the servant or slave caste.

Ṣūfi: A member of an Islamic spiritual order who follows a mystical, spiritual "path" (tariqa) and who progresses through several stages and initiations leading to direct knowledge of God, spiritual illumination, and, eventually, union with Allah. Ṣūfism became a more formalized movement after the ninth century.

Sunna: In Islam, a reference to the examples of the Prophet which give guidance to the Islamic community and eventually were written down in collections known as Hadith and which inform Islamic law (Sharīᶜah).

Sunni: The major body of Islam, comprising 80 percent of Muslims worldwide who recognize the first form caliphs as the true successors of Muhammad. They are divided into four schools of law: Ḥanafī, Mālikī, S̲h̲āfiʿī and Ḥanbalī.

Śunyāta: Literally, "emptiness," referring to the absence of substantial independence. A key concept in Mahāyāna conceptions of reality.

Śūnya-vāda: An alternative name for the Mādhyamika school of Buddhism meaning "all is void."

Sūrah: Islam term referring to a chapter in the Qurʾān. There are 114 sūrahs in the Qurʾān.

Sūtras: Authoritative texts in Hinduism and Buddhism, often including aphorisms.

Svarūpa: Used in Hinduism to describe essential nature.

Takbīr: *See* Allāhu Akbar.

Taṇhā: Literally, "thirst." Refers to human cravings which Buddhists attribute as the cause of suffering in the Four Noble Truths.

Ṭarīqas: Spiritual or mystical "path" in Ṣūfism leading to direct knowledge and communion with God.

Taṣawwuf: Islamic term for Ṣūfism. *See* Ṣūfī.

Tat twam asi: A phrase which can be translated as "you are that" which is used repeatedly in the Upanishads to reinforce the identity of one's ātman with Brāhman, the all-pervading reality of the universe. *See* Brāhman.

Tathāgata: Honorific title for the Buddha after his Enlightenment, meaning "one who has gone to Awakening." Mahāyāna apply the term more broadly to anyone who has achieved Buddhahood.

Tathatā: The focal point of consciousness in the Yogācāra school of Buddhism.

Tawḥīd: Doctrine of the unity of God which, in the Islamic context, refers to a strict non-Trinitarian monotheism.

Tetralemma: Nāgārjuna's famous doctrine of causation which reduces all philosophies to one of four categories for the purpose of refuting all philosophies that posit any form of causation. *See* Nāgārjuna.

Than ka: Painted scrolls in Tibetan Buddhism which are used to aid the development of the mental disciplines.

Theotokos: Literally, "God-bearer," used widely as a devotional title for Mary, the mother of Jesus. *See* Nestorianism.

Theravāda: Literally, "the Elders," referring to the more ancient, monastic expression of Buddhism. *See* Hīnayāna.

Thomism: In Roman Catholicism, the systematic expression of the theological work of Thomas Aquinas.

Three Baskets: *See* Tripiṭaka.

Three Cardinal Virtues: The virtues of compassion *(karuṇā)*, loving-kindness *(maitri)*, and giving/charity *(dāna)* which form the basis of Buddhist ethical teachings.

Trikāya: Three bodies of Buddha in Mahayana thought. *See* Dharma-kāya, Saṃbhoga-kāya, and Nirmāṇa-kāya.

Tripiṭaka: Three "baskets" or divisions in the Pali canon of Buddhism: Vinaya, Sutta, and Abhidhamma. *See* Pali canon.

Uddaka: One of the two high-caste Brahmins under whom Siddhartha Gautama studied prior to his enlightenment. *See* Āḷāra.

'Ulama': The collective term for the experts in Islamic canon law and theology. *See* ilm.

Upanishad: Literally, "to sit down near," referring to a collection of mostly philosophical and reflective writings which were attached to the ends of the various strands of Vedic literature and which form the basis for much of the development of Hindu philosophical thought.

Vaiśeṣika: One of the six orthodox schools of Hindu philosophy, known as the atomistic school; assumes the reality of the many, varied constituents in the universe.

Vaiśya: The merchant caste; one of the four castes or varṇas in Hinduism. *See* caste.

Vedānta: One of the six orthodox schools of Hindu philosophy. Its two most important branches are Śaṅkara's advaitism (non-dualism) and Rāmānuja's viśiṣṭādvaitism (modified non-dualism).

Vedas: A term that frequently refers to the entire structure of Vedic literature, including the Saṃhitās, the Brāhmaṇas, the Āraṇyakas, and even, at times, the Upanishads. Some writers apply the term exclusive of the Upanishads and some even use the term to refer only to the Saṃhitās.

Vidyā: A term for knowledge that is widely used in all Indian religions.

Vijñānavāda: Another name for the Yogācāra school of Buddhist thought, meaning "mind-only." *See* citta.

Viśiṣṭadvaita: Literally, modified non-dualism; refers to another major branch of Vedānta and is often associated with the Hindu philosopher Rāmānuja.

Viṣṇu: Hindu deity who first appears in the Ṛg-Veda but gradually assumes a more prominent role and is the source of the most important avatārs in Hinduism today.

Vyavahārika: In advaitism, a form of dependent or contingent reality.

Wālī: In Islam, a friend of God or one who is "near" to God. For Shiʿites it forms part of an important title of ʿAli, the "friend of Allah."

Yajurveda: The third of the four main Saṃhitās in Vedic religion, a precursor religion to Hinduism. The Yajur contains various hymns and formulas which were spoken by the priests during the ritual sacrifices.

Yathrib: Pre-Islamic name of Medina, the city of the Prophet. *See* Hejira.

Yogācāra: Major school of Buddhist philosophy which emphasizes the mind and the nature of consciousness, also called Vijñānavāda.

Yogi: A person who is physically, mentally, and spiritually disciplined.

Yugas: The four ages in Indian cosmology, known respectively as Kṛta, Tretā, Dvāpara, and Kali.

Zakat: Annual alms tax of 2½ percent of one's income in Islam levied to provide assistance to the poor and to further Islamic causes. The third of the five pillars of Islam.

Bibliography

Al-Madinah, Mushaf, and an-Nabawiyah, trans. *The Holy Qur-an: English Translation and the Meanings and Commentary.* Saudi Arabia: King Fahd Complex for the Printing of the Holy Qurʾān, n.d.

Alston, A. J., ed. *Śaṅkara on Creation.* London: Shanti Sadan, 1980.

———. *Śaṅkara on the Absolute.* London: Shanti Sadan, 1980.

———. *Śaṅkara on the Soul.* London: Shanti Sadan, 1981.

Amaladoss, Michael. "Dialogue and Mission: Conflict or Convergence?" *International Review of Mission* 75, no. 299 (July 1986): 222–41.

Anderson, J. N. D. *Christianity and Comparative Religion.* Downers Grove, Ill.: InterVarsity, 1971.

Animanada, B. *The Blade.* Calcutta: Roy and Son, 1947.

Baillas, L. J. *World Religions: A Story Approach.* Mystic, Conn.: Twenty-Third Publications, 1991.

Baljon, J. M. S. *Religion and Thought of Shah Wālī Allah Dihlawi, 1703–1762.* Leiden: Brill, 1986.

Barnard, L. W. *Justin Martyr.* Cambridge: Cambridge University Press, 1967.

Barrett, David. "Annual Statistical Table." *International Bulletin of Missionary Research* 25, no. 1 (January 2001): 24–25.

Bediako, Kwame. "The Doctrine of Christ and the Significance of Vernacular Terminology." *International Bulletin of Missionary Research* 22, no. 3 (July 1998): 110–11.

———. *Theology and Identity: The Impact of Culture upon Christian Thought in the Second Century and in Modern Africa.* Oxford: Regnum, 1992.

Besant, Annie, trans. *The Bhagavad-Gītā.* Wheaton: Theosophical Publishing House, 1998.

Bonner, Anthony, ed. and trans. *Selected Works of Ramon Llull (1232–1316).* 2 vols. Princeton: Princeton University Press, 1985.

Boyd, Robin. *An Introduction to Indian Christian Theology.* Delhi: ISPCK, 1994.

———. *India and the Latin Captivity of the Church.* Cambridge: Cambridge University Press, 1974.

Brockington, J. L. *Hinduism and Christianity.* New York: St. Martin's Press, 1992.

Carman, John. *The Theology of Rāmānuja.* New Haven: Yale University Press, 1974.

Carter, John, trans. *The Dhammapada.* Oxford: Oxford: Oxford University Press, 2000.

Caspar, Robert. *Trying to Answer Questions.* Rome: PISAI, 1989.

Chatterjee, S., and D. Datta. *An Introduction to Indian Philosophy.* 8th ed. Calcutta: University of Calcutta, 1984.

"Christians in Dialogue with Men of Other Faiths." *International Review of Mission* 59, no. 236 (October 1970): 382–91.

Cobb, John B., and Christopher Ives, eds. *The Emptying God: A Buddhist-Jewish-Christian Conversation.* Maryknoll, N.Y.: Orbis, 1990.

Conze, Edward, ed. *Buddhist Texts.* New York: Philosophical Library, 1954.

Corless, R., and P. Knitter, eds. *Buddhist Emptiness and Christian Trinity.* New York: Paulist, 1990.

Cox, James. "Faith and Faiths: The Significance of A. G. Hogg's Missionary Thought for a Theology of Dialogue." *Scottish Journal of Theology* 32 (1979): 241–55.

———. "The Influence of A. G. Hogg over D. G. Moses: A Missionary Message for India." *Religion and Society* 27, no. 4 (December 1980): 66–79.

Cragg, Kenneth. *The Mind of the Qur'ān.* London: George Allen and Unwin, 1973.

Dabney, Robert L. *The Westminster Confession and Creeds.* Dallas: Presbyterian Heritage, 1983.

Davids, R., trans. *Saṃyutta-Nikāya.* London: Oxford University Press, 1922.

Deane, S. N., trans. *Anselm: Basic Writings.* LaSalle, Ill.: Open Court, 1966.

deBary, William Theodore. *The Buddhist Tradition in India, China and Japan.* New York: Vintage, 1972.

Demarest, Bruce. *General Revelation.* Grand Rapids: Zondervan, 1982.

Deutsch, E. and J. A. B. van Buitenen, eds. *A Source Book of Advaita Vedānta.* Honolulu: University of Hawaii Press, 1971.

Dharmaraj, Jacob, and Glory Dharmaraj. *Christianity and Islam: A Missiological Encounter.* Delhi: ISPCK, 1998.

Doniger, Wendy, trans. *The Laws of Manu.* New Delhi: Penguin India, 1991.

Farah, Caesar. *Islam.* 6th ed. Hauppauge, N.Y.: Barron's Educational Services, 2000.

Farquhar, J. N. *The Crown of Hinduism.* 1913. Reprint, New Delhi: Oriental Books Reprint Corporation, 1971.

Fernando, Antony. *Buddhism Made Plain.* Rev. ed. Maryknoll, N.Y.: Orbis, 1985.

Feuerbach, Ludwig. *The Essence of Christianity.* New York: Harper and Brothers, 1957.

Feuerstein, G. "The One and the Many: A Fundamental Philosophical Problem in the Principal Upanishads." *Hinduism* 88 (1980): 1–10.

Forman, Robert K. C., ed. *Religions of the World.* 3d ed. New York: St. Martin's, 1993.

Frazer, Robert W. *Indian Thought.* London: T. F. Unwin, 1915.

Gairdner, W. H. T. *God as Triune, Creator, Incarnate, Atoner.* Madras: CLS, 1916.

Gamghirananda, S., trans. *Brahma Sūtras Bhasya of Shankaracharya.* Calcutta: Advaita Ashrama, 1993.

Geisler, Norman, and Abdul Saleeb. *Answering Islam: The Crescent in the Light of the Cross.* Grand Rapids: Baker, 1993.

George, Timothy. *Is the Father of Jesus the God of Muhammad?* Grand Rapids: Zondervan, 2002.

Gispert-Sauch, Gilbert. "The Sanskrit Hymns of Brahmabandhav Upadhyay." *Religion and Society* 19, no. 4 (December 1972): 60–79.

Goldziher, Ignaz. *Introduction to Islamic Theology and Law.* Princeton: Princeton University Press, 1981.

Graham, Dom Aelred. *Conversations: Christian and Buddhist.* New York: Harcourt, Brace and World, 1968.

Griffith, Ralph, trans. *The Hymns of the Ṛg-Veda.* 2 vols. Delhi: Low Price Publications, 1995.

Griffiths, Bede. *Christian Ashram.* London: Darton, Longman and Todd, 1966.

Grimes, John. "Radhakrishnan and Śaṅkara's Māyā." *Scottish Journal of Religious Studies* 10 (spring 1989): 50–56.

Gross, Rita, and Terry Muck, eds. *Buddhists Talk about Jesus—Christians Talk about the Buddha.* New York: Continuum, 2000.

Hackett, Stuart. *The Reconstruction of the Christian Revelation Claim.* Grand Rapids: Baker, 1984.

Hawley, J. "Thief of Butter, Thief of Love." *History of Religions* 18, no. 3 (February 1979): 203–20.

Hay, Stephen, ed., *Sources of Indian Tradition.* Vol. 2, 2d ed. New York: Columbia University Press, 1988.

Heine, S., ed. *Buddhism and Interfaith Dialogue.* London: MacMillan, 1995.

Heinegg, Paul, trans. *Christianity and World Religions.* Maryknoll, N.Y.: Orbis, 1993.

Herman, A. L. "Indian Theodicy in Śaṅkara and Rāmānuja on *Brahma Sūtra* II.1.32–36." *Philosophy East and West* 21 (1971): 265–81.

Hick, John. *An Interpretation of Religion.* New Haven: Yale University Press, 1989.

Hick, John, and Brian Hebblethwaite. *Christianity and Other Religions.* Philadelphia: Fortress, 1980.

Hick, John, and Paul F. Knitter, eds. *The Myth of Christian Uniqueness.* Maryknoll, N.Y.: Orbis, 1987.

Hillman, Ed. *The Wider Ecumenism: Anonymous Christianity and the Church.* New York: Herder and Herder, 1968.

Hogg, A. G. "Notes of the Month." *Madras Christian College Magazine,* n.s., 7, no. 4 (1907): 202.

———. "Some Fundamentals of Christianity." *Madras Christian College Magazine.* Quarterly series 3, no. 1 (1923): 15–26.

———. "The God That Must Needs Be Christ Jesus." *International Review of Missions* 6 (January 1917): 62–73.

———. *Karma and Redemption.* 1909. Reprint, Madras: Christian Literature Society, 1970.

———. *The Authority of Faith.* Madras: Christian Literature Society, 1939.

Huntington, C. W., Jr. *The Emptiness of Emptiness: An Introduction to Early Indian Mādhyamika.* Honolulu: University of Hawaii Press, 1989.

Hussein, M. Kamel. *City of Wrong: A Friday in Jerusalem.* Trans. Kenneth Cragg. Oxford: One World, 1995.

Jacob, G. A. *Handbook of Popular Maxims.* Bombay: Tukaram Javaaji, 1907.

Jenson, Robert. *The Triune Identity.* Philadelphia: Fortress, 1982.

Kalupahana, David. *Nāgārjuna: The Philosophy of the Middle Way.* New York: SUNY Press, 1986.

Kelly, J. N. D. *Early Christian Creeds.* New York: Longmans, Green, 1950.

Khan, Abrahim H. "Muhammad as Object and Subject." *Studies in Religion* 7, no. 4 (fall 1978): 373–85.

Khan, Muhammad Muhsin, trans. *The Translation of the Meanings of Sahih Al-Bukhārī.* Vols. 1–9. Dar Ahya: Us-Sunnah, Al Nabawiya, n.d.

King, Richard. "Brāhman and the World: Immanence and Transcendence in Advaita Vedānta." *Scottish Journal of Religious Studies* 12 (autumn 1991): 107–26.

Kraemer, Hendrick. *The Christian Message in a Non-Christian World.* London: Edinburgh House, 1938.

Kulandran, Sabapathy. *Grace: A Comparative Study of the Doctrine in Christianity and Hinduism.* London: Lutterworth, 1964.

Kumarappa, B. *The Hindu Conception of Deity.* London: Luzac, 1934.

Lazarus, F. K. *Rāmānuja and Bowne.* Bombay: Chetane, 1962.

LeSaux, H. *Hindu-Christian Meeting Point.* Bangalore: National Press, 1969.

Lipner, Julius. *The Face of Truth.* Albany, N.Y.: SUNY Press, 1986.

———. "The Christian and Vedantic Theories of Originative Causality: A Study in Transcendence and Immanence." *Philosophy East and West* 28 (1978): 1–16.

Lopez, Donald, Jr., and Steve Rockefeller. *The Christ and the Bodhisattva.* Albany, N.Y.: SUNY Press, 1987.

Lott, Eric J. "The Conceptual Dimensions of *Bhakti* in the Rāmānuja Tradition." *Scottish Journal of Religious Studies* 2, no. 1 (spring 1981): 97–114.

Macdonell, A. *Practical Sanskrit Dictionary.* London: Oxford University Press, 1954, 1969.

Macnicol, N. "Some Hindrances to Theism in India." *The Indian Interpreter* 7, no. 2 (July 1912): 81–88.

———. *Indian Theism.* Oxford: Oxford University Press, 1915.

Mahadevan, T. M. P., trans. *Pañcadaśī.* Madras: Sri Ramakrishna Math, 1967.

Malkovsky, B. "The Personhood of Śaṅkara's *Para Brāhman.*" *The Journal of Religion* 77, no. 4 (October 1997): 541–62.

Massanari, Ronald. "A Problematic in Environmental Ethics: Western and Eastern Styles." *Buddhist-Christian Studies* 18 (1998): 37–61.

Massignon, Louis. *The Passion of al-Hallaj.* Vols. 1–4. Trans. Herbert Mason. Princeton: Princeton University Press, 1982.

May, Peter. "The Trinity and *Saccidānanda.*" *Indian Journal of Theology* 7, no. 3 (July–September 1958): 92–98.

McDermott, Gerald R. *Can Evangelicals Learn from World Religions?* Downers Grove, Ill.: InterVarsity, 2000.

McGrath, Alister. "The Challenge of Pluralism for the Contemporary Christian Church." *JETS* 35, no. 3 (September 1992): 361–73.

———. "The Christian Church's Response to Pluralism." *JETS* 35, no. 4 (December 1992): 487–501.

McLean, George, ed. *The Existence of God.* Washington, D.C.: Catholic University of America, 1972.

McNeill, John T. , ed. *Calvin: Institutes of the Christian Religion.* 2 vols. Philadelphia: Westminster, 1960.

Muhammad, Ṣuwar min Ḥayat. *Images from the Life of Muhammad.* Dar al-Ma'arif, Egypt: Amin Duwaidar, n.d.

Müller, Max. *Origin and Growth of Religion.* Varanasi: Indological Book House, 1964.

Nash, Ronald. *Is Jesus the Only Savior?* Grand Rapids: Zondervan, 1994.

Neill, Stephen. *Christian Faith and Other Faiths.* London: Oxford University Press, 1961.

Netland, Harold. *Dissonant Voices.* Grand Rapids: Eerdmans, 1991.

Newbigin, Lesslie. *The Gospel in a Pluralist Society.* Grand Rapids: Eerdmans, 1989.

———. *The Finality of Christ.* Richmond: John Knox; London: SCM, 1969.

Newport, John P. *Life's Ultimate Questions.* Dallas: Word, 1989.

Nicholson, R. A. *Studies in Islamic Mysticism.* Cambridge: Cambridge University Press, 1921, 1989.

Nikata, Samyutta, trans. *The Connected Discourses of the Buddha.* Boston: Wisdom Publications, 2000.

O'Flaherty, Wendy, ed. *Hindu Myths.* New York: Penguin, 1975.

Oden, Thomas C. *The Living God.*, Vol. 1. of *Systematic Theology.* San Francisco: Harper and Row, 1987.

Otto, Rudolph. *The Idea of the Holy.* 5th ed. Trans. John W. Harvey. London: Oxford University Press, 1928.

Oxtoby, Willard, ed. *World Religions: Eastern Traditions.* Oxford: Oxford University Press, 1996.

Pandit, Moti Lal. *Transcendence and Negation.* New Delhi: Munshiram Manoharlal, 1999.

———. "Śaṅkara's Concept of Reality." *Indian Theological Studies* 17, no. 4 (December 1980): 8–16.

Panikkar, R. G. *The Unknown Christ of Hinduism.* London: Darton, Longman and Todd, 1964.

———. "The Brāhman of the Upanishads and the God of the Philosophers." *Religion and Society* 7, no. 2 (September 1960): 12–19.

Parrinder, Geoffrey. *Jesus in the Qur'ān.* London: Faber and Faber, 1965. Reprint, Oxford: One World, 1995.

———. *Avātar and Incarnation.* Oxford: One World, 1997.

Pickthall, Muhammad Marmaduke, trans. *The Glorious Qur'ān.* Mecca: Muslim World League, 1977.

Pinnock, Clark. *A Wideness in God's Mercy: The Finality of Jesus Christ in a World of Religions.* Grand Rapids: Zondervan, 1992.

———. "Toward an Evangelical Theology of Religions." *JETS* 33, no. 3 (September 1990): 359–68.

Pomazansky, M. *Orthodox Dogmatic Theology.* Plantina, Calif.: St. Herman of Alaska Brotherhood, 1983.

Pontifex, Don Mark. *Belief in the Trinity.* New York: Longmans, Green, 1954.

Radhakrishnan, S., ed. *The Principal Upanisads.* Delhi: Harper Collins, 1996.

Rahner, Karl. *Theological Investigations.* 20 vols. New York: Seabury, 1966–83.

Rahula, Walpola. *What the Buddha Taught.* New York: Grove Weidenfeld, 1974.

Ramachandra, Vinoth. *The Recovery of Mission.* Carlisle, England: Paternoster, 1996.

Robert, Dana. "Shifting Southward: Global Christianity since 1945." *International*

Bulletin of Missionary Research 24, no. 2 (April 2000): 50–58.
Roberts, Alexander, and James Donaldson, eds. *The Ante-Nicene Fathers.* 10 vols. Peabody, Mass.: Hendrickson, 1999.
Robinson, J. A. T. *Truth Is Two-Eyed.* London: SCM, 1979.
Robinson, Richard H., and Willard L. Johnson. *The Buddhist Religion.* 2d ed. Belmont, Calif.: Dickenson, 1977.
Robinson, Richard H., and Willard L. Johnson. *The Buddhist Religion: A Historical Introduction.* 3d ed. Belmont, Calif.: Wadsworth, 1982.
Rushdie, Salman. *The Satanic Verses.* London: Viking, 1988.
Sanders, John. *No Other Name: An Investigation into the Destiny of the Unevangelized.* Grand Rapids: Eerdmans, 1992.
Schaff, Philip, ed. *A Select Library of the Nicene and Post-Nicene Fathers of the Christian Church.* 14 vols. Grand Rapids: Eerdmans, 1954.
Schaff, Philip, and Henry Wace, eds. *Nicene and Post-Nicene Fathers.* Peabody, Mass.: Hendrickson, 1999.
Schumann, Hans. *Buddhism.* Wheaton, Ill.: Theosophical Publishing House, 1974.
Scott, David, ed. *Keshub Chunder Sen.* Madras: CLS, 1979.
Sharpe, Eric. *The Theology of A. G. Hogg.* Madras: Christian Literature Society, 1971.
Shehadi, Fadlou. *Ghazali's Unique Unknowable God.* Leiden: Brill, 1964.
Smart, Ninian. *World Religions: A Dialogue.* Baltimore: Penguin, 1966.
Soeng, Mu, trans. *The Diamond Sūtra.* Boston: Wisdom Publications, 2000.
Stanton, H. S. *The Teaching of the Qur'an.* London: SPCK, 1969.
Stewart, P. J. *Unfolding Islam.* Reading, England: Garnet, 1994.
Swidler, Leonard, ed. *Muslims in Dialogue: The Evolution of a Dialogue.* Lewiston, N.Y.: Edwin Mellen, 1992.
Swing, A. T. *The Theology of Albrecht Ritschl.* New York: Longmans, Green, 1901.
Tappert, Theodore, ed. and trans. *Table Talk.* Vol. 51 of *Luther's Works.* Philadelphia: Fortress, 1967.
Tennent, Timothy. *Building Christianity on Indian Foundations.* Delhi: ISPCK, 2000.
Thibaut, George. *The Vedānta Sūtras with the Commentary by Rāmānuja.* Sacred Books of the East, vols. 34 and 38. London: Oxford University Press, 1904.
Upadhyay, Brahmabandhav, trans. *Pañcadaśī.* Calcutta: n.p., 1902.
———. *Sophia: A Monthly Catholic Journal.* Vol. 1, no. 1 (January 1894)–vol. 6, no. 3 (March 1899). Karachi: Phoenix Press.
———. *Sophia: A Weekly Review of Politics, Sociology, Literature and Comparative Theology.* New series. Vol. 1, no. 1 (16 June 1900)–vol. 1, no. 23 (1 December 1900). Calcutta: K. C. Nan.
———. *The Twentieth Century: A Monthly Review.* Vol. 1, no. 1 (January 1901)–vol. 1, no. 8 (August 1901). Calcutta: K. C. Nan.
Urquhart, W. S. *Vedānta and Modern Thought.* London: Oxford University Press, 1928.
van Rooy, J. A. "Christ and the Religions: The Issues at Stake." *Missionalia* 13, no. 1 (April 1985): 3–13.
Verdu, A. *The Philosophy of Buddhism.* The Hague: Martinus Nijhoff, 1981.
Vireswarananda, S., and S. Adidevananda, eds., *Brahma Sūtra Bhasya According to Sri Rāmānuja.* Calcutta: Advaita Ashrama, 1995.
Vivekananda, Swami. *Essentials of Hinduism.* Mayavati: Advaita Ashrama, 1947.
Waines, David. *An Introduction to Islam.* Cambridge: Cambridge University Press, 1995.
Walls, Andrew. "Eusebius Tries Again: Reconceiving the Study of Christian History." *International Bulletin of Missionary Research* 24, no. 3 (July 2000): 105–11.
———. *The Missionary Movement in Christian History: Studies in the Transmission of Faith.* Maryknoll, N.Y.: Orbis, 1996.
Watson, Burton, trans. *Lotus Sūtra.* New York: Columbia University Press, 1993.

Williams, J. A. *The Word of Islam.* Austin: University of Texas Press, 1994.

Williams, Paul. *Mahāyāna Buddhism: The Doctrinal Foundations.* London: Routledge, 1989.

Wilson, R. M., ed. *The New Testament Apocrypha.* Vol. 2. Philadelphia: Westminster, 1964.

Zacharias, Ravi. *Jesus among Other Gods.* Nashville: Word, 2000.

———. *Jesus Talks with the Buddha: There Is One God and Who Is His Prophet?* Sisters, Ore.: Multnomah, 2001.

Zaehner, R. C. *Hinduism.* Oxford: Oxford University Press, 1966.

Zago, Marcello. "Mission and Interreligious Dialogue." *International Bulletin of Missionary Research* 22, no. 3 (July 1998): 98–101.

Zebiri, Kate. *Muslims and Christians Face to Face.* Oxford: One World, 1997.

Zwemer, Samuel. "The Allah of Islam and the God Revealed in Jesus Christ." *The Muslim World* 36 (October 1946): 306–18.

———. *The Moslem Doctrine of God.* New York: American Tract Society, 1905.

Subject Index

ahismā. *See* ethics, foundation for Buddhist ethics
al-Hallaj, 150–51, 186
Allah. *See also* God
  essence of, 148–49. *See also* monotheism, absolute; tawḥīd
  identification with Yahweh, 147–48, 152–53
  immutability of, 179–80. *See also* God, immutability of
  interchangeability with "God", 205–8
    linguistically, 205
    positionally, 206
    revelationally, 205–6
  knowledge of, 149, 165. *See also* God, knowledge of
  ninety-nine beautiful names of, 148
  relational capacity of, 153–55, 159–60
  as title or name, 208
  union with, 165–66
  worship of, 147, 206. *See also* God, worship of
Ambedkar, B. D., 123–24
Amitābha. *See* Buddhism, Amitabha
analogies, usefulness of, 162–63
anonymous Christians, 21, 25, 237. *See also* inclusivism
Anselm, 103–4
Aquinas, Thomas, 24, 212–13, 226
Arianism, 181
Arius. *See* Arianism
Arundhatī, 42–43
Augustine, 26
Avatar, 59–60
Barth, Karl, 51, 136. *See also* revelation, personal vs. propositional
Bediako, Kwame, 196, 203–4
Being, 218. *See also* saccidānanda; Upadhyay, Brahmabandhav
Black Stone, 144, 144 n. 8
Bliss, 219–21. *See also* saccidānanda; Upadhyay, Brahmabandhav
bodhisattvas. *See* Ultimate Reality, worship of
Brāhman. *See also* God
  body of, 58
  knowledge of, 48–53. *See also* God, knowledge of
  nirguṇa, 41–45
  ontological confusion within, 57–60
  saguṇa, 41–45
  worship of, 57–58. *See also* God, worship of
Brunner, Emil, 51. *See also* revelation, personal vs. propositional
Buddha
  founder of Buddhism. *See* Buddhism, origin of
  insight of, 125
  source of Buddhist ethics. *See* ethics, foundation for Buddhist ethics
Buddhism
  Amitābha, 109, 235–37
  doctrine of dependent arising, 91–92, 100–101, 125
  doctrine of no-soul/no-self, 92, 124–27, 130–32
  Eightfold Path, 116
  four noble truths, 91
  Hīnayāna, 93

Mahāyāna, 93–95
Mādhyamika school, 95–96
Yogācāra school, 96–97
origin of, 90–91
Therevāda. *See* Buddhism, Hīnayāna
three cardinal virtues, 116
compassion, 119–20, 131, 133
giving/charity, 121
loving-kindness, 120–21
Buford, Grace, 9

Calvin, John, 26
caste system, 65, 123
Christianity, exclusiveness of, 22. *See also* exclusivism
conversion, 15–16
Cragg, Kenneth, 207
creation
biblical account of, 81, 133–34
ex nihilo, 70–71
Hindu doctrine of
identity approach. *See* Panentheism; Pantheism; Puruṣa Man; Rāmānuja, doctrine of creation
separation view. *See* Śaṅkara, doctrine of creation

Deism, 73
dharma-kāya, 99–101
dialogue. *See also* witness
conservative approach to, 11–13. *See also* exclusivism
ecumenical, 197
genuine, 14, 16, 53, 239–41
historical, 197
interior, 15
interreligious, 9–33, 197, 239–41
ground rules for, 31–32
liberal approach to, 13–16. *See also* inclusivism; pluralism

emptiness, 105–6
Enlightenment, the, 242
ethics, 115
environmental ethics, 131, 133–34
ethical relativism, 134
foundation for Buddhist ethics, 116–18, 127, 130
foundation for Christian ethics, 128–30, 132–33
goal of Buddhist ethics, 118–19
reality of agent and recipient of ethical action, 124–25, 128–29, 131–32. *See also* Buddhism, doctrine of no-soul/no-self
exclusivism, 16–20
critique of, 25–26
engaged exclusivism, 26–27

faith, 231–32, 236. *See also* Hogg, A.G.
faith commitment, 14
Farquhar, J. N., 19, 234
Feuerbach, Ludwig, 104–5
fulfillment theology, 18–19

Gautama, Siddhārtha. *See* Buddhism, origin of
Geisler, Norman, 12, 207
God. *See also* Allah; Brahman; Ultimate Reality
differentiation within, 158–59, 161–66
as "Father," 156–57
immutability of, 105, 107–8, 182. *See also* Allah, immutability of
interchangeability with "Allah," 205–8
linguistically, 205
positionally, 206
revelationally, 205–6
knowledge of, 48–53, 164–65. *See also* Allah, knowledge of
Orthodox theology of, 50, 52–53
worship of, 206. *See also* Allah, worship of; Brahman, worship of; Ultimate Reality, worship of
gospel message, translatability of, 195

Hackett, Stuart, 20
Ḥanīfs, 143. *See also* Islam, origin of
Hick, John, 10, 22–23
Hinduism
advaita, 40–43, 45–46. *See also* Sankara
bhakti, 49
viśiṣṭadvaita, 43–45. *See also* Ramanuja
Hogg, A.G. 197, 231–35. *See also* faith

imposter theory, 189–92. *See also* Jesus Christ, Qurʾānic doctrine of; Jesus Christ, death of
incarnation. *See* avatar; Jesus Christ, incarnation of
inclusivism, 20–22, 236. *See also* Hogg, A.G.
critique of, 23–25

Islam
origin of, 142–44, 151–52, 174
Shiʿite, 149
similarities to Christianity, 152–53
Ṣūfism, 150, 159–61
Qadirite theology, 185–87
Sunni, 159
Īśvara, 42, 45

Jainism, 116
Jesus Christ, 17, 113
death of, 190–92
deity of, 60, 165, 171, 192–93
incarnation of, 25–26, 58–60, 129, 170–71, 178–82, 192, 195, 233. *See also* Arianism; Monophysitism; Nestorianism
Qurʿānic doctrine of, 171–76, 178, 182–83
agreement with Christian doctrine, 177–78, 184–85
birth of, 173
death of, 188–90
deity of, 175, 178–79, 188–89
as prophet, 174–75, 188
as "Son," 156–57
titles of, 203–4
worship of, 193
Jili. *See* Islam, Sufism; Islam, Qadirite theology

Kaʿbah, 144, 144 n. 8
Karma, 74–79, 84–86, 124
King Negus, 152–66
Knitter, Paul, 13–14, 22
Kraemer, Hendrick, 17–19, 22, 24, 26, 234–35
Kung, Hans, 152, 166–67

language
usefulness of in describing God, 48–52. *See also* Brahman, knowledge of; God, knowledge of
līlā, 73–75. *See also* problem of evil; Ramanuja, doctrine of creation
Llull, Raymond, 27
logos, 165. *See also* Martyr, Justin
in Greek philosophy, 200
in John's Gospel, 200–201, 203–4
in works of Justin Martyr, 201–2
logos spermatikos. *See* logos
Luther, Martin, 27–29

Madjid, Nurcholic, 25 n. 39
Martyr, Justin, 18, 196, 199–202. *See also* logos
māyā, 81–83. *See also* Sankara, doctrine of creation
middle way of emptiness. *See* emptiness
modalism, 159, 162
Monier-Williams, Monier, 19
Monophysitism, 180
monotheism
absolute, 145–46, 156. *See also* tawḥīd
trinitarian, 146–47, 153–57, 161–65, 213–14. *See also* Jesus Christ, incarnation of
Indian expression of. *See* saccidānanda; Upadhyay, Brahmabandhav
linguistic issues, 156–57
misunderstood in the Qurʾān, 154–55
Muhammad
coming prophesied by Jesus, 183–84
essence of, 185–87, 189
knowledge of the Bible, 176–77
life of, 143–44. *See also* Islam, origin of
as prophet, 146–47
relationship with Jews, 174
Muller, Max, 19

Nāgārjuna, 95–96
Nash, Ron, 10, 18
Nestorianism, 181
Nestorius. *See* Nestorianism
nihilism, 102–3, 105–6
nirvana, 122

Otto, Rudolph 51. *See also* revelation, personal vs. propositional

Pañcadaśī, 217–18. *See also* saccidānanda; Upadhyay, Brahmabandhav
Panentheism, 71–72
Pantheism, 71
Paul, the apostle, on Mars Hill, 14, 72
Peter, the apostle, 26
Pinnock, Clark, 22–23
pluralism, 22
critique of, 23, 239–40, 242–43
postmodernism, 242–43
problem of evil, 68, 73–77, 85
Puruṣa Man, 65–66

Qurʾān, 144–45
Christology of, 184–85. *See also* Jesus Christ, Qurʾānic doctrine of

Rahner, Karl, 21. *See also* anonymous Christians; inclusivism
Rāmānuja. *See also* Hinduism, visistadvaita
doctrine of creation, 67–68, 70. *See also* līlā
doctrine of God, 43–46, 55–56
relativism, 14, 23, 56–57. *See also* ethics, ethical relativism
relativistic theology of, 56–57. *See also* relativism
revelation
corruption of Jewish and Christian revelation, 147–48
general, 17–26, 216, 236–37
Jesus Christ as revelation, 233–35, 237
personal vs. propositional, 50–52
special, 17–26, 236
Ritschl, Albrecht, 234

saccidānanda, 214–18, 222–28. *See also* Upadhyay, Brahmabandhav
God as Ānanda, 219–21, 227–28
God as Cit, 218–19, 226–27
God as Sat, 218, 225–26
Saleeb, Abdul, 12, 207
salvation, 17–23, 32
Śaṇkara. *See also* Hinduism, advaita
doctrine of creation, 68–69, 80–81. *See also* māyā
doctrine of God, 40–43, 47–48
Sen, Keshab Chandra, 215. *See also* saccidānanda; Upadhyay, Brahmabandhav
Slater, T. E., 19
Smart, Ninian, 27
Socrates, 201–2

Table Talk, 28–29. *See also* Luther, Martin
tawḥīd, 145–46, 158–59, 164. *See also* Allah, essence of; monotheism, absolute
Tertullian, 11, 26
truth
absolute truth, 14–16
truth claims, 13–16, 22–23

Ultimate Reality. *See also* God
objectivity of, 102–7
transcendence of, 102, 106–7
worship of, 108–12. *See also* God, worship of
Upadhyay, Brahmabandhav, 196. *See also* saccidānanda
"Canticle to the Trinity," 222–28
life of, 211–13
theology of, 214–21, 233
Upanishads, 39

Vedas, 39
development of. *See* Vedic period
Vedic period, 64
vicarious suffering, 124. *See also* Buddhism, three cardinal virtues; Buddhism, compassion
Vivekananda, Swami, 15, 25 n. 39

witness, 240–41
worship, 54. *See also* God, worship of

Scripture Index

Genesis

1:1 37, 47, 81, 200
1:3 63
1:4 81
1:9 81
1:11 134
1:12 81
1:18 81
1:21 81, 134
1:24 134
1:25 81
1:26–27 128
1:27–28 133
1:31 81
12:8 147
14 20

Exodus

3:14 165, 192
32:32 119

Leviticus

19:2 132
20:8 132
22:32 132

Deuteronomy

6:4 141

Joshua

2 20

1 Kings

10 20–21

Psalms

19 134
19:1 162
24:1 133
102:26–27 108
148 134

Isaiah

6:3 162
26:13 157

Jeremiah

10:12 108

Daniel

7 193 n. 45
7:13–14 193 n. 45

Jonah

3 20

Matthew

5:17 19
7:12 115
16:27 193 n. 45
19:28 193 n. 45
24:27 193 n. 45
24:30 193 n. 45
25:31 193 n. 45
26:39 147
26:64 193 n. 45
28:9 193
28:16–17 193
28:17 193 n. 45

Mark

4:1–20 136
16:15–16 17, 25

Luke

10:25–37 132–33
22:66–71 193
24:38 193
24:52 193 n. 45

John

1 13
1:1 47, 165, 169, 171, 200
1:3 201
1:4 169
1:14 113, 171, 179, 184, 184 n. 22, 201
1:18 165
3:16 20, 169, 170, 184, 184 n. 22
3:16–18 17
3:18 184 n. 22
3:36 17
4:6 171
5:23 157
6:62 170
7:14 171
8:42 170
8:54–59 192
8:58 165, 170, 192
10:33 165
10:36 170
11:33 171
11:35 171
11:38 171

13:34 171
14:6 17, 113
14:9 113, 186 n. 27
14:16 183 n. 19, 184
14:17 132, 184
15:9–13 171
15:11 171
15:26 183, 183 n. 19
16:7 183 n. 199
16:13 132, 183
16:14 183
17:1–26 171
17:5 157
17:8 170
18:37 15
19:28 171
19:33 192
19:34 192
20:28 193
21:12–13 193

Acts

2:31–32 17
4:12 17
10 21
14:17 21
17 13, 72
17:28 14, 71
20:21 24

Romans

1:20 81
2:15 21
9:3–4 119
10:13 24
10:14–15 24
10:18 24
11:33 108
11:33–36 48
14:17 161

1 Corinthians

2:1–2 136
3:1–2 136
10:4 21
13:12 166
15:6 193
15:12–20 193

2 Corinthians

5:19 17

Ephesians

2:12 17

Philippians

2:1–11 129

Colossians

1:13 210
1:20 17
2:3 108
2:9 60

1 Timothy

3:16 179
6:16 164
6:20–21 136

Hebrews

1:3 83, 171
1:6 171
1:12 108
2:18 171
3:3 162
5:8 171
8:10 132
11:3 72, 89

1 Peter

2:24 113
3:15 26, 241

2 Peter

3:9 20, 24

1 John

2:23 206
4:14 179
4:16 128
4:19 128
4:20–21 129
5:11–12 17

Jude

3–4 161